THE FATHERS
OF THE CHURCH

A NEW TRANSLATION

VOLUME 35

THE FATHERS
OF THE CHURCH

A NEW TRANSLATION

EDITORIAL BOARD

Hermigild Dressler, O.F.M.
Quincy College
Editorial Director

Robert P. Russell, O.S.A.
Villanova University

Thomas P. Halton
The Catholic University of America

Robert Sider
Dickinson College

Sister M. Josephine Brennan, I.H.M.
Marywood College

Richard Talaska
Editorial Assistant

FORMER EDITORIAL DIRECTORS

Ludwig Schopf, Roy J. Deferrari, Bernard M. Peebles

SAINT AUGUSTINE

AGAINST JULIAN

Translated by
MATTHEW A. SCHUMACHER, C. S. C.

THE CATHOLIC UNIVERSITY OF AMERICA PRESS
Washington, D.C.

NIHIL OBSTAT:

JOHN A. GOODWINE
Censor Librorum

IMPRIMATUR:

✠ FRANCIS CARDINAL SPELLMAN
Archbishop of New York

September 17, 1957

Library of Congress Catalog Card No. 77-081347
ISBN 8132-0035-0

Copyright © 1957 by
THE CATHOLIC UNIVERSITY OF AMERICA PRESS, INC.
All rights reserved

Second Printing 1977
Third Printing 1981
First Paperback Reprint 2004
ISBN 0-8132-1400-9
ISBN-13: 978-0-8132-1400-9 (pbk.)

CONTENTS

BOOK 1 3

Augustine proposes to defend the doctrine of original sin set forth in Book 1 of *De nuptiis et concupiscentia,* against Bishop Julian, who had attacked it in four volumes and who had called its defenders Manichaeans. Such a charge would fall, therefore, upon the most famous of the Fathers, Greek and Latin, as Augustine shows by citing their own testimony, with particular explanation of passages from Basil and John Chrysostom which Julian believes favor his view. Actually, it is certain rash statements of Julian that strongly support the Manichaean heresy.

BOOK 2 55

Augustine refutes the five arguments of the Pelagians against original sin from the pronouncements of earlier famous Church authorities: the ten illustrious bishops—Irenaeus, Reticius, Olympius, Hilary, Gregory Nazianzen, Ambrose, Basil, John of Constantinople, Innocent, and Jerome.

CONTENTS

BOOK 3 105

Augustine answers Book 1 of Julian so that it becomes clear that, although the true and good God is the Creator of men, and marriage is good and is instituted by God, yet the concupiscence by which the flesh lusts against the spirit is evil. Conjugal modesty uses this evil well, and more holy continence does better by not using it at all. This evil is not in us from another substance which God did not make, as the Manichaeans say, but arose and is transmitted through the disobedience of Adam, and is expiated and healed through the obedience of Christ. Everyone born incurs a deserved punishment in bondage to this evil; the reborn is released from it by a gratuitous grace. He shows from Julian's own words that lust is evil, for Julian acknowledges remedies against it, wants it to be restrained by reason, and says that glorious combats are fought against it by the continent.

BOOK 4 167

Augustine considers each argument in this reply to Julian's Book 2, omitting only those statements that have no bearing on the question. He proves two things: that the virtues of unbelievers are not true virtues; and that concupiscence is evil. Through his opponent's very argument he also proves this from the words of the Gentiles. He shows how grace is not given according to merits, yet may not be attributed to fate; and how we are to understand the words of the Apostle that God wishes all men to be saved.

CONTENTS

BOOK 5 241

In dealing with Julian's Book 3, Augustine shows first why Christians despise the new heresy which rejects original sin. Concupiscence does not deserve praise merely because man's disobedience is punished through it; it is a fault and, even in those who do not consent to its wicked activities, it is always evil. He shows how we should understand the words of the Apostle: 'That each one may know how to possess his vessel,' and so forth. There is true marriage without union of bodies, as was the marriage of Mary and Joseph. Julian's attempt to argue by Aristotelean Categories against the sin derived from our first parents is without avail. Augustine shows how the flesh of Christ differs from the flesh of other men. Catholics by no means favor the Manichaeans when they acknowledge original sin and the evil of lust; this is true, instead, of the Pelagians when they say: 'Sins do not arise from that which is free from sin.'

BOOK 6 307

Augustine answers Book 4 of Julian, as well as his cavilings and calumnies against *De nuptiis*. That man is born with sin is shown from the baptism of infants, from the rite of exorcism and exsufflation in the baptism of infants, from the words of the Apostle to the Romans and the Corinthians. The aptness of the illustration of the olive and the oleaster shows how from regenerated and just parents are born children who must be regenerated. Original sin was voluntary in the first parents; in us it is another's sin by the ownership of action, but it is our sin by the contagion of offspring. It is because of this sin that the human race from infancy is afflicted by these great miseries, and that infants who die without the grace of regeneration are excluded from the kingdom of God. Sanctification is now conferred through baptism on both soul and body, yet the corruption of the body, which also presses down the soul itself, is not removed in this life. He shows how concupiscence remains in act, passes in guilt; and he gives the Catholic interpretation of the Apostle Paul which Julian expounded in an incorrect sense.

WRITINGS
OF
SAINT AUGUSTINE

VOLUME 16

INTRODUCTION

S T. AUGUSTINE WROTE this work in the closing years of a life busied with three great controversies—Manichaeism, Donatism, Pelagianism, the last ending with the *Contra Julianum* and the *Opus imperfectum contra Julianum*. The year 411, which, for all practical purposes, saw the end of Donatism—a result largely due to Augustine—finds him beginning in earnest the conflict with Pelagianism, which was to occupy his time in sermons and a number of important writings for the rest of his days.

The Council of Carthage (411) condemned the teachings of Celestius, the disciple of Pelagius. The councils of Carthage were sleeplessly active against the errors of Pelagianism, for, when the doctrines of Pelagius were accepted by John, Bishop of Jerusalem, and also by the Council of Diospolis as in harmony with the teaching of the Church, a new Council of Carthage (416) reaffirmed the previous condemnation. This action and a similar action by the Council of Milevis (416), at which Augustine was present, urged Pope Innocent I to ratify their decision. When word came from the Pope that on January 27, 417, he had condemned Pelagius and Celestius, Augustine in the course of a sermon proclaimed thankfully and wistfully: *'Inde etiam rescripta venerunt, causa finita est. Utinam aliquando finiatur error.'* The usual form of the statement, *'Roma locuta, causa finita,'* is, according to Battifol, 'less rich in tenor than the authentic version.'[1] *'Utinam aliquando finiatur error'* had not been fully realized, for it required another Council of Carthage (418), with its nine canons summarizing the Catholic teaching on the important points of original sin, the need and action of grace, denial of the unlimited power of the human will, and considerable letter-writing, before Pope Zosimus in *Epistola Tractatoria*, issued in May, 418, approved the council's action and condemned the Pelagian teachings.

Eighteen Italian bishops refused to sign the Pope's document, and they were excommunicated and deposed. Julian, Bishop of Eclanum, was the leader of the dissident group. According to Cayré, Julian was 'a fine humanist, keenly interested in all matters of speculation, somewhat pedantic, who exalted the rights of reason to the detriment of faith.'[2] St. Augustine characterized Julian: *'in disputatione loquacissimus, in contentione calumniosissimus, in professione fallacissimus.'*[3]

This discussion from 418 to the year of Augustine's death, 430, between two persons who never met during this time, is best set forth in three sources from Augustine's writings: The Preface to the *Opus imperfectum contra Julianum*, where he states briefly what he had in mind in the *Contra Julianum;* in the eighty-eighth heresy described in *De haeresibus*, in which we have his understanding of the doctrines of Pelagianism; and the *Contra Julianum* itself, giving Augustine's specific purpose and plan. The Preface follows:

'I wrote a book entitled *De nuptiis et concupiscentia* to

[1] P. Battifol, *Le Catholicisme de Saint Augustine* (Paris, 1924) 404.
[2] F. Cayré, *Manual of Patrology and History of Theology* I (Belgium, 1936) 632.
[3] *Sermo* 131.10.

INTRODUCTION   xiii

Count Valerius against the Pelagian heretics, who assert that, even if Adam had not sinned, he would have died in body, and that the human race was not vitiated in him—whence it follows that they contend that death, deadly diseases, and all the evils which we see infants also suffer, would have existed in paradise, even if no one had sinned. I wrote this book because I knew the report had reached him that the Pelagians say we condemn marriage. In this book, using my strongest arguments, I distinguished the good of marriage from the evil of carnal concupiscence, which conjugal modesty uses well. When the illustrious Valerius had received this book, he sent me a memorandum containing several statements selected from the work of Julian, a Pelagian heretic who thought to answer in four volumes the one volume which, as I said, I wrote about marriage and concupiscence. These statements were sent to Valerius by some unknown person who had taken it upon himself to select what he chose arbitrarily from Julian's first volume. Valerius asked me to answer them as soon as possible, and thus I came to write a second volume under the same title. Julian, with his usual prolixity, composed eight more volumes against it. These volumes I shall now answer in his own words, replying to the individual passages that seem to call for refutation, although, after I received his four volumes, I refuted them sufficiently and fully and in six volumes.'[4]

In *Contra Julianum,* Augustine sets forth his purpose:

'I shall so arrange my argument that I may first show how many great doctors of the Catholic Church you do not hesitate to insult intolerably by the name of Manichaeans, attacking them with me and hurling your sacrilegious weapons against them. Then I shall show that you yourself so support the damnably and abominably impious error of the Manichaeans that they cannot find such a defender even among

---

4 Migne, *Patrologia Latina* 45.

their own adherents. In the third place, as briefly as I can, I shall refute all your subtleties and elaborate arguments, not by my own statements, but by those of men who lived before us and defended the Catholic faith against the wicked. Finally, since, if you do not reform, it will be necessary for you to attack even those doctors of the Catholic Church and to contend that not even they held the Catholic truth in this matter, I shall, God helping me, defend their faith and ours against you. And here even this shall become clear, that not only you in your own words, which I said I would prove in the second place, but the very doctrine of Pelagianism, which is common to all of you, greatly supports Manichaeism.'[5]

Augustine stresses in the first two books the traditional teaching of the Church as found in the Fathers, in contrast to the rationalism of Pelagianism. His reaction to their teaching is thus expressed: 'It would be more endurable if with your evil tongue you tore to pieces our names than our faith through whose merit our names are written in heaven.'[6]

Augustine at the end of the second book gives a brief summary of the important doctrines discussed:

'But now let us briefly sum up as best we can what we have discussed throughout this whole book. We proposed here by the weight of authority of holy men, who were bishops before us, and strenuously defended the Catholic faith not only by their words while they were living in this world, but also by their writings which they left for posterity, to refute your arguments in which you say: "If God creates men, they cannot be born with any evil. If marriage is good, nothing evil arises from it. If all sins are forgiven in baptism, those born of the reborn cannot contract original sin. If God is just, He cannot condemn in the children the sins of the

---
[5] See below, 1.1.3.
[6] See below, 1.4,13.

parents, since He forgives the parents their own sins as well. If human nature is capable of perfect justice, it cannot have natural faults." To this we reply that God is the Creator of men, that is, of both soul and body; and that marriage is good; and that through the baptism of Christ all sins are forgiven; and that God is just; and that human nature is capable of perfect justice. Yet, although all these things are true, men are born subject to the vitiated origin which is derived from the first man, and therefore go to damnation unless they are reborn in Christ. And this we have proved by the authority of Catholic saints who assert what we say about original sin and also confess that all these five statements are true. Therefore, it does not follow that this is false because those are true. Indeed, such great men according to the Catholic faith, which of old was spread throughout the world, confirm the truth both of this and of those; and so your fragile and, as it were, oversubtle novelty is crushed by their authority alone, in addition to what they say, so that truth itself bears witness that it is speaking through them. But now your obstinacy must first be checked by their authority, and checked in your presumptuous attack, and in some way wounded, so that when you finally believe that such men of God could not commit such an error in the Catholic faith that they would say something from which it would follow that God is not the Creator of men, that marriage is to be condemned, that not all sins are forgiven in baptism, that God is unjust, that we have no hope of perfect virtue—all or any of which it is wicked to think—you may restrain your headlong boldness, and, as it were, recovering from madness, may begin to consider and recognize and resume the truth in which you were nurtured.'[7]

A statement of the issue involved and one of a number of efforts made by Augustine to bring Julian to the truth: 'I

---

[7] See below, 2.29.31.

beg you to consider now, I say now, so that wholesome truth may win you over. Put aside all craving for victory and consider whether you ought to accept our opinion rather than yours. The whole point between us in this controversy is whether the thing of which good use is made is good or evil. In this controversy I do not want you to reject the outstanding judges who, as I have shown above, are learned in sound doctrine, and have impartially expressed sentence on this matter . . . Listen once more to my short and clear answer. When I say this concupiscence is a disease, why do you deny it, if you concede that a remedy for it is necessary? If you acknowledge the remedy, acknowledge the disease. If you deny the disease, deny the remedy. I beg you, yield at last to the truth which even you yourself have spoken. No one provides a remedy for health.'[9]

'Does lust deserve to have both your friendship and your opposition, so that you attack it in yourself yet defend it against me? Your opposition is latent; your friendship is patent; the latent makes the patent suspect. How can you ask us to believe in this warfare you say you wage under cover when we see your friendship in the open? How do you want us to think you oppose the sting of lust when you fill books with the praise of lust? But I shall overcome my suspicion. I believe you attack what you praise, but I am sorry to see you praise what you attack. From this evil, then, and with it, is generated man, whom you deny is saved by regeneration. For this is the evil which the married use well, and which celibates do better in not using at all. If that by which the flesh lusts against the spirit and which you also admit the legion of Apostles combatted is an evil, it follows that when the married make good use of it they cannot be using a good well, but an evil. Children generated from and with this evil are to be regenerated so that they may be

---

[8] See below, 3.21.42.

delivered from evil. Their parents were also born guilty of this original evil, though they were delivered from the guilt by rebirth. What would we have them beget, not from that whence they were reborn, but from that whence they were born, except what they themselves were at birth? Therefore, they beget the guilty, and, since they generate from that whence they were born, they cannot generate something different from what they themselves were at birth. But, whence they were reborn, thence they were delivered from the guilt with which they were born. Therefore, the offspring which liberated parents generate as guilty must itself be delivered by that same regeneration, because as guilty was it born from the evil which the reborn use well in order that men may be born to be regenerated. If you do not combat this evil, believe those who are combating it. If you also do so, acknowledge the adversary and do not in praising the disease hold as a friend what in combat experience shows to be an enemy.'[9]

A concise resume of the discussion and a final appeal to Julian to accept the truth closes the work:

'If you are not too obstinate, Julian, I believe you will see I have answered and refuted all the arguments you have brought forth in your four volumes to show that we should not believe in original sin, and that we cannot regard the concupiscence of the flesh as evil without also condemning marriage. It has been shown that he alone is not bound by the ancient paternal debt who has changed inheritance and father; where he who is himself adopted through grace discovers the sole co-heir who is heir through nature; that carnal concupiscence does not inflict death after death on him alone who in the death of Christ has found the death by which he dies to sin and escapes the death by which he had been born in sin.

---

9 See below, 3.26.66.

'One died for all, therefore all have died; and He died for all. Nor can there ever live any for whom He did not die, who, Himself alive, died for the dead. Denying these things, attacking them, trying to destroy these defenses of the Catholic faith and to rend the very sinews of the Christian religion and of true godliness, you dare assert you are waging war on the ungodly, when as a matter of fact you are using the weapons of ungodliness against the mother who gave birth to you spiritually. You dare join the line of the holy Patriarchs, Prophets, Apostles, martyrs, and priests, even when the Patriarchs say to you: Sacrifices for sins were offered even for new-born infants; not even an infant of one day upon the earth is clean of sin; when the Prophets say to you: "We are conceived in iniquities"; when the Apostles say to you: "All we who have been baptized into Christ Jesus have been baptized into his death," so that "we are dead to sin but alive to God in Christ Jesus"; when the martyrs say to you: "Those born carnally according to Adam contract the contagion of the ancient death in their first birth, so that not their own, but another's sins are remitted for infants in baptism"; when the priests say to you: "Those formed in carnal pleasure come under the contagion of sins even before they experience the gift of this life." You presume to associate yourself with these men whose faith you seek to destroy. You say that any association with the Manichaeans would conquer you, yet you have so strengthened them that you and they stand or fall together. You are mistaken, my son, wretchedly mistaken, if not also detestably mistaken. When you overcome the animosity that possesses you, you will possess the truth that has overcome you.'[10]

We might say Pelagianism is age-old. For man it began in the primal transgression and it will be young until the last transgression is recorded. That is why this work of Au-

---

10 See below, 6.26.83.

gustine will always have *actualité*. And since this perennially present and personal subject is given in the clear presentation and masterly method of the Bishop of Hippo, we have something that is as absorbing as it is enlightening. To many, St. Augustine is here at his best as genius and teacher; the work is a sort of synthesis of the great truths he meditated so long and so well and expressed so helpfully for all who would know *how* to do, resting firmly on a knowledge of *what* to do. A constant storm, this life, but reasonable peace here, and assured peace in due and unending days.

The text used for the *Contra Julianum* is that of Migne. As there stated, this text has been compared with various manuscripts, especially the five Vatican and eight Gallican manuscripts. The comparatively few variant readings in these are of no special significance.

Thanks and appreciation are due to Ann Condit, Ph.D., for assistance in the production of the translation; and to Stella Lange, Ph.D., for collaboration in part. They were both students of mine in the School of Theology at St. Mary's College, Notre Dame, Indiana.

SELECT BIBLIOGRAPHY

Text:

Sancti Aurelii Augustini Hipponensis Opera Omnia, ed. J. P. Migne, in *Patrologia Latina* 44 (Paris 1865), cols. 641-874.

Secondary Writings:

Battifol, P., *Le catholicisme de saint Augustin* (Paris 1924).
Cayré, F., *Manual of Patrology and History of Theology* 1 (Paris 1936).
Froget, J., 'Julien d'Eclane,' *Dictionnaire de théologie catholique* 8 (Paris 1927), cols. 1926-1931.

Gilson, E., *Introduction à l'étude de saint Augustin* (Paris 1943).
Healy, P., 'Julian of Eclanum,' *Catholic Encyclopedia* 8 (New York 1913) 557-558.
Hedde, R., and E. Amann, 'Pelagianisme,' *Dictionnaire de théologie catholique* 12 (Paris 1927), cols. 702-707.
Julian of Eclanum, *Liber subnotationum in verba Juliani; Dissertatio prima; Dissertatio sexta*, ed. J. P. Migne, in *Patrologia Latina* 48 (Paris 1865), cols. 121-171, 277-286, 622-626.
Noris, H. Cardinal, *Historia Pelagiana* (Padua 1873).
Pohle, J., 'Pelagius and Pelagianism,' *Catholic Encyclopedia* 11 (New York 1913) 607-608.
Portalié, E., 'Augustine of Hippo,' *Catholic Encyclopedia* 2 (New York 1913), 84-104.
Portalié, E., 'Augustin (saint),' *Dictionnaire de théologie catholique* 1 (Paris 1927), cols. 2268-2472.
Tillemont, L. de, *Mémoirs pour servir à l'histoire ecclésiastique* (Paris 1710).
Tixeront, J., *History of Dogma* 2 (St. Louis 1923).

SAINT AUGUSTINE

AGAINST JULIAN

Translated by
MATTHEW A. SCHUMACHER, C.S.C., S.T.B., Ph.D., LL.D.
St. Mary's College
Notre Dame, Indiana

BOOK I

Chapter 1

 SHOULD LIE IF I SAID that I despise your insults and evil words, Julian, which you breathed forth, burning with wrath, in your four books. For how could I despise them, when I see, in considering the testimony of my conscience, that I ought either to rejoice for myself or to grieve for you and for those whom you deceive? Who, indeed, despises the occasion of his rejoicing or grief? And we by no means despise that which in part causes us gladness and in part sadness. Now the cause of my joy is the promise of the Lord, who says: 'When they say all manner of evil against you falsely for my sake, rejoice and exult, because your reward is great in heaven.'¹ And again, the cause of my grief is the feeling of the Apostle, who writes: 'Who is weak and I am not weak? Who is made to stumble and I am not inflamed?'² But even you can say this for your doctrine, which you think to be the truth. So, if you will, let us put aside these common sentiments, which can

---
1 Matt. 5.11,12.
2 2 Cor. 11. 29.

3

be expressed by either side, although they cannot be spoken truthfully by both sides.

(2) First, I ask you why you boast that you have at least externally replied to my book when in your four books you have not even touched upon a quarter of my one book to refute it, and have taken such leaps in sidetracking my arguments that you seem not to expect there will be any reader of either my work or yours who will discover them. Finally, even those few points which comprise, as I said, scarcely the fourth part of my book—and which you evidently considered the weaker and so, with the clatter of your four great volumes, sought to overwhelm and crush them as if with onrushing chariots—are found to remain unshaken by the consideration of the far greater number of the others you feared to attack. It is almost superfluous to demonstrate this. For we should rather warn those who wish to understand that they may not be reluctant to read both what I have written and what you wished to reply. The matter itself is so clear and evident that those would be indeed slow of comprehension who would ask us to demonstrate it.

(3) Now, therefore, since I see you abandoned by the truth and turning to abuse, I shall so arrange my argument that I may first show how many great doctors of the Catholic Church you do not hesitate to insult intolerably by the name of Manichaeans, attacking them with me, and hurling your sacrilegious weapons against them. Then I shall show that you yourself so support the damnable and abominably impious error of the Manichaeans that they could not hope to find such a defender even among their own adherents. In the third place, as briefly as I can, I shall refute all your subtleties and elaborate arguments, not by my own statements, but by those of men who lived before us and defended the Catholic Church against the wicked. Finally, since, if you do

not reform, it will be necessary for you to attack even those doctors of the Catholic Church and to contend that not even they held the Catholic truth in this matter, I shall, God helping me, defend their faith and ours against you. And here even this shall become clear; namely, that not only you in your own words, which I said I would prove in the second place, but the doctrine of Pelagianism itself, which is common to all of you, greatly supports Manichaeism.

Chapter 2

(4) Consider, a little, the first part of my plan and how I shall follow it out. In regard to the purpose of my book, to which you boast that you have replied in your four, the matter for discussion between us is this: that I say that marriage should be so praised that no blame or censure should accrue to it from the fact that all men are born subject to the sin of our first parents. He who denies this strives to overturn the very foundations of Christian faith. As a result, I wrote a book about marriage and concupiscence, distinguishing, as you see, the good of marriage from that evil through which original sin is contracted. But you say that marriage is without doubt condemned unless that which is born of it is free from all obligation under sin. You thus boast that you have refuted my one book by your four. In these books, wishing to turn men from established Catholic belief and to lead them to the novelty of your error, you often insinuate into the minds of the readers the horror of the Manichaean plague, as though he agreed with the Manichaeans about a 'natural evil,' who says that infants born physically according to Adam contract the contagion of the ancient death by their first birth, and for this reason have need of the second, so that they may first be purged through

the laver of regeneration by the remission of original sin, and, adopted as sons of God, be transferred into the kingdom of His only-begotten son. This charge of Manichaeism was also brought by Jovinian,[1] who denied that Mary's holy virginity, which had existed when she conceived, remained while she was giving birth, as if we believed with the Manichaeans that Christ was a phantasm when we say that in His birth His mother's virginity remained inviolate.[2] But with the aid of the Saviour Himself, just as Catholics scorned even the most ingenious arguments brought forward by Jovinian and believed that holy Mary was not corrupted in giving birth, and that the Lord was not a phantasm, but that she remained a virgin after giving birth, although the true body of Christ came from her—so may they scorn your slanderous vain talk, not inventing a natural principle of evil, with the Manichaeans, and in no way doubting, according to the ancient and true Catholic faith, that Christ in blotting out the handwriting of the paternal debt is the liberator of infants.

Chapter 3

(5) Consider, you who so often accuse us of Manichaeism, if you are alert, whom and what kind of men and what great

---

1 Jovinian presented the doctrine of salvation by faith without works, denied the Virgin Birth, and put marriage on a par with virginity.
2 Many Manichaeans professed to be Christians, and for this reason were regarded as heretics because of their false teaching about specifically Christian doctrines. Their unsound teaching about marriage is well expressed by Augustine's words: 'I ask why it should displease you for a man to put aside his wife, when you do not believe a man should take a wife for the faithfulness of matrimony, but for the crime of concupiscence. It was indeed named "matrimony" from this: that a woman ought to marry for no other reason than that she may become a mother, which is hateful to you. You believe that in this way a part of God which has been conquered and subjugated in battle with your race of darkness is also bound in fetters of flesh' (*Contra Faustum Manichaeum* 19.26).

defenders of the Catholic faith you dare insult with such a detestable charge. Indeed, I do not promise that I will gather the opinions of all on this matter, nor all the opinions of those whom I shall mention; it would take too long and I do not think it necessary. But I shall cite a very few, by which, however, our adversaries may be compelled to blush and to yield, if they have any fear of God or shame before men that can overcome that great evil of their obstinacy. Irenaeus, Bishop of Lyons, lived not long after the time of the Apostles. He says: 'Men cannot be saved in any other way from the ancient wound of the Serpent except by believing in Him who according to the likeness of sinful flesh was lifted up from the earth on the tree of testimony and drew all things to Himself and gave life to the dead.'[1] Again he says: 'Just as the human race was bound to death by a virgin it is released through a virgin, the obedience of a virgin evenly counterbalancing the disobedience of a virgin. For the sin of the first-formed was wiped out by the chastisement of the First-born,[2] the wisdom of the Serpent was conquered by the simplicity of the dove, and we were released from the chains by which we were bound to death.'[3] Do you understand the ancient man of God, and what he thinks about the ancient wound of the Serpent, and about the likeness of sinful flesh through which the wound of the Serpent is healed in the sinful flesh, and about the sin of the first-formed by which we had been bound?

(6) The blessed martyr, Bishop Cyprian, speaks much more

---
1 Irenaeus, *Adversus haereses* 4.5.
2 The terms, 'the first-formed,' which means Adam, and 'the First-born,' who is Christ, are often used by some of the early Fathers, especially those whose language was Greek, to emphasize the importance of the idea of re-establishing, or bringing under one head, all things in Christ (Eph. 1.0, *anakephalaiōsasthai*), in the sense that the human race is given a new Head in the Son of God, who was born perfect man, for the salvation of man, after the fall of the first man.
3 Irenaeus, *Adversus haereses* 5.19.

openly about the same belief. 'If anything,' he says, 'could prevent man from attaining grace, it would be rather those who are adult and advanced in years, and the aged, who might be prevented by serious sins. But if men guilty of very serious crimes and those who have previously committed many sins against God are granted remission of sins when they later come to believe, and no one is forbidden baptism and grace, how much more should infants not be forbidden, who, just born, have committed no sin except that, having been born physically according to Adam, they have contracted the contagion of the ancient death by their first birth? They come to receive remission of sins all the more easily because they are forgiven not their own, but another's, sin.'[4]

(7) Reticius of Autun was a bishop of great authority in the Church during his episcopacy. This is shown to us by his ecclesiastical activities, when in Rome he served as judge with others in the court presided over by Melchiades, Bishop of the Apostolic See, and condemned Donatus, who had been the orginator of the Donatist schism, and absolved Caecilianus, bishop of the church at Carthage. Reticius, when discussing baptism,[5] spoke as follows: 'No one is unaware of the fact that this is the chief forgiveness in the Church, in which we put away the whole weight of the ancient crime and blot out the former evil deeds of our ignorance and also strip off the old man with his inborn crimes.' You notice the expressions, 'the weight of the ancient crime,' 'the former evil deeds,' 'the old man with his inborn crimes'—and you dare set up against these a destructive novelty.

(8) Olympius, a Spanish bishop, a man of great glory in the Church and in Christ, says in one of his ecclesiastical sermons: 'If faith had remained ever incorrupt upon earth and had followed the tracks which were formed and im-

---

4 Cyprian, *Epistola* 64, *ad Fidum.*
5 This work is not extant.

printed, but from which it departed, it would never have scattered by the death-dealing transgression of the first-formed the fault in the seed, resulting in this, that sin is born with man.[6] Is there anything you think you can say against me, which you are not forced to say also against him, or, rather, against them? For there is in all the one Catholic faith, and they believe with one heart and confess with one mouth that through one man sin entered into the world, in whom all have sinned,[7] and with their Catholic antiquity they overthrow your presumptuous novelties.[8]

(9) Hear, also, what may move you more and trouble you, and, would that it might, change you for the better. Who does not know that the Gallic bishop Hilary is to be revered as the keenest defender of the Catholic Church against the heretics? Note what he says when dealing with the flesh of Christ. 'Therefore, when He was sent in the likeness of sinful flesh,[9] He did not have the sin though He had the flesh. But, since all flesh comes from sin—namely, descended from the ancestral sin of Adam—He was sent in the likeness of sinful flesh, not that the sin existed in Him, but the likeness of sinful flesh.' Again he says in his exposition of Psalm 118, when he comes to the words: 'Let my soul live and praise thee':[10] 'He does not think he lives in this life, for he had said: "Behold I have been conceived in iniquities, and in sins did my mother bear me."[11] He knows that he was born of sinful origin and under the law of sin.' Do you understand what you hear? Do you ask what you should say? If you have any sense of shame, do you dare accuse on this matter of

---
6 This work is not extant.
7 Cf. Rom. 5.12.
8 For a concise summary of this reading of Rom. 5.12, cf. F. Prat, *The Theology of St. Paul* (Westminster, Md. 1950) I 213, and 215, footnote.
9 Rom. 8.3.
10 Ps. 118.175.
11 Ps. 50.7.

original sin a man so gloriously outstanding among Catholic bishops and so conspicuous in fame and honor?

(10) But, again, listen to another excellent steward of God, whom I reverence as a father, for in Christ Jesus he begat me through the Gospel, [12] and from this servant of Christ I received the laver of regeneration. I speak of the blessed Ambrose, whose grace, constancy, labors, dangers, whether in works or in speech, for the Catholic faith, I myself have experienced, and together with me the Roman world does not hesitate to proclaim them. When this man was explaining the Gospel according to Luke, he said: ' "The Jordan turned backwards" '[13] signified the future mysteries of the laver of salvation, through which infants who are baptized at the beginning of their natural life are reformed from badness.'[14] Again, he says in the same work: 'No union with a man disclosed the secrets of the virginal womb, but the Holy Spirit infused the immaculate seed into the inviolate womb. For the Lord Jesus, alone of all born of woman, is holy in all things. He who did not experience the contagions of earthy corruption in the newness of His immaculate birth, and who expelled it by His heavenly majesty.'[15] And again, he says in the same work: 'In Adam we all die, because through one man sin entered into the world and through sin death, and thus it has passed unto all men; in whom all have sinned. His guilt, therefore, is the death of all.'[16] And in another passage on the same Gospel: 'Beware, therefore, lest you be stripped as Adam was stripped, deprived of the protection by the heavenly commandment and putting off the garments of faith, and so receiving a mortal wound in which he would have slain all the human race, unless that Samaritan

---

12 Cf. 1 Cor. 4.15.
13 Ps. 113.3.
14 Ambrose, *Expositio evangelii secundum Lucam* 1.36.
15 *Ibid.* 2.56.
16 *Ibid.* 4.67, on Luke 4.58.

had descended and cured its grievous wounds.'[17] Again, in another place of the same work, he says: 'Adam was, and in him we all were. Adam perished and in him all perished.'[18] Again, he says in the book about the Prophet David: 'Before we are born we are stained by contagion, and before seeing the light we receive the injury of our very origin, we are conceived in iniquity. He does not say,' comments Ambrose, 'whether that of our parents or our own. And in sins his mother gives birth to each one. Nor does he state here whether the mother gives birth in her own sins or whether there are already some sins in the one being born. But, consider whether both are not to be understood. The conception is not without iniquity, since the parents are not without sin, and if not even a child of one day is without sin, so much more are those days of the maternal conception not without sin. Thus, we are conceived in the sin of our parents and are born in their iniquities. But birth itself also has its own contagions, and the nature itself has not merely one contagion.'[19] In his exposition of the Book of Tobias, he says: 'Who is this usurer of sin except the Devil, from whom Eve borrowed sin and obligated the whole human race, that is, the succeeding posterity which is subject to the interest?' Again, in the same work, he says: 'The Devil deceived Eve that he might ensnare her husband and put his inheritance under obligation.'[20] He also says in his exposition of Psalm 48: 'Our iniquity is one thing, another that of our heel, in which Adam was wounded by the tooth of the serpent and left by his wound an obligated inheritance for the human succession, so that we are all lamed by that wound.'[21]

---
17 *Ibid.* 7.73, on Luke 10.30.
18 *Ibid.* 7.234, on Luke 15.24.
19 *Apologia prophetae David.* 11.
20 Ambrose, *De Tobia* 9, 23.
21 Ambrose, *Enarrationes in XI psalmos Davidicos*, in Ps. 48.6.

Chapter 4

(11) Go, now, and make objections about original sin. Disagree with them, pretend you do not know what they say, and in view of so many great teachers who, after leading a most noble life and combating the errors of their times, most gloriously departed from this life before you came into being —as if you did not see them while you are attacking me, and, as if you did not know that they are being defamed under my name, you insult them with impunity. I confess that I would believe you ignorant of the evil you are doing and would attribute it to your imprudence rather than your impudence that you dare pursue with hostility these shining lights of the City of God which you ought to have followed with fidelity; I would believe, I say, that you commit this great crime in ignorance, if I had not set forth a very clear account of the discussion of St. Ambrose[1] in that book which you think, or wish to be thought, to have refuted. Or did you not read there that, when the above-mentioned bishop spoke of the Virgin Birth of Christ, he said: 'Therefore, as a man He was tempted in all things and in the likeness of men He endured all things, but as born of the Spirit He abstained from sin. For every man is a liar[2] and no one is without sin except God alone. It remains true, therefore, that from man and woman, that is, through that union of bodies, no one may be seen to be without sin. But He who is without sin is also without this kind of conception.'[3] If you did not there read these words of the venerable Ambrose, how could you undertake to refute the book in which they are written? But, if you read them, why do you rage against me and criticize him first of all in me? Why do you strive to rend my name and,

---

1 *De nuptiis et concupiscentia* 1.40.
2 Ps. 115.2.
3 Ambrose, *Expositio Isaiae prophetae.*

without mentioning his name, make of Ambrose a Manichaean?

(12) Surely you see with whom I endure your insults, you see with whom I make common cause, while without sane consideration you strive to attack and overthrow them by calumnies. You see how ruinous it is for you to accuse such men of so horrible a crime, and how glorious for me to be accused of any crime whatsoever together with such men. If you have eyes to see, note it and finally be silent. Silence the Pelagian tongue with so many Catholic tongues, shut your impudent mouth before so many venerable mouths. If, like Polemo,[4] you had entered the school of Xenocrates inebriated from late carousing, should you not be checked by reverence for so many holy men as he was by that assembly? Surely the reverence here ought to be so much greater as a greater wisdom is learned here. The countenances of so many venerable bishops are so much more to be revered than that of Xenocrates alone as Christ their teacher is greater than Plato the teacher of Xenocrates. Indeed, I do not forget Memor, your father of blessed memory, who was joined with me in no slight friendship through literary pursuits, and caused you to be very dear to me, and when I saw you in your books, not drunk with late carousing, but disturbed with mad wrangling, I brought you to be calmed and healed—not into the hall of a philosopher, but into the peaceful and honorable assembly of holy fathers. Let it be worth while, I pray you. Look at them, as it were, regarding you and gently and kindly saying to you: Are we, then, Manichaeans, son Julian? I ask you, what will you answer? With what eyes will you look at them? What arguments will come to your mind? What Categories of Aristotle, with which you wish to appear

---

4 An Athenian philosopher who was later head of the school of Plato. When he was about thirty, still a dissolute young man, he burst into the school during a discourse on temperance and, as here related, was converted to the study of philosophy.

adept that you may spring upon us as an ingenious disputer? What glassy edge or leaden dagger of your arguments will you dare draw forth in their sight? What arms will not desert you and leave you unprotected? Or will you, perhaps, say you did not name any of them in this charge? And what will you do when they say to you: It would be more endurable if you tore our names to pieces with your evil tongue rather than our faith, by whose merit our names are written in heaven? Or perhaps you will say to them: I have not violated your faith by any such charge. But with what confidence will you dare say this, you who say it is a Manichaean notion to confess that all who are born contract from Adam the sin by way of origin, which they confessed and professed, which they learned in the Church of Christ at the time of their beginnings, which they taught the Church of Christ in the time of their honor, they who through the Holy Spirit gave remission of so many sins to all whom they could baptize, and gave to so many infants remission of original sin only? Again I admonish you, again I ask, look at the great number of defenders and doctors of the Catholic Church; see on whom you inflict so serious and so wicked an injury.

(13) Or do you think that they are to be despised because they all belong to the Western Church and I have not mentioned any Eastern bishops among them? What, then, shall we do, since they are Greek and we Latin? I think that that part of the world should suffice for you in which the Lord wished to crown with glorious martyrdom the first of His Apostles. If you had been willing to listen to the head of that Church, blessed Innocent, you would already have withdrawn your perilous youth from the Pelagian snares. For, what could that holy man answer the African councils except what the Apostolic See and the Roman Church together with the others have steadfastly held from of old? Yet you accuse his successor (Zosimus) of prevarication because he

was unwilling to oppose the apostolic doctrine and the judgment of his predecessor.⁵ But I say nothing of this at present, lest by the praises of him who condemned you I should exasperate your mind, which I wish to cure rather than irritate. Consider what you will reply to St. Innocent, who knows nothing else of this matter except the opinion of those into whose company I introduced you, if that is of any avail. He, too, is on their side; though later in time, yet higher in place. In regard to freeing wretched infants by the grace of Christ from the orginal evil which is contracted from Adam, he holds with them the true and Christian doctrine. He said that Christ by the laver of His baptism purged away all the former fault, that is, of the first man, who by free will plunged into the depths,⁶ and finally defined that infants,⁷ unless they eat the flesh of the Son of Man, can by no means have life.⁸ Answer him, or rather, the Lord Himself, who used that bishop as witness, and tell why the image of God is punished with this capital punishment, that it is deprived of life, if original sin is not contracted by those who are born. But what will you say or what will you reply, for, even if you dare it in the case of blessed Innocent, you will not dare call Christ a Manichaean.

(14) Thus, there is no reason why you should appeal to the Eastern bishops, because they themselves are also Christians and in both parts of the world this faith is one faith, for this faith is Christian; and certainly the Western land brought you forth and the Western Church regenerated you. What do you wish to bring to it which you did not find in it when you came among its members? Or, rather, what do you seek to take away from it, which you yourself also

---

5 Cf. the Introduction, on the treatment of Pelagius by Innocent and Zosimus.
6 *Epist.* 181.7, *inter Augustinianas.*
7 *Epist.* 182.5, *inter Augustinianas.*
8 Cf. John 6.54.

received in it? For the original sin which you deny, to the destruction of other infants, at whatever age you were baptized was itself remitted for you, or, at any rate, was also remitted. But if it is true, as we have heard, that you were baptized as an infant, then even you, although innocent of personal sins, yet, because you were born physically of Adam, contracted the contagion of the ancient death by your first birth, and you were conceived in iniquity and then exorcised and exsufflated[9] so that, rescued from the power of darkness, you might be transferred into the kingdom of Christ. O my son, ill born of Adam but well reborn in Christ, you attempt to take from your mother the sacraments by which she bore you. Was she Manichaean when she bore you in this way in which you no longer wish her to bear; and do you reproach her manner of bearing, so that you close for others her bowels of mercy from which you yourself were born? You divide for her the name of her husband, so that for the regeneration of infants He is only Christ, for adults Christ Jesus, because, as you know, Jesus means Saviour,[10] and this is what you do not wish Him to be for infants, since you teach that they have nothing from which He may save them.

Chapter 5

(15) But you shall not lack a famous bishop of great reputation and highest renown from the East, a man whose statements, deservedly very popular, were translated into Latin and have become famous everywhere. Let St. Gregory,

---

9 This concise technical term naming the act of breathing upon the baptized, to signify the expulsion of the Devil, is used throughout this translation.
10 This use of the meaning of the name is warranted by Matt. 1.21; cf. remarks on this text in *Commentary on the New Testament* (Paterson, N.J. 1943).

then, also sit with these Fathers and bear with them the odium of your senseless accusation, while he, too, brings a remedial argument against your baneful novelty. Hear, then, what he says: 'The image of God will purge away the stain of this bodily flood and will lift up with the wings of the word of God the flesh joined to it. And although it would have been better not to need this kind of purging, but to have remained in that first dignity to which we hasten once more after our present purification, and it would have been better not to fall from the tree of life by the very bitter taste of sin, nevertheless, as the second course, it is better to be cured and corrected after the fall than to remain in sins.' And again he says: 'As we all died in Adam, so in Christ we are all brought to life. Let us, then, be born with Christ and crucified with Christ and buried with Him in death so that with Him we may also rise to life. It is necessary that we endure this useful and necessary change, so that, just as we fell from happiness into wretchedness, so we are restored from wretchedness to better things. For, where sin abounded, grace abounded yet more, so that those whom the taste of the forbidden tree condemned may be justified through more abundant grace by the cross of Christ.' Again, he says: 'Revere the birth through which you are set free from the bonds of earthy birth. Honor Bethlehem, weak and small, through which the return to paradise has been opened for you.'[1] Likewise, he says elsewhere, speaking of baptism: 'Let the word of Christ persuade you of this, also, as He says that no one can enter into the kingdom of heaven unless he is "born again of water and the Spirit."'[2] Through Him the stains of the first birth are cleansed away, through which we are conceived in iniquity and in sins have our mothers brought us forth.' Are you going to say that he, too, savors of Manichaeism or spreads poison? You

---

1 Gregory Nazianzen, *Oratio in natalem Christi.*
2 John 3.5.

hear how all with one heart, one mouth, one faith, say the same thing, and that this is the Catholic faith, established without a dissenting witness.

(16) Or does it seem to you that there is too little authority in Gregory alone of all the Eastern bishops? He is a personage of such importance that he could not say this unless it were well known to all from the Christian faith, and they would not consider him so brilliant and venerable unless they recognized these statements of his to be in accordance with the rule of the well-known truth. But, if you wish, we shall add to him St. Basil as well; indeed, whether you wish or not, he must be added, especially since in the fourth volume of your work you decided to say something about a passage from his book against the Manichaeans which is not in any way relevant to the matter of original sin entering into the world by one man and passing on through all men. He is dealing there with the truth that evil is not to be considered as a substance having its own matter, as the Manichaeans hold. Thus he says: 'It is not a substance, but a mode of behavior coming from the will alone'—not to those who have contracted the contagion of the ancient death by their first birth—'to those who through their own will have adopted an unhealthy way of living'; that is, those already grown up and having the use of reason and free will: 'This mode of behavior, accidental as it is,' he says, 'can very easily be separated from the will of those who are thus afflicted.' He adds: 'If this evil had come about so that it was no longer possible to be removed from the will, that is, though it had been added as an accident, if it had been so added that it was no longer possible to be separated from the will, it could properly be said that indeed there is no substantial evil, but that the substance itself could not now exist without the evil inhering in it as an accident. But if it is added as an accident,' he says, 'and the source of this addition is not the substance, but

the will, the evil can easily be separated from the substance, so that even the substance subject to the will can be possessed clean through all, so that not even the signs of any evil remain.' This was so rightly said by St. Basil that it can well be understood even of that evil which through Adam entered into the world and passed to all men, for this, too, was added accidentally to human nature. For it was not thus created at first, and the source of this addition is not a substance, but a will, whether of the woman who was seduced by the Serpent or of her husband who consented to his wife who had been tempted to sin. But what he says: 'that the evil can easily be separated from the will or from the substance'—it is not easy for the human will, but for the mercy of God. And this is quite sufficient against the Manichaeans, who think it is impossible for what they call the nature of evil to be changed to good. Therefore, St. Basil does not say that the will of man, or his substance or nature, can easily separate the evil from itself, but 'it can easily be separated from it,' so weighing his words that he might confute the Manichaeans against whom he was arguing, and might not lift up human pride against divine grace. Indeed, that almighty One, for whom according to the Gospel that is easy which is impossible for men,[3] will so destroy by the abundance of His grace the evil which befalls us, either from the first man or from our own will thereafter, 'that the substance even subject to the will,' as you quoted Basil as saying, 'can be possessed clean through all, so that not even the signs of any evil remain.' So may it be; this is the undoubted hope of the faithful. But when it is accomplished it is a matter of the Catholic faith. For then it shall be said to the last enemy, Death: 'Where is thy victory? Where is they sting?'[4]

(17) Thus, in regard to what you recall that Basil said: 'If

---
3 Matt. 19.26.
4 1 Cor. 15.55.

chastity is a virtue and the body were really substantially evil, it would be impossible to find a chaste body, for the body of shamefulness could not become the body of virtue. But when it is sanctified, it becomes the body of virtue and virtue shares with the body and the body with virtue, through which it also becomes the temple of God. Hence, if every body were the body of fornication, it would be impossible to find chastity in bodies, and then, indeed, we could attribute substantial evil to the nature of bodies. But, if the merits of the body have advanced so far and it has been adorned with so much honor and has received such a garment of modesty that it deserves to be the house of its Creator and becomes the bridal chamber of the Son of God, so that the Father and the Son come and deign to choose the body for their habitation, how could the Manichaean argument not prove detestable and ridiculous?' What could be said that is truer and more in accord with the Catholic rule? For it is spoken against the Manichaeans, who hold and affirm that bodies have their origin from a 'race of darkness,' which they describe as an evil nature co-eternal with the good God, holding also that bodies themselves are unchangeable evils. He was speaking against these men, I say, and not against those who hold the true and truly Christian faith; that now, indeed, the body is corruptible and presses down the soul,[5] but not that it was first created so when placed in paradise, and not that it will always be so, but will be changed to incorruption and immortality, and that even now it is beginning to be a temple of God, adorned with the modesty of a wife or widow or even of a virgin; since, though the flesh lusts against the spirit, the spirit also lusts against the flesh, so that it does not yield the members of the body to sin as weapons of iniquity.[6]

(18) But hear what is truly relevant to the present subject;

---

5 Wisd. 9.15.
6 Gal. 5.17; Rom. 6.13.

what St. Basil says without any ambiguity about that sin of the first man which also pertains to us. Although I found it in translation, I prefer for the sake of greater fidelity to truth to translate it word for word from the Greek. In a sermon on fasting,[7] he says: 'Fasting was established in paradise by law. For Adam received the first commandment: "From the tree of the knowledge of good and evil you must not eat."[8] But, "you must not eat" means fasting, and the beginning of the Law. If Eve had fasted from the tree, we should not need this fast. For it is not the healthy who need a physician, but they who are sick.[9] We have fallen ill through sin; we are healed by penance. But penance without fasting is vain. The accursed earth shall bring forth thorns and thistles for thee. Are you not ordained for sorrow and not for delights?' And a little later in the same sermon he says: 'Because we did not fast we fell from paradise. Let us fast, therefore, that we may return to it.' If you had read these and other similar words of St. Basil, or if you had wished to consider them faithfully after reading them, you would not have written in your book, with what purpose I know not, statements from his writings to becloud the minds of the ignorant, statements entirely irrelevant to the question with which we are dealing. You hear that we should not need this fast if man had not transgressed the law of fasting in the happiness of paradise, and you deny that other men are born subject to the sin of those men. You hear what he adds: 'For it is not the healthy who need a physician,' and you deny that we have lost by the sin of those men the health in which we were created. You hear that the sentence pronounced against the first man when he sinned: 'The earth shall bring forth thorns and thistles for thee,' applies to us also, and you deny that they are subject

---

7 Basil, *Sermo* 1.
8 Gen. 2.17.
9 Matt. 9.12.

to the sin whom you perceive to be subject to the same sentence. You hear that we must return to the paradise from which we fell and you deny that the sin of those who then were the only men dwelling in paradise, in whom we also were, pertains to us?

(19) Why say more of this? See whether these voices from the Eastern Church are enough for you; men so outstanding and endowed with such great sanctity, and, as the report is, even brothers in the flesh.[10] But suppose you say they are not enough. We have fourteen other Eastern bishops—Eulogius, John, Ammonianus, Porphyry, Eutonius, Porphyry, Fidus, Zoninus, Zoboennus, Nymphidius, Chromatius, Jovinus, Eleutherius, Clematius—whom we have found together in one place and can introduce into this assembly, the very ones who sat as judges over Pelagius, and as men who thought him a Catholic, with no adversary pressing on from the other side, pronounced him a Catholic. But if he had not in their sight and hearing condemned those who say that the sin of Adam harmed him alone and not the human race; and that new-born infants are in that state in which Adam was before he sinned; and that infants even if they are not baptized have eternal life—then he would by no means have gone from there uncondemned. For what does it profit you that you apply I know not what handles and hooks by the tricks of I know not what complexity in order that simple things may not be plain and clear truths may not shine forth? Who does not see how those judges could accept these things, namely, according to the Catholic faith, which everywhere by exorcising and exsufflating infants rescues them from the power of darkness—and not as these things are explained or, rather, invented by you? Yet you could say: 'The sin of Adam

---

10 Augustine's information is incorrect; Basil's brother was Gregory of Nyssa, not Gregory of Nazianzen, from whose writing these quotations are taken.

harmed the human race not through propagation but through imitation, and new-born infants are not in that state in which Adam was before he sinned because he was able to receive a commandment and these are not yet so.' With these foggy statements Pelagius thinks he has set at naught that judgment, and you nod agreement with all your might to this crime, and laugh that he has made sport of so many bishops. But could you by any cleverness twist into something else or cover with any fig leaves the statement that 'infants even if they are not baptized have eternal life'? Pelagius could do nothing but condemn before Catholic judges those who say this, and what he thought, he condemned before men, fearing to be condemned by men. For, if you do not think this, then you entirely agree with us. But, because you do not agree with us, you unquestionably think this. And herein Eastern judges condemn you. Pelagius, fearing to be condemned by them, condemned those who think this, and he is certainly to be condemned with those whom he condemned, because he held in his heart what he denied with his mouth. For what is anathematized in his words is found in his writings. But I am not now dealing with him. What do you say, you with whom I am now concerned? See, here are a number of Eastern judges; we read the records of the Church which have been preserved about them. We read that it was charged against Pelagius that 'He says infants even if not baptized have eternal life.' We read that Pelagius condemned those who say this, for otherwise he could not have escaped those judges. Now, what do you yourself say? Will infants have eternal life even if they depart from this life without being baptized, or will they not? If you say they will, then the words of your Pelagius will condemn you, and all those by whom he feared to be condemned. But if you say they will not, I ask for what reason the innocent image of God will be punished by being deprived of life if no sin is contracted by human propagation. But, if it is actually contracted, why are those called Manichaeans who think this, by whom Pelagius would have been condemned if he had not pretended to think this?

(20) Meanwhile, you have before your eyes bishops not only of the West but also of the East. For we have found many of the East, whom we seemed to lack. They all believe in one and the same way, that by one man sin entered into the world and through sin death, and thus it has passed unto all men; in whom all have sinned, and the way is this, that all are believed to be born subject to the sin of that one first man. If you call him who says this a Manichaean, look at these, blush before them, spare them, or rather yourself, lest He who rules them and dwells in them may, perchance, not spare you. But, if you do not call them Manichaeans, you can find no reason to call me so. For you call me this for no other reason than that I believe what they believe, I hold what they hold, I teach what they teach, I preach what they preach about the sin of the first man, to which all men are subject by their carnal birth and from which none is released except by spiritual birth. Yield to them and you will not strike me; agree with them and you will leave me alone. Finally, if you do not wish to be my friend through them, I ask only that you not become their enemy through me. But how will you not become that if you remain in this your error? How much better to abandon this in order that you may join them. Have Pelagius and Celestius such power over you that you dare not only to desert, but even to call Manichaeans, so many great doctors and defenders of the Catholic faith, ancient and contemporary, from the rising of the sun to its setting, some fallen asleep and others still with us? I wonder how this can ever come from your mouth—which the perverseness of your error yet compels you to proclaim. It is strange indeed that in the face of a man there is so great a distance between his brow and his tongue that in this case the brow does not subdue the tongue.

Chapter 6

(21) But I know what you are muttering. Speak now, speak and let us hear it. At the end of your work with which we are now dealing, that is, in the last part of Book 4, you say: 'St. John of Constantinople says there is no original sin in infants. In a homily which he delivered about the baptized, he says: "Blessed be God, who alone hath done wondrous things, who hath made all things and changed all things. Behold, they enjoy the serenity of freedom who a little while ago were held captive, and they are citizens of the Church who were strangers and wanderers, and they are in the state of justice who were in the confusion of sin. For they are not only free but also holy, not only holy but also just, not only just but also sons, not only sons but also heirs, not only heirs but also brothers of Christ, not only brothers of Christ but also co-heirs, not only co-heirs but also members, not only members but also a temple, not only a temple but also instruments of the Spirit. You see how many are the benefits of baptism; some think the heavenly grace consists only in the remission of sins, but we have enumerated ten honors. For this reason we baptize even infants, though they are not defiled with sin, in order that there may be given to them holiness, justice, adoption, inheritance, and the brotherhood of Christ, that they may be His members." '[1]

(22) Do you, then, dare to set these words of the holy bishop John in opposition to so many statements of his great colleagues, and separate him from their most harmonious society, and constitute him their adversary? Far be it, far be it from us to believe or say such an evil thing of so great a man. Far be it from us, I say, to think that John of Constantinople, on the question of the baptism of infants and their liberation by Christ from the paternal handwriting,

---

[1] John Chrysostom, *Homilia ad neophytos.*

should oppose so many great fellow bishops, especially the Roman Innocent, the Carthaginian Cyprian, the Cappadocian Basil, the Nazianzene Gregory, the Gaul Hilary, the Milanese Ambrose. There are other matters on which at times even the most learned and excellent defenders of the Catholic rule do not agree, without breaking the bond of the faith, and one speaks better and more truly about one thing and another about another. But this matter about which we are now speaking pertains to the very foundations of the faith. He who would overthrow in the Christian faith what is written: 'Since by a man came death, by a man also comes resurrection of the dead. For as in Adam all die, so in Christ all will be made to live,'[2] strives to take away all that we believe in Christ. Christ is fully the Saviour of infants as well. They shall certainly perish unless redeemed by Him, for without His flesh and blood they cannot have life. This John, too, thought and believed and learned and taught. But you twist his words according to your doctrine. He said that infants do not have sins—he meant sins of their own. This is why we rightly call them innocents, according to what the Apostle says, that those not yet born had not done aught of good or evil; not according to what he says: 'By the disobedience of the one man the many were constituted sinners.'[3] Even our Cyprian could say the same thing about infants as John, when he wrote: 'The new-born infant has not committed any sin, and he is forgiven not his own sins, but those of another.'[4] Therefore, John, comparing them to adults whose personal sins are forgiven in baptism, said they do not have sins—not as you quote him: 'are not defiled with sin,' where you want it understood to mean they are not defiled by the sin of the first man. But I should not attribute this to

---

2 I Cor. 15.21,22.
3 Cf. Rom. 9.11; 5.16.
4 Cyprian, *Epistola*, 64, *ad Fidum*.

you but to the translator, although in some manuscripts which have the same translation we read not 'sin' but 'sins.' Therefore, I wonder if one of your party did not prefer to write the singular number so that that one sin might be understood of which the Apostle says: 'For the judgment was from the one unto condemnation, but grace is from many offenses unto justification.'[5] There he wishes us to understand the 'one' to mean nothing else but the offense; not wishing men to believe that infants are defiled by it, you preferred to say: 'not defiled by sin,' so that the one sin of the first man might come into our mind, not that they do not have sins, as John says, lest we understand their personal sins, or read 'They are not defiled with sins,' as the same passage reads in other manuscripts. But let us not deal with suspicions, and here we may suppose an error of the copyist or a variation in the translation. I shall quote the Greek words themselves as John wrote them: *'Dia touto kai ta paedia baptizomen, kaitoi hamartêmata ouk echonta,'* which is, in [the English translation of the] Latin,[6] 'Therefore, we also baptize infants, though not having sins.' You certainly see that he did not say: 'Infants are not defiled with sin' or 'sins,' but 'not having sins,' meaning sins of their own; there is no difficulty. But you will say: Why did he himself not add 'their own'? Why, I think, except that he was speaking in the Catholic Church and did not believe that he would be understood in any other way, since no one had raised such a question, and he spoke more carelessly since you were not yet disputing.

(23) Do you wish to hear what he, too, said quite openly about this matter? Listen, I add him also to that number of saints. Listen, I set him among my witnesses, or among your judges, whom you considered your patron. Listen, you would even call him a Manichaean. Come in, St. John, come in, and

---
5 Cf. Rom. 5.19.
6 *Ideo et infantes baptizamus, quamvis peccata non habentes.*

sit down with your brothers, from whom no argument and no temptation have separated you. We need your opinion, also, and yours especially, since in your writings this young man thinks he has found the means to overthrow and make void the opinions of so many of your great fellow bishops. But, if he had really found something of the sort, and it became clear that you think what he thinks, we could never prefer you alone—pardon me for saying so—to so many men of such great importance in this case, about which Christian belief and the Catholic Church have never varied. But far be it from you to have another opinion and thus stand out as peculiar in this. Say something by which this young man may be confounded and abashed when he seeks to stain my reputation, and pardon me when, after I have explained to him what you think in this matter, he will also seek to stain yours. For he says it is a Manichaean notion to believe that infants need the help of Christ as liberator, that they may be freed from damnation, to which they are subject from the sin of the first man. And when he learns that you, too, think so, he will through this repent of his Pelagian error or will accuse you of Manichaeism. But, in order to confer a true benefit on him, let us not care about his false reproach.

(24) Now hear, Julian, what John says in agreement with the other Catholic doctors. Writing to Olympia, he says: 'When Adam sinned that great sin, and condemned all the human race in common, he paid the penalties in grief.' Again, on the raising of Lazarus, he says: 'Christ wept because mortality had transgressed to the point that, cast out from eternity, it loved the world of the dead. Christ wept because the Devil made mortal those who could have been immortal.'[7] What could be said more clearly? What will you answer to this? If Adam by his great sin condemned all the human race in common, can an infant be born otherwise than

---

7 John Chrysostom, *Homilia de Lazaro resuscitato*.

condemned? And through whom except Christ is he freed from this condemnation? And if even in Lazarus he says that mortality, cast out from eternity, loved the world of the dead, who of mortals is not touched by this fault and mischance by which the first man fell from everlasting life, which he would have received if he had not sinned? If the Devil made mortal all who could have been immortal, why do even infants die if they are not subject to the sin of that first man? And can even infants be saved from the power of death except through Him in whom all shall be made to live?

(25) This same John treats in one of his sermons the question why beasts harm men or kill them, although the saying of the Lord is clear by which He subjects beasts to men that he may have power over them.[8] He solves this question by saying that, before sin entered [the world], all beasts were subject to man, and the fact that now they harm men is punishment of the first sin. The treatise is long—therefore, I shall not include it in this work—but it is fitting to set forth a part of it. He says: 'We fear and dread beasts; I do not deny it. And we have fallen from our lordship; this, too, I admit. But this does not show that the law of God is false, for in the beginning things were not so arranged, but they feared and trembled and were subject to their master. And since we fell from our trust, so we also fell from our honor. What is the proof for this? God brought the beasts to Adam to see what he would call them, and Adam did not recoil as if in fear.' And a little later: 'This is one sign,' he says, 'that in the beginning the beasts were not terrifying to man; a second is even clearer than this: namely, the conversation of the woman and the Serpent. For, if beasts had been terrifying to men, the woman surely would not have stayed when she saw the Serpent; she would not have taken its advice and would not have talked with it so trustfully, but would im-

---
8 Cf. Gen. 1.28.

mediately have been terrified and have fled at the very sight of it. Now she converses and is not afraid, for that fear did not as yet exist. But since sin entered, the properties of honor were taken away.' Again, a little later: 'Indeed, as long as he trusted in God he was terrifying to the beasts, but because he transgressed he now fears even the lowest of his fellow servants. If this is not so,' he says, 'then show me that, before man sinned, beasts were terrifying to him. You cannot do so. But if, after all this, fear entered, this, too, is under God's care. For if, after the commandment which had been given was removed and broken by man, the honor which had been given to him by God had remained unmoved, he would not easily have risen again.'[9] Surely it is clear that St. John has shown in this discussion that that sin which entered through one man became common to all, since the fear of beasts is common to all, and beasts by no means spare even infants, whom certainly, according to this treatise of St. John, they should in no way harm or frighten unless infants were held by the bonds of that ancient sin.

(26) Now, Julian, call him also a Manichaean (why do you hesitate to do so?) since he wrongs this very excellent nature whose innocence you defend, and asserts the propagation of condemnation.[10] Nay, rather, restrain yourself and make amends if there is anything of sound reason in you, and at last understand how John could say that infants do not have sins; not that they are not bound by the sin of the first parents, but that they have not committed any personal sins. And in this same homily, if you have read the whole of it, I do not

---

9 John Chrysostom, *Homilia 9, in Genesim.*
10 Here, as elsewhere, the phrases *propago mortis, propago condemnationis,* and others of the same kind, have been translated literally to retain the allusion to one of the Pelagian phrases against the doctrine about original sin—a reference to their argument that sin cannot be transmitted by way of natural propagation, but must be voluntary by the will of the one to whom it is imputed.

know how it could have escaped you, or, if it could not have escaped you, I wonder why you have not made amends if the authority of John is of any importance with you. But if you read the whole sermon, and are familiar with the passage which I have mentioned, and yet thought that you should hold to your opinion, then why did you quote him in your work? Or was it that you might induce us to read the whole and to find the means of discovering and refuting your deception? For what is clearer than what he said there: 'Christ came once and found us bound by the paternal handwriting which Adam wrote. He showed the beginning of the debt; through our sins the interest increased'?[11] Do you hear this man, learned in the Catholic faith and teaching, distinguishing the debt of the paternal handwriting which has clung to us as our inheritance, from those debts whose interest increased though our sins? Do you hear from what infants are released in baptism, who have not as yet contracted debts of their own and yet could not have been immune from the paternal handwriting? His words, not translated, are as follows, in Greek: '*Erchetai hapax ho Christos, heuren hêmôn cheirographon patrôön, ho ti egraphen ho Adam. Ekeinos tên archên eisêgagen tou chreious, hêmeis ton daneismon heuxêsamen tais metagenesterais hamartiais.*' Translated word for word, this reads as follows: 'Christ came once; He found our paternal handwriting, which Adam wrote. He caused the beginning of the debt; we increased the interest by our later sins.'[12] Was he content to say 'the paternal handwriting' without adding 'our,' so that we might know that before we increased the interest by our later sins, the debt of that paternal handwriting already pertained to us?

11 John Chrysostom, *Homilia ad neophytos*.
12 The Latin reads: *Venit semel Christus, invenit nostrum chirographum paternum, quod scripsit Adam. Ille initium induxit debiti, nos fenus auximus posterioribus peccatis.*

(27) Read, also, how this same holy man explains this same passage of the Apostle, where it is written: 'Through one man sin entered into the world.' For there the truth of his Catholic faith is clearer than light. Since it would be too long to quote the whole of it in this work, I shall mention only a few points. 'It is clear,' he says, 'that it is not the sin which comes from transgression of the law, but that sin which comes from the disobedience of Adam, which has defiled all.' And a little later he says: ' "Death reigned from Adam to Moses even over those who had not sinned." How did it reign? "After the likeness of the transgression of Adam, who is a figure of him who was to come."'[13] For this reason Adam is also a figure of Christ. How is he a figure? they ask. Because, just as Adam became the cause of death to those who were born of him, even though they did not eat of the tree—that death which was brought about through the food—so Christ, for those who are of Him, even though they have done nothing just, became the purveyor of justice which He bestowed on us all through the Cross.' In another part of the same sermon he says: 'So that when a Jew says to you: "How was the world saved by the virtue[14] of one man, Christ?" you can say to him: "Just as the world was condemned by the disobedience of the one man, Adam"—although grace and sin are not equal, nor are death and life on a par, nor are God and the Devil equal.' And again, a little later: 'But not like the offense,' he says, 'so also is he gift. For, if by the offense of the one many died, much more has the grace of God and the gift in grace of the one man, Jesus Christ, abounded unto the many.' What he means is this. If sin had power, and the sin of one man, then

---

13 Cf. Rom. 5.14.
14 Augustine uses the term *virtus* in the larger sense which it has in Latin, namely, general excellence and power, by which it may mean both virtue and strength. It is useful to recall this in passages about strength made perfect in weakness, relying on one's own virtue, and the like.

grace and the grace of God, and not only of the Father but also of the Son, should certainly have more power. This is much more reasonable, for that one should be condemned for another certainly does not seem to make much sense, but that one should be saved for another seems much more fitting and reasonable. But, if the former happened, then much more the latter. And again, elsewhere in what follows: ' "The judgment," he says, "was from one man unto condemnation, but grace is from many offenses unto justification." This is the same,' he says, 'as to say that sin could bring about death and damnation, but grace destroyed not only that one sin, but also the sins that came in afterwards.' And a little later, on the same matter, he says: 'Therefore, he shows that many goods were brought in, and not only that that sin was destroyed, but also all the rest, saying: "But grace is from many offenses unto justification." ' And after a little, he says: 'At first he said that, if the sin of one destroyed all, then much more the grace of one could save. And after this he shows that not only this sin was destroyed by grace, but also all the rest, and not only were the sins destroyed, but justice was bestowed, also. And Christ did not benefit us merely as much as Adam harmed us, but much more, and more abundantly.' After this, in the same work, when he was discussing baptism, he quoted the words of the Apostle, who said: " 'Do you not know, brethren, that all we who have been baptized into Christ Jesus have been baptized into his death? For we were buried with him by means of baptism into death." What does this mean: "We were baptized into his death"? That we, too, shall die as He died, for baptism is a cross. Thus, what the cross and the tomb were to Christ, baptism has become for us. But not in the same way, for He died and was buried in the flesh, but we both died and were buried in sin. Therefore, he does not say "united with him in death," but "in the likeness of death." For both are a death, but not in the same thing. The one is the death of the flesh of Christ, but ours is of sin. Therefore, just as the former is true, so the latter is also true.'

(28) Can you any longer doubt that St. John is as far from your teaching as he is close to Catholic teaching? Is there in his argument, in which he explains the passage of the Apostle which is most necessary for the matter we are discussing, the words: 'Through one man sin entered into the world,' and the whole context, any trace of what you say, that this refers to imitation and not to physical birth? Does he not say that by that one sin all things were defiled, and so distinguish it from the others committed and introduced later, which you say pertain to imitation and not to propagation, that he says that not only those but this and those also were destroyed through the grace of Christ? Does he not so explain the words of the Apostle: 'All we who have been baptized into Christ Jesus have been baptized into his death,' in such a way that he says that he who is baptized into Christ so dies to sin as Christ died to the flesh, because to be baptized into the death of Christ is nothing else than to die to sin? To what sin, then, does the infant die, if it has not contracted original sin? Or are infants, perhaps, not baptized into the death of Christ, although the Apostle does not say 'certain ones,' but 'all we who have been baptized into Christ have been baptized into his death'? Or, when they are baptized with Christian baptism, are you going to say that they are not baptized into Christ, lest Bishop John silence you by his definition, when he says that, for those who are baptized into Christ, baptism is what the cross and the tomb were for Christ, so that we may understand them to have died to sin just as He died in the flesh? Consider how great in the Christian faith and defense of this Catholic teaching is the man to whom you wished to attribute your teaching, as if he had said that

infants are not defiled with the sin of the first man, when he said: 'They do not have sins.' That he meant only sins of their own is plainly proved by considerable evidence.

Chapter 7

(29) What good has it done you to quote the testimony of John of Constantinople as though he agreed with you? Is it that you may with keen cunning seize upon one word of his, spoken, as it were, in passing, and bring upon yourself such a great heap of his words by which you may be overwhelmed? While you were so imprudent and careless that you did not notice that in the very homily in which you could find scarcely one piece of evidence which deceived you because you did not understand it rightly and by which you deceived others, St. John of Constantinople very clearly stated that all men, aside from their own debts, are debtors of the paternal handwriting. Yet, after you quoted his words, by which you thought your opinion gained some support, you went on to say: 'Since then, it is crystal clear that this is the sound and true doctrine, which in the first place reason and then the authority of Scripture supports and which the learning of holy men has always sustained—who, however, attributed authority to the truth itself and not by their own agreement, but received testimony and glory from their association with it—let not a conspiracy of the wicked disturb any of the prudent.' Of what use are these words of yours except to show either how in this matter you have neglected to learn the opinions and statements of Catholic doctors, or, if you took the pains to learn them, by what fraud you try to deceive the ignorant? For, leaving aside reason and the authority of holy Scripture, has the learning of holy men always sustained that opinion by which you deny that infants are born subject

to the sin of the first man? This is not indicated by the number of testimonies of the many holy and learned men which I have cited; on the contrary, I think that you now see how far you are deceived in this opinion, if you are not trying to deceive, and did not know this long ago. But let me believe better of you; if you have learned this now for the first time, if you see now for the first time that so many holy and learned men have learned and taught what we also learn and teach on the subject of the sin of the first man, namely, that infants who are generated physically are bound by it and are not released from it except by spiritual regeneration, then change this opinion of yours, forget this error and near madness, with which you insult so many great Fathers by calling them Manichaeans. If you have done this in ignorance, why do you not cast aside your wretched stupidity; if you have done it knowingly, why do not put away your blasphemous boldness?

(30) You are convicted on every side. The numerous testimonies of the saints are clearer than daylight. See into what assembly I have introduced you. Here is Ambrose of Milan, whom your teacher Pelagius praised so highly that he said: 'In his books the Roman faith shone out most clearly, who bloomed as a beautiful flower among the Latin writers, so that not even his enemy would dare censure his faith and his most pure interpretation of the Scriptures. Here is John of Constantinople, whom you quoted as outstanding among the learned and holy men in this very work which I am refuting. Here is Basil, whose words, which do not have anything to do with the matter in hand, you thought gave you support. Here are others whose general agreement ought to move you. This is not, as you write with an evil pen, a conspiracy of the wicked. They were famous in the Catholic Church for their pursuit of sound doctrine; armed and girded with spiritual arms, they carried on strenuous warfare against heretics. After they had faithfully completed their labors in

this world they fell asleep in the arms of peace. 'One,' you say, 'came forth' (meaning me) 'who wishes it to be understood that the crisis of the battle depends on him.' Listen, not I alone, but a great many holy and learned doctors answer you for me and with me, and for the salvation of all of us and your own, if you are wise.

(31) It is not, as you slander, that we set only the murmur of the populace against you—although the populace itself murmurs against you for the reason that this is not a question which can escape the popular knowledge. Rich and poor, high and low, learned and unlearned, men and women, know what is forgiven to each age in baptism. Hence, too, mothers in all the world run daily with their little ones not only to Christ, that is, the Anointed, but to Christ Jesus, that is, the Saviour also. But see to what I have introduced you: the assembly of these saints is not a popular multitude; they are not only sons but also fathers of the Church. They are of that number of whom it is prophesied: 'In the place of thy fathers sons are born to thee, thou shalt set them as princes over all the earth.'[1] From her, sons are born to learn these things; they became her fathers that they might teach.

(32) Why do you boastfully say that you rejoice that this truth, which you consider error or wish to consider so, can find no supporter in such a great multitude? As if it were a slight proof that in this most sure and ancient foundation of the faith the very multitude scattered over the whole earth does not disagree. But, if you seek supporters for it among those who have produced something of literary value, and whose teaching is famous, then here is a memorable and venerable assembly and agreement of supporters. St. Irenaeus says that the ancient wound of the Serpent is healed by the faith of Christ and the cross, and that we were bound by

---
1 Ps. 44.17.

original sin as if by chains. St. Cyprian says that the infant perishes unless he is baptized, although it is not his own sins that are forgiven him, but those of another. St Reticius says that the old man whom we stripped off has not only old, but inborn, sins. St. Olympius says that the fault of the first-formed was scattered in the seed, so that sin is born with man. St. Hilary says that all flesh comes from sin, with the exception of Him who came in the likeness of sinful flesh, without sin. He says that he is born of sinful origin and under the law of sin, whose words are: 'I was conceived in iniquity.'[2] St. Ambrose says that those infants who are baptized are re-formed from wickedness at the beginning of their natural life. He says that, alone of those born of woman, our holy Lord Jesus experienced no contagions of earthy corruption in the newness of His immaculate birth. He says that in Adam we all die because through one man sin entered into the world, and his guilt is the death of all. He says that by his wound Adam would have slain all the human race unless that Samaritan, descending, had healed its grievous wounds. He says that Adam was and in him all were; Adam perished and in him all perished. He says that we are stained by contagion before we are born and that no human conception is without sin, because we are conceived, he says, in the sin of our parents and are born in their transgressions. And birth itself has its contagions and the nature itself has not only one contagion. He says that the Devil is the usurer by whom Eve, duped, obligated the whole human race in the subsequent posterity, which is subject to the interest. He says that Eve was deceived by the Devil in order to deceive her husband and put his inheritance under obligation. He says Adam was so vitiated by the bite of the Serpent that we are all lamed by that wound. He says that through the bodily union of man

---

[2] Ps. 50.7.

and woman no one is without sin. But He who is without sin, that is, the Lord Christ, is also without this kind of conception. St. Innocent tells you that by the laver of regeneration all former fault is cleansed away which came through him who, falling by free will, was plunged into the depths. He says that infants cannot have life unless they eat the flesh of the Lord and drink His blood. St. Gregory says that it would have been better not to have fallen from the tree of life by the very bitter taste of sin, but that, after the fall, we must amend our lives. He says that we fell from good into misery and wishes us to return from misery to better things, so that those who were condemned by the taste of the forbidden tree may be justified through more abundant grace by the cross of Christ. He says that that birth is to be revered through which we are delivered from the bonds of our earthly birth. He says that by the regeneration through water and the Spirit the stains of the first birth, by which we are conceived in iniquity, are cleansed away. St. Basil says that we have contracted the disease of sin because Eve did not wish to fast from the forbidden tree. He says, finally, that we have fallen from paradise because we have not fasted, and he teaches that we should fast in order to return there. They say to you with one mouth, so many holy bishops—Eulogius, John, Ammonianus, Porphyry, Eutonius, the other Porphyry, Fidus, Zoninus, Zoboennus, Nymphidius, Chromatius, Jovinus, Eleutherius, Clematis: We did not acquit Pelagius except because he condemned those who say that infants even if they are not baptized have eternal life. Now, answer whether the just God could deprive of eternal life His own image, if not subject to any sin.

(33) Finally, the holy Bishop John says—he whom you mentioned honorably, whom you praised as holy and learned, of whom you said that he received testimony and glory from

his association with truth—even he says that Adam so sinned that great sin that he condemned all the human race in common. He says that at the death of Lazarus Christ wept because mortality, cast out from eternity, loved the world of the dead, and because the Devil made mortal those who could have been immortal. He says that before the sin of man beasts were subject in all ways to man, but, after that sin entered, we began to fear beasts, and thus far did he wish it understood that that sin of the first man pertains to all men; for who does not see it follows that no beast would harm infants unless their physical birth bound them also with the chain of that sin? He says, in the same sermon by which you wished to deceive the incautious, that Christ found us bound by our paternal handwriting, which Adam wrote, and by our own later sins. He explains the passage of the Apostle on which this whole question depends, which reads: 'Through one man sin entered into the world,'[3] and the rest of the context of this passage. Nor does he in his long discussion say what you say, that this sin passed to all men, not by propagation of the race, but by imitation; on the contrary, he shows by not disagreeing with the teaching of his fellow bishops that the truth is quite otherwise. For he says that all were defiled by the sin of the first man, and lest anyone think that this happened not by physical generation,[4] but by moral imitation, he says that Adam was called a figure of him who was to come because, just as he became the cause of the death induced by the food to those born of him although they do not eat of the tree, so Christ, for those who are of Him, even though they have done nothing just, became the purveyor of justice which He bestowed on all through the cross. He

---

[3] Cf. Rom. 5.12.
[4] Augustine seldom uses *generatio* in the more common sense of 'generation' as the result of the process of generation. In nearly every instance in this book, 'generation' signifies the less usual English meaning of the act and process of generating or begetting.

says that a Jew who denies that the world can be saved by the virtue of one man, Christ, can be refuted by the sin of the first man, since by the one, Adam, when he disobeyed, the world was condemned. He says it seems not to make much sense that one should be condemned for another, yet that happened through Adam; hence, he argues that much more plausibly should we find it more fitting and reasonable that one should be saved for another, which was fulfilled in Christ. But who does not see that, if the sin of the first man passed unto all men not by propagation but by imitation, then no one is condemned for another's sin, but each one for his own, not a sin transmitted to him by another through generation, but which he himself of his own will committed by imitation. He says that grace destroyed not only that one sin of the first man, but also the sins that came in afterwards. Here he sufficiently distinguishes later sins, which we can say are committed by imitation, from that one which passed to men by propagation, and shows that both are destroyed by grace, so that, according to the intention of the Apostle, we see that regeneration brought more benefit than generation brought harm. Thus he explains what has been written: 'But not like the offense is the gift. For the judgment was from one man unto condemnation, but grace is from many offenses unto justification.'[5] By this statement, that imitation of yours, which is the new contrivance of the Pelagian error, is refuted by the writings of the Apostle Paul and the explanation of Bishop John. And he also says about baptism itself, explaining what the Apostle says: 'All we who have been baptized into Christ Jesus have been baptized into his death,'[6] that to be baptized into the death of Christ is nothing else but to die in sin, as He died in the flesh. Hence, it is necessary either that infants are not baptized into Christ, or, if they are

---
5 Cf. Rom. 5.16.
6 Rom. 6.3.

baptized, they are baptized into His death; thus, they also die to sin and, since they have no personal sin, they are cleansed from the contamination of another's sin, that is, original sin, which has become common to all.

(34) Walled about by such a mound of holy and learned men, do you still think that our cause 'could find no defender in such a great multitude'? Or will you call so complete an agreement of Catholic priests 'a conspiracy of the wicked'? Nor will you think St. Jerome deserves your scorn because he was but a priest, yet learned in Greek and Latin, and even in Hebrew eloquence, and going from the Western to the Eastern Church lived until extreme old age in holy places and in sacred writings, and read all or nearly all who before him in both parts of the world had written on the teachings of the Church, and held and expressed no other doctrine on this matter. When he was explaining the Prophet Jonas, he said very plainly that even infants are held subject to the sin which Adam sinned.[7] Are you, then, so in love with your error, into which you fell carelessly in youthful confidence and human frailty, that you not only dare to disagree with these priests of Catholic unity and truth, men from all parts of the earth, agreeing with each other in such harmony of faith, and in so important a matter, wherein the sum and substance of Christian religion consists—but that you even dare in addition to call them Manichaeans? If you do not do this, then you are not doing it to me justly, since you see that in the same matter I have followed in their footsteps by my arguments which have made you fiercely angry at me. But if you heap such opprobrium upon me alone for no other reason except that I think what they think about the sin of the first man and hold what they hold and preach what they preach, then who does not see that you are casting open insult at me, but secretly judge the same of them? If you

---

7 Jerome, *In Jonam* 3.

consider, to say nothing of the rest, either the words of Bishop John about our paternal handwriting which Adam wrote, words I believe you found in that sermon from which you took what you wished, or of Bishop Ambrose, that no one coming from the union of man and woman can be without sin, which you read in my book but feared to touch upon in yours—and if your face is bold before men—yet your mind will blush before God.

(35) But I, in view of the love I have for you, which by God's mercy you shall not remove from the fibres of my heart by any insults, I should prefer, my son Julian, that you might conquer yourself by a better and stronger youth and overcome by a more powerful piety that pride (what is it but human?) because of which you wish your opinion to prevail, whatsoever it may be, just because it is yours. And just as Polemo, gradually taking from his head and flinging aside the garlands of luxury, hid his hands under his cloak and changed his face and expression to one of modesty, and finally gave himself up wholly as disciple to him whom he had intended to mock, so do you—since so many venerable men are speaking to you, especially Bishop Ambrose, praised in the integrity of his Catholic faith even by the mouth of your wicked teacher and deceiver, and also Bishops Basil and John, whom you also by truthful testimony placed among the holy and learned men—cast aside like the garlands of drunken men the praises of the Pelagians by which you are lifted up as their great defender. Break your abusive pen, to put it mildly, with repentant hand, not merely hiding it, as it were, under the cloak of modesty; and give back your heart, as one who has withdrawn, not giving it up as one coming for the first time, not to the Platonist Xenocrates, but to these Christian bishops, or, rather, through them to the Lord Christ to be filled with the truth. If this advice of mine displeases you, do as you please. If you repent, which is what I most desire, I shall have great and abounding joy; but if, what

I deprecate, you remain in this perverseness, I shall have gained from your insults an increase of heavenly reward for me and the sting of sorrowing pity for you.

Chapter 8

(36) Since I have shown how many great and worthy men, defenders and teachers of the Catholic faith, you falsely make Manichaeans, hear a little how you aid the true Manichaeans by your ignorant boldness. For I promised that I would prove this in the second part of my argument. The Manichaeans (and you have sufficiently shown that you know this) teach that there are two natures, one of good and the other of evil, coming from two different and hostilely opposed co-eternal principles—a sacrilegious vanity of an evil error. In oposition to them the Catholic faith teaches that the nature of God alone is without beginning, that is, the nature of the supreme and changeless Good, namely, of that ineffable Trinity. And it holds that by this aforesaid supreme and changeless Good all creation was established, and all natures good, although unequal to the Creator, because they were created from nothing and thus are changeable; so that there is no nature at all which is not either Himself or made by Him; so that, however great or of whatever sort a nature is, in so far as it is a nature, it is good.[1]

---

[1] Since Julian thought that the phrase, 'natural sin' and similar uses of the word 'natural' betrayed Manichaeism in Augustine's position, it is useful to mention the chief significations by which Augustine indicates various aspects of the same reality in his varied use of the terms *natura* and *naturale,* although this is usually evident from the text itself. 'Nature' is sometimes used here to mean the intrinsic principle by which things in general, or a particular thing, becomes and is what it is and is preserved and perfected. It may also be used to mean a special kind of being that has an existence of its own. Again, it may also be used to mean the individual existing in a special nature, where 'nature' is taken in the second sense.

(37) They ask us, then, whence comes evil. We answer, from good, but not from supreme and changeless Good. Therefore, evils arose from inferior and changeable goods. Though we understand, indeed, that these evils are not natures but faults[2] of natures, at the same time we understand that they cannot exist except from and in natures, and that evil is not anything but a falling away from goodness. But a falling away of what, except of some nature, without a doubt? Because even an evil will is certainly the will of some nature or other. Both angel and man are surely natures. It cannot be a will of no one when there is a will. And these same wills are of so much worth that they constitute qualities of those natures whose wills they are. For, if one asks of what sort is an angel or a man of evil will, it is correct to answer, 'evil,' taking the name of the quality from the evil will rather than from the good nature. The nature is the substance itself which is capable both of good and of evil. It is capable of goodness by participation of the good by which it was made. It receives evil not by a participation of evil, but by privation of good, that is, not when it is mixed with a nature which is an evil something, because no nature inasmuch as it is a nature is evil, but when it falls away from the nature which is the supreme and unchanging Good, because it was made not of that nature but of nothing. Otherwise, it could not even have an evil will, if it were not changeable. Now, a nature would not be changeable if it were of God, and not made by Him of nothing. Therefore, God is the author of goods when He is the author of natures, whose spontaneous falling away from the good does not indicate whom they were made by, but whence they were made. And this is not some-

---

2 Augustine uses *vitium* both for the more general idea of a fault and for the special idea of a vice, in accordance with the Latin usage. The term has usually been translated here as 'fault,' the better to render his intentional references to his doctrine that evil itself consists in defect.

thing, since it is absolutely nothing; therefore, it cannot have an author, because it is nothing.

(38) Therefore, as the Manichaean is opposed to the Catholic faith, that is, the faith of truth and true piety, since he says that good and evil are so opposed to each other that he will not say a nature becomes evil when it falls away from good, and that this falling away itself is an evil of it; but says, rather, that evil itself is a nature, and, what is more senseless, a nature everlasting and without beginning, and he calls it a body and spirit; namely, a body whence the spirit operates and a spirit which operates from the body—so it is impossible to say how much this adversary of the faith is aided by him who denies that evils arise from goods, and interprets in this way the words of the Lord: 'A good tree cannot bear bad fruit.' For God our teacher does not mean the tree to be a nature from which the fruit of which He speaks comes, but the will, whether good or evil, and the fruits the works, which cannot be evil if the will is good, or good if the will is evil. This is what He means by saying: 'A good tree cannot bear bad fruit, nor can a bad tree bear good fruit,'[3] as though He should say: An evil will cannot do good works, nor can a good will do evil works. For, if we seek the origin of the trees themselves, that is, of the wills themselves, what are they except natures, which God made good? Therefore, evils arose from goods; not evil works from good wills, but evil wills from good natures. What, then, does the Manichaean so hope to hear as this, that evils cannot come from goods, so that, because we cannot deny there are evils, nothing is left except that they must come from evils, if they cannot come from good natures; and thus, without beginning, evils have an origin of their own, namely, a nature of evil which has always existed without beginning, and there are two natures, one of good, and the other of evil. For it is necessary either that

---
3 Matt. 7.18.

there are no evils, or they must come from good natures or from evil ones. If we say there are no evils, than we say in vain to God: 'Deliver us from evil.'[4] But if we say that evils arise only from evils, the Manichaean plague will triumph and will destroy everything and will violate the nature of God Himself by a mixture of an evil nature, as though His were a mutable nature.[5] Therefore, it remains for us to admit that evils come from goods, because, if we deny this, then they must come from evils, and we shall quite agree with the Manichaeans.

(39) Thus, when you say: 'Since according to the saying of the Gospel a tree should be known by its fruit, do you think we should listen to him who, declaring that nothing but evil comes forth from marriage, says it is a good?' you wish us to think of marriage as a good tree from which as bad fruit you will not have man born bound by the contagion of original sin, and you do not see you must needs make adultery a bad tree if marriage is a good tree. Therefore, if he who is born of marriage is the fruit of marriage and must then be without fault, lest bad fruit be born from a good tree, it follows that he who is born of adultery should not be born without fault, lest good fruit be born from a bad tree, since the Lord by divine authority says that bad fruit cannot come from a good tree or good fruit from a bad tree. So, in order to get out of this difficulty, because you say that a man cannot be born with a fault, even if born of adultery, you must deny that adultery is a bad tree, lest it seem that he who according to you is born of adultery without fault is born as good fruit from a bad tree, contrary to the definition of the

---
4 Matt. 6.13.
5 A consequence of the doctrine that the soul, which the Manichaeans said is of the nature of God, has been mixed by force with a creature of the substantial principle of evil and thus compelled to commit sins, although the soul itself was said to have the nature of the divine goodness.

Lord. Therefore, deny that marriage is to be called a good tree, and admit you erred in saying this. But you will say a man born through adulterous union is not born of adultery. Whence, then? Of human nature, you will say, which even in adulterers is the work of God and not their own work. Why, then, do you not understand in the same way that a man born through the union of marriage is not born of marriage, but likewise of human nature, which in the married also is the work of God, not their own, and it is therefore not to be attributed to the goodness of marriage that those born contract evil from the fault of the nature, just as it is not attributed to the wickedness of adultery that those born derive good from the institution of the nature? But you understand by the good tree not what Christ wished us to understand, namely, the good will of man, but the work of God itself, that is, the marriage of men or their nature. And because these works of God are good, you say that evil cannot come from them, because a good tree cannot bear bad fruit. And thus the Manichaean concludes his argument against you on behalf of his dogma. You aid him so much by these words of yours that he desires nothing more than to hear that evils cannot come from goods. For, if this is accepted, he draws his conclusion and says to you: If evil cannot come from good, whence will it come except from evil? For evils cannot suddenly spring up of themselves without an author. But you say that evil cannot come from good, lest, contrary to the saying of the Gospel, a good tree bear bad fruit. It remains, he says, that there is an everlasting nature of evil, which can generate evils, because you admit they cannot come from good.

(40) Are you now willing to change your opinon which you have expressed for the assistance of the Manichaean plague, not because you favored the Manichaeans, but because you did not know what you were talking about? For how could

Christ have said: 'Either make the tree good and its fruit good, or make the tree bad and its fruit bad'[6]—since He said this to men whom He Himself had created—if, from His good work which is man, evil could not come, as you think when you make the good tree the good work of God, that is, the marriage of men, or their nature; and thus say that evil cannot be born from this, because, if we say that evil is born from good, we contradict, as you think, Him who said: 'A good tree cannot bear bad fruit,' although you know that from the good natures of the angel and the man whom no evil parents generated, but God supremely good had created from no parents, not merely bad fruit but the bad trees themselves came forth, from which bad fruit was to be born? But the Lord Jesus conquers the Manichaeans, because one man, that is, one nature, can produce either tree, and He also conquers you, because a bad tree can come from a good nature. From this is proved wrong what you say in favor of the Manichaeans, that 'Evils cannot come from goods,' which results in their saying evils cannot be supposed to come from anything else but the evil nature which their evil error introduces.

(41) And not only in one passage, where you mentioned the good tree in the Gospel, but also in other places in your argument you give support to the Manichaeans by your perverseness; for instance, in that passage where you say once more: 'Sin cannot be contracted through the nature, because the work of the Devil is not permitted to pass through the work of God.' To this I reply: How is the work of the Devil permitted to remain in the work of God, if it is not permitted to pass through the work of God? For who can doubt that it is worse for it to remain there than for it to pass through there? Perhaps you ask how the work of the Devil can remain in the work of God. Look no further; consider the Devil himself.

---
6 Matt. 12.33.

Certainly, the angelic nature is the work of God, but envy is the work of the Devil himself, and this work proceeded from him and remains in him. Therefore, it is false to say as you say: 'The work of the Devil is not permitted to pass through the work of God,' where you see it even remains. Do you not as yet see how grateful the Manichaean is to you? Are you not yet awake? For the Manichaean strives to show that evil cannot arise from the good work of God, so that, as he wishes, we may believe that evil cannot come from anywhere but from evil. Here you are of wonderful assistance to him. You say: 'Evil is not permitted to pass through the work of God,' so that he concludes very easily that far less can it arise from that through which it is not even permitted to pass.

Chapter 9

(42) Hear something else similar to this, even more serious, in which you again support the Manichaeans. You say: 'Original sin has vanished, because the root of evil cannot be located in that which you say is the gift of God.' See how I shall refute this by the plain truth. Are not man's senses the gift of God? Yet, that enemy sower placed the root of evil there when by the Serpent's deceit he persuaded man to sin.[1] For, if the human senses had not then received the root of evil, there would not have been assent to the evil persuasion. What shall I say of avarice, the root of all evils? And where is this except in the soul of man? And what is the soul of man except a gift of God? How, then, can you say, except by not considering what you are saying: 'The root of evil cannot be located in the gift of God?' But listen to what the Manichaean, whom these inconsiderate statements of yours strongly support, will say to you. If to be a rational creature

---

1 Cf. Gen. 3.1-6.

is a gift of God, and you say the root of evil cannot be located in the gift of God, with how much greater probability can it be said that the root of evil cannot arise from the gift of God? And thus with your support the Manichaean introduces a root of evil from that nature of evil which he imagines as not created by God, but co-eternal with God. For, if you say that the root of evil arose from the free will of a good nature created by God (which the Catholic truth teaches), he will very easily overcome you with those words of your own in which you say: 'The root of evil cannot be located in a gift of God,' since free will also is without doubt a gift of God. By this statement, 'The root of evil cannot be located in a gift of God,' you have given the Manichaean an argument against you. For, if evil cannot be located in good, as you say to me, much less can evil arise from good, as he says to you. Thus, he will conclude that evil cannot come from anywhere but from evil, in which he will consider himself the victor, and he will be so in fact unless both he and you are refuted. Thus, the truth of the Catholic faith conquers the Manichaean, in your words, only because it also conquers you. For, if it did not overcome you when you say: 'The root of evil cannot be located in the gift of God,' much less could it overcome the Manichaean when he says that the root of evil cannot arise from the gift of God. But, that it may overcome both of you, it says that the root of evil cannot arise from anywhere else or be anywhere else except from and in a rational nature, for a rational nature cannot be anything but a gift of God. But, since it was created from nothing by the supreme and unchanging Good, so that it might be a good, even though changeable, its falling away from the Good by which it was created is the root of evil from it or in it, because evil is nothing else but privation of good.

(43) Farther on, where you say: 'The reasoned order of things does not permit that evil be produced from good or

the unjust from the just,' you are using the words of the Manichaeans. For this is what they assert, that evil can be produced only from evil, and their whole vicious sect is built upon this foundation; that they first contend that evil cannot be produced from good. If we grant them this on your authority, we shall have no further means to refute their evil doctrines; and 'the unjust from the just' is the same thing as evil from good. Thus, the Catholic faith, in order to resist both you and them, says that evil was produced only from good, and the unjust from the just, for the angel and the man, from whom these were produced, were first good and just. Therefore, we cannot refute the Manichaeans unless we hear you admit that evils arose only from goods, and that these evils are not substances, but the faults of created substances by which they fall away from the good because, being made from nothing, they are changeable. This is the sound Catholic teaching by which the poison of the Manichaean plague is expelled.

(44) Hence, that teacher of mine, Ambrose, who is praised even by the mouth of your evil teacher, in the book he wrote, *Isaac and the Soul,* says: 'What, then, is evil but privation of good?' And again he says: 'Therefore, evils arose from goods. For there are no evils except things deprived of goods; by evils, however, goods stand out pre-eminently. Therefore, privation of good is the root of evil.'[2] You see how blessed Ambrose refutes the Manichaeans with the true reasoning of the Catholic faith. You see how, although he does not name them in the same discussion, he refutes them by the truth of his short statements. Behold what a man of God, whom, because of original sin, which he as a Catholic defends in Catholic fashion, you insult in a spirit of evil madness with the name of the Manichaeans, when he, in opposition to the support you lend them, brings invincible aid to the Catholic

---

2 Ambrose, *De Isaac et anima* 7.60.

defenders who are opposing them. For he, in opposition to the Manichaeans, exclaims: 'Evils arose from goods,' and you exclaim against him in favor of the Manichaeans: 'That from which and through which bad fruit appeared must needs be evil'; and 'The work of the Devil is not permitted to pass through the work of God'; and 'The root of evil cannot be located in the gift of God'; and 'The reasoned order in things does not permit that evil be produced from good or the unjust from the just.' These things you cry out for the Manichaeans against the voice of the Catholic truth proclaimed through the bishop of God, so that, if you should be heard, the Manichaeans would conquer, saying, not to mention other things: 'If the reasoned order of things does not permit that evil be produced by good, then evils came not from goods, as Ambrose says, but, as we say, from the nature of evil.' Behold the whirlpool into which you have fallen by misunderstanding what the Lord meant when he said: 'A good tree cannot bear bad fruit,' since this does not refer to the nature or marriage, which God instituted, but to the good will of man, by which no evil deeds are done.

(45) But, lest you or someone else should say: 'How can it be that bad fruit does not come from the tree which man makes, that is, from a good will, yet from the nature which God makes comes a bad tree, which itself produces bad fruits'—as though man should make something better, from which bad fruit cannot come, than that which God makes, from which a bad tree can come—lest anyone should err in this way, let him listen carefully to what Ambrose says: 'What is evil but privation of good? For there are no evils except things deprived of goods, because privation of good is the root of evil.' Let him understand, therefore, that the bad tree is an evil will, evil because it has fallen away from the supreme Good, where the created good is deprived of the creating Good, so that the root of evil in it is nothing else but

the privation of good. But the good tree is the good will, because through it man is turned to the supreme and unchanging Good and is filled with good that he may bear good fruit. And hereby God is the author of all goods, that is, of both the good nature and the good will, which man does not produce unless God works in him, because the will is prepared by the Lord.³

(46) I now see that the order of my arrangement demands that I do, God willing, what I promised to do in the third place, namely, by the teachings of the Catholic bishops who lived before us—those I can find who are concerned with the matter with which we are dealing—to break down your brittle subleties and fragile arguments, because of which you think yourself very clever and brilliant. For this purpose I shall make a new beginning, concluding this lengthy book.

---

3 Cf. Prov. 8 (Septuagint).

BOOK II

Chapter 1

NOW I MUST UNDERTAKE what I have put in the third section of my treatise, to overcome by the help of the Lord your machinations, Julian, by means of teachings of the bishops who have most gloriously dealt with the holy Scriptures. Not that I shall show that they believed about original sin according to the Catholic faith, for I have already done this in the first part of this work so that I might show to how many great men, holy and famous doctors of the Church, you impute the crime of Manichaeism, and, when you wish to defame me in the opinion of the ignorant, accuse of the wicked crime of heresy those who defended the Catholic faith against the heretics. But now we must refute by the statements of the saints your arguments in which you contend that the first birth of men must not be believed to be bound by original sin. It is fitting that the Christian people rate the statements of these men higher than your unholy novelties and choose to cling to them rather than to you.

(2) Surely these are, it would appear, the topics of your

dreadful arguments by which you terrify the weak and, less than is expedient for you, those versed in sacred literature. For you say that we 'by asserting original sin, say that the Devil is the creator of men who are born, condemn marriage, deny that in baptism all sins are forgiven, convict God of the crime of injustice, and make men despair of perfection.' You contend that all these things follow if we believe that infants are born bound by the sin of the first man, and for this reason are subject to the Devil unless they are reborn in Christ. 'For the Devil creates them,' you say, 'if they are created from this wound which the Devil inflicted on the human nature which was first created; and marriage is condemned if we believe men have something by which they are generated as damnable; and all sins are not forgiven in baptism if there remains in the baptized parents an evil by which their children are generated as evil. And how is God not unjust if He forgives the baptized their own sins and condemns an infant because, though created by Him, the infant, without knowledge or will, contracts another's sins from those parents whose sins have been forgiven? And we must believe that virtue, which is understood to be the contrary of vice, cannot be perfected because it is incredible that inborn vices and faults, which no longer are to be considered faults, can be destroyed, for he does not sin who cannot be other than he was created.'

(3) If you would diligently investigate these things and not oppose with unbelieving boldness those things which are founded on the ancient truth of the Catholic faith, then, nourished by the grace of Christ, you would come to those things which have been hidden from the wise and prudent and revealed to the little ones.[1] For great is the extent of the sweetness of the Lord, which He did not begrudge, yet hid for those who fear Him, and accomplished for those who

---
1 Matt. 11.25.

hope not in themselves but in Him.² Therefore we say what that faith holds, of which it is written: 'Unless you believe you will not understand.'³ Not the Devil, but the true and truly good God, is the Creator of men, ineffably producing the clean even from the unclean, although no man is born clean; hence, until he is cleansed by the Holy Spirit, he is obliged to be subject to the unclean spirit. And no uncleanness of the natures, however great it be, is any crime of marriage, for the proper good of marriage is plainly distinct from many faults of the natures. And no guilt of sin remains which is not removed by the regeneration which is made in Christ, although a weakness remains, and he who is reborn, if he makes progress, fights against this within himself. Nor is God unjust, since He renders what is due to sins either original or personal;⁴ rather would He be shown to be unjust or weak if He Himself, without preceding sin either original or personal, put 'the heavy yoke upon the children of Adam, from the day of their coming out of their mother's womb until the day of their burial into the mother of all,'⁵ as is written, under which yoke His image is defaced, or if someone else put it upon them against His will. Nor is the perfection of virtue to be despaired of through the grace of Him who can change and heal a nature vitiated from its origin.

Chapter 2

(4) So I shall begin to fulfill my promise. And I shall not

---

2 Ps. 30.20.
3 Isa. 7.9 (Septuagint).
4 In this book the Latin word *originale,* which for the sake of clarity and adherence to custom, is here translated by the English 'original,' is seldom used with the meaning 'first,' or 'initial,' as is often true in ordinary English usage, but is best read as 'by way of origin' or 'by means of origin.' 'Origin' itself most often means 'origination,' signifying the action of arising from a source.
5 Eccli. 40.1.

undertake to refute one by one with the testimonies of the saints these five arguments of yours in which you tie together the various points against the Catholic faith which you discuss in this matter; but such of these as can be nullified and overthrown, even as I bring forward one by one testimonies from the works of Catholic bishops, these shall be nullified and overthrown, whether it be one or two or more or all, according to the value of what is brought forward. For instance, there is the remark made by blessed Ambrose in the book he wrote about Noah's ark: 'This announces the salvation to come to all nations through the one Lord Jesus, who could not have been the only just One, when all human generation was in sin, unless, being born of a virgin, He was not bound by the law of the bound generation. "Behold, " he says, "I was conceived in iniquities, and in sins did my mother bring me forth,"[1] says he who was considered just above the others. Whom, therefore, could I call just but one free of these chains, whom the chains of the common nature do not bind? All were under sin; from Adam death reigned over all. May there come the only One just in the sight of God, of whom it may be said, not with the exception that "He sinned not by his lips,"[2] but "He did no sin." '[3] Say to him, if you dare, that he makes the Devil the creator of men born by the union of the sexes, since he excepts only Christ, because He was born of a virgin, from the chains of the bound generation; all others being born from Adam under the bondage of sin, since the Devil certainly sowed this sin. Charge him with condemning marriage, since he says that only the Son of a virgin was born without sin. Accuse him of denying that virtue can be perfected, since he says that faults are engendered in the human race at the very beginning of conception. And say to him what you think you said very

---
1 Ps. 50.7.
2 Job 1.22.
3 1 Peter 2.22.

aptly and cleverly against me in your first volume: 'And they who are said to sin do not sin at all, since by whomsoever they were created they necessarily live according to what they were created and do not go against their nature.' Say all these things to Ambrose or about Ambrose which you say about me so proudly and abusively and boldly and impudently. (For perhaps it cannot be said that by his words he defames even the sacrament of baptism, saying that full remission of sins is not given in it, or makes God unjust because He condemns in the children the sins of others which He forgave in the parents; because when he said this he was not speaking of the offspring of baptized persons.) Furthermore, if St. Ambrose was not one of those who consider the Devil the Creator of men or condemn marriage, or think human nature incapable of virtue, but, rather, one of those who recognize and confess that God the supreme and supremely good is the Author of the whole man, that is, of the whole soul and the whole body, and who honor marriage in the goodness of its own degree, and do not despair of the perfect justification of man, then these your three arguments are overthrown by the authority of this great man, and are no longer to be used against us who say of original sin what he said, who neither attributed the creation of man to the Devil nor condemned marriage, nor despaired of the perfection of justice in the nature of man.

Chapter 3

(5) About your two remaining arguments which concern baptism we shall soon see what that man thought, and how he crushes you by the vast weight of his authority. For he says in his book against the Novatians:[1] 'All men are born under

---
1 Ambrose, *De poenitentia* 1.3.13.

sin, our very origin is in a fault, as you read where David says: "Behold I was conceived in iniquities and in sins did my mother bear me." This is why the flesh of Paul was the body of death, as he himself says: "Who will deliver me from the body of this death?"[2] But the flesh of Christ condemned sin, which He did not experience in His birth and crucified in His death, so that in our flesh there might be justification through grace where previously there was impurity through guilt.' Here truly all your arguments are overthrown at once. For, if all men are born under sin, our very origin being in a fault, why do you accuse me of saying that the Devil is the creator of men? And if David, because the origin of man is in a fault, said: 'Behold I was conceived in iniquities and in sins did my mother bear me'—and this statement does not condemn the union of marriage, but original sin—why do you say I condemn marriage, which you would not dare say of Ambrose? If, because all men are born under sin and our very origin is in a fault, the flesh of Paul was the body of death, as he himself says: 'Who will deliver me from the body of this death?' do you finally see that the Apostle wished also to indicate himself in these words[2] of his? Thus, while his inner man was delighted with the Law of God, he saw another law in his members warring against the law of his mind, and therefore he called his flesh the body of death. Therefore, in his flesh no good dwelt, because he did not the good that he wished, but performed the evil that he hated. Behold, your whole case is overthrown, ruined, crushed, and like the dust which the wind sweeps from the face of the earth[3] it is swept from the hearts of those whom you attempted to deceive, if they are willing to put aside their desire of contention and consider these things. For was not the Apostle Paul baptized? Or had he not been forgiven every

---

2 Cf. Rom. 7.15-24.
3 Cf. Ps. 1.4.

sin whether original or personal, either of ignorance or of knowledge? Why, then, did he say such things unless what I said in my book, which you boast you have refuted, is altogether true? Indeed, this law of sin which is in the members of the body of this death, is forgiven by spiritual regeneration, yet also remains in the mortal flesh, forgiven indeed, because its guilt is remitted by the sacrament through which the faithful are reborn; but it remains, because it produces desires against which the faithful struggle. This is the thing which completely overthows your heresy. And this you see and fear so much that you attempt to escape these words of the Apostle only by asserting with all your might that here we must not understand the person of the Apostle himself, but of a Jew still under the Law and not under grace, against whom the habits of his evil conduct were fighting—as though the force of habit itself were laid aside in baptism and the baptized themselves did not struggle against it, and all the more strongly and fiercely the more they strive to be pleasing in the eyes of Him by whose grace they are aided, lest they be overcome in this contest. And if you would consider this attentively and without stubbornness, truly you would find in the force of habit itself how concupiscence is remitted in its guilt and remains in its action. For we cannot say nothing happens in a man when he is disturbed by the goading of his concupiscence even when he does not consent. But it was not because of the force of habit that the Apostle called his flesh the body of death, but because of what Ambrose rightly understood, that we are all born under sin, and our very origin is in a fault. He could not doubt that the guilt of this fault had been forgiven him in baptism, but, fighting against its disturbance, he feared first to be defeated and overcome by it and then, rather than fighting a long time, even invincibly, he preferred not to have an enemy, when he said: 'Unhappy man that I am, who will deliver me from the body of this death? The grace of God through Jesus Christ our Lord,' knowing that we are healed of the activity of concupiscence by the grace of Him who healed us of the original guilt of it by spiritual regeneration. This war which we have undertaken to fight within ourselves is experienced within themselves—and they cannot deny it—by the keenest opponents of lust, not by its most shameless eulogizers.

(6) Finally, even the most glorious Cyprian says in his Epistle on the Lord's Prayer: 'We pray that the will of God may be done in heaven and on earth, both of which concern the consummation of our safety and salvation. For, since we possess a body from earth and a spirit from heaven, we are ourselves earth and heaven, and we pray that in both—that is, in body and spirit—the will of God may be done. For there is a struggle between the flesh and the spirit, and a daily warfare between them as they disagree with each other, so that we do not the things we will; while the spirit seeks the heavenly and divine, the flesh desires the earthly and worldly. And so we pray that, by the aid and assistance of God, harmony may be established between these two, so that while the will of God is done in both, the spirit and the flesh, the soul which has been reborn through Him may be saved. This the Apostle Paul declares openly and plainly in his words: "The flesh," he says, "lusts against the spirit and the spirit against the flesh, for these are opposed to each other, so that you do not do what you would." [4] See how the noble doctor instructs the baptized people (for what Christian does not know that the Lord's Prayer concerns the baptized?), that they may understand that man's safety and the salvation of his nature consists in this, not that the flesh and the spirit, as though by nature hostile to each other as the Manichaean

---

4 Gal. 5.17.

foolishly thinks, may be separated, but that they may be healed of the fault of discord and be in harmony. For this it is to be delivered from the body of this death: that what is not the body of death may become the body of life, death itself dying in it; an end of discord, not of the nature. Hence it is also written: 'Death, where is thy victory?'[5] That this is not accomplished in this life the same martyr testifies in his Epistle on Mortality, where he says that for this reason the Apostle Paul 'desires to be dissolved and to be with Christ, that he may no longer be subject to any sins and faults of the flesh.' Do you see how watchfully he explains this passage in the Lord's Prayer against your doctrine, in which you trust in your own strength? For he teaches: 'This is rather to be asked of the Lord than presumed of our own strengh, that not human virtue but divine grace may establish harmony between the flesh and the spirit'; wholly agreeing with the Apostle who says: 'Who will deliver me from the body of this death? The grace of God through Jesus Christ our Lord.'

(7) St. Gregory also attests this when he says: 'For when the soul is in labor and difficulty, when it is beset in hostile manner by the flesh, then it flees to God and learns whence it should seek aid.' And lest anyone suspect that in these words of Bishop Gregory the flesh besetting in hostile manner comes from a contrary nature of evil according to the madness of the Manichaeans, let him see how Gregory agrees with his brothers and fellow doctors, teaching that the spirit lusts against the flesh for no other reason than both may be recalled to their Author after that very serious conflict between them in this life, in which the life of every saint labors. In his *Apology* he says: 'I do not mention those blows by which we are assailed within ourselves by our own vices and passions and are attacked day and night by the fiery goads of this lowly body, the body of death, now secretly and now

---
5 I Cor. 15.55.

even openly, provoked and excited everywhere by the enticements of visible things, by the dregs of this filth in which we are mired and which exhales the stench of its loathesomeness from its spacious veins, but also by the law of sin, which is in our members and wars against the law of the Spirit, seeking to lead captive the royal image which is within us, so that whatever it is which flowed into us by the benefit of that divine and first creation may fall prey to its arms. Only with great difficulty may one guiding himself by a long and severe course of philosophy and gradually recovering the nobility of his soul recall and reflect back to God the nature of light which is in him conjoined to this lowly and shadowy clay; or, if he act with the favor of God, he will certainly recall both alike, provided that by long and careful meditation he becomes accustomed always to look up and to lift up that matter which is joined to him by close bonds and which always drags and presses him down.'[6] Recognize, son Julian, the Catholic voices that are in agreement, and cease to disagree with them. When blessed Gregory says: 'We are assailed within ourselves by our own vices and passions and are attacked night and day by the fiery goads of this lowly body, the body of death,' a baptized person is speaking and he is speaking of the baptized. When he says: 'the law of sin which is in our members and wars against the law of the spirit,' a baptized person is speaking and he is speaking of the baptized. This is the battle of faithful Christians, not of infidel Jews. Believe it, if you are not fighting, and by this fight also cast out the rebellious pride of the Pelagian error. Do you now see, do you now understand, do you now return to your senses, and realize that in baptism there is remission of all sins, and in the baptized person there remains, as it were, a civil war of interior faults? For they are not the kind of faults which ought to be called sins, provided concupiscence does not

---

6 Gregory Nazienzen, *Apologeticus primus de sua fuga.*

draw the spirit to unlawful works and does not conceive and bring forth sin, yet they are not outside us. These we must strive to conquer, if we make progress as we toil in this contest; they are ours, they are passions, they are faults, they are to be bridled, checked, cured, but while they are being cured they are dangerous. And though, as we advance to better things, they are diminished more and more, yet, while we live here, they do not cease to exist. When a godly soul departs hence they will perish; in the risen body they will not return.

Chapter 4

(8) Let us return, then, to blessed Ambrose. 'Even the flesh of Paul,' he says, 'was the body of death, as he himself says: "Who will deliver me from the body of this death?" ' This is the opinion of Ambrose, of Cyprian, of Gregory—to say nothing at present of other doctors of similar authority. To this death it will be said at the end: 'Death, where is thy victory?' But this is the grace of the regenerated, not of the generated. 'For the flesh of Christ,' Ambrose continues, 'condemned sin, which He did not experience in His birth and crucified in His death'—He did not experience it in Himself in His birth and He crucified it in His death. Thus, the law of sin warring against the law of the mind, which existed also in the members of so great an Apostle, is forgiven in baptism, not ended. From this law of the flesh warring against the law of the mind the body of Christ drew nothing to itself, because the Virgin did not conceive from this law. From this law of the flesh warring against the law of the mind there is none who by his first birth does not draw with him this same law itself, because no woman conceives except from this law. And thus the revered Hilary did not hesitate to say that all flesh comes from sin; but did he therefore deny that

it comes from God? Just as we say flesh comes from flesh, and also flesh comes from man—do we hereby deny that it comes from God? It is also from God because He creates it, and it is from man because he generates it, and it is from sin which corrupts it. But God who begat the Son co-eternal with Himself, the Word which was in the beginning, through whom He created all that was not, also created Him man without fault, born of a virgin, not of the seed of man, and in Him He regenerates generated man, and heals vitiated man, from guilt at once, and from weakness little by little. And he who is regenerated, if he has the use of reason, strives as in a contest against his weakness, God watching and helping him, for strength is made perfect in weakness when against this part of us which departs from justice war is waged by that part of us which progresses toward justice, so that the whole rises to the better with victorious progress, sinks to the worse with non-victorious defection. But an infant who as yet has not the use of reason is indeed neither in good nor in evil by his own will, because he does not turn his thoughts to either; in him both the natural good of reason and the original evil of sin are inactive and dormant. But as he grows older and reason awakes, the commandment comes and sin revives, and, when it begins to fight against him as he grows, then appears what was latent in the infant; it either conquers—and he will be condemned, or it is conquered, and he will be healed. Yet, this evil would not have been without harmful effect even if the infant had departed from this life before it had begun to manifest itself in him, because the guilt of this same evil—not guilt by which the evil itself is guilty, but by which it makes him guilty in whom it is—as it is contracted by generation, so it is not removed except by regeneration. This is the reason infants are baptized, not only that they may enjoy the good of the kingdom of Christ, but also that they may be delivered from the evil of the kingdom of death. And this cannot be done except through Him who 'in His flesh condemned sin, which He did not experience in His birth and crucified in His death; that in our flesh there might be justification through grace where previously there was impurity through guilt.'

(9) According to these words of blessed Ambrose, then, the Devil did not in his goodness create man, but corrupted man in his wickedness; nor did the evil of concupiscence take away the good of marriage; nor is the guilt of any sin left unremitted in the sacrament of baptism; nor is God unjust who condemns by the law of justice him who is made guilty by the law of sin, even though he is born of that law which is no longer able to make his parent guilty because the parent has been reborn. And why, if these things are true, should we despair of that strength [virtue] which is made perfect in weakness,[1] since through the flesh of Christ, which condemns the sin He did not experience in His birth and crucified in His death, justification through grace is made also in our flesh, in which previously there was impurity through guilt? In consequence, those five arguments of yours by which you particularly terrify men will not be able to trouble others or you, if you believe Ambrose, Cyprian, Gregory, and other holy and famous Catholic doctors, nay even yourselves, also, that the law of sin which dwells in the members of man, warring against the law of the mind, the law by which the flesh lusts against the spirit, forces even upon baptized saints the necessity of fighting: and against what, if not evil?—not a subtance, but the fault of a substance, which by the grace of God regenerating us is not imputed to us, which by the grace of God aiding us is to be bridled, and which by the grace of God rewarding us is to be healed.

---

1 2 Cor. 12.9.

68   SAINT AUGUSTINE

Chapter 5

(10) But perhaps you may say that the baptized fight rather against this which they have themselves caused by the evil habits of their former life, not against that with which they were born. Yet, if you say this, you already without doubt see and admit that there is in man something evil which is not itself taken away in baptism, but only the guilt which had been contracted from it. However, since it contributes little to the solution of this problem unless it is proved to have been born in us from the sin of the first man, listen to what St. Ambrose says more plainly in another place, in his *Exposition of the Gospel according to St. Luke,* when he is dealing[1] in various ways, yet not at variance with the one rule of faith, with that passage[2] where the Lord says that in one house three shall be divided against two and two against three: 'We can see,' he says, 'the flesh and the spirit divided from the odor, touch, and taste of luxury, separating themselves in one house from the opposing vices and subjecting themselves to the Law of God and removing themselves from the law of sin, and their dissension turned to nature through the transgression of the first man, so that they could not agree with each other in equal zeal for virtue; yet through the Cross of the Lord our Saviour, who made void the enmities as well as the Law of the commandments, they accorded in mutual harmony after Christ our peace, descending from heaven, made both one.'[3] Again, in the same work, when speaking of the spiritual and incorruptible food, he says: 'Reason is the food of the mind, and a noble and sweet nourishment, which does not burden the body, and changes not into something shameful in nature, but into something glorious, when

---
1 Ambrose, *Expositio Evangelii secundum Lucam* 7.141-143.
2 Luke 12.52.
3 Cf. Eph. 2.14.

the wallowing place of lust is changed into the temple of God, and the inn of vices begins to be the shrine of virtues. This takes place when the flesh, returning to its nature, recognizes the nurse of its strength and, putting aside the boldness of its obstinacy, is joined to the will of the regulating soul—such as it was when it received the secrets of dwelling in paradise, before it was infected with the poison of the pestilent Serpent and knew that wicked hunger, and through gluttonous greed brushed aside the memory of the divine commandment which inhered in the senses of the soul. It is hence, we are told, that sin flowed from body and soul as though from its parents; the nature of the body being tempted, the soul suffered with the body's disorderly health. For, if it had restrained the appetite of the body, the soul would have destroyed in its very beginning the origin of sin; but the soul, in its now corrupt vigor, heavy with burdens not its own, gave birth to sin as though in an evil pregnancy by the action of the male, the body.'

(11) Here, surely, the teacher Ambrose, so highly praised by the mouth of your teacher, most openly and fully declared both what original sin is and whence it is, and whence came the first confusion which was the disobedience of the flesh disagreeing with the soul—and this disagreement is healed by the grace of God through Jesus Christ our Lord. You see whence the flesh lusts against the spirit, you see whence comes the law in our members warring against the law of the mind. You see that the discord of the soul and the flesh turned to nature, and through these enmities wretchedness flowed upon us which can be ended only by the mercy of God. Do not oppose me now, for, if you still do so, you see whom you are opposing at the same time. Indeed, you said that I strove for nothing more than that I might not be understood. And in some passages you interpret my meaning rather according to your own ideas, abusing men of somewhat

slower minds, who do not understand that you are unwilling to be silent rather than able to reply to my book in your four. See how Ambrose pours forth a clear and lucid stream of eloquence; there is no place where the reader can be at a loss, where the listener can fail to hear. He says most clearly that the Apostle said: 'Who will deliver me from the body of this death?' because we are all born under sin and our very origin is in a fault. He says most clearly that the Lord Christ was without sin because, being born of a virgin, He was not bound by the chains of the bound generation and the common nature, and that He condemned sin, which He did not experience in His birth. He says most clearly that the disagreement of flesh and soul through the trangression of the first man turned to nature. He says most clearly that the flesh, the wallowing place of lust and the inn of vices, is then changed into the temple of God and the shrine of virtues when, returning to nature, it recognizes the nurse of its strength and, putting aside the boldness of its obstinacy, is joined to the will of the regulating soul, such as it was when it received the secrets of dwelling in paradise, before it was infected with the poison of the pestilent serpent. Why do I pile up these books against you, you ask? Look at him, dare oppose him, who confronted the poisons of your heresy before it was brought forth and has prepared these antidotes by which it can be expelled. If these are not enough, listen further.

(12) In his *Isaac and the Soul* he says: 'Therefore, a good driver restrains and checks the bad horses and urges on the good. The good horses are four: prudence, temperance, fortitude, justice. The bad horses are anger, lust, fear, injustice.'[4] Does he say a good driver has good horses and does not have bad ones? No, he says: 'He urges on the good horses; he restrains and checks the bad.' What are these horses? Surely,

---

4 Ambrose, *De Isaac et anima* 8.65.

if we call or think them substances we favor or adhere to the madness of the Manichaeans. That this may be far from us, we understand that, according to the Catholic teaching, by these horses he means our faults, which from the law of sin resist the law of the mind. These faults will not be separated from us and exist somewhere else; if they are healed in us they will be nowhere. Why do they not perish in baptism? Will you not yet admit that their guilt perishes but their weakness remains; not a guilt by which they themselves were guilty,[5] but by which they made us guilty in the evil deeds to which they had drawn us? And their weakness does not remain as if they were certain animals which are made weak; they are our own weakness itself. And we must not think that by the one bad horse is meant that injustice which is destroyed in baptism, for that was the injustice of the sins which we committed, which are all forgiven, and now no longer exist, whose guilt remained after they themselves came into being and passed away. But that law of sin whose guilt was remitted in the sacred font he called 'injustice,' because it is unjust that the flesh should lust against the spirit, although in our renewal there is justice, because it is just that the spirit should lust against the flesh, so that we may walk by the spirit and not fulfill the lusts of the flesh. This justice of ours we find named among the good horses.

(13) Hear, also, what he says in the book he wrote about Paradise:[6] 'Perhaps,' he says, 'the reason Paul said: "Secret words that man may not repeat,"[7] was that he was still confined in the body, that is, he saw the passions of this body, he saw the law of his flesh warring against the law of his mind.' And again, in the same work: 'When he says the

---
5 For the sense of this passage, which refers to an argument drawn by Julian from a problem he truly found in the matter, see Book 6, chapter 17.
6 Ambrose, *De paradiso* 11.53.
7 2 Cor. 12.4.

Serpent was more cunning,[8] you understand whom he means, that is, that Adversary of ours who, however, has the wisdom of this world. But pleasure and delectation may also properly be called "wise," because we also read about "the wisdom of the flesh," where it is written: "Because the wisdom of this flesh is hostile to God."[9] And they who desire pleasures are clever in seeking out varieties of delectation. Or you may understand whatever kind of delectation is contrary to the divine commandment and hostile to our senses. Whence St. Paul says: "I see another law in my members, warring against the law of my mind and making me prisoner to the law of sin."[10] What kind of pleasure this teacher is speaking of in this passage is clear, because, in order that we might understand, he refers to the testimony of the Apostle, who says: 'I see another law in my members, warring against the law of my mind and making me prisoner to the law of sin.' This is that pleasure whose defense you have taken upon yourself, although even you find fault with its excess. Where and of what sort it is you clearly admit, but you defend and praise it in its moderate form with such adornment of words as if it had fixed this measure for itself, and not the spirit which lusts against its onslaught. He bravely stood out against it who exclaimed: 'I see another law in my members, warring against the law of my mind.' If this force warring against it were slackened, into what impurities would it fall? Over what precipices would it not draw and hurl itself? Even now, as it makes its onslaught, behold, not some Jew as you think, but according to blessed Ambrose, the Apostle Paul says of himself: 'I see another law in my members, warring against the law of my mind and making me prisoner to the law of sin.' Again, in another passage in the same work, the

---
8 Gen. 3.1.
9 Rom. 8.7.
10 Rom. 7.23.

same teacher says: 'Paul is attacked and he sees the law of his flesh warring against the law of his mind and making him prisoner to the law of sin; and he does not presume on his own conscience, but by the grace of Christ he trusts he will be delivered from the body of death. And still you think that no one can sin knowingly? Paul says: "For I do not the good that I wish, but the evil that I do not wish, that I perform."[11] And still you think that knowledge profits a man when it increases the jealous hostility of sin?' In the same work this same bishop, addressing all of us and diligently pleading our common cause, also says: 'For the law of the flesh wars against the law of the mind, and we must toil with all our might to chastise the body and bring it back into servitude, and plant the things which are spiritual.'[12]

(14) In another book which he wrote, *On the Sacrament of Regeneration, or on Philosophy*,[13] he says: 'Blessed is the death which delivers us from sin that it may reform us to God. "For he who is dead is acquitted of sin."[14] Is anyone acquitted of sin merely by the ending of his natural life? By no means, since a sinner who dies remains in his sin, but he for whom all sins are remitted in baptism is acquitted of sin.' Have you anything to say to this? Do you see how the venerable man expresses the truth that in baptism the death of man becomes blessed when all sins are remitted? But listen to something else; listen to what you do not wish to hear. 'We have seen,' he says, 'what mystical death is. Now let us consider what the burial ought to be. For it is not enough that our faults die, unless the luxury of the body decays and the tissue of all carnal bonds is dissolved, and all the cords of bodily uses are cut. Let no one flatter himself that he will

---

11 Rom. 7.19.
12 Ambrose, *De paradiso* 12.60; 15.77.
14 Rom. 6.7.

put on another form, will receive mystical precepts, will apply his mind to the practice of continence. We do not what we would, but what we hate, that we perform. Sin works many things in us. Very often, pleasures revive and rise up against us though we resist them. We must struggle against the flesh. Paul struggled against it, and at last he said: "But I see another law in my members, warring against the law of my mind and making me prisoner to the law of sin." Are you stronger than Paul? Have no confidence in the sedulous flesh and do not entrust yourself to it, since the Apostle exclaims: "For I know that in me, that is, my flesh, no good dwells, because to wish is within my power, but I do not find the strength to accomplish what is good. For I do not the good that I wish, but the evil that I do not wish, that I perform. Now if I do what I do not wish, it is no longer I who do it, but the sin that dwells in me."[15] However great the obstinacy of mind by which you are carried away, Julian, however great the stubborness with which you oppose us in defending the Pelagian error, you are surrounded by so much factual evidence given by blessed Ambrose, you are so refuted by the clarity of his statements, that surely, if no reason, reflection, religious consideration, piety, humanity, or regard for truth you may have recalls you from your stubborn purpose, you show how powerful a thing it is in human evils to have reached a point where you do not wish to stay, yet from which you are ashamed to retreat. For I believe that this is how you will feel when you read this. Oh, if the peace of Christ might only conquer in your heart and a good repentance carry off the prize over an evil shame!

---

15 Rom. 7.18-20.

Chapter 6

(15) But now note for a moment how from this law of sin, whose activity the mortal nature even of celibates is compelled to endure; upon which the chastity of marriage strives to place a rule of moderation; whence the concupiscence of the flesh and the pleasure you praise makes its attacks against the purpose of the will whenever it is aroused, even if it does not accomplish its acts, since it is bridled—note, I say, how every man is generated from this law of sin and hence contracts original sin, as St. Ambrose explains in this same book of his *On the Sacrament of Regeneration, or on Philosophy.* 'There is,' he says, 'a house which wisdom builds and a table filled with heavenly sacraments, at which the just man dines upon the food of divine pleasure, drinking the sweet cup of grace, if he rejoices in the abundant progeny of everlasting merits. Generating these children, David shunned those births of bodily union, and so he desired to be cleansed by the watering of the sacred fountain that he might wash away the stain of earth and the flesh by the grace of the spirit. "Behold," he said, "I was conceived in iniquities and in sins did my mother bear me."[1] Evilly did Eve give birth, thereby leaving to women the inheritance of childbirth, and the result that everyone formed in the pleasure of concupiscence and conceived in it in the womb and fashioned in it in blood, in it wrapped as in swaddling clothes, first undergoes the contagion of sin before he drinks the gift of the life-giving air.' If you are not destitute of all human judgment you see what he states about the pleasure of concupiscence, to which you give your most shameless approval, this famous teacher Ambrose, praised by the testimony of your teacher, as I must often repeat: that in it each one is formed and in it conceived in the womb, in it fashioned in blood, and he is

---
[1] Ps. 50.7.

wrapped in swaddling rags, not woolen or linen cloths, or anything of that sort in which infants already born are wrapped, but, as it were, in the hereditary rags of his vitiated origin, that he may undergo the contagion of sins before he breathes this life-giving air, into which everyone who is born is cast as into a vast fountain of common and never-failing nourishment after the hidden breathing in his mother's womb; to weep at birth for the guilt which he contracted before his birth. Should not those first men have blushed, then, at the activity of this concupiscence, which plainly showed that they themselves were guilty, and also foretold that their children would be subject to the sin of their parents? And just as they blushed to leave exposed those parts of their bodies in which they perceived the disobedience of lust, so may you in obedience to the Catholic faith blush to praise what is shameful.

(16) Note, also, what this same teacher wrote about this same covering of fig-leaves in his book *On Paradise*: 'Even more important,' he says, 'according to this interpretation, we find that Adam girded himself where he should rather have girded himself by the fruit of chastity. For in the loins where we are girded there are said to be certain seeds of generation; therefore, Adam was evilly girded with useless leaves to designate not the future fruit of future generation, but certain sins.'[2] Here the holy man certainly nullified your most elaborate and most careful argument against our believing that after their sin Adam and Eve with open eyes girded their loins.[3] For, that you might there strive with much eloquence, you went against the common sense of all and wished to ensnare them with the din of much talk. For what is so evident as that by girdles or loin cloths, called *perizomata* in Greek, and which are popularly called *muniturae*, men cover

---
2 Ambrose, *De paradiso* 13.67.
3 Gen. 3.7.

or gird their loins. And that man of God with whose eloquence we refute you did not trouble to explain this fact as though it were obscure, but only showed what it designates. He says: 'For in the loins where we are girded there are said to be certain seeds of generation, and therefore Adam was evilly girded there with useless leaves.' Why evilly? He continues: 'to designate not the future fruit of future generation, but certain sins.' Do you have anything to say to this? Behold whence came that confusion; behold whence the covering and girding with leaves; behold whence the original sin in their posterity.

(17) But St. John, Bishop of Constantinople, in so far as modesty could permit, clearly expressed this whole matter of the shame of the first men in two words, saying: 'They were covered with the leaves of the fig tree, hiding the outward appearance of sin.' Who does not see what and what kind of outward appearance of sin they had to cover in the region of the loins in their shame, when they were not ashamed by the nakedness of their bodies before they sinned? I beg you, understand; nay rather, permit men to understand what they understand with you, and do not compel us to argue any longer in almost shameless fashion about shameful things.

(18) Rightly the same blessed John tells us, just as the martyr Cyprian did,[4] that circumcision was commanded for a sign of baptism. 'And see,' he says, 'how because of the threat the Jew does not defer circumcision, because every soul not circumcised on the eighth day shall be destroyed from his people.'[5] 'But you,' he says, 'defer a circumcision not wrought by hand, but through putting off the body of the flesh, although you hear the Lord Himself saying: "Amen, amen I say to thee, unless a man be born again of water and the Spirit, he cannot enter into the kingdom of God." '[6]

---
4 Cyprian, *Epist.* 64, ad Fidum.
5 Gen. 17.14.
6 John 3.5.

You see how a man versed in the doctrine of the Church compared circumcision with circumcision, threat with threat. Therefore, what it is not to be circumcized on the eighth day is the same as what it is not to be baptized in Christ, and to be destroyed out of his people has the same significance as not to enter into the kingdom of God. And yet you deny that in the baptism of infants this putting off the body of the flesh, that is, the circumcision not wrought by hand, is solemnized, because you contend they have nothing which they need to put off. For you do not admit that they are dead in the circumcision of their flesh, which signifies sin, especially that which is contracted by way of origin. For through this our body is the body of sin, which the Apostle says is destroyed through the cross of Christ.[7]

Chapter 7

(19) Now, I have undertaken to attack you with the opinions of bishops who lived before our time and who faithfully and memorably dealt with these divine precepts. Let us return, then, to Bishop Ambrose, who does not doubt that men, that is, the souls and bodies of men, are the work of God, and who honors marriage, and who teaches that in the baptism of Christ all sins are forgiven, and who recognizes that God is just, and does not deny that human nature is capable of virtue and perfection through the grace of God. These you make your five arguments, contending that none of these five things can be true, unless it is false that those who are born contract original sin. Yet, this very thing which you try to take away by your five arguments he states where necessary in his sermons, so that it is sufficiently clear to anyone what the Catholic truth is accustomed to preach and

---

[7] Rom. 6.6.

what profane novelty tries to overturn. Or do you perhaps doubt that Ambrose himself also knew and taught that God is the Creator of men, both of soul and of body? Hear, therefore, what he says in his book *On Philosophy* against the philosopher Plato, who asserted that the souls of men are put back into beasts and considered God the creator only of souls, saying that the creation of bodies was entrusted to lesser gods. 'I am surprised,' he says, 'at so great a philosopher, that he shuts up the soul, to which he attributes the power of conferring immortality, in owls and frogs and clothes it in the fierceness of beasts; since in *Timaeus* he says that it is the work of God, made by God among things immortal, but asserts that the body does not seem to be the work of God, because the nature of human flesh does not differ in any way from the nature of the body of beasts. But, if the soul is worthy of being believed the work of God, how can it be unworthy of being clothed by a work of God?' Consider, Ambrose asserts against Platonists, that not only the soul, as they also say, but also the body, which they deny, is the work of God.

(20) Or are you going to say that he condemns marriage, because he says that what is born therefrom, being formed in the pleasure of concupiscence, undergoes the contagion of sins? Then hear the opinion of Ambrose on marriage in his book about holy David.[1] 'Marriage is good,' he says; 'the union is holy. But let those who have wives be as if they had none. The marriage bed is undefiled, and neither should deprive the other of it, except perhaps for a time, that they may give themselves to prayer. Yet, according to the Apostle, no one can give himself to prayer at the time when he exercises this bodily function.'[2] Listen to another statement in his book *On Philosophy*. 'Continence,' he says, 'is good, being as it were a kind of support of piety, for it makes stable the

---

1 Ambrose, *Apologia prophetae David.* 11.56.
2 Cf. 1 Cor. 7.29,5.

footsteps of those who slip on the precipices of this life; it is a careful watcher, lest anything unlawful creep up on them. But the mother of all vices is incontinence, which turns even the lawful into vice. Therefore, the Apostle not only warns us against fornication, but also teaches a certain moderation in marriage itself, and prescribes times of prayer. For he who is intemperate in marriage, what is he but the adulterer of his own wife?' You see how he says marriage should have true soundness even within itself.[3] You see how he says that incontinence turns even the lawful into vice, where he shows that marriage is lawful, and he does not wish incontinence to defile what is lawful in it. You notice how you should understand with us in what disease of desire the Apostle was unwilling that one possess his vessel, not like the Gentiles who do not know God.[4] But to you lust seems culpable only toward one other than one's wife. What will you say of Ambrose, who calls intemperance in marriage a kind of adultery of one's wife? Do you honor marriage more in which you would allow a very licentious range to lust, lest, perchance, the one offended might find another defender for herself?[5] For you did not wish to touch even with a word what I mentioned the Apostle granted to husband and wife as pardonable (where, doubtless, a fault is noted, even though it is pardoned), nor did you dare mention in your reply the fact that the husband and wife are admonished to abstain from this act in order to give themselves

---

3 In regard to this entire subject, it is useful to note that the word translated throughout this book as 'modesty' is *pudicitia,* by which Augustine usually means the virtue of chastity in its fullest sense; thus, it exceeds the meaning of the English word, and includes the less general virtue of modesty proper, which concerns the outward signs of the things unseemly because of the activity of lust, as well as the virtue of chastity itself, and also the disposition called bashfulness, an auxiliary of chastity. St. Thomas discusses Augustine's use of this term in *Summa theologica,* 2-2 q. 151, a. 4.
4 Cf. 1 Thess. 4.4,5.
5 An allusion to conscupiscence, personified as Julian's protege.

to prayer,⁶ which I recorded entirely; fearing, I believe, that your defense might seem false if on your admission it should appear that even the prayers of husband and wife are impeded by lust, which you are not ashamed to defend. Thus, since you desired to answer me on its behalf but did not dare resist the Apostle and were not able to twist his testimony into another meaning as you usually do, you preferred to be completely silent about it. Who, then, honors marriage more: you, when you deface its dignity by making it a blameless wallowing place of carnal concupiscence; or he who, while he says marriage is not only lawful but also good and its union holy, yet recalls that the Apostle recommended times of prayer and abstinence from the pleasure of lust, and who does not wish husbands and wives to be given up to that disease whence original sin is contracted? Thus, according to the same Apostle, he wishes those who have wives to be as if they had none, and he does not hesitate to call an intemperate husband the adulterer of his wife; weighing all the good of marriage not by the lust of the flesh but by the faith of chastity, not by the disease of passion but by the contract of union, not by the pleasure of lust but by the will for offspring. He asserts that woman was given to man only for the purpose of generation, a matter which you thought it necessary to argue so long in vain, as if any of us denied this statement. These are his words on the subject, written in his book *On Paradise*:⁷ 'If woman is the source of guilt for man, how can we think she was given for a good? If you consider, however, that God cares for the universe, you will find that this must please God more in which there is the cause of the universe than that is to be condemned in which is the cause of sin. Therefore, because the propagation of the human race could not be from the man alone, God said it is not good for

---

6 Cf. 1 Cor. 7.6,5.
7 Ambrose, *De paradiso* 10.47.

man to be alone.⁸ For God preferred that there be many for Him to save and forgive their sins, than Adam alone, who might be free of guilt. Finally, because the same One is the Author of both works, He came into this world that He might save sinners. Last of all, He did not permit Cain, guilty of fratricide, to perish before he had generated children. Therefore, woman was given to man for the sake of the generation of human posterity.'

(21) There you have Ambrose, my teacher, and greatly praised by yours, not only admitting but also defending the opinion that every man and the flesh of man is the work of God, and that marriage as such is good. But that through original sin he by no means detracts from holy baptism I have shown above when I quoted his words, where he says: 'He for whom all sins are remitted in baptism is acquitted of sin.' Where does he not teach that God is just, or what Catholic can doubt this, which nearly all the ungodly also confess?

Chapter 8

(22) The fifth point remains: Whether Ambrose thinks human nature is capable of justification and perfection, and is not shaken in this opinion because he often and in many ways says that every man is born under sin and that his very origin is in a fault. But I showed this above¹ where I recalled that in the same passage, a little farther on, he says: 'The flesh of Christ condemned sin, which He did not experience in His birth and crucified in His death, so that in our flesh there might be justification through grace where previously there was impurity through guilt,' There he showed that human nature, even that which is born under sin and whose

---

8 Cf. Gen. 2.18.

1 Cf. above, 2.5.

origin is in a fault, is capable of justification, but surely through grace, although this fact is hateful to you, the cruel enemies of this same grace. But if you have not heard enough, listen to what he says in his *Explanation of the Prophet Isaias.* 'Let us see,' he says, 'whether our regeneration be not after the course of this life, of which it is said: "In the regeneration when the Son of Man shall sit on the throne of his glory."[2] For, even as we speak of the regeneration of the laver, through which we are renewed by removal of the impurity of sin, so this seems to speak of a regeneration through which, purified from every stain of corporal matter, we are with purified soul regenerated unto life eternal.' Truly, the holy and truthful man has distinguished the justification of this life, which takes place through the laver of regeneration, from its perfection, when our bodies also are renewed by immortality. Therefore, Ambrose, although he admits the fault in the origin of those born, does not despair of our perfect justification. For, as human nature can be fashioned by God the Creator, so it can be healed by God the Redeemer.

(23) But you are in a hurry, and in your hurry you desert your presumption. For you wish man to be perfected here, and would have that indeed by the gift of God—not a free gift, but one dependent on the decision of man's own will. You think you are far from this perfection, you say, but there is deceit in your mouth, whether you say you are sinners and wish to be thought just, or whether you profess a perfection of justice you by no means perceive in yourselves. Now, justification in this life is given to us according to these three things: first by the laver of regeneration by which all sins are forgiven; then, by a struggle with the faults from whose guilt we have been absolved; the third, when our prayer is heard, in which we say: 'Forgive us our debts,'[3] because,

---
2 Matt. 19.28.
3 Matt. 6.12.

however bravely we fight against our faults, we are men; but the grace of God so aids us as we fight in this corruptible body that there is reason for His hearing us as we ask forgiveness. You do not think that this mercy of God toward us is necessary for you, because you are of that number of whom it is said in the psalm: They 'trust in their own strength.'[4] But how much better we hear Ambrose in his *Flight from This World,* where he says:[5] 'We often talk of fleeing from this world; would that our disposition were as careful and solicitous as our speech is easy. But, what is worse, there frequently creeps upon us the enticement of earthy desires and the flood of vanities occupies our mind, so that you think about what you seek to avoid and turn it over in your mind. It is difficult for man to avoid this, and to strip it off entirely is impossible. That it is rather a matter of firm purpose than of actual effect is shown by the Prophet who says: "Incline my heart to thy precepts and not to avarice."[6] For our heart is not in our power, nor are our thoughts which, unexpectedly darkened, confuse our mind and soul, and draw them elsewhere than we intend. They recall them to the worldly, implant the earthy, force sensual matters upon us, and weave enticements—and at the very time we are trying to lift up our minds they introduce vain thoughts, and we are often cast down to the earth.' If you do not suffer these things— forgive us, but we do not believe you—but recognize in these words of St. Ambrose a kind of mirror of common human infirmity, and that, even if we are making progress. But if we should believe you and say: Pray for us that we also may not suffer these things—we would find you so lofty and haughty that you would answer us not only that you do not suffer theses things, but also that is is in man's power not to suffer

---

4 Ps. 48.7.
5 Ambrose, *De fuga saeculi* 1.1,2.
6 Ps. 118.36.

these things and there is no reason why he should ask the help of God for this.[7]

(24) How much better again to hear Ambrose as he confesses the grace of God and does not trust in his own strength, and, after saying this, adds: 'But who is so blessed that he always tends upward in his heart? Indeed, how can anyone do this at all without divine aid? It is completely impossible. Finally, the Scriptures say about this matter: "Blessed is the man whose help is from thee, Lord; his heart tends upward." '[8] Again, he says in his book *On the Sacrament of Regeneration*: 'What but the soul uses the flesh for acting? Therefore, the soul is by nature the ruler and mistress of the flesh, and should subdue and govern the flesh. Therefore, supported by the help of the Holy Spirit, the soul says in the psalm: "I will not fear what flesh can do against me."[9] And it says similarly in St. Paul: "But I chastise my body and bring it into subjection."[10] Therefore, Paul chastises what is of him and not what is himself. For what is of him is one thing, what is himself is another. He chastises what is of him, so that he, being just, may bring about the death of bodily wantonness.' Was not St. Ambrose, when he said this, struggling against his faults? Was he not overcoming his faults? Was he not like a good soldier of Christ fighting within himself against an army of various desires? Was he not chastising his own body? Was he not in the conquest and

---

7 In the second book of *De peccatorum meritis et remissione,* dealing with freedom from sin in this life, St. Augustine answers four questions. (1) Man is able to be without sin in this life, with the aid of divine grace (2.6.7), but (2) as a matter of fact, Scripture says no man is without sin in this life (2.7.8.). (3) Man shows himself unwilling to be without sin when obliged to combat constantly against concupiscence and ignorance (2.17.26). (4) Christ the Mediator alone is without sin in this life, because He alone was born without sin (2.20.34).) See *Summa theologica,* 1-2 q. 109, a. 8, 9, 10 for a more explicit presentation of this doctrine.
8 Ps 83.6.
9 Ps. 55.5.
10 1 Cor. 9.27.

overthrow of the works of the Devil, seeking the peace of justice between the work of God and the work of God, that is, the soul and the flesh? And thus, not trusting in his own strength, but, as he says, 'supported by the help of the Holy Spirit,' he says: 'I will not fear what flesh can do against me.' Behold how human nature is shown to be capable of justification; behold how strength is made perfect in weakness.[11]

(25) But let us also hear on this matter that most glorious martyr Cyprian, in his *Epistle on Mortality*: 'We must contend,' he says, 'with avarice, with immodesty, with anger, with ambition; we must constantly carry on a troublesome struggle with the vices of the flesh and with worldly enticements. The mind of man, besieged and surrounded on all sides by the invading forces of the Devil, scarcely can meet the individual assaults and scarcely can resist. If avarice is overcome, lust rises up; if lust is overpowered, ambition enters; if ambition is scorned, anger inflames, pride puffs up, drunkeness invites, envy destroys harmony, jealousy breaks friendship. You are urged to curse, which the divine law forbids; you are driven to swear, which is not permitted. So many persecutions the soul daily endures, by so many dangers is the heart oppressed; yet you are pleased to stand longer here among the weapons of the Devil, when, instead, you should desire and will to hasten more quickly to Christ by the help of death.' Yet, far be it from us to think St. Cyprian was a miser because he struggled with avarice, or immodest because he struggled with immodesty, or wrathful because he struggled with anger, or ambitious because he struggled with ambition, or carnal because he struggled with the sins of flesh, or a lover of this world because he struggled with worldly enticements, or lustful because he struggled with lust, or proud because he struggled with pride, or a drunkard because he struggled with intemperance, or envious because

---

11 Cf. 2 Cor. 12.9.

he struggled against envy. Actually, he was none of these things, precisely because he stoutly resisted these evil impulses coming partly from our origin and partly from habit, and did not consent to be what they tried to force him to be. Yet, in so dangerous and laborious a contest as this he did not escape the stroke of all hostile weapons, as he says in his *Epistle on Almsgiving*: 'Let no one flatter himself that his heart is so pure and immaculate that, relying on his innocence, he does not think medicine should be applied to his wounds, since it is written: "Who shall glory that he has a chaste heart? Or who shall glory that he is pure from sins?"[12] And again, let John write in his Epistle: "If we say that we have no sin, we deceive ourselves, and the truth is not in us."[13] But if no one can be without sin, and whoever says he is blameless is either proud or foolish, how necessary and how kind is divine mercy, which, since it knows that those who have been healed afterwards receive wounds, has given us over and over again salutary remedies to cure and heal our later wounds.' O most famous teacher and glorious witness, so you have taught, so you have advised, so have given yourself to be heard and imitated! Deservedly, when all other struggles with desire were ended and all wounds healed, you fought against the last and greatest of all desires of this life, for the truth of Christ, and you conquered by the abundance of His grace toward you. Your crown is secure, your doctrine is victorious, in which you also conquer those who trust in their own strength. For they exclaim: 'The perfection of our strength is from ourselves,' but you reply: 'No one is strong by his own powers, yet by the forgiveness and mercy of God he is safe.'

(26) Hear, also, most blessed Hilary, when he expresses his hope for the perfection of man. When he was speaking

12 Prov. 20.9.
13 1 John 1.8.

of the peace of the Gospel,[14] where the Lord says: 'My peace I give to you,'[15] he said: 'Because the Law was the shadow of good things to come, therefore through this prefigured meaning he taught that we cannot be clean in this earthy and mortal dwelling which is the body unless through the washing of celestial mercy we obtain cleansing when, after the change of our earthy body in the resurrection, our nature has been made more glorious.' Again, in the same discourse, he says: 'That the Apostles themselves, although cleansed and sanctified by faith, were not without evil through the condition of our common origin He taught when He said: "If you, evil as you are, know how to give good gifts to your children." '[16] You see how the venerable Catholic teacher does not deny our cleansing in this life, yet hopes for a more perfect human nature, that is, having received a more perfect cleansing, in the final resurrection.

(27) But hear what he says in a homily on the book of holy Job, hear how he asserts that the constant war of the Devil himself against us results from this; that he arouses against us the evils that are in us. He wishes to teach us that this is for our own good, since the divine mercy uses the malice of the Devil for our purification. 'For so great and admirable is the goodness of God's mercy toward us,' he says, 'that he through whom in the sin of Adam we lost the nobility of that first and blessed creation; through him, I say, we may deserve to obtain again what we lost. For then in his envy the Devil harmed us; now, when he strives to harm us, he is overcome. For through the infirmity of our flesh he hurls all the weapons of his power, when he stirs us to lust, entices us to drunkenness, urges us to hatred, provokes us to avarices, excites us to murder, goads us to curses. But when

---
14 Hilary, *Expositio ps. 118* 18.115.
15 John 14.27.
16 Matt. 7.11.

all these temptations that come upon us are checked by a firm mind, we are cleansed from sin through the glory of this victory. For it has been said: "Or can he that is born of woman cleanse himself?"[17] If there is no war there will be no victory. And if we do not obtain victory over the faults that strive against us there will not be any cleansing from faults, for, if we conquer temptation in these snares of our body, we are purged of the strife of passions that war against us. Therefore, remembering and knowing that these very bodies of ours are the material of all vices, through which we are besmirched and soiled so that we have nothing clean, nothing harmless in us, we rejoice that we have an enemy, in striving against whom we fight a kind of war against the war in ourselves.'

(28) In his explanation of Psalm 1, the same teacher does not hesitate to say that our own nature, namely, that which contracts disease from disease, is drawn to sin, so that in order not to commit sin we fight against our nature in a certain way, by our service to the faith. He says: 'There are many who, although they have been parted from wickedness by confessing God, are not hereby free from sin, not observing the teachings of the Church, such as the avaricious, the turbulent, insolent, proud, greedy, the drunkards, hypocrites, liars. And to these vices the impulse of our nature urges us, but it is to our advantage to depart and not to tarry in the way to which we are drawn. Thus, "Blessed is the man who has not stood in the way of sinners," for our nature carries us toward this way, but our service to the faith carries us far back out of it.'[18] Shall we then think he was an accuser of the nature which God created? By no means. For this Catholic man did not doubt that human nature is the work of God, but he certainly accused the faults with which

---

17 Job 25.4.
18 Hilary, *Expositio ps. 1* 1

we are born, holding to the statement of the Apostle: 'For we too were by nature children of wrath, even as the rest.'[19] But, if these words which I have quoted from the sermon of St. Hilary were my own, how much would you say against me, and with what noisy outcries would you impute to me the name and crime of the Manichaeans? And now, lest the stomach of your wrath burst with repletion of undigested curses, send forth at him, if you dare, your slanderous falsehoods and lying madness. 'To these vices,' he says, 'the impulse of our nature urges us.' What is this nature? Is it the race of darkness which the fable of the Manichaeans introduces? No, indeed. A Catholic is speaking; a famous doctor of the Church is speaking; Hilary is speaking. Therefore, it is our own nature, vitiated by the transgression of the first man, not to be separated by any kind of division from another nature, but itself to be healed. You falsely say we make the Devil its author, whereas you grudge it Christ as Saviour, and contend that its life here can be led in perfection so that it is absolutely without any sin.

(29) But listen to what blessed Hilary tells you beyond this. When he was explaining Psalm 51, he said:[20] 'Hope in the mercy of God is forever and ever. For those very works of justice do not suffice to merit perfect blessedness, unless the mercy of God even in this will to do justice does not impute the faults of human changes and movements. Hence, this saying of the Prophet: "Thy mercy is better than lives." '[21] Do you see that the man of God is one of that number of the blessed of whom it was foretold: 'Blessed is the man to whom the Lord has not imputed sin, and in whose mouth is no guile'?[22] For he confesses even sins of the just, asserting

---
19 Eph. 2.3.
20 Hilary, *Expositio ps. 52* (towards the end).
21 Ps. 52.4.
22 Ps. 31.2.

that they rather put their hope in the mercy of God than trust in their own justice, and therefore there is no guile in his mouth, nor, indeed, in the mouths of all those to whose truthful humility or humble truth he bears witness. This guile abounds in your mouth. For, where there is no virtue and so much boastfulness there is hypocrisy, and where there is hypocrisy there surely is guile. Truly, as much as the saints trust in the mercy of God, which is great, so much do you trust in your own strength, which is non-existent. And as much as they, assisted by the grace of God, wage war against inborn faults, so much do you wage war against this same grace of God. Would that as it conquers you in its own affairs, so, making you its own, it may also conquer you in yourselves.

(30) Thus, you dare say in your hearts that when men hear you they are inspired to virtue, but when they hear these others, men of such quality and importance, Cyprian, Hilary, Gregory, Ambrose, and other priests of the Lord, they are overcome by despair and give up the pursuit of perfection?[23] Do such monstrous thoughts arise in your hearts and not make you feel ashamed? Then, do you honor the saints of God, the Patriarchs, Prophets, and Apostles, in your praise of the nature, and do these lights of the Church dishonor them by their censure of the nature in saying that in the body of this death, in order to hold fast the good of chastity, they fought against the inborn evil of concupiscence, which through the grace of God must first be conquered in combat and then cured in the final regeneration? You think it is a Jew who said: 'For I do not the good that I wish,' and this you say with the excellent intention of 'not turning impurity

---

23 Julian's contention that the Catholic position denies the possibility of human virtue is not merely speculative; it is obvious that the Pelagians accused the Catholics of permiting and even encouraging immorality among the people, as the Manichaeans are said to have done.

of conduct to a hatred of the nature, or finding comfort for foulness in insulting the Apostles and all the saints.' And this evil, which you do not do, Ambrose did together with his colleagues who held the same doctrine, when he understands that the blessed Apostle speaks of himself when he says: 'I do not the good that I wish, but the evil that I do not wish, that I perform,' and 'I see another law in my members, warring against the law of my mind,'[24] and other remarks of this sort? Therefore, do these holy men in teaching such things 'undermine,' as you accuse me, 'the wall of modesty,' while you, for preaching perfection, are hated? But, as you write, you are much comforted 'because it is a kind of glory to displease one who did not spare the Apostles.' If, in saying such things, I did not spare the Apostles, then neither did Ambrose spare the Apostles, nor did his fellow bishops, who held the same doctrine. But, if they learned these things from the Apostles and taught them according to the Apostles, why do you attack me alone? Look at them, consider them again and again, putting aside a little your pride of mind. And thus, O most self-confident young man, should you take heart or mourn because you are displeasing to such men?

Chapter 9

(31) Now let us briefly sum up as best we can what we have discussed throughout this whole book. We proposed here by the weight of the authority of holy men, who were bishops before us, and strenuously defended the Catholic faith not only by their words while they were living in this world, but also by their writings which they left for posterity, to refute your arguments, in which you say, 'If God creates men, they cannot be born with any evil. If marriage is good, nothing

---

24 Rom. 7.19,25.

evil arises from it. If all sins are forgiven in baptism, those born of the reborn cannot contract original sin. If God is just, He cannot condemn in the children the sins of the parents, since He forgives the parents their own sins as well. If human nature is capable of perfect justice, it cannot have natural faults.' To this we reply that God is the Creator of men, that is, of both soul and body; and that marriage is good; and that through the baptism of Christ all sins are forgiven; and that God is just; and that human nature is capable of perfect justice. Yet, although all these things are true, men are born subject to the vitiated origin which is contracted from the first man, and therefore go to damnation unless they are reborn in Christ. And this we have proved by the authority of Catholic saints who assert what we say about original sin and also confess that all these five statements are true. Therefore, it does not follow that this is false because those are true. Indeed, such great men, according to the Catholic faith which of old was spread throughout the world, confirm the truth both of this and of those, so that your fragile and, as it were, oversubtle novelty is crushed by their authority alone, in addition to what they say, so that truth itself bears witness that it is speaking through them. But now your obstinacy must first be checked by their authority, and checked in your presumptious attack, and in some way wounded, so that when you finally believe that such men of God could not commit such an error in the Catholic faith that they would say something from which it would follow that God is not the Creator of men, that marriage is to be condemned, that not all sins are forgiven in baptism, that God is unjust, that we have no hope of perfect virtue—all or any of which it is wicked to think—you may restrain your headlong boldness, and, as it were, recovering from madness, may begin to consider and recognize and resume the truth in which you were nurtured.

(32) Blessed Ambrose says that only one man, the Mediator between God and men, because He was born of a virgin and did not experience sin in His birth, is not subject to the chains of the bound generation. But all men are born under sin, and their very origin is in evil, because, formed in the pleasure of concupiscence, they first suffered the contagion of sin before they breathed the vital breath of this air. He says that this concupiscence, as the law of sin in the body of this death, wars against the law of the mind, so that not only all the good and faithful but also the great strength of the Apostle fought against it, so that the flesh being subjected to the spirit by the grace of Christ may be brought back to harmony, because through the transgression of the first man discord was brought about between these two who were first created without sin. Who is it that says this? A man of God, a Catholic, and a most keen defender of the Catholic truth against heretics, even unto danger of death, one so highly praised by the testimony of your teacher that he said not even an enemy would dare find fault with his faith and his clear understanding of the Scriptures. He asserted that God is the Creator not only of souls but also of bodies, against the error of Platonic philosophers. He preached that marriage is good and that it was divinely instituted for the sake of the propagation of the human race, and that its union is holy through conjugal modesty. He said that none is acquitted of sin but one whose every sin is forgiven in baptism. He justly worshiped the just God. He was far from despairing of and hindering the perfection of man in virtue and justice, but it is in another life that he hopes for that perfection to which nothing is lacking, which shall be consummated by the resurrection of the dead. In this life he placed human justice in a kind of warfare and battle not only against hostile powers of the air, but also against our own lusts, through which those external enemies themselves strive to overthrow us or

enter into us. In this war he says the flesh itself is a dangerous adversary, whose nature as it was first created would have remained in harmony with us if it had not been vitiated by the sin of the first man, but it now strives against us in a kind of sickness. In this war the holy man warns us to flee from the world, and shows the great difficulty—rather, the very impossibility—of this flight, unless we are aided by the grace of God. He says that our faults are dead through the forgiveness of all sins in baptism, but that we must take care, as it were, of their burial. In this same work he recounts that we have such a conflict with our dead faults that we do not what we wish, but do what we hate; that sin works many things in us while we struggle with it; that pleasures often revive and rise again; that we must struggle against the flesh against which Paul was struggling when he said: 'I see another law in my members warring against the law of my mind.' He teaches us not to trust our flesh, not to rely on it, since the Apostle exclaims: 'I know that in me, that is, in my flesh, no good dwells, because to wish is within my power, but I do not find the strength to accomplish what is good.'[1] See what a fight we have with our dead sins, as that active soldier of Christ and faithful teacher of the Church shows. For how is sin dead when it works many things in us while we struggle against it? What are these many things except foolish and harmful desires which plunge those who consent to them into death and destruction?[2] And to bear them patiently and not to consent to them is a struggle, a conflict, a battle. And between what parties in this battle if not between good and evil, not of nature against nature, but of nature against fault, which is already dead but still to be buried; that is, entirely healed? How, then, do we say this sin is dead in baptism, as this man also says, and how do we confess

---
1 Rom. 7.23,18.
2 Cf. 1 Tim. 6.9.

it dwells in our members and works many desires against which we struggle and which we resist by not consenting to them, as this man also confesses, except that it is dead in that guilt by which it held us, and until it is healed by the perfection of its burial it rebels even though dead? However, it is called sin, not in such a way that it makes us guilty, but because it is the result of the guilt of the first man and because by rebelling it strives to draw us to guilt, unless we are aided by the grace of God through Jesus Christ our Lord, lest even the dead sin so rebel that by conquering it revives and reigns.

Chapter 10

(33) The reason that we who toil in this war as long as human life is a trial on the earth[1] are not without sin is not that that thing called sin works in our members in this way, warring against the law of the mind, even though we do not consent to unlawful acts (for as much as pertains to us, we would always be without sin until this evil is healed if we never consented to evil); but that wherever we are overcome by the rebellious element, even though not mortally but only venially, we are nevertheless overcome, and herein we contract something, whence we daily say: 'Forgive us our trespasses.'[2] For instance—husband and wife when for the sake of pleasure alone they exceed the limit necessary for procreation; or celibates when they linger with some delight in such thoughts, not indeed deciding to commit crime, but not turning away the intention of the mind as they should in order that they do not fall into sin, or not tearing it away if it falls. About this law of sin which in another way is also

---
1 Cf. Job. 7.1.
2 Matt. 6.12.

called sin, and which wars against the law of the mind, about which blessed Ambrose had much to say, St. Cyprian, Hilary, Gregory, and many others have also spoken. Therefore, he who is born in Adam and must be reborn in Christ, dead in Adam and to be revived in Christ, is bound by original sin because he is born of the evil by which the flesh lusts against the spirit, not of the good by which the spirit lusts against the flesh.[3] Why, then, it is strange if a man must be reborn, since he is born of that evil against which the reborn fights and by which the reborn himself would also be held in guilt if he were not set free by being reborn? This evil is not the matter of God the Creator, but the wound of the Devil vitiating this matter. This is not an evil of marriage, but the sin of the first men transmitted to their posterity by propagation. The guilt even of this sin is remitted by the sanctification of baptism. And if the just God imposed evils so great I cannot at present recount them, upon infants who contract no sin, He would rather seem unjust. And man's perfect capacity for justice is not denied, because none could despair of the most complete healing of all faults under the care of the almighty physician. Because of this Catholic truth, holy and blessed priests, famous in their treatment of sacred doctrine, Irenaeus, Cyprian, Reticius, Olympius, Hilary, Ambrose, Gregory, Innocent, John, Basil, to whom I add, whether you wish it or not, the priest Jerome, omitting those who are still alive, have pronounced against you their opinion about the succession of all men which is bound by original sin, whence no one can rescue them except Him whom a virgin conceived without the law of sin warring against the law of the mind.

(34) What reason have you to rejoice and gloat over me as victor, as though I could not find anything to do, any place to flee, if I were overwhelmed by the power of the judges,

---

[3] Gal. 5.17.

if I stood in the midst of the learned with you, if the trumpet of sound reason, as you say, blown I suppose by you, the greater trumpeter, and the arms of the listeners standing about and supporting you should make a great clamor? For so you envisage our contest in argument, and imagine as you please that I have nothing to answer your arguments. Thus the vain and insane imagination of your heart talks to you, as if you set me with you before Pelagian judges, with whose applause you can raise up your voice like a trumpet and speak against the Catholic faith and against the grace of Christ, by which both infants and adults are delivered from evil—an error common to you and them in this ungodly novelty. Such judges within the Church of God, and that not without an opponent representing the other side, your teacher Pelagius succeeded in finding. From this judgment he himself, so far as concerns the opinion of men, came forth cleared, but your teaching was openly condemned. But wherever you are, wherever you may read this, I place you, deep within your heart, before these men whom I have constituted judges, not my advocates in this our debate, since they are not my friends and your enemies and in any way prejudiced in my favor or prejudiced against you because of your offense. And I have not, with empty imagining, invented such persons as have never existed and do not exist, or whose teachings on the matter about which we are arguing are uncertain, but holy bishops famous in the holy Church, and I have quoted them by name as was fitting, men versed in sacred Scripture, not in Platonic or Aristotelean or Stoic or other such studies, either Greek or Latin—although some of them were that, also. And I have arranged their doctrines as seemed sufficient to me, expressed without any ambiguity, that in them you may fear not themselves but Him who made them useful vessels for Himself, and holy temples; and they then judged the case when no one can say they were wrongly prejudiced for or against anyone. For you had not as yet been born, against whom we were to undertake the argument on this question; you were not in existence to say what you say in your books: that we lie about you to the multitude and that we terrify men by the name 'Celestians' or 'Pelagians,' and by terror force assent from men. Certainly, you yourself said that all judges ought to be free from hatred, friendship, enmity and anger. Few such could be found, but we must believe that Ambrose and the others, his colleagues, whom we mentioned with him were of this calibre. But even if they were not so in the cases brought before them for trial during their lifetime and on which they passed judgment, they were so in this case, for they were involved in no friendship or enmity with us or with you; they were not angry at either of us, they felt no pity for either of us. What they found in the Church they held; what they learned they taught; what they received from the fathers they handed down to the sons. We were not as yet involved with you before these judges; they tried our case. Neither we nor you were known to them; we recite their judgments delivered in our favor against you. We were not as yet contending with you; we were victorious by their pronouncements.

(35) You say that if I were overwhelmed by the power of judges—such as you imagine for yourself—I should not know what to do and where to turn; I should not be able to find any means of meeting your arguments. I certainly did know what to do. I knew where to turn. I called you forth from the Pelagian darkness to these brilliant Catholic lights, and I do so now again. So do you answer what you yourself can do; tell me where you will turn. I turn from the Pelagians to these; to whom will you turn from these? Or because you think that 'opinions should be not numbered but weighed,' and add (what, again, I grant to be true), that 'to find something a multitude of blind men is of no use,' will you

dare call even them blind? Has the long day so confounded the highest with the lowest, and shall darkness be called light and light darkness to such an extent that Pelagius, Celestius, and Julian see, and Hilary, Gregory, and Ambrose are blind? But whatever kind of man you are, yet, because you are a man, I think that I sense your feeling of shame (if, indeed, all hope of health is not dead in you) and, after a fashion, hear your voice. You answer: 'Far be it from me either to think or to call those men blind.' Then weigh their opinions. I do not wish them to be many so that it will be irksome for you to count them; but they are not unimportant, so that you will not disdain to weigh them; rather, they are so important that I see you are burdened with their weight. Are you going to say also of them that I in my weakness am trying to create opinion of a force supporting me, and as if overcome by fear, I name my accomplices?

(36) You say that, when judgment is passed, the noise of crowds must be removed, that for the discussion of such matters we must choose from all sorts and conditions of men, whether priests or governors or rulers, and not mere names but prudence and small numbers must be honored, whom reason, learning, and liberty elevate. It it true, as you say. But I do not disturb you by the large numbers of the multitude, although by the grace of God, about this faith which you oppose, even the multitude of the Catholics has sound judgment. In this, many, where they can and in whatever way they can, as they are given divine assistance, constantly refute your vain argument. Hence, I shun that arrogance of which you accuse me; far be it from me to promise, one for all, to carry on this case against you. However, you yourself do this among the Pelagians, not blushing to say and to write that it is to your greater glory before God to defend deserted truth. They are brought very low and truly deserted and depend very much on you if they do not consider it intolerable arrogance

by which you put yourself above Pelagius and Celestius, the teachers of all of you, as if they had already given way and you alone remained to defend what you consider the deserted truth. But because it pleases you not to count numbers but to weigh the few, I shall exclude the judges of Palestine who condemned your heresy in acquitting Pelagius when they compelled him, overwhelmed with fear, to condem the Pelagian doctrines; and I set against you as judges in this case ten bishops (now deceased) and one priest who passed judgment on this matter while they were alive. If we consider your small numbers, they are many; if we consider the multitude of Catholic bishops, they are very few. Of these you will perhaps try to remove Pope Innocent and the priest Jerome— the former, because he condemned Pelagius and Celestius; the latter, because he defended the Catholic faith with pious zeal against Pelagius in the East. But read what Pelagius said in praise of blessed Pope Innocent, and see whether you can easily find other such judges. But of that holy priest who, according to the grace that was given him, labored so much in the Church to assist Catholic learning in the Latin tongue by many necessary works, Pelagius does not usually say much except to envy him as a rival. But I do not wish you to think that for this reason he should be removed from the number of these judges. For I have not quoted from those doctrines which he stated when defending his teaching against your error at the time of hostility, but what he wrote in his books, free from all partisanship, before your damnable doctrine sprang up.

(37) About the others there is certainly no objection you could make. Were Irenaeus and Cyprian and Reticius and Olympius and Hilary and Gregory and Basil and Ambrose and John gathered in hostility against you 'from the plebian dregs of the mechanics,' as you jest in Ciceronian fashion? Were they soldiers, vagrant students, sailors, shopkeepers, fishmon-

gers, cooks, porters? Are they dissolute youths from among the
monks? Are they a crowd of nondescript clerics, whom you
satirize by your polished wit or, rather, despise 'because they
cannot judge about dogmas according to the Aristotelean
Categories?' And if you, who loudly complain that an examination and the judgment of the bishop is denied you, might
find a council of Peripatetics in which a dialectical sentence
might be pronounced about the matter in hand, and the
point involved in it against original sin, these are bishops,
learned, serious, holy, zealous defenders of the truth against
garrulous vanities; in whose reason, learning, liberty—three
qualities you say are necessary for a judge—you can find
nothing to despise. If an episcopal synod were gathered from
the whole world, it would be surprising if so many men of
such calibre could be members of it. For these did not all
live at one time, but God, as it pleases Him and He judges
expedient, Himself distributes His stewards, faithful, few, more
excellent than many, in diverse ages, times and places. So you
see them gathered from various periods and regions, from the
East and the West, not at a place to which men are obliged
to travel, but in a book which can travel to men. The more
desirable these judges would be for you if you held the Catholic faith, which they sucked with their mother's milk, which
they took in their food, and they have ministered this milk and
food to great and small, openly and bravely defending it
against its enemies—even you who were not then born;
whence you now stand revealed. With such planters, waterers,
shepherds, fosterers, the holy Church grew after the time of
the Apostles. This is why she feared the profane voices of
your novelty, and, being cautious and sober as a result of
the Apostle's warning, lest, as the Serpent seduced Eve by
his cunning, her mind be seduced from the chastity which is
in Christ;[4] she shuddered at the toils of your doctrine creeping

---

4 2 Cor. 11.3.

toward the virginity of the Catholic faith like the head of a serpent; she trod upon it, crushed it, cast it away. Therefore, by the statements and the great authority of holy men you will either be cured—God's mercy granting it, and He who may accomplish it knows how much I desire it for you—or, what I deprecate, if you persevere in this your wisdom which is really great folly, you will no longer merely seek judges before whom you may justify your cause, but before whom you may accuse so many famous and brilliant holy teachers of the Catholic truth: Irenaeus, Cyprian, Reticius, Olympius, Hilary, Gregory, Basil, Ambrose, John, Innocent, Jerome, and the others, their comrades and colleagues, and, in addition the whole Church of Christ, to which divine family they faithfully ministered the food of the Lord and thus grew famous in the glory of the Lord. But against this wretched madness, which I pray God may remove from you, I see that your books must be so answered that the faith of these men is defended against your attacks, just as the Gospel itself is defended against the ungodly and professed enemies of Christ.

BOOK III

Chapter 1

ERE ARE SAINTLY MEN, many and great, learned in sacred letters, brilliant, highly honored and praised for their remarkable government of the Church. If you will not now yield and accept their authority, you must surely assert that they erred, whether you choose to insult them as you insult me, or more gently show them a certain personal

---

1 Since Augustine begins in this book to refute, one at a time, the arguments advanced by Julian, it is not difficult to reconstruct the arguments contained in the lost work by Julian from the statements Augustine quotes in his replies, if Julian's two principal objectives are recalled; namely, his intention to refute the Catholic position stated by Augustine in *De nuptiis et concupiscentia*, and his hope of establishing his own doctrine. His general attack on Augustine is based on the five arguments well summarized above in 2.1. The positive doctrine he wishes to establish, and the means he uses, seem to follow the outline given by Augustine in *Contra duas epistolas Pelagianorum* (4.2.2). 'In all these charges, whatever they say about the praise due the creature and marriage, they try to relate to this: that there is no original sin. Whatever they say about the praise due to the Law and free will, they wish to relate to this: there is no grace except where there is merit first, and thus grace is no longer grace. Whatever they say about the praise due the saints, they try to relate to this: that mortal life in the saints has no sin, and it is not necessary for them to beseech God to forgive their trespasses.'

respect. Therefore, I am duty bound to answer you, Julian, my son, and, God willing, so to refute your books and your arguments that you will see, if you are able, that the thing of which you have tried to persuade others is something of which you yourself were badly persuaded, and will do wholesome penance for your youthful and rash advance and fall. Your emendation will not only be good for you, but also for many others, if you realize and confess how truthfully and not vainly this large number of great rulers and doctors of the Christian peoples learned and taught in the Church of God that which you, who were deceived by a novelty resembling the truth, were eager to overthrow. But, God forbid, if you keep your heart so clouded that you cannot understand, or if you are of that number whom the truth describes in the holy psalms, when it says, 'He would not understand that he might do well,'[2] of those of whom it is written, 'A slave will not be corrected by words: because he understandeth what thou sayest, and will not answer,'[3] my efforts, or those of the same mind who through the grace of Christ are defending the Catholic faith against your error, will not be unfruitful. If there are some subverted and disturbed by unusual error, there is a greater number whom the defense of the ancient truth will either instruct or correct. I shall not repeat all you said, lest the book be too long. But with the Lord's help, I shall let none of your supposedly astute arguments go unsolved and unvanquished.

(2) Let us consider the judges before whom you say you cannot conduct your case, 'because he who does not show himself free of partisan hatred or anger or friendship is not a good judge of doubtful matters.' Those who will judge your case, you complain, will not be so qualified 'because they began to hate it even before they began to know it.' We have

---

2 Ps 35.4.
3 Prov. 29.19.

already answered your complaint.⁴ If you are looking for the kind of judges described by Sallust, from whom you took the definition, you must certainly accept Ambrose and his fellow bishops, whose hearts were devoid of hatred for you in this cause, and devoid of friendship and of anger, and, to offer another qualification which Sallust named, although you did not mention it, they were devoid of mercy for you or against you when they passed their true and tranquil judgments about it. But you think it a small matter that you are unwilling to have these men as judges, unless you also regard them as culprits. How, I ask you, did these men who condemned your cause begin to hate it before they knew it? Undoubtedly, those men hated it because they knew it. They knew you to say there is no evil in infants at birth which must be purged by rebirth. They knew you to say that the grace of God is given according to our merits, so that grace would not longer be grace, because it is not given gratuitously, but rendered as something due.⁵ They knew you to say that a man in this life can be without sin, so that what the whole Church says in the Lord's prayer, 'Forgive us our trespasses,'⁶ is not necessary for him. These things they knew in you, and these things they very rightly hated. If they know you have corrected these errors, they will love you. It is not true, as you say, that 'If anyone either says there is free will in men or that God is the Creator of those merely born, he is called a Pelagian or Celestian.' A Pelagian or Celestian is he who does not attribute to the grace of God the freedom to which we have been called, and who denies that Christ is the deliverer of infants, and who says that a certain petition in the Lord's prayer must be made by every just man in this life, but not for his own sake. Whoever takes the name attached to this error is partaker of its fault.

---

4 See above, 2.10.34.
5 Cf. Rom. 11.6.
6 Matt. 6.6.

(3) It is not necessary for us here to name the Catholic lights you dare to defame with the crime of Manichaeism, whether you are unaware of doing so or only pretend to be ignorant. If, as you say, 'The emperor has spoken for our side,' why do you not further allege the public authority to show that it is you whose faith the Christian prince has approved? If, however you understand the law of God not as it is in itself, but as it is your good pleasure, what wonder if you behave likewise about the law of the emperor? But you promise that you will carry out these actions more fully elsewhere. If you do so, they will be either refuted as deceitful or despised as futile.

(4) You seem to rejoice much as you say that 'One source hopes that men will think him the center of the battle;' that is, you want to seem David while I shall be Goliath. If you have made this compact and agreement with the Pelagians, it follows that, if you are vanquished, that will end their daring. God forbid that I should ever challenge your side to single combat, since, wherever any of you appears, the ubiquitous army of Christ routs you. That army routed Celestius at Carthage when I was not present, and it routed him at Constantinople, far from Africa. That army routed Pelagius in Palestine, where, in fear of his own condemnation, he condemned your cause and your whole heresy fell to the ground. Since He, of whom David was a figure, fights against His adversaries in all His soldiers, He has beheaded your error with His sword, even by the tongue of Pelagius, a prostrate and fallen man. For Pelagius—no, the Lord Himself, through Pelagius' tongue—has destroyed your complaint that 'The reason you are said to be new heretics is that you say no evil defined as "sin" is in the nature, but in the will alone.' In other words, Pelagius, fearing his own condemnation, condemned all who say infants have eternal life even if they are not baptized. Therefore, you who deny there is in an infant

any evil which is washed away by baptism must tell why a non-baptized infant is committed to eternal death. Can you do anything except curse Pelagius? Suppose you curse him, and he replies; 'What would you have had me do? When Christ said, "Unless you eat my flesh and drink my blood, you shall have not have life in you,"[7] should I have said an infant who ends this life without the sacrament will have life?' I think you will regret his whole error.

(5) Do not invoke the wretched argument used by all heretics whom the laws of Catholic emperors restrain from pernicious licence. All of them say, as you yourself have said: 'The other party suffers from poverty of argument. It refuses to consult the prudent in conducting its case, and invokes terror to extort blind assent from the timid.' You are new heretics, to be sure, but you, with all the rest, know how to use the old voice of nearly every heretic. You deceive neither yourselves nor anyone else into thinking you have against us as we had against the Donatists, whom we compelled through imperial commands to meet with us in conference.[8] Their fury had taken possession of all Africa, and, while they were terrifying all men, working immense destruction by forceful aggression, pillaging, ambush on the highways, rapine, fire, and massacre, they would not suffer Catholics to preach the truth against their error. We were able to accomplish nothing with them in the episcopal courts, since we did not have bishops in common with them. The people no longer remember what our elders had to encounter in those men nearly one hundred years ago. This necessity, therefore, compelled us to crush their shame-

---
7 John 6.54.
8 St. Augustine's important conflict with the Donatists centered on their misconception of the sacraments and the Church, which involved sacraments administered by an unworthy minister and the false notion that sinners could not be members of the Church. The Donatist schism itself was finally suppressed after the great Conference of Carthage, held in 411, and attended by 286 Catholic bishops and 279 Donatist bishops.

lessness and to repress their daring, at least by the transactions of our conference. But your case has been closed by the competent judgment of bishops common to you and us, and, so far as a right to a trial is concerned, we have no further business with you except that you shall follow peacefully the sentence which has been passed upon the matter. If you are unwilling to do so, you shall be restrained from turbulence and sedition. But you more nearly resemble the Maximianists who, to console themselves for their insignificance, hoped, by being permitted to enter into discussion with us, at least by their recognition to seem of importance in the eyes of those who held them in contempt.[9] When they appeared with letters and challenged us, we treated them with scorn. They were more eager to have a name than fearful of being vanquished in contest; they did not hope for the glory of victory, but sought the reputation associated with a conference, for they lacked the prestige of number. If, therefore, you think you are victors because you have not been accorded the trial you desire, the Maximianists have anticipated you in this kind of idle talk. Yet the Catholic Church has indeed accorded you such judgment as was due, where your case was closed. She did not give them a hearing, because they had separated from the Donatists, not from us, as you have done. If from the Maximianists you see it does not follow that those not permitted to confer in a given case should be thought to rest secure in the truth, throw aside your vain taunts and let it suffice for you that the Catholic Church which has sustained you in maternal gentlesness has also condemned you with judicial severity, or, rather, out of remedial necessity.

(6) Lest we delay in superfluous details, I shall pass over the tumult of insults and abuse which is found not only at the beginning of your work, but almost everywhere throughout

---

9 A sect in schism from the Donatists themselves, supporting Maximian, a Donatist claimant to the see of Carthage against the Donatist Primian.

the four volumes. I do not want earnest men to feel that neither of us is earnest in this disputation, that both of us are shallow litigants. Let us see what reason you have to offer for your statement that I attribute the authorship of men and of marriage to the Devil.

Chapter 2

(7) It is your custom to quote my words for the purpose of refuting them. After proposing them as though to answer them, you try to prove that I contradicted myself: that after saying in my own defense that the new heretics accuse us of condemning marriage and the divine work, I later withdrew this statement by saying that 'Man at birth is possessed in half-shares by God and the Devil, or, better, that the whole is possessed by the Devil, to the total exclusion of God as if from His universal possession, which is man.' Where is the acumen by which you have mastered the Aristotelean Categories and the keenness of the art of dialectics? Do you not see that an enemy of the truth can use your objection to me about infants, against both of us about evil adults? I ask you what you will answer about a very evil man who has not yet been regenerated. You concede that he at least must be under the Devil unless he shall be reborn in Christ—or will you also deny this? If you deny it, I ask whom God has freed from the power of darkness and transferred to the kingdom of the Son of His charity? If you concede it, I ask whether God has any power over this man who is still in the power of darkness. If you answer that He has not, then God has been excluded by the Devil from His possession. If you answer that He has, then God and the Devil possesses man in half-shares and such hatred will be stirred up against you among the ignorant as you, who wish to seem wise, have been trying to stir up against

me in respect to new-born infants. Behold the great ease with which your first argument has been destroyed because of your failure to see that men are indeed under the power of the Devil before they are redeemed by Christ, but in such a way that not only they, but even the Devil himself, cannot withdraw from the power of God.

Chapter 3

(8) You complain that our falsehoods have made baptism odious· to the ignorant. I can scarcely say how smoothly you have evaded and turned this hatred away from yourselves by conceding that infants must be baptized, because, as you say, 'The grace of baptism is not to be changed for special cases, because it dispenses its gifts relatively to the capacity of those who approach it. Christ, therefore, who is the redeemer of His own work, increases His benefits to His image in continual lavishness. Those whom He made good by creation, He makes better by renovation and adoption.' Is this your only reason for believing no one can stir up hatred against you concerning the baptism of infants?—as though any of us says you deny infants must be baptized; yet in your remarkable wisdom you say such extraordinary things as: they are baptized in the sacrament of the Saviour, but not saved; they are redeemed, but not delivered; they are bathed, but not washed; they are exorcized and exsufflated, but not freed from the power of the Devil. These are the marvels of your judgments; the undreamed of mysteries of your new dogmas; these are the paradoxes of the Pelagian heretics, more wonderful than those of the Stoic philosophers. While you are thus declaiming, are you afraid to hear: 'If they are saved, what was sick in them? If they are delivered, what held them in the bonds of slavery? If they are washed, what unclean thing lay hidden in them? If

they are freed, why were they under the power of the Devil when they were not guilty of any wickedness of their own—unless it is because they contracted original sin, which you deny?' And you deny, not that you may declare them saved, free, pure, subject to no enemy—for your false testimony does not help them in any way before the true judge—but that you may follow your new vanity, while they remain in their old evil. The true judgment is not yours, but His who said: 'Unless a man be born again of water and the Spirit, he cannot enter the kingdom of God.'[1]

(9) You, who are such excellent lovers of that life which will be eternal with Christ, think it no punishment for the image of God to be eternally exiled from the kingdom of God. If you were to say it is a small punishment, yours would not be the voice of a blessed lover of the kingdom, but the words of a wretched railler; yet, as suffices in this case, if you concede that a great punishment, that is, for the image of God not to be permitted to enter into the kingdom of God, is at least a small punishment, then I beg you to open whatever kind of eyes you have and see by what justice such punishment can be inflicted of an infant whom, with your eyes closed, you deny is subjected to original sin. I shall not describe here the evils nearly all infants suffer in this transitory life, and how we are to explain the words: 'A heavy yoke is upon the children of Adam from the day of their coming out of their mother's womb until the day of their burial into the mother of all.'[2] Under the just and almighty God, these evils would not be visited upon His image—evils that could not lead to practice of virtue in infants—if nothing calling for punishment were contracted from parents. Without a glance you pass by these evils which befall infants; and these are not the evils you deny infants have, but the evils all of us

---
1 John 3.5.
2 Eccli. 40.1.

see them suffer. You pass by, exercising your learned wit and skillfull tongue in praise of the nature, but that nature, fallen into such great and manifest misery, must necessarily have Christ for its saviour, deliverer, cleanser, redeemer—not Julian, not Celestius, not Pelagius for its encomiast. You would not concede that that nature must be redeemed in infants if Celestius, who could not withstand Christian testimony, had not confessed this in the ecclesiastical transactions at Carthage. I ask you, therefore, how this redemption can be understood unless it be redemption from evil, by Him who redeemed Israel from all his sins?[3] When we hear of redemption, we also think of price; and what is the price but the precious blood of the immaculate lamb, Jesus Christ?[4] Must we seek elsewhere why this price was paid? Let the Redeemer Himself answer; let the Buyer speak. He says: 'This is my blood which is being shed for many unto the forgiveness of sins.'[5] Go on, then, go on and say that they are baptized in the sacrament of the Saviour, but not saved; they are redeemed, but not delivered; they are bathed, but not washed; they are exorcised and exsufflated, but not freed from the power of the Devil. Declare, likewise, that the blood is also shed for them for forgiveness of sins, but they are not cleansed by forgiveness of any sin. Wondrous are the things you say. New are the things you say. False are the things you say. We gape at wonders. We are wary of novelties. We convict falsity.

Chapter 4

(10) Did you not declare: 'The administration of the body is committed to the soul in such a way that the result of the

---

3 Cf. Ps. 129.8.
4 Cf. 1 Peter 1.18,19.
5 Matt. 26.28.

operation is shared by the two, and the soul will sense either the joys of the use of virtue or the punishments for insolence together with affliction of the flesh which it did not rule well in this life.' Answer, therefore, why the soul of an infant is tormented in this very life by afflictions of the flesh, although nothing deserving this torment can yet be imputed to the infant on the ground that he has not ruled his flesh well. You say: 'At the beginning of life, human nature is adorned with the gift of innocence.' We agree wholeheartedly, so far as personal sins are concerned. But, since you also deny that an infant is subject to original sin, you must answer why such great innocence is sometimes born blind; sometimes, deaf. Deafness is a hindrance to faith itself, as the Apostle says: 'Faith is from hearing.'[1] 'Indeed, if nothing deserving punishment passes from parents to infants, who could bear to see the image of God, which is, you say, adorned with the gift of innocence, sometimes born feeble-minded, since this touches the soul itself? Or is each of you feeble-minded, so that none thinks feeble-mindedness an evil, although as Scripture says: 'The mourning for the dead is seven days, but for a feeble-minded man and ungodly man all the days of their life.'[2] Does anyone not know that those whom people call 'morons' are so dull by nature that some have almost as little wit as cattle? Yet you do not wish to say that from the beginning, when the human race deserted God, it contracts the offense of its condemned origin, which fully deserves to suffer all these punishments it endures except where the inscrutable wisdom of the Creator spares it, mysteriously, according to His plan. Nor does He withold the good of His work from that universal mass of perdition, so that out of evil faults He forms, though together with faults, yet formed by Him in so far as it is itself good, a mortal and rational nature, of which He alone

---
1 Rom. 10.17.
2 Eccli. 22.13.

can be the Creator, and in the condemned generation He presents the help of regeneration to vessels of mercy.

Chapter 5

(11) There is no basis for your judgment that 'There cannot be offense in infants, because there can be no offense without will, which they no not possess.' This assertion may be correctly made about a personal sin, but not about the contagion by way of origin of the first sin. If there were no such sin, then infants, bound by no evil, would suffer nothing evil in body or in soul under the great power of the just God. Yet, this evil itself took its rise from the evil will of the first man; so that there is no other origin of sin but an evil will. If you understand the meaning of these things, you will simply and truthfully confess the grace of Christ in regard to infants, and you will not be forced to the ungodly and absurd assertions either that infants ought not to be baptized, which you may very well be driven to say at some later time, or that so great a sacrament is mockery in them, with the result that they are baptized in the Saviour, but not saved; are redeemed by the Deliverer, but not delivered; are bathed by the laver of regeneration, but not washed; are exorcized and exsufflated, but not freed from the power of darkness; their price is the blood which was shed for the forgiveness of sins, but they are not cleansed by the forgiveness of any sins. You must bear this whole burden of absurdity and ungodliness because you are afraid to deny that they should be baptized, lest not only your face be dirtied by the spittle of men, but also your head be pulverized by the slippers of women.

(12) We declare that the reason whoever is born must be under the power of the Devil until he be reborn in Christ is the contagion of sin from his origin. But you who deny it:

Consider some plain facts. Consider why some infants suffer from a demon—unless you want to deny that there are such infants or that they are under the power of the Devil. Nor will the Gospel remind you, when, perhaps for your sake, our Lord asked what He already knew so that the father of the boy might answer that his son from infancy had been grievously vexed by so powerful a demon that Christ's disciples could not expel it.[1] I do not say that marriage causes infants to be under the power of the Devil, as you calumniously say I do. Marriage has indeed its own order and its own goodness, and these could not be lost at the entrance of sin. But at least answer, if you can, why an infant who is very plainly vexed by the Devil, in such a way that some infants die in this vexation, is under the power of the Devil. You do not wish to admit that anyone undergoes punishment for the sins of another, lest your admission make it credible that the contagions of sins also pass from those who beget to those who are born.

Chapter 6

(13) As an outstanding dialectician, however, you say you will not suffer me to escape, but will ask me briefly and to the point whether I hold an action or the nature to be guilty in infants. You yourself answer both alternatives, saying that, if it is an action, I must show what acts infants perform; if it is the nature, I must show who made it. You speak as though an evil action, too, made only the nature guilty. In truth, the one made guilty by a man's action is man, but man is a nature. Therefore, just as adults become guilty by a sinful action so minors become guilty by contagion from adults. The former become guilty from what they do; the

---

1 Cf. Mark 9.16-26.

latter, from those from whom they take their origin. It is a good in an infant that he is man; and he would not be man at all if not created by Him who is supremely good. But, if he contracted no evil from his origin, he would never be born with even bodily faults. For God, who is the creator of souls, is also the creator of bodies, and He would never undeservedly inflict faults on human nature in its very creation. Moreover, our Lord's words[1] about the man born blind—that this did not happen because of his own sin or the sin of his parents, but that the works of God were to be made manifest in him—cannot be applied to the innumerable infants born with such great variety of faults in soul and body. For, indeed, there are many who are never healed at all, but die with those same faults, at another age, or even in infancy; and some infants already reborn retain the faults with which they were born, while other evils of the same kind may also be added—God forbid we say this is done without its being deserved. Let us conclude, instead, that their being reborn profits them in regard to the other world, while because of the fault of human pride, through which man apostatized from God,[2] the plan of this world is executed in a variety of human evils, in 'the heavy yoke upon the children of Adam, from the day of their coming out of their mother's womb until the day of their burial into the mother of all.'[3]

Chapter 7

(14) When your book tries to teach how dialecticians construct syllogisms, a question no one has asked, you displease

---
1 Cf. John 9.3.
2 Cf. Eccli. 10.11,15.
3 Eccli. 40.1.

earnest readers as much as you please yourself. Worse than that, you pretend that I say what I do not say, that I conclude what I do not conclude, concede what I do not concede, and you draw conclusions which I reject.[1] When have I ever denied that the nature of the men is praiseworthy—in so far as they are men? When have I ever said that they are guilty from the mere fact of existence—since they would surely exist, yet not be guilty, if no one had sinned? When have I ever said that fecundity must be censured—when it pertains to the blessing of marriage? How could I ask you to concede what I myself have never asserted?

(15) Your remark that I assume all union of bodies is evil is nothing less than to assert that I must also find fault with the union of wine and water when our drink is tempered, because here is unquestionably a union of bodies. If I had said that all union of bodies is evil, I should not have omitted this kind of union. I have never censured the union of the two sexes if it is lawfully within the boundaries of marriage. There could be no generation of human beings without such union, even if no sin had preceded it. As to the second proposition you add as mine, that children are born of the union of bodies: this I do say indeed, but the conclusion you wish to draw as mine is not mine. I do not say that children, coming from an evil action, are evil, since I do not say that the activity in which married persons engage for the purpose of begetting children is evil. As a matter of fact, I assert that it is good, because it makes good use of the evil of lust, and through this good use, human beings, a good work of God, are generated. But the action is not performed without evil, and this is why the children must be regenerated in order to be delivered from evil.

---

[1] The first of the formal arguments Julian constructed by means of propositions he selected from Augustine's writing and attributed to Augustine, in order to show Manichaeism in his reasoning.

(16) You proceed to construct your second syllogism; I say it is yours, since the first syllogism was also yours, not mine.[2] You say: 'The reason for the existence of the sexes is the union of bodies,' and you want me to concede this to you. I do concede it. You continue: 'If the union of bodies is always evil, the condition of bodies in the different sexes is a deformity.' If this argument were good, it would not disturb me, for I do not say that nuptial union—that is, union for the purpose of procreating—is evil, but even say it is good. But it does not follow, if the union of the two sexes is always evil in fact, that the condition of the bodies in the different sexes is a deformity. If men were subject to the evil of lust to such an extent that if the honesty of marriage were removed, all of them would have intercourse indiscriminately, in the manner of dogs, the condition of the bodies, of which God is the author, would not be a deformity merely because all sexual union happened to be evil. Even now, in evil adulterous union, we see that the work of God in the condition of the bodies is good. Yon see how logically you have said nothing, but that is no reflection on the art of dialectics from whose principles you have much departed. You use it to glorify yourself and shock the inexperienced in your desire to appear what you are not. But, even if you were an excellent dialectician, you would be at a loss as to how these matters should be discussed; as matters stand, you are both inept and unskilled. If you were a good dialectician, you would still be an inept artist. Yet you advance to the combat as though you were laden with the darts of dialectics, and you hurl these leaden daggers, saying: 'If intercourse is always evil, the condition of bodies in the different sexes is a deformity.' When you add that I cannot deny this, you do not see that what you have called a

---

2 The second of the syllogisms by Julian is the first part of a *reductio ad absurdum* which is completed by the third syllogism below.

necessary argument is not consequent. What is it that I cannot deny, unthinking man? What am I unable to deny? It is this, which you cannot deny—if you grasp it even so tardily: that, if the intercourse of adulterers is evil, it is not therefore true that the condition of those born of it is a deformity. Evil union is the work of the men operating evilly from their good members. The condition of the newborn is the work of God operating well from evil men. If you say that, even when there is adultery, the union is good in itself, since it is natural, but adulterers use it evilly, why will you not acknowledge that in the same way lust can be evil, yet the married may nevertheless use it well for the purpose of begetting children? Will you assert there can be evil use of good, but there cannot be good use of evil? We see how well the Apostle used Satan himself, when he delivered a man over to him for the destruction of the flesh, that his spirit might be saved in the day of the Lord, and when he delivered others up to him that they might learn not to blaspheme.[3]

Chapter 8

(17) How did you want us to understand your words: 'God cannot be the author of an evil'? God himself spoke better than you when he said through the Prophet that he creates evils.[1] Regardless of the meaning of your words, how can they apply to me, when I do not concede the proposition with which you connect them, and I have shown it does not follow that the condition of bodies is a deformity, even if granted that every union of bodies, by which I mean union of the two sexes, were evil? Does it follow that

---
3 Cf. 1 Cor. 5.5.

1 Cf. Isa. 45.7.

He is not the author of the condition of bodies, which I have by no means conceded to be evil, since none of my earlier concessions compelled me to say this? Your inference that 'All bodies must then be ascribed to an evil author' is vain and foolish. It is truer to conclude that if not even the evil union of adulterers makes the condition of bodies evil, or, if the union of the two sexes is good even in adultery where evil men use it evilly, then, since it is much more consequent that the condition of bodies cannot be evil, it is right to attribute the authorship of bodies to God. You see there is no abyss that would cause me in fear to return to the way you would have me follow. You must tell me what this way is, and give your reason.

Chapter 9

(18) You say: 'The good God, through whom all things were made, formed the members of our body.' This is most true. You continue by saying: 'But he who made the bodies also distinguished the sexes. That which he intended to join in action he distinguished in kind, and he made the dissimilarity of the members the cause of the union.' I also concede this. You then infer: 'The union of bodies giving the origination of bodies is from God.' Who denies it? You say that, when I have unwillingly conceded this point, 'It follows that the fruits of this multitude of goods—bodies, sexes, and union—cannot be bad.' This is also true, for the fruit of these goods is man, and, in so far as he is man, he is something good. The evil that is in him, from which he must be healed through the Saviour, and delivered through the Redeemer, and washed through the laver, and rescued through exorcism, and absolved through the blood which was shed for the forgiveness of sins, is not the fruit of bodies, sexes, and union, but of the old and original sin.

Now, if I should declare about the offspring of adulterers: 'There could be no good fruit of so many evils; of lust, ugliness, and crime,' it would be correct for you to answer that man born of adulterers is not the fruit of lust, ugliness, and crime, whose author is the Devil, but of bodies, sexes, and union, and these are goods whose author is God. In the same way I say to you in highest truth that the evil with which a man is born is not the fruit of bodies, sexes, and union, for these are goods whose author is God; it is the fruit of the first prevarication, whose author is the Devil.

(19) God forbid we should say, as you calumniate us: 'Men are made by God for the purpose of being subject by legitimate right to the Devil.' Although it would be more the work of the divine than the diabolic power to make the unclean generation subject to the unclean prince unless it be cleansed by regeneration, nevertheless God did not make men so the Devil might in some way have his own household. God made man by the goodness through which He gives to all natures the gift of existence and through which He gives subsistence to the Devil himself. If God withdrew His goodness from things, they would forthwith be nothing at all. Consider, for example, that God does not create animals in the herds and flocks of ungodly men so that they may be immolated to demons, although He knows those men will immolate them to demons; in like manner, when He sees generation subject to sin, He does not withhold His creative goodness from it, all in harmony with the very beautiful order in which He ordered the ages.

Chapter 10

(20) After this argument, in which you deceive yourself and think you have scored an important point, you inject

your customary abuse, saying: 'He will probably assert we should use the testimony of Scripture, not syllogisms, to prove that offspring born of the union of bodies must be ascribed to the divine work'; as though anyone denying this truth could be a Christian. As though it were part of our controversy, you try through testimonies of Scripture to show something we most heartily profess and most gladly proclaim, and you labor vainly, not to answer us, but to fill out your books. Your statement, however, that 'Expressing his faith in the works, the Prophet nearly endangered his modesty when he said: "They shall be two in one flesh," '[1] I ought to give you good warning that there would have been nothing shameful in the works of God if there had not first been a reason why human nature had to be ashamed of the deformity it had deserved.

Chapter 11

(21) You say, praising lust: 'It was restored to Abraham and Sara by the gift of God when they were stricken with old age and their bodies were dead.'[1] With malicious voice you proclaim that if I were able, I should declare what I see God confer sometimes for a gift to be the work of the Devil. Now, if God resuscitated a lame man, and restored to life one no longer able to limp because dead, it might seem that lameness itself was bestowed as a gift. In the same way, if the bodily vigor of their youth was restored, it was certainly restored in accordance with the condition of the body of this death, for it was not fitting to restore the state in which Adam was before sin, so that they might

---
1 Gen. 2.24.

1 Cf. Rom. 4.19.

be able to procreate children without the law in the members which wars against the law of the mind.

(22) Yet, we should also understand that Abraham's body was said to be dead because he was not able to beget children of a female able to conceive. Advancing age is said to bring it about that an old man may be able to beget of an adolescent female when he is no longer able to do so of an older woman, though she may at that time be able to conceive of a younger man. But those living as long as human beings lived at that time doubtless became so decrepit that eventually they could not be roused to union at all, if this can happen in a healthy man because of his age. In regard to this matter we have heard a report of a man eighty-four years of age who, after living religiously and in continence with a religious wife for twenty-five years, suddenly bought himself a Lyristria[2] to satisfy his lust. Considering the short life span of men of this era, he was of more advanced age than Abraham was at the age of a hundred, when he had another seventy years to live. Thus, it is more prudent to hold that God gave His servants the fecundity they lacked. Indeed, two reasons are given for Sara's inability to conceive and the deadness of her womb. The first was the barrenness present from her youth. The other was her age—not that she was ninety years old, but because it had ceased to be with her after the manner of women; for it is agreed that, if the internal menstrual flow has ceased because of age, women are no longer able to conceive, even if they were fruitful before menstruation ceased. Scripture were unwilling to pass this fact by in silence, wishing to increase the glory of the miracle God was to work in their offspring. But when Sara gave her handmaid to her husband in the hope of receiving offspring from the servant because she could not herself give birth she was motivated by her own barrenness, not by her age. For Scrip-

---

2 A female player of the lyre.

ture says: 'But Sara, the wife of Abraham, had brought forth no children.' Her own words to her husband are, 'Behold, God has closed my womb so that I do not bear children.' If, however, we consider their ages at that time, we see that they would have been decrepit according to the present lifespan. Abraham was about eighty-five years old, and Sara was about seventy-five, since it is written: Abraham was fourscore and six years old when Agar brought him forth Ishmael.'[3] Therefore, it was about a year earlier when he took the handmaid and Ishmael was conceived. Do any spouses of our era generate at this age unless a miracle be divinely wrought? Yet those two would then have been able to beget if Sara had not been barren, since Abraham was able to beget of Agar, and Sara had not yet reached the age when menstruation would cease. Therefore, Abraham's body was dead in that he could not beget of Sara, even if she had been fecund, yet so that she was approaching the age when the menstrual flow would cease; for medical authors state that women who no longer have this flowing cannot conceive. If this were false, Scripture would not have taken care to write: 'It had ceased to be with Sara after the manner of women,' when it had already said: 'Abraham and Sara were both old.'[4] Considering the measure of that era, then, when men lived a far longer time than now, we see that Abraham and Sara were no longer able to generate when Abraham was one hundred and Sara was ninety, even if she had not been barren and they had come together the year before, when, perhaps, she might still have been able to conceive if her husband had been young. But, at the time in question, she could not have conceived because Abraham's body was so dead with age that a female of Sara's age could not have conceived from it, although he himself could have begotten of an adolescent female, as later, of Cetura,[5] although here, too, it could be

---

[3] Gen. 16.1,2,16.
[4] Gen. 18.11.
[5] Cf. Gen. 25.1.2.

said that he retained the gift of fecundity he received in order that Isaac be born. By the measure of a lifetime in this era, when human beings live a far shorter length of time, it is said they are able to generate within the hundred years of the two spouses. But if their combined years exceed one hundred, it is asserted that they cannot procreate, even if the woman is fruitful, and, provided she menstruates, able to procreate from a young man; thus it has also been established by the law that no one shall have the *jus liberorum* except when the combined age of the two spouses is greater than one hundred.[6]

(23) Therefore, a miracle of God was wrought in order that Isaac be conceived. It did not consist in the restored lust of his parents, but in the fecundity which was given them; for lust could have existed even in those years, but fecundity could not have existed with so many causes to impede it. As we have already noted, however, lust would also have revived in the dead senile members when these were brought back to life, as it were, by the gift of God. But this lust would certainly have followed the condition of the corruptible flesh, so that in the body of this death would be the lust which could not have existed in the body of that life in paradise, before sin. In accordance with the penal condition of this body, God does not now bestow fecundity according to the happy state in which, since it was fitting that there be peace and not war in the nature of man before sin, there was nothing in the flesh which might lust against the spirit, and which would have to be restrained by the

---

[6] The *jus liberorum* named here seems to have been a legal right possessed by childless spouses only after reaching a certain age, a right by which the spouse might receive the whole amount of the testament made in his or her favor by the other spouse, without the usual restrictions and penalities arising from the absence of children. Records of such laws are extant, although they seem to make the age limit for men 60 years, for women, 50.
(Cf. Ulpian, *Fragm. tit.* 16; Isidore, *Orig.,* 5.)

spirit's lusting against it. Here your idle effort rests on the supposition that we could have said Isaac was begotten without the concupiscence of the flesh, or without the seed of a man. We do not say this and we shall not comment further on the contemptible conclusions you draw.

Chapter 12

(24) Thinking you have discovered another telling point, you say: 'If the Devil created men, they would not be evil by any guilt of their own, and, therefore, they would no longer be evil, for no one can be other than what he is by birth, and it is not just to demand more of him than he can accomplish.' We ourselves often say the same in opposition to the Manichaeans, who do not say the evil nature their fables describe is actually a vitiated good nature, but for them it is a nature that is evil without beginning and unchangeably. According to the Catholic faith, however, human nature was made good, but was vitiated by sin and deservedly condemned. It is neither remarkable nor unjust that the condemned root brings forth the condemned, unless they be tended now as then by the liberating mercy of their Creator; the mercy you begrudge when you say infants have no evil from which they must be delivered.

(25) But, surely, you who oppress wretched infancy by a false defense of it and attack it with pernicious praise must tell why, if they are not baptized, you will not admit into the kingdom of God the vast number of images of God in infants who deserve no evil. Do they fail themselves by not performing what they are wholly unable to perform, so that they must be deprived of the kingdom and punished by the most grievous of exiles? Where would you place them, for they do not have life, because they did not eat the flesh and drink

the blood of the Son of Man?[1] As I have already said, Pelagius would have left the ecclesiastical court a condemned man, if he had not condemned those who say that 'Infants have eternal life even if they are not baptized.' I ask you by what justice must an image of God that has in no way transgressed the law of the God be estranged from the kingdom of God, from the life of God? Do you not hear how the Apostle detests certain men, who, he says, are 'estranged from the life of God through the ignorance that is in them, because of the blindness of their heart'?[2] Is a non-baptized infant bound by this sentence or not? If you say he is not bound, they you will be vanquished and punished by the evangelical truth and by the testimony of Pelagius himself, for where is the life of God except in the kingdom of God, into which none but those born again of water and the Spirit can enter?[3] But, if you assert that he is bound, you acknowledge the punishment. Then you must acknowledge the guilt. You confess the torment—confess, then, that it is deserved. You will find no answer in your teaching. Finally, if there is any Christian sense in you, acknowledge the progeny of death and condemnation in infants also, which is to be punished with due justice and to be delivered gratuitously by the grace of God. The mercy of God can be praised in the redemption of infants, but the truth of God cannot be accused in their perdition, because all the ways of the Lord are mercy and truth.[4]

Chapter 13

(26) You divide, you define, you give a kind of clinical

---
1 Cf. John 6.54.
2 Eph. 4.18.
3 Cf. John 3.5.
4 Cf. Ps. 24.10.

dissertation on the genus, the species, the mode, and the excess of concupiscence, asserting that 'Its genus is in the vital fire; its species is in the genital action; its mode is in the conjugal act; its excess is in the intemperance of fornication.' Yet, after all this supposedly subtle and truly prolix disputation, when I ask you briefly and openly why this vital fire plants the root of warfare in man, so that his flesh lusts against his spirit, and it becomes necessary for his spirit to lust against his flesh[1]—why he who wills to consent with the vital fire receives a mortal wound—I think the black ink in your book must turn red with blushing. Behold the vital fire which not only does not obey at the decision of soul, which is the true life of the flesh, but for the most part rises up against the soul's decision in disorderly and ugly movements, so that unless the spirit lusts against it, this vital fire destroys our good life.

(27) After a long discussion you say, as though in conclusion: 'Therefore, it is correct to state that the origin of concuspicence is in the vital fire; it follows that carnal concupiscence must be attributed to the fire through which carnal life is compounded.' You speak as though you were able to prove, or were insolent enough to suspect, that in the first creation of man, before the merited condemnation followed his guilt, such carnal concupiscence either existed in paradise or produced its base warfare against the spirit by means of the disorderly activity of which we are now aware. You say: 'The guilt of such appetite is not in its genus or its species or its mode, but in its excess, because the genus and species are the work of its Maker, and its mode pertains to honest decision, but its excess comes from fault of the will. How elegantly your empty words sound, but only for him who does not consider what they say. If the mode of this

---

1 Cf. Gal. 5.17.

appetite pertains to honest decision, we ask whether any married man chooses that this appetite be aroused except when needed? Yet, what he wishes he cannot accomplish. What honest celibate chooses that this appetite ever be aroused? Yet, what he wishes he cannot accomplish. Thus a man cries out: 'To wish is within my power, but I do not find the strength to accomplish what is good.'[2] In the very movement of this appetite, then, it has no mode answering to the decision of the will, while in the effect it is not itself moderate, but the honest spirit must impose a mode on it, by watchful combat. Evil men, why do you praise it and do not cry out to God: 'Deliver us from evil'?[3]

Chapter 14

(28) What do you gain by saying that 'Lust is diminished by debility,' as though it were not wholly extinguished by death, when no contest is required, but the vanquished must now pay the penalty? This is the bitter thing; this is where you do not understand the progeny of the death which still does battle, for that unhealthy activity exists when we are healthy. You say: 'In the married it is exercised honestly; in the chaste it is restrained by virtue.' Is this your experience of it? Is, then, this evil (your good) not restrained by the married? Indeed, since it is very pleasant, let the married effusively and impetuously seek each other whenever it titillates; let not this appetite be denied or put off until the proper time for such commerce; let the union of bodies be legitimate whenever this, your natural good, spontaneously acts. If you led this kind of married life, rely no more on your own

---
2 Rom. 7.18.
3 Matt. 6.13.

experience, but choose instead to learn from others how it should be led or taught.[1] If you did not restrain even adulterous desires, did you not at least sense they ought to be restrained? Since conjugal modesty itself also restrains this pest, because of the boundless sloughs of lust and the damnable craving even in marriage, lest something be committed beyond the natural use of the spouse, why did you say: 'In the married it is exercised honestly,' as though to say this appetite were always honest in a spouse, and there were nothing to concede, at least by way of pardon, as the Apostle says?[2] How much better to say: 'In the moderateness of the married it is exercised honestly.' Were you afraid this also might lead to recognition of the evil which the married themselves restrain by careful moderation? Since you are now living in celibacy, recognize the bad horse in the chariot described by Ambrose,[3] and do not praise in heart or mouth that which you are obliged to restrain by virtue. You say: 'The fourth, which is the excess of that pleasure, is practiced by the lascivious; and because this is done in insolence, not from nature, it is condemned by law.' From whose insolence, I ask, does it arise—that of lasciviousness or of concupiscence? Lest you offend the protege you have taken to yourself, you will say it is lasciviousness only when there is consent to concupiscence. But is not a thing evil if to consent to it means commission of sin? This evil truly exists in the flesh lusting against the spirit, even though it does not exist in a spirit not consenting and lusting back against it. Cry out, then, 'Deliver us from evil,' and do not add to this evil the evil of false praise.

---
1 It is known that Julian married in his youth, but after the death of his wife lived in continence.
2 Cf. 1 Cor. 7.6.
3 See above 2.5.12.

Chapter 15

(29) As a mean between lasciviousness and celibacy you expressly name conjugal chastity, which, you say, 'is indignant at the unlawful acts of the one extreme, and marvels at the other's despising even the lawful. Its domain lies on the farthest boundary, whence it execrates the barbarousness of those who go beyond the limit, and venerates the striking brilliance of those above itself; it modestly soothes the ardent and praises those who do not need this remedy.' I take great pleasure in this very eloquently phrased truth, but I beg you to see that, just as you say, very well and truly, the reason conjugal modesty praises celibates is that they do not need the remedy it sees itself to have needed, as the Apostle says: 'But if they do not have self-control, let them marry.'[1] Why do you acknowledge a necessary remedy for concupiscence, yet contradict me when I say concupiscence is a disease? If you acknowledge the remedy, acknowledge the disease. If you deny the disease, deny the remedy. I ask you at last to yield to the truth which speaks to you even through your own mouth. No one provides a remedy for health.

Chapter 16

(30) You say truly: 'On close examination, we see that marriage cannot be pleasing if it is praiseworthy only by comparison with evil.' This is true. Marriage is by all means good in its own kind, but the reason it is good is that it keeps the faith of the marriage bed; that it unites the two sexes for the purpose of begetting offspring; and that it shrinks

---

1 1 Cor. 7.9.

from the impiety of separation.¹ These are the good properties of marriage, by which marriage itself is a good, and, as we have often said, such marriage could have existed even if no one had sinned. After sin, however, and not happily but from necessity, a combat came to marriage, so that marriage by means of its own good must now war against the evil of concupiscence, not permitting it to do anything unlawful, though concupiscence itself, acting now slackly, now with great violence, never ceases to urge marriage to the unlawful, even when marriage makes good use of the evil of concupiscence in the propagation of offspring. Who can deny this is an evil except one unwilling to hear the Apostle's warning: 'But this I say by way of concession, not by way of commandment,'² when the married are overcome by desire, not for offspring, but to satisfy lust for carnal pleasure? This may not be praised, but when marriage intercedes and pleads, it may be forgiven in comparison with what is worse.³

Chapter 17

(31) Next, I know not why, you return to the example of Abraham and Sara, which I think I have already fully answered. You forgot something and wanted to add it when

---

1 A description of the three elements in which Augustine places the goodness of marriage, and to which Pius XI refers throughout his 1930 Encyclical, *Casti Connubii*.
2 1 Cor. 7.6.
3 Augustine held that the only worthy motive for entering into Christian marriage is the remedy it provides against incontinence by permitting the marriage act, though only for the purpose for which marriage was instituted. In this passage he seems to state that spouses may without mortal sin perform the act of marriage even when they do not positively intend to beget children, provided they do nothing directly to impede conception. (For information about Augustine's doctrine about the motive for marrying, which is not the same thing as the purpose of marriage itself, see *De bono conjugali*, and others of his writings dealing specifically with marriage.)

you remembered it. This is human and it happens often, so let us hear what it was. You say: 'A prophecy is now being fulfilled in the region of Africa: neither the spouse nor the chastity of the beautiful and holy woman, who was a figure of the Church, was safe, but by divine means she was there preserved unharmed.' I shall not spend time over all these words of yours. You address him to whom you are writing, and say: 'We must pray God, most blessed brother Turbanus, fellow priest, that the powers remain constant even in this storm, and that He delay not to preserve the Catholic Church, the mature, the fruitful, the chaste and comely bride of His Son, from abduction into Africa or from Africa by Manichaean brigands.' This is indeed our own prayer against Manichaeans and Donatists and other heretics, and against all enemies of the Christian and Catholic name who may be found in Africa. Are we, then, brigands come out of Africa against you, because against you, a pest come to us from overseas, and a pest to be conquered by Christ the Saviour, we oppose one martyr from here, Cyprian, through whom we prove we are defending the ancient Catholic faith against the vain and profane novelty of your error? Oh, the wickedness here! Did the Church of God located in Africa need your prayers when most blessed Cyprian proclaimed the truths you are attacking? Were they lacking when he said: 'Much more ought no one to forbid baptism to a new-born infant who has committed no sin except that, since he has been born carnally according to Adam, he has contracted the contagion of the ancient death in his first birth, so that not his own, but another's, sins are remitted for him.'[1] When Cyprian learned and taught these things, did he need the help of your prayers to preserve Sara unharmed in the region of Africa, and to deliver the beauty of the Church from abduction by the Manichaeans, who by your reasoning de-

---

[1] *Epist. 64,* ad Fidum.

ceived Cyprian himself before the name of Manichaeus was heard from Roman soil? See what monstrous and frenzied charges you make against the very ancient Catholic faith in your inability to find anything else to say.

(32) No matter how you shift your ground, O Pelagian heresy, devising new attacks against the ramparts of the very ancient truth, and contriving new devices, 'A Punic debater,' as your defender insultingly names me, a Punic debater, I say, not I, but Punic Cyprian, 'slays you with this blow, and requires punishment from the polluted dogma.'[2] What if I should name as many bishops from Africa as I have named from the other parts of world? What if there were many Africans among these very bishops? Of the bishops whose consensus from the East and from the West confounds you, one is from Africa, and the rest from elsewhere, yet you have become so blind in obstinacy you cannot see it is you yourselves who wish to corrupt the ancient beauty of the Church; that is, the ancient faith which resembles the chastity of the old and very beautiful Sara. For, if Manichaeans have ravished the Church through holy bishops of God, and through the memorable doctors Irenaeus, Cyprian, Reticius, Olympius, Hilary, Ambrose, Gregory, Basil, John, Innocent, and Jerome, then tell me, Julian, who gave birth to you? Was she a chaste woman or a harlot who through the womb of spiritual grace brought you into the light you have deserted? Is it to defend the Pelagian dogma that you defame the womb of the bride of Christ, who is your mother, by a wicked impulse not of error, but of madness? For this deformed novelty with its constant lies against the ancient beauty of Sara charges with the blasphemy of Manichaeism the consensus of so many glorious Catholic bishops, in the

---

2 An allusion to Virgil, *Aeneas* 12.946-947.

face of overpowering evidence of their teachings. Some of these never heard the name of Manichaeus.³

(33) But from this digression, to which the impulse, not of grief but of shamelessness, carried you away, you say you will return to the ravings you had first intended, giving testimony from the Apostle⁴ and trying to confirm what you said earlier about the dead members of Abraham and Sara. I shall be content with my previous answer. What Christian does not know that 'He who made the first man from dust makes all men from seed'? But He makes them from seed already vitiated and condemned, which in part remains in torment, through truth; and in part is delivered from evil, through mercy. It is not true, then, as you think and conclude, that 'The assertion of natural sin has been choked' in your nets. Your defense in vain words, expressing a new-found dogma, does not cleanse the nature debased by the will of the first transgressor. This is accomplished by the grace of God through Jesus Christ our Lord.

Chapter 18

(34) This is why I do not hold what you calumniously attribute to me, namely, that the married generate without the heat of bodies, and I do not say God did not make man, or God made man by means of the Devil, or the Devil made man, because not even the parents are able to make man; God makes man from the parents. The Devil cannot withdraw himself from God's power; much less, then, is he able to withdraw human nature, which he makes subject to himself

---
3 In *Opus imperfectum contra Julianum*, Augustine says that Manes, or Mani, the founder of the sect of the Manichaeans, used this form of the name when he associated with those who spoke Latin.
4 Rom. 4.19.

only through the penalty deserved by sin, after God's condemnation. Since these things are so, you, not I, convict yourself, not of worshiping the Devil as you say I do, but of assisting the Devil, no matter how severely you accuse him. It is you who contend by your own unsound doctrine that infants are sound, and that it is not necessary for all infants to be healed through Christ for the evil through which they are under the power of the Devil. According to the sound faith, however, I say that Isaac was also formed from this same pleasure of concupiscence from which come all other men, excepting only Him through whom we are delivered from evil. I do not deny that Divine Providence reaches from end to end mightily, and orders all things sweetly, and no defiled thing comes into her.[1] Therefore, Providence works what it wishes, even from the unclean and contaminated, while it remains itself clean and uncontaminated. You need not enter into minute details to prove to me what I concede. But answer, if you can, why Isaac's soul would have perished from his people if he had not been circumcised on the eighth day by the sign of the baptism of Christ.[2] Explain, if you can, the reason why he would have suffered so great a punishment if not delivered by the sacrament. You cannot deny that God gave life to the dead womb of Sara for the reception of seed, and to the dead body of Abraham for generation in the way in which young men generate, in order that offspring might be born of the old age of the parents. But why did Isaac, born innocent as to personal sins, who would have born innocent in this respect even if born of adulterers, deserve that his soul should perish from his people if he were not circumcised? Do not wander off through a multitude of obscurities, perplexities, and superfluities; answer this one plain, simple and necessary question.

---

1 Wisd. 8.1; 7.25.
2 Gen. 17.14.

(35) You introduce the testimony of the Apostle, not for the purpose for which he wrote it, but for your arbitrary use. Let this be as it may; we merely note that you insert the passage where he says: 'And how is God to judge the world? For if through my life the truth of God has abounded unto his glory, why am I also still judged as a sinner?'[3] You say: 'By these words the Apostle shows that if God did not observe the proper manner of commanding, He would lose the right of judging.' You conclude: 'The Apostle says this in order to restrain those asserting that the sins of mortals advance the glory of God, and that the reason God commanded the impossible was to prepare materials for His mercy.' You continue: 'The Apostle shows, then, that the reason men are rightly judged is that they have failed to fulfil possible commandments. It would be unjust to judge them as failing to carry out impossible commands.' What can you say about Isaac, who received no commandment, possible or impossible, yet who would have been punished by the loss of his own soul if he had not been circumcised on the eighth day? Will not see even now that the commandment given in paradise at the beginning was possible and easy of fulfilment; but after it was despised and violated, all, from one man, have that sin in common as in the mass of their origin; thence came 'the heavy yoke upon the children of Adam from the day of their coming out of their mother's womb until the day of their burial into the mother of all'?[4] Since no one from that generation condemned in Adam is delivered unless he be regenerated in Christ, Isaac would have perished if he had not received the sign of this regeneration, and would have perished deservedly, as one departing without the sign of regeneration, from this life into which he entered condemned, through the condemned generation. If this is not

---
3 Rom. 3.6,7.
4 Eccli. 40.1.

the reason, you must give us another. God is good; God is just. He can deliver some men not meriting good, because He is good. He cannot condemn any man not deserving evil, because He is just. The eight-day-old infant had nothing deserving of evil from personal sins. Why would he have been condemned if not circumcised, unless he contracted sin from his origin?

Chapter 19

(36) Proceed on your merry way of invention, but remember you are giving fiction, not Scripture. When you say: 'We see that perfect ignorance may be called justice, when God says to Abimelech who, not knowing Sara was the wife of another, intended to lie with her: "And I know that thou didst it with a sincere heart."[1] It follows that the state of the new-born is not damaged by the will of those who generate them, because even if the will were evil, the new-born could have no knowledge of it.' Why do you not then call them just, if perfect ignorance is to be called justice? Nothing is more perfect than the ignorance of infants; hence, let nothing be called more just. Where is the proposition you once thought should be asserted: 'Infants are born neither just nor unjust; these qualities will appear later in their actions; the only endowment of infancy is innocence'? Do not your words say: 'Man is indeed born replete with innocence, but only with capacity for virtue, and he will deserve praise or blame according to his later intentions'? Are you going to assert that justice is not virtue? If an infant has the fullness of ignorance, which you say is justice, how can you say he lacks the fullness of virtue and has only the capacity for virtue, unless you deny that justice is a virtue? Should not this absurdity arouse you to regret your statement? The words

---
1 Gen. 20.6.

of the Lord are wakeful, but you are asleep. He did not say that He knew the king had a just heart, since it is written: 'Blessed are the pure in heart, for they shall see God,'[2] but you proposed Abimelech as an example of a sinner. God says: I know that thou didst this with a sincere heart'; God did not refer to everything, nor to any other thing but this in which Abimelech was not conscious of adultery.

(37) I marvel that, while you are trying to accomplish something you cannot accomplish by your example, you fail to see what you do not want to hear. You are trying to make men believe that desire was returned to the women at Abraham's prayer, because it it written: 'For the Lord had closed up every womb of the house of Abimelech, on account of Sara, Abraham's wife.'[3] You want us to understand the closing to mean that lust was taken from the women when God became angry, although the words themselves more plainly insinuate that the womb was closed by a disorder of some kind, so that a woman about to be impregnated, or ready to give birth, was not able to do so. You who will not admit that by divine judgment someone can be punished for sins not personal but another's do not see how it could come to pass that Abimelech sinned, although not with an adulterous heart, yet God avenged his sin, no matter how venial, on the women of his household. You see the contagion of sin pass from the man to the women with whom he had intercourse or whom he ruled, yet you do not want sin to pass to the offspring from the very parents from whose seeds the offspring is propagated. Consider the inscrutable depth of the judgments of the wisdom and the knowledge of God,[4] and then cease to babble about the secrets of original sin.

---

2 Matt. 5.8.
3 Gen. 20.18.
4 Cf. Rom. 11.33.

Chapter 20

(38) You begin next to discuss the excess of concupsicence, which you say is reprehensible, as though in its moderation, when a married man uses it well, the horse itself which is evil should be praised and not the driver. What benefit do you derive from the testimonies from Scripture where it is shown how God either forbids or condemns the excess of lust? Look rather at this: that the concupiscence of the flesh, unless it be restrained, can effect all those things that horrify us in the most vicious crimes having to do with the reproductive members; and these effects it produces by means of those very movements which it causes, to our sorrow, even in sleep, and even in the bodies of chaste men.

(39) You ask: 'For what reason would God have sought out the just men in Sodom, if He had made them such by nature?'[4] You speak as though we said the concupiscence of the flesh cannot be restrained by the more excellent nature of the mind. We answer that concupiscence is such an evil that it must be vanquished in actual combat until, like a wound in the body, it shall be healed by a perfect cure.

(40) If you believe, as you say, that 'The Apostle has praised lust, because he said that the use of the woman is natural, where he says: "Some, abandoning the natural use of woman, have burned in their lusts one towards another,"'[2] you will be obliged to praise every use of woman. Thus, you will have to praise all perverse acts committed with woman, because there, too, the use is certainly natural, although it must be condemned because it is not lawful; this is why illegitimate children thus born are called natural children. The Apostle is not here praising the concupiscence of the

---
1 Gen. 18.26.
2 Rom. 1.27.

flesh. He merely calls the use from which human nature comes into being by birth the natural use.

(41) You say: 'The Sodomites also sinned in the creature of bread and wine,' and thus you want us to understand that lust is good, although it is sinful to use it evilly. You do not understand what you are saying, so that you do not see that the creature of bread and wine does not lust against the spirit. This creature enters the body from outside, and it is coveted unsoundly by those who use it evilly. The reason it should be used sparingly and with restraint is that the concupiscence which is an evil within us and part of us may not rise up more vehemently and invincibly against us when the corruptible body with greater mass exerts heavier pressure on the soul. This evil, which is shown to be evil not only by him who fights against it, but also by him whom it subjugates, is the evil which a parent uses well when he begets a child in chastity, and which God uses well when in His providence He creates a man.

Chapter 21

(42) I beg you to consider now; I say now, so that wholesome truth may win you over. Put aside all craving for victory and consider whether you ought not to accept our opinion rather than yours. It is well, you say, for you briefly to remind us what you have accomplished in your entire volume, so that the reader will retain it. This brief admonition, in your own words, is: 'He who holds to the mode of natural concupiscence uses a good well. He who does not hold to the mode uses a good evilly. But he who in love of holy virginity also despises the mode itself does better in not making use of a good, for, indeed, relying on his own health and strength, he has despised the remedies so that he may engage

in glorious combats.' I answer your words thus: He who holds to the mode of carnal concupiscence uses an evil well. He who does not hold to the mode uses an evil evilly. But he who in his love of holy virginity despises also the mode itself does better in not making use of an evil, for, indeed, relying on the divine assistance and gift, he has despised the least of the remedies so that he may engage in glorious combats. The whole point between us in this controversy is whether the thing of which good use is made is good or evil. In this controversy I do not want you to reject the outstanding judges who, as I have shown above, are learned in sound doctrine, and have impartially passed sentence on this matter. But, since you will undoubtedly accuse or, to speak more mildly, censure them if you are not put right, I shall make you yourself the judge between our opinions, and from your own book, and with this very passage. You say: 'Holy virginity, relying on its own health and strength, has despised the remedies so that it may engage in glorious combats.' I ask you to name the remedies it has despised. You will answer: Marriage. I ask the disease for which the remedies are necessary. The word 'remedy' is derived from mede-ing [*medendo*], that is, medicating. Thus both you and I see that there is a remedial aspect of marriage. Why do you praise the disease of lust, when you see a man will die of it unless the restraint of celibacy or the conjugal remedy resists it? I discussed the matter with you earlier when you expressly placed conjugal chastity between lasciviousness and celibacy, saying: 'Conjugal chastity which soothes the ardent with shy modesty, and praises those who do not need such a remedy.' I shall repeat what I said there; listen once more to my short and clear answer. 'When I say this concupiscence is a disease, why do you deny it, if you concede that a remedy for it is necessary? If you acknowledge the remedy, acknowledge the disease. If you deny the disease, deny the remedy.

I beg you, yield at last to the truth which even you yourself have spoken. No one provides a remedy for health.'[1]

(43) In what do your 'glorious combats' of the holy virgins consist, except that they are not conquered by evil, but conquer the evil in good? I prefer to call these combats more glorious, not merely glorious, for conjugal chastity also has its victory, although lesser, from the subjugation of this evil. It, too, combats carnal concupiscence lest it exceed the proprieties of the marriage bed; it combats lest concupiscence break into the time agreed upon by the spouses for prayer. If this conjugal chastity possesses such great power and is so great gift from God that it does what the matrimonial code prescribes, it combats in even more valiant fashion in regard to the act of conjugal union, lest there be indulgence beyond what suffices for generating offspring. Such chastity abstains during menstruation and pregnancy, nor has it union with one no longer able to conceive on account of age. And the desire for union does not prevail, but ceases when there is no prospect of generation. But if an act is done in regard to the spouse, not contrary to nature, yet passing beyond the limit of the matrimonial code, then, according to the Apostle,[2] it is something pardonable, because the carnal limit is not exceeded, yet, lest the limit itself be exceeded, there must be warfare against evil of concupiscence, which is so evil it must be resisted in the combat waged by chastity, lest it do damage.

(44) Unless I am mistaken, you are also in this combat, and because you think you are fighting faithfully you fear defeat. By what, I ask? By good or evil? Or do you so fear to be overcome by me that you continue to deny to be evil and praise as good that which you fear will defeat you? You are forced into great straits between two adversaries, wishing to conquer me through eloquence, and to conquer lust through

---
1 Above, p. 133.
2 Cf. 1 Cor. 7.6.

continence. But in fighting against lust, you confess the evil; in praising it, you desert the good of truth. I shall conquer you, who both attack and praise this evil, by placing you before no other judge than yourself. You want to conquer concupiscence by routing it, and to conquer me by praising it. I answer: that he who praises may be conquered, let him who fights be the judge. If concupiscence is evil, why praise it? If it is good, why attack it? As long as you oppose lust, you judge for my side against yourself. Perhaps, lest you be conquered in your combat with me, you will decide not to fight against lust, telling yourself it is better not to fight than to show by fighting that what you praise is evil. Do not do this, I pray you. What am I, whom you desire to conquer at so great a price? Let the truth conquer you, instead, that you may conquer lust, for if you cease to war against it, you will be conquered, I say, and drawn to all manner of uncleanness. Since this is an evil to be abhorred, it will not conduct you to what you desire, for even in this way you will be conquered by me—actually by the truth I proclaim. But you who praise concupiscence and attack concupiscence will be conquered by your own judgment if you praise the evil in the rout of which you glory. If, however, you cease to fight, lest the voice of praise be silenced in the effort of warfare, I shall conquer the captive of concupiscence, the deserter of continence, no longer by his own judgment, but by the judgment of wisdom.

(45) Thus our case is closed. No matter how highly you praise the concupiscence of the flesh, as long as you fight against it you must perceive the truth of the words of the Apostle John about it, and it alone, that 'It is not from the Father.'[3] If, as you say: 'He who does not hold to the mode of it uses a good evilly,' then it must also be good in those who use it evilly. What, then, is that which is not from the

---

[3] 1 John 2.16.

Father? Do you also intend to praise that thing, however you understand it? Furthermore, if it is evil, where will it be evil, and when will it be evil? For it must be good even when some one uses it evilly, and you say that not it, but the man who uses the good evilly, is evil. Thus, it was in vain that John said the concupiscence of the flesh is not from the Father, for you contend that it is good, and, therefore, from the Father, even when someone uses it evilly, because he uses a good evilly. You cannot say that when it is moderate it is from the Father, but when it is immoderate it is not from the Father, because here you say again that it is a good which an evil man uses evilly. But you will be freed from these straits if you heed your fighting rather than your voice, for continence is from the Father, and concupiscence would not be attacked by continence unless concupiscence were not from the Father. This concupiscence, therefore, against which you fight bitterly, if you live in continence, is not from the Father; for you would not fight against it unless it fought against you, nor would it fight against you when you accomplish something given and loved by the Father if it were from the Father.

(46) From and with this concupiscence is born a man, a good work of God, but not born without the evil which the origin of generation contracts and which the grace of regeneration heals. Therefore, I had good reason for saying: 'The goodness of marriage cannot be accused on account of the evil by way of origin which it there contracted, just as the evil of adultery and fornication cannot be excused on account of the natural good which is born therefrom.'[4] I was referring to the natural good which you praise with me, and the evil by way of origin against whose activity you fight alongside me; by praising which you fight against me. The fact of your birth is not an evil, but that with which you were

---
4 *De nuptiis et concupiscentia* 1.1.

born and against which you fight spiritually because you were reborn, is evil. The fact of your birth pertains to God's creative power and the fecundity of your parents. That against which you fight, because you have been reborn, pertains to the prevarication which was sowed by the Devil's cunning; from which the grace of Christ delivered you, so that you once used this evil well in marriage, and you now oppose it in yourself; no longer guilty of it as you were at birth, but freed from the guilt only because of rebirth, so that after your redemption you might be able to reign with Christ—provided this heresy does not cause you to perish with the Devil. We desire far more than you that you confess the evil against which you fight, so that when this evil is gone, not separated as though it were an alien nature, but entirely healed in you, you may be happy in everlasting peace.

(47) I am not, as you say, a charlatan, promising, as it were, to show a beast that consumes itself. Beware, however, lest that bestial movement against which you seem to fight in your flesh consume you if you set it free, just as it is perverting you when you praise it. I did not say, as you calumniously assert, that 'Marriage is both a great good and a great evil,' as though this statement were to consume itself like the medicine man's beast. I said that in one and the same man the nature is good; the fault, evil. You yourself certainly admit this in adulterers, where you neither condem the nature on account of the fault nor approve the fault on account of the nature. I said that marriage, from which you were born, is good; the evil against which you, reborn, wage war is not derived from marriage, but from a vitiated origin.

(48) It is ridiculous for you to say that I follow the Epicurean way and brush aside all forces by which covetings are restrained. What if I should praise the pleasure of the body! What Epicurus did crudely and without finesse you

do quite eloquently, as though the reason you oppose him were that he lacked artistry in saying what you say. I notice, also, that you have gone to some length to appear an encomiast of pleasure, but not an Epicurean. Give yourself no further trouble; I shall relieve you of that burden. You are not an Epicurean, because Epicurus put the whole of man's good in the pleasure of the body, while you try to put the major part of human good in virtue; but you do not understand true virtue, which is the virtue of true piety, for God has said to man: 'Behold, piety is wisdom.'[5] This comes only from Him of whom is written: 'The Lord maketh the blind wise,'[6] of whom we also read: 'If any of you is wanting in wisdom, let him ask it of God.'[7] But if you who with Epicurus praise pleasure are not an Epicurean, how much less am I, who agreed with Ambrose about the pleasure of the flesh,[8] that it is an enemy of justice, and that a man fashioned in the pleasure of concupiscence is under the contagion of offenses before he is born? But what are our morals, how we live, is easily discovered by those with whom we live. We are concerned here with Catholic dogma and faith. Let none of the deserter's perfidy be found in you. I confess that I teach men what I learned in the apostolic writings: 'If we say that we have no sin, we deceive ourselves, and the truth is not in us.'[9] I confess that in the people of God and with the people of God I strike my breast and say truthfully: 'Forgive us our trespasses.'[10] You may not scoff at us for this; indeed, you are heretics because these things displease you. We rely on the true mercy of God; you, on your own false virtue. You say that the grace of God is given according to our merits, but, if Pelagius had not condemned this, he would

---

5 Job 28.28.
6 Ps. 145.8.
7 James 1.5.
8 Above, pp. 71-72.
9 1 John 1.8.
10 Matt. 6.12.

have been condemned by the Catholic bishops. We confess that grace is given gratuitously and for this reason it is called grace, and all the merits of the saints come from it, as the Apostle says: 'By the grace of God I am what I am.'[11] This is the reason you laugh at us and despise us in comparison with your stubborn selves. We are a reproach to the rich and contempt to the proud.[12] You have confounded the counsel of the poor man, but the Lord is his hope.[13]

(49) I do not see why you say in this matter that I brush aside all the forces by which covetings are restrained, since I declare that all covetings must be restrained with every force of virtue according to the grace of God which is given to men. I ask you whether the covetings you say must be restrained, and to which you say I give free rein, are good or evil. I do not think they are covetings of horses or of any other but human animals; they are our own. Therefore, in us there are evil covetings which we restrain by living well. You accuse me, then, of the crime of undermining the forces by which evil, not good, covetings are restrained. One of these is the concupiscence of the flesh, from which and with which infants are born, and on account of which they are reborn. I say that chaste spouses use this evil well; adulterers use it evilly. But you say adulterers use this good evilly, and chaste spouses use it well. We both say continence does better in not using it at all. But I am referring to this evil; you, to this good. Although God alone knows our conscience, while our conduct is known also by those among whom we live, we both profess continence, and, if we both practice what we profess, we restrain concupiscence, we war against its rebellious movements, we overcome it, if we are to make progress. There is a difference, however. I say what I am restraining is an evil; you say it is a good. I say an evil is

---
11 1 Cor. 15.10.
12 Cf. Ps. 122.4.
13 Cf. Ps. 13.6.

opposing me; you say a good opposes you. I fight an evil; you, a good. I desire to subdue an evil; you, a good. It would seem that you seek rather to arouse concupiscence by your praise than restrain it by continence.

(50) You profess to engage in glorious combats through continence. I ask what you oppose. What can you answer except that you oppose the concupiscence of the flesh? As friend or enemy? Can you say other than as enemy? 'For the flesh lusts against the spirit and the spirit against the flesh, for these are opposed to each other,'[14] as the Apostle says. Perhaps your praising it while opposing it is only pretense. I do not see how you could in good faith praise and oppose it at the same time, for you would be praising it as a friend and opposing it as an enemy. We shall believe one of the two, but you must choose which one. If you fight wholeheartedly, then you do not praise wholeheartedly. But if your declaration is sincere, you must be jesting in your combat. I am not your enemy as the evil which dwells in your flesh is your enemy, and I most earnestly desire that you shall overcome this evil with sound doctrine and holiness of life. Of the two, you can do only one wholeheartedly; the other would be pretense. I should prefer that your praise of concupiscence were pretense rather than your opposition to it, for it is better to be wrong in speech than in living, and wrong in judgment than in continence. You are counterfeiting this praise in your opposition if you are not counterfeiting the chastity by which you oppose your own concupiscence. Thus, it may come to pass that you will no longer speak falsely against me, if you wage war truthfully against lust. But, whether you are counterfeiting in reference to the only one of them or to both (I do not see how you could sincerely fight against what you praise, and also praise what you fight against without some kind of counterfeit), I shall accept the milder view about you and proceed on the

---

14 Gal. 5.6.

supposition that I am dealing with an opponent of lust. I do not say, then, that marriage is evil, but that it uses an evil well. You say marriage uses a good well, declaring that the concupiscence of the flesh is a good, although you show it to be evil by opposing it in yourself. I have already described how the married, who use it well, must also war against it.

Chapter 22

(51) Since these things are so, we see that marriage, as marriage, is good, and man, be he born of marriage or of adultery, is good in so far as he is man, because, in so far as he is a man, he is the work of God; yet, because generated with and from the evil which conjugal chastity uses well, it is necessary that he be freed from the bond of this evil by regeneration. Why do you ask where original sin is, when the lust against which you fight in yourself speaks to you more eloquently than you yourself speak when you praise it? Why do you ask: 'Whence does man, whom God made, come to be under the power of the Devil?' Whence does he come under a death which God did not make? You ask: 'What does the Devil recognize as his own, if he made neither what was made, nor whence it was made?' What was made is man; whence it is made, the seed of man. Both are good; the Devil made neither, but sowed the fault of the seed. The Devil does not recognize there his own good, because the good we both praise is not his; but he recognizes his own evil, against which we both fight, and it is not right that what we both fight against is praised by one of us. Surely you realize that when you ask me: 'Among so many goods, whence comes the evil in infants?' you pass by what I wrote in the same book you are answering; among the statements you are now answering I quote the Apostle's words: 'Through one man

sin entered into the world, and through sin death, and thus passed unto all men; in whom all have sinned.'[1] You do not want anyone to hear or to read this in that passage where it is most necessary, lest they recognize their own faith, and despise your arguments.

Chapter 23

(52) You say I declared: 'If a man is born of fornication, he is not guilty; if born of marriage, he is not innocent.' This is extravagant and open calumny. I declare that, according to the Catholic faith which the Fathers most openly defended against you before you were born, we assert that, no matter whence born, a man is innocent because there is no personal sin, and he is guilty through original sin. I declared that the substance of his nature, of which God is the author, is good even in great sinners, who are evil also because of the personal sins they have added to the evil with which they were born. Why should I fear the objection you raise, that I impute the sins of all parents to all their children? Even if the proposition be true (referring not to those exercising free will, but to the new-born), the substance of the nature, whose author is God, would by no means be evil, but only the faults that are in that nature, and against which you also, to use your own words, 'engage in glorious combats.'

(53) You say: 'When adulterers beget offspring, a man is born from the power of the seeds, not from the depravity of their unlawful act.' In the same way, when the married beget, a man is born from the power of the seeds, not from the soundness of marriage. If this is not true, and man is born from both elements in marriage, it follows that man is born from both elements in adultery. But, if we consider

---
[1] Rom. 5.12.

the very essence of marriage, we must say the fruit of marriage itself is not the generation of men, who can also be born of adultery, but the orderly begetting of offspring. Why, then, do you say my statement is entirely false when I say that the goodness of marriage cannot be accused on account of the evil by way of origin thence derived? Not only is it true that, in order that you be born, your parents made good use of the evil you oppose; we must also say the evil thence derived would have remained as guilt in you if you had not been reborn. Thus, the married who use the evil well cannot be accused, and the offspring must be regenerated in order that they may be delivered from evil. If the goodness of marriage were only good use of a good, we might well wonder how evil can be thence derived. But, since the goodness of marriage is good use of an evil, it does not surprise us that from the evil which the goodness of marriage uses well is derived the evil which is original sin. It is a matter of wonder that though the Apostles were the good odor of Christ, both good and evil were thence derived. To some they were the odor of life unto life; to others the odor of death,[1] although this odor was not the use of evil, but of good; they were the good odor of Christ because they used the grace of Christ well. Therefore, your statement: 'If evil is thence derived, the source can be accused; it cannot be excused,' is false, because original evil is thence derived when good is also thence derived, the good which is the orderly propagation of offspring. The reason this evil is thence derived is not simply that marriage is good, but that among the goods of marriage there is also the use of evil. Nuptial union was not instituted for the sake of carnal concupiscence, as you think, but for the sake of the good which is made from that evil. This good would exist without that evil if no one had sinned, but, as it is, this good cannot exist without that evil; yet,

---

1 Cf. 2 Cor. 2.15,16.

the good is not therefore evil. Conversely, there can be no evil without a good; yet, evil is not therefore good, for the work of God in the nature is a good, without which, however, there cannot be an evil will. Thus, just as adultery cannot exist without the good of nature, yet adultery is not therefore good, so the marriage union cannot now exist without the evil of concupiscence, yet marriage is not therefore evil. Hence, even if we should grant you your premiss that every cause of evil is destitute of good, you could not apply this principle to marriage, which is not a cause of evil. Marriage did not produce the evil of concupiscence, but only found it there to be used well.

Chapter 24

(54) You say: 'Nothing which brings guilt to other things associated with it can escape penalty.' Applied to the concupiscence of the flesh, this is not absurd. Faithful spouses use this evil well, yet the offspring generated from this evil contracts guilt, and that is why the offspring, too, must be regenerated. But neither can this evil escape penalty. Its penalty will be punished together with the generated if they have not been regenerated; it will cease to exist in the regenerated when they are completely healed. You declare: 'If original evil is derived even from marriage, then the marital union is a cause of evil.' What if some one said that, if an evil will be derived from a nature, the constitution of natures is a cause of evils? Is this not absolutely false? Your inference is likewise false, although, as a matter of fact, original evil is not derived from marriage, but from carnal concupiscence. This is the evil you combat, and which spouses use well when they come together only for the purpose of procreation. Moreover, if the sin which has passed unto all men had not come first, there

would not have been an evil for spouses to use well, yet they would have come together to procreate offspring.

(55) I think the first part of my book[1] has fully exposed your error about the good and the bad trees. Since this part of your argument merely revives difficulties already solved, we need not waste time in useless repetition. You ask: 'Where does the sin in infants come from?' You enumerate many goods, but are silent about the evil you combat; yet even in your silence you cry out, for you write: 'Parents who by their union produce a cause of sin are rightly condemned since by their act the Devil gains mastery over men.' You could make the same complaint to God Himself, not because He creates men who contract original sin, since you deny original sin, but because He feeds and clothes innumerable ungodly men who He knows will persist in their ungodliness. If He did not preserve them, the Devil would surely not have any men to serve him. Perhaps you will say that in caring for such men God attends to nothing but the good of which He is the author, namely, that they are men. We say, then, that when parents beget offspring they think only of this good, namely, that they are men; especially true here, since they know nothing of what awaits their children. In other words, as you also agree, there would be no sin if no evil will came first, because there would have been no sin by way of origin (as we assert, but you deny) if the nature had not been vitiated by the evil will of the first man. But there would have been no evil will if there had not first been a nature, angelic or human. Do you want to say in consequence that God is the cause of sins because His will is the cause of mutable natures? The fact that rational natures fall away from good is not imputed to God the Creator, although the fact that they are good is imputed to Him. In the same way, the fact that children are born with the evil of concupiscence is not to be attributed to the parents

---

1 Cf. above, 8.38-41.

who beget them, and who use this evil well, although the fact that the children are a good is imputed to the parents. It does not follow, as you think it does, that because it is said the origin of the sin without which no man is born is from the Devil, the origin of those who are born is from the Devil, in so far as they are men. That the origin of death is from the Devil does not imply that the origin of mortals is from him.

(56) You say you are looking for 'a crack in the many ramparts around innocence by which sin could have entered,' although the Apostle Paul shows you, not a crack, but a wide-open door, when he says: 'Through one man sin entered into the world and through sin death, and thus death has passed unto all men.' But you bypass these words for your own: 'Because the work of the Devil is not permitted to pass through the work of God'; although men are the work of God, yet sin, which the Apostle says passed to all of them, is the work of the Devil. You cry out: 'If the nature is from God, there cannot be original evil in it,' as though someone else might not think it more religious to cry out that if the nature is from God no evil can arise from it, or that there can be no evil in it. Yet this is false, because evil can only come from a nature and can exist only in a nature. I declare, then, that he who is born is the work of God, even though contracting original evil, since what in him is the work of God is good, because the work of God is good even when it is with evil, not only in infancy but at any age whatsoever; the substance, the form, the life, the senses, the power of reason, and all the rest are goods, even in an evil man, no matter who he may be. Who brings it about that a man live, unless it be He in whom we live and move and have our being?[2] But this takes place in a certain operation of His beneficence which is hidden from us except in those visible foods by which we are sustained from outside. Therefore, He who

---

2 Acts 17.28.

brings it about that a man live, even if he lives a vicious life, also brings about the birth of man, although by vitiated origin.

Chapter 25

(57) What do you mean by arbitrarily selecting words from my book and pretending I say that, before Adam's sin, the institution of marriage was different; that it could have existed without concupiscence, without activity of bodies, and without need of the two sexes? Subtract from marriage the concupiscence by which the flesh lusts against the spirit, subtract the evil you oppose when you engage in glorious combats by means of the virtue of continence, and you need not subtract the rest, if you are looking for the kind of marriage which could have existed before the sin of the first men. Has anyone ever conceived of marriage without activity of bodies and without need of the two sexes? We say, however, that the war which the chaste, be they celibates or spouses, experience in themselves would by no means have existed in paradise before sin. Therefore, the very same kind of marriage exists even now, but at that time it would have used nothing evil in generating offspring, while it now uses well the evil of concupiscence. Marriage has not by this evil lost its own goods, which are found in the faith of chastity, and in the contract of union, and in the fruit which is offspring. At that time, also, a husband would have cleaved to his wife to beget offspring. They would not have had the activity of turbulent lust in their flesh, however, but only the movement of peaceful will by which we command the other members of the body.

(58) You accuse me of saying that the infants who have filled the world, and for whom Christ died, are the work of the Devil, and are born of disease, and are guilty from their

very origin. Infants are not the work of the Devil, as to their substance, but by the work of the Devil they are guilty by way of origin. This is why Christ also died for infants, a fact you yourself confess, because the blood which was shed for the forgiveness of sins[1] also applies to them. You estrange them from this blood when you deny they contract the sin by way of origin. Moreover, you should not take offense at my saying concupiscence is disease, since you also admit a remedy has been provided for it. The origin of infants, from which they were to be born, was in Adam. This source being vitiated and condemned through sin, Christ instituted another origin, from which they might be reborn.

Chapter 26

(59) You say: 'If, before sin, God created that whence men are born, while the Devil made that whence parents are aroused, then we cannot hesitate to ascribe sanctity to the new-born, and guilt to those who generate.' What do you mean by saying the parents are aroused? If they are aroused by the godliness of will by which a man hopes to beget children, this was also instituted by God. If they are aroused by the agitation of lust, which the decision of their will is not sufficient either to excite or to remove, this is the wound of the nature, inflicted by the prevarication to which the Devil persuaded the man. Thus I had good reason for saying, 'The semination of children in the body of that life would have been without that disease without which semination cannot exist in the body of this death.'[1]

(60) You argue: 'Children pertain to the good of fecundity, which, before the disease of lust, was instituted by God's blessing; they do not pertain to the disease of lust, if

---

1 *De nuptiis et concupiscentia* 1.1.

it is something added later after men sinned. Therefore, sanctity must be ascribed to the new-born, and guilt to those who generate.' You do not see that the whole of the nature from which the offspring was to come was changed for the worse by that great sin. By your argument you could also say that Eve, not the other women, was to feel the pains of childbirth because the blessing in which it was said: 'Increase and multiply,'[2] from which the children are procreated, was made before the female sex was punished by that curse. But if you use this argument, someone will surely retort that from the curse also, just as from the sin, the entire nature was changed for the worse; whence were derived original sin and the heavy yoke upon the sons of Adam.

(61) It is not true, as you argue, that the Apostle was describing a Jew placed under the law when he said: 'I know that in me, that is, in my flesh, no good dwells,' and 'It is no longer I who do it, but the sin that dwells in me,' and 'Evil is at hand for me,' and 'I see another law in my members, warring against the law of my mind.' He was describing human nature in this corruptible flesh, and human nature as God's work was not first instituted with a fault, but was damaged by the fault coming from the voluntary choice of the first men. Whose are the words, 'Unhappy man that I am! Who will deliver me from the body of this death? The grace of God through Jesus Christ our Lord'?[3] Are these the words of a Jew? God forbid. Undoubtedly, they are the words of a Christian; therefore, so are the others from which this follows as a consequence. He who said: 'I see another law in my members, warring against the law of my mind,' also said: 'The grace of God will free me from the body of this death, through Jesus Christ our Lord.'

(62) Perhays you think they are the words of a cate-

---
2 Gen. 1.28.
3 Rom. 7.18,20,23-25.

chumen still hoping for the laver of regeneration; that after the laver he will have no law of sin in his members, warring against the law of his mind; although you yourself, as you wish us to believe, engage in glorious combats through the good of continence against the evil of concupiscence, after the laver of regeneration. Consider his words to the Galatians, who were certainly baptized. 'But I say: Walk in the Spirit, and you will not fulfill the concupiscences of the flesh.' He does not say they are not to have them, because they were unable to be without them; he says: 'Do not fulfill them,' that is, do not carry out their works by consent of the will. 'For the flesh lusts against the spirit,' he says, 'and the spirit lusts against the flesh, for these are opposed to each other so that you do not do what you would.' See whether he does not write to the Romans; 'I do not the good which I wish, but the evil that I do not wish, that I perform.' Writing to the Galatians, he makes an addition and says: 'If you are led by the Spirit you are not under the law.'[4] See whether he does not write to the Romans: 'It is no longer I who do it' and 'I am delighted with the law of God according to the inner man' and 'Let not sin reign in your mortal body so that you obey its lusts.'[5] For, if a man does not obey the concupiscences which must exist in the flesh of sin and in the body of this death, he will not fulfill what the Apostle forbids him to fulfill when he says: 'Do not fulfill the concupiscences of the flesh.' The works described in the entire passage are in wonderful sequence: 'Now the works of the flesh are manifest, which are fornication, uncleanness, licentiousness, idolatry,'[6] and the rest. Therefore, although the concupiscences of the flesh are realized in their movements, they are not fulfilled in works if the will does not consent to them. It

---

4 Gal. 5.16-18.
5 Rom. 7.15,20,22; 6.12.
6 Gal. 5.19,20.

follows that when the flesh lusts against the spirit and the spirit lusts against the flesh, and we do not the things we wish, then neither are the concupiscences of the flesh fulfilled, although they indeed come into being; nor are our good works fulfilled, although they also actually come into being. For just as the concupiscence of the flesh is fulfilled only when the spirit consents to it in evil works, so that the spirit does not lust against the flesh but lusts with it; so, too, our good works are fulfilled only when the flesh in no way lusts against the spirit. This is the effect which we will when we long for the perfection of justice, and we ought always to maintain this intention. But because we cannot arrive at this perfection in this corruptible flesh, he says to the Romans: 'To wish is present with me, but I do not find the strength to accomplish what is good,' or, as the Greek codices have it: 'To wish is within my power, but not to fulfiill the good.'[7] He does not say he is unable to do good, but unable to fulfill the good, for to do good is to go not after thy lusts,[8] but to fulfill the good is to be free from concupiscence. Therefore, the exhortation to the Galatians: 'Do not fulfiill the concupiscences of the flesh,' is put to the Romans conversely: 'I do not find the strength to fulfill the good.' Concupiscences are not fulfilled in evil when the assent of our will is withheld from them; and our will is not fulfilled in good as long as their activity, to which we do not consent, perseveres. This conflict, in which the baptized must also fight as in a combat, when the flesh lusts against the spirit and the spirit lusts against the flesh; when the spirit does a good work in not consenting to evil concupiscence, but does not fulfill the good because it does not destroy the evil desires themselves; and when the flesh has an evil desire, but does not fulfill it, because, when the

---

7 Rom. 7.18.
8 Cf. Eccli. 18.30.

spirit does not consent to it, the flesh does not fulfill damnable works—this conflict is not given to Jews, nor to any others, but it is manifestly the conflict of Christian believers, who fight in this combat by living well. The Apostle demonstrates this briefly to the Romans when he says: 'Therefore I myself with my mind serve the law of God, but with my flesh, the law of sin.'[9]

(63) If this is our condition in the body of this death (which was certainly not the condition in paradise in the body of that life), then without any doubt it is plain enough whence infants born carnally contract at birth the obligation of sin which is dissolved only when they are reborn spiritually. They do not contract this obligation from human nature as produced by God, but from the wound which the Enemy inflicted on human nature; not an enemy which, as the Manichaeans say, emerged from a nature of evil God did not make, but an enemy angel, once good as the work of God, now evil from his own work. This enemy first wounded and felled himself so that he made others to be, like himself, outcast, and through evil suasion inflicted the wound of prevarication from which the human race limps even in those who walk in the way of God.

(64) You are incensed because I said: 'This concupiscence, shamelessly praised by shameless men, is something to be ashamed of,'[10] and you use many angry words, even more shamelessly extolling yourselves and, saying your purpose is to exhort men to strive for virtue, when you try, in agreement with holy Scripture and with most evident reason, as you say, to show there is no evil in the nature. You say no height of virtue is so lofty a believing mind cannot reach it with God's help. You say the reason you insist there is not in the flesh what you call a necessity coming from evil is that man

---
9 Rom. 7.25.
10 *De nuptiis et concupiscentia* 1.1.

made in honor will blush to lead a deformed life, and, thus, 'modesty will confront base sloth with praise of inborn nobility,' and many other eloquent phrases. You press the argument against us and say no one can doubt that the overthrow of sanctity, the contamination of chastity, and the defiling of morals are in accord with and even inherent in our teachings. You think I cannot deny this because, as you assert, I turn the sordidness of evil conduct to the disadvantage of nature, that I may relieve sinners of fear. You think I console sinners for their obscenities to the injury of the Apostles and all the saints because I state that the golden vessel, Paul the Apostle, often said: 'I do not the good that I wish, but the evil that I do not wish, that I perform';[11] and this does not exhaust your calumnies.

(65) But, while you are praising yourselves and accusing us, you are fighting against the evil of concupiscence, and in this fighting you confess what you deny in words. You wish it to appear that you have reached the height of virtue, and from the summit itself on which you think you stand, are warring against pursuing concupiscence as though from a fortress, so that, no matter how superior your position, you never cease to combat the internal enemy. Yet you do not blush to praise concupiscence, which will unquestionably make your destruction more complete if it conquers you—and that against Him who seeks you who have been lost, even when it conquers. This is most evident when at end of your book you say my only intention is to swear by the sacraments of the vices to wage war on the virtues; to strive with all cunning and fury for the fall of the City of God; to terrify those who combat baseness by making them despair of achieving chastity; to invent lies about the forces of an obscene lust so great that reason cannot rule and restrain it, and not even the legion of Apostles could oppose it.

---

11 Rom. 7.19.

Complete lies about me! I do not wage war on virtues; but to the best of my ability I do indeed wage war on vices and declare that war must be waged on them. If you, also, do this, why do you praise that against which you fight? How shall I believe you are subduing by virtue the enemies you fear to oppose vigorously in word? If both of us attack concupiscence, why do we not both revile it? Why will you not condemn by statement what you boast of expelling by continence? You say I invent lies about forces of lust so great that reason cannot rule and restrain it. I do not say the forces of lust are so great that human reason, divinely helped and aroused, cannot rule and restrain it. But you—why do you deny that to be evil which slays if not restrained? Attend, with all my force I proclaim what you say I deny: The legion of Apostles warred against lust, which indeed warred against them. You slander us and seem to be indignant, as though we had injured the Apostles. Why do you honor their enemy and yours with praises? Who but an enemy of the Apostles would defend what the legion of the Apostles opposed?

(66) Does lust deserve to have both your friendship and your opposition, so that you attack it in yourself, yet defend it against me? Your opposition is latent; your friendship is patent; the patent makes the latent suspect. But can you ask us to believe in the warfare you say you wage under cover, when we see your friendship in the open? How do you want us to think you oppose the sting of lust, when you fill books with the praise of lust? But I shall overcome my suspicion. I believe you attack what you praise, but I am sorry to see you praise what you attack. From this evil, then, and with it, is generated man, whom you deny is saved by regeneration. For this is the evil which the married use well, and which celibates do better in not using at all. If that by which the flesh lusts against the spirit and which you also

admit the legion of the Apostles combated is an evil, it follows that when the married make good use of it they cannot be using a good well, but an evil. Children generated from and with this evil are to be regenerated so that they may be delivered from evil. Their parents were also born guilty of this original evil, though they were delivered from the guilt by rebirth. What would we have them beget, not from that whence they were reborn, but from that whence they were born, except that which they themselves were at birth? Therefore, they beget the guilty, and, since they generate from that whence they were born, they cannot generate something different from what they themselves were at birth. But, whence they were reborn, thence they were delivered from the guilt with which they were born. Therefore, the offspring which liberated parents generate as guilty must itself be delivered by that same regeneration, because as guilty it was born from the evil which the reborn use well in order that men may be born to be regenerated. If you do not combat this evil, believe those who are combating it. If you also do so, acknowledge the adversary and do not in praising the disease hold as a friend what combat shows by experience to be an enemy.

BOOK IV

Chapter 1

ET US NOW BEGIN at the beginning of the second volume, and look at the rest of the arguments with which you try to refute my book. In accordance with our plan, we shall confine ourselves to real difficulties, avoiding superfluities, so as not to discourage the reader by too many words and prevent his paying adequate attention. In the foregoing book we said enough to make clear to those able to judge properly that the true and good God is the Creator of men; that marriage is a good which God instituted in the state and union of the two sexes, and which He blessed with fecundity; that the concupiscence of the flesh by which the flesh lusts against the spirit is evil. Conjugal modesty uses this same evil well, and more holy celibacy does better in refraining from its use. This evil is not a mixture in us of another substance which God did not make, as Manichaeus raves, but had its origin and was transmitted through the disobedience of one man, and must be expiated and healed through the obedience of one Man. A deserved punishment involves man at birth in subjection to this evil, while unmerited grace frees man at rebirth. In praising this evil, opposing me, you seem my adversary, while in warring against it in yourself you are my witness; but if you do not war against it you are your own enemy. I think I have made suffcient reply to your first book, which covered the whole matter, yet, lest it seem that we were unable to answer your other three books, we shall consider their vain pretensions.

(2) You exult over some words from my book,[1] that 'By the testimony of the Apostle, conjugal modesty is a gift of God,' as though the Apostle praised the evil you praise, by which the flesh lusts against the spirit,[2] and which conjugal modesty uses well. I answered this in a former book. It is no small gift of God when this evil is so restrained that it is used for nothing unlawful but serves only for the generation of children who are to be regenerated. Its force is not self-moderating, for no one abstains from unlawful acts if he follows its lead. Hence it is praised, not for its disquieting activity, but for the restrained and good use made of it by the individual.

(3) When married believers use well that evil from whose guilt they have been freed by the gift of the Savior, then those born by the gift of that same Creator are not, as you object to me, 'made subject to the kingdom of the Devil,' but, rather, are prepared to be rescued from it and transferred to the kingdom of the Only-begotten. This is and ought to be the intention of godly married persons: to prepare birth for rebirth. If, however, this evil which parents sense in themselves, the evil against which, in your words, 'the legion of the Apostles warred,' did not pertain to the children, they would be born without it. But, since they are actually born with it, why do you marvel that they must be reborn in order to be absolved from its guilt, and either be

---

[1] *De nuptiis et concupiscentia* 1.3.
[2] Cf 1 Cor. 7.7., Gal. 5.17.

taken from this life free from this evil or be obliged to fight against it in this life, as free men, and be rewarded as victors in the end?

(4) Who ever theorized that 'the conjugal relationship was invented by the Devil?' Who has ever believed that 'the union of bodies is the result of the evil of the prevarication,' since marriage could by no means exist without these elements and there would be no evil of this kind if no one had sinned? Raise objections to what I actually said, and I shall clear myself; if you object to what I never said, when shall we end the discussion?

(5) 'It follows,' you think, 'that the gift of God is harmful if a man is born with an evil, since no one is born except by the gift of God.' Then listen and understand. The gift of God by which a man exists and lives harms no one. But the evil of concupiscence cannot exist except in him who exists and lives. Evil, then, can exist in the gift of God, to be healed by another gift of God. Hence, there can exist in man, who exists and lives by the gift of God, an evil which is contracted by generation and must be healed by regeneration. No infant could be born with a demon if he were not born, nor may we think that his being born is the cause of the evil. He is born by the gift of God, but he is born with a demon by a judgment of God which is indeed hidden —but is it unjust?

Chapter 2

(6) When I said: 'If one does not possess the conjugal good, he should ask this, too, from the Lord'[1] (and who except he for whom it is necessary?), I seem to you to have

---
1 *De nuptiis* 1.3.

said that 'he should ask for the power to have intercourse.' But I said a man should ask God for conjugal modesty to be used in lawful mode, not in unlimited intercourse. If someone is not able to have intercourse it were better for him not to seek a wife, since, when the Apostle says: 'If they do not have self control, let them marry,'[2] he wants marriage to be a remedy, as you also do, against the disease of concupiscence, which fact you do not accept, though you say there must be a remedy for it.[3] This remedy does not produce concupiscence where it does not exist, but restrains it from issuing forth into unlawful acts. We can make use of the petition we make in the Lord's Prayer here, too: 'Lead us not into temptation,' because 'Everyone is tempted by his own concupiscence,'[4] as the Apostle James says, although we pray: 'Deliver us from evil.'[5] The married pray that, delivered from evil in their mind, they may use properly the evil in their flesh (since they know that in their flesh no good dwells[6]), so that afterwards, when all corruptibility has been healed, all evil will be consumed. Why do you triumph as over a defeated enemy? Conquer, rather, the internal enemy you praise, for my victory over you is certain while the evil is fighting on your side. You dare not say that he who stands for the true is defeated by him who supports the false. I say the concupiscence against which you fight is evil; you say it is good. Your warfare admits the evil your tongue deceitfully calls good, and you add one lie to another by claiming that I also say it is good. I could not have called good that concupiscence of the flesh which the Apostle John said is not from the Father,[7] but I call conjugal modesty

---

2 1 Cor. 7.9.
3 See above, p. 133.
4 James 1.14.
5 Matt. 6.13.
6 Cf. Rom. 7.18.
7 Cf. 1 John 2.16.

good which resists the evil of concupiscence lest, when aroused, it draw men to unlawful acts.

(7) But, realizing how shallow your argument is, you, not I, 'pounce upon the other part of the statement,' and say: 'If the reproductive heat, the minister of conjugal honor, is withheld from immoderate acts by the effort of the faithful as well as by the power of the gift, and if it is not extinguished, but restrained through grace, it is acceptable in its own kind and its own mode, and is censurable only in its excesses.' In making these assertions you fail to notice the reason why the union of the married for the purpose of generating is a praiseworthy good, namely, that it sets a lawful limit for the evil of concupiscence. Why is it not better to admit that it is evil, even if there is no consent to it, and that it will be so until we come to where it is no longer found? Let us not try to think what good may come from the concupiscence of the flesh, but what evil it produces. For conjugal modesty permits the lawful and restrains the unlawful to that eager concupiscence which is always seeking pleasure. This is good; not a goodness of concupiscence, but the goodness of him who uses concupiscence well. What concupiscence itself does is evil, whether the goal for which it burns is the lawful or the unlawful. This is the evil which conjugal modesty uses well, and which virginal continency uses better by refraining from its use.

(8) You say: 'If the reproductive heat were something naturally evil, it would be something to eradicate, not to quiet.' See how you do not want to speak of restraint, as before, but prefer to talk about quieting. You are aware that no one would restrain it unless he warred against it; by changing the word, your fear has admitted the evil which wars against the good. You call it reproductive heat because you are ashamed to call it lust, or, as sacred writing usually calls it, the concupiscence of the flesh. You should say, 'If the concupiscence of the flesh were naturally evil, it should

be eradicated, not quieted.' In this way those who know only everyday language can at last understand what you are saying. But you speak as though all whose reason for marrying is that, not bearing the effort involved in the kind of continency by which the evil is resisted, they choose rather to use the evil well than to do better by refraining from its use, would not prefer to eradicate concupiscence if they could. But if in the body of this death this evil necessary for the married because the good of generation cannot exist without it, then let celibates eradicate the concupiscence of the flesh. You yourself, who talk and do not attend to what you are saying, ought to eradicate lust in your members. It is not necessary for you, nor are its desires good, for if you consent or yield to them you will perish.

(9) Indeed, if that in you against which you fight, which you oppose, and which you expel when you overcome it is evil, then it were better for you to refrain from using the evil they use well, they in whom you hold it is a good. Here you are either lying or mistaken, since you are not going to say lust is good in the married but evil in holy virgins and celibates. We note that you have already said: 'He who follows the moderated way of natural concupiscence is using a good thing well; he who does not follow this way is using a good thing badly. But he who despises even the moderated way, out of love of holy virginity, does better in refraining from use of a good; for, confident of his own health and strength, he despises the remedies, for the opportunity to engage in glorious combats.' With this you declare unambiguously that concupiscence of the flesh exists in both the married and the celibate; you say it is a good which the married use well and which celibates use better by refraining from its use. I say it is an evil. But in holy virgins and celibates the concupiscence of the flesh reveals itself as an evil, since, as you

say, they 'engage in glorious combats' against it; hence, they do better by refraining from use, not of a good, but of an evil. The same applies to the married use, and it is not a good they are using. The whole dispute (if there is any dispute) concerns the question whether, in those who have vowed celibacy to God, the concupiscence of the flesh about which we are arguing is something good or evil. What is true for celibates is also true for the married, because celibates do better in refraining entirely from the use of what the married use well. Therefore, with all the power of your penetrating intellect and open mind, answer, if you can, that the thing against which 'the legion of Apostles warred,' as you admitted in the foregoing book, is good; that is, when you reproached me as though I said: 'The forces of lust are so great that not even the legion of the Apostles warred against it.' This admission would be rather in my favor, because a legion, not of just any saints, but of the Apostles themselves warred against that evil which you say is good. Who would have believed this evil would have an encomiast from the very ranks of its attackers? God forbid that it enlist one of ancient times, or an Apostle, or saint. But, remarkably, there is at least one of the new heretics who inexplicably professes himself to be two things at once—that is, an adversary and also a defender of lust; a man who, remaining in the Pelagian heresy, tries to show that he gives heartful praise to the very thing, which, if not expelled, destroys his heart and soul, and, at the same time, that he is expelling from his soul the thing which, unless praised, would nullify his own teaching.

(10) I ask you, as a human being, whether sin is evil, yet the desire to sin is good? What does concupiscence arouse in the flesh of celibates except desires to commit sin—and by not consenting to them they 'engage in glorious combats,' as you admit? For one who professes celibacy, even the desire

for the act of marriage is evil. What does it do there, where whatever it does is evil, and if there is consent to it, what does it bring to completion? What does concupiscence accomplish there, where nothing good is sought by means of it? It is said to exist in the married without unseemliness since, if they attain the loftiest height of conjugal modesty, they accomplish something good through it, although they do nothing for its sake. I ask you: What does the protege of your folly, your adversary in your wisdom, accomplish where of itself it never accomplishes any good and no good comes from it? What does it accomplish in those in whom whatever is desired according to it is evil? What does it accomplish in those whom it compels to watch and to war against it; where, if any assent is wrested from them even in sleep, they upon waking say with sigh after sigh, 'How my soul is filled with illusions'?[8] When dreams delude the sleeping senses, even the chaste fall into base assents—I know not how. If the Most High were to impute such assents to us, who could live chastely?

(11) I speak, then, about the evil which you will not call good unless you grow so deaf to every sounding truth that you proclaim it is good to desire evil; something you would not even proclaim among the deaf. Why, you ask, is not the evil eradicated from the flesh of celibates? Why is not 'the whole thing removed by the power of the mind'? You say that 'this would have to be done, if it were evil.' Because it is not eradicated in the married, where there is, however, necessary restriction of it, you think that it is good, although you note that it remains where there is not even a restricted use of it, and to the extent of its remaining is harmful—not to such an extent as to deprive one of holiness if he consents not to it, yet diminishing spiritual delight of holy souls, of which the Apostle says: 'I am delighted with the law of God, according

---
8 Ps. 36.8.
9 Rom. 7.22.

to the inner man.'⁹ Such delight is surely diminished when the soul, even if not following concupiscence for carnal pleasure, but, rather, opposing it, is engaged in glorious combats which themselves keep it from delight in intellectual beauty. Since in our present state of misery pride is a worse enemy, calling for continual care, we venture to say that perhaps concupiscence is not wholly extinguished in the flesh of holy celibates in order that, while the soul is fighting against concupiscence, it may be mindful of its dangers and thus escape a false security. This must continue until it attains that perfection of sanctity where it is no longer disturbed by the thought or the swelling of pride. 'For strength is made perfect in weakness'¹⁰—and fighting is of weakness. The more easily one conquers, the less one needs combat. But who would fight within himself if there were no opposition from self? And why is there opposition from self if nothing remains in us to be healed and cured? Therefore, the sole cause of our fighting is weakness in ourselves. Again, weakness cautions against pride. Truly, that strength and virtue by which a man is not proud in this life where he could be proud is made perfect in weakness.

(12) This is why we say the married use well what celibates do better by not using. Hence, the evil which the married use well exists in them, since they use it well, and it exists also in celibates, since they do better by refraining from its use. It exists in them so that they may not become proud. 'Only the excesses of lust are censurable'—that is, in him who lacks restraint they are censurable—but concupiscence of itself is censurable in its very movement and must be opposed lest there be excess. It is not true that 'Modesty about a matter which is harmful of its very nature does not promote innocence.' But not to consent to evil does in fact promote innocence, nor can we therefore say the thing to which consent

---

10 2 Cor. 12.9.

is denied is not evil. It is unquestionably evil, since not to consent to it is good. What evil would a man commit if he consented to a concupiscence which were good, when, as it is, he commits no evil when by the conjugal act, and that not without the evil of concupiscence, he sows a man, the good work of God? You could not say that 'Lust produces the seed.' He who creates the seed of man creates man from seed; but the whence makes a difference. There are hidden and fearful contagions of this evil, even though regeneration has rescued some men from the crime of it, just as those born from them must be rescued.

(13) I truly said what you quote from me about conjugal modesty, and I do not regret it: 'Since these gifts are demonstrably from God, we learn from whom we ought to ask them if we do not have them, and whom we should thank when we have them.' We give thanks, not 'for the origination of concupiscence,' as you say, since its origination is man's first evil, 'but for its regulation.' This you admit to be true, since you mention both of them: 'either its origination or its regulation.' Therefore, we give thanks for the regulation of concupiscence because it is overcome as it resists. But that which resists a good will is not good. Who would deny this to be evil except he who does not have that good will which he acknowledges is attacked only by evil?

Chapter 3

(14) You quote other passages from my book where, after stating that conjugal modesty is a gift of God and teaching it by the testimony of the Apostle, I did not wish to overlook the question arising as to what we should say about some of the ungodly, who also seem to live chastely with their

spouses.¹ For you, who deny that the virtues by which a man lives rightly are gifts of God, and attribute them to human nature and will, not to the grace of God, are accustomed to argue that unbelievers sometimes have these virtues; in this way you try to nullify our assertion that no one lives rightly except by faith through Jesus Christ our Lord, the one Mediator of God and men, and thus you most plainly profess yourselves His adversaries. Let us not get too far afield; we shall see whether I am mistaken, by what you say to these statements. I wrote: 'He who does not keep the faith of marriage with his wife, and do so for the sake of the true God, cannot truthfully be called chaste.' I added the way in which I showed this to be true, and the proof seemed to be an important evidence. 'Since modesty is a virtue whose contrary evil is immodesty, and since all the virtues, even those which function through the body, dwell in the soul, by what true reason may a body be called modest when the soul itself is disloyal to the true God?' Then, lest one of you deny that the soul of an unbeliever is disloyal, I gave testimony from the holy Scripture: 'Behold, they that go far from thee shall perish; thou hast destroyed all them that are disloyal to thee.'² But you, who, as you say, 'intend to pursue all the arguments I thought pointed,' passed over this one completely, as though I considered it dull. You must decide which premiss you will deny. You most readily confess that conjugal modesty is a virtue. You do not deny that all virtues, even those which function through the body, dwell in the soul. He who openly professes enmity to holy Scripture can deny that the soul of an unbeliever is disloyal to God. From all this we conclude either that true modesty can exist in the soul of one disloyal—you see how absurd this is —or that there cannot be true modesty in the soul of an un-

1 *De nuptiis* 1.4.
2 Ps. 72.27.

believer; yet when I state this, you pretend to be deaf. I do not, then, according to your slander, 'praise the gifts with the purpose of reviling the substance.' The substance of man would not be capable of the divine gifts unless it were good; the very faults of that substance testify to its natural good, for a fault is displeasing in proportion as it detracts from or diminishes what is pleasing in the nature.

(15) Therefore, when a man is divinely aided, not only is he 'given aid towards obtaining perfection,' as you yourself have written, thereby implying that a man by himself, without grace, can begin that which grace makes perfect, although we had better repeat the Apostle's words that *He who has begun a good work in you will keep bringing it to perfection until the end.*[3] You want a man to glory, not in the Lord, but in his own free will, for you want him to be 'aroused by the stirrings of a noble heart to what is praiseworthy,' so that he would first give, that recompense should be made him, and in this way grace would no longer be grace,[4] because it is not gratuitous. You say: 'The nature of man, which merits the assistance of this grace, is good.' I would gratefully accept this if you said that this is because man's nature is rational, for the grace of God through Jesus Christ our Lord is not given to stones or sticks or cattle. Man as the image of God merits this grace: not because the good will of man comes first, without grace, and thus there is something prior to grace and calling for reward, and then grace would no longer be grace, not given as gratuitous, but as something due. Why did you decide, in your usual manner, that I 'locate the divine gifts in the effectiveness of the will,' as though the will of man could be moved toward good without the grace of God, and thus God would repay man by giving him the effectiveness of will. Have you forgotten what

---

3 Cf. Phil. 1.6.
4 Cf. Rom. 11.33,6.

we quoted against you from Scripture: 'The will is prepared by the Lord,'⁵ or that God works in us also the will? Ingrates to the grace of God! Enemies to the grace of Christ, and to the very name of Christian! Does not the Church pray for her enemies? I ask you: What does she pray for? If she prays that they be repaid by their own will's being made effective, they will receive great punishment. What is against them is not for them. But she prays for them. Thus, she does not pray for them because their will is good. She prays that the bad will may be changed to a good will, for, as the Apostle says: 'The will is prepared by the Lord' and 'It is God who works in you also the will.'⁶

(16) Most bitter enemies of grace, you offer us examples of ungodly men who, you say, 'though without faith, abound in virtues where there is, without the aid of grace, only the good of nature even though shackled by superstitions. Such men, by the mere powers of their inborn liberty, are often merciful, and modest, and chaste, and sober.' When you say this you have already removed what you thought to attribute to the grace of God: namely, effectiveness of will. You do not say those men will to be merciful, modest, chaste, sober, and are not such because they have not obtained through grace the effectiveness of their will. If they both will to be such and actually are such, we already find in them both will and effectiveness of will. What, then, is left for grace in those clearly evident virtues in which you say they abound? If it pleases you so much to praise the ungodly that you say they abound in true virtues—as though you did not hear Scripture saying: 'They that say to the wicked man: thou art just, shall be accursed by the people, and the tribes shall abhor them'⁷—it were much better for

---
5 Prov. 8 (Septuagint).
6 Phil. 2.13.
7 Prov. 24.24.

you, who say they abound in virtues, to confess that these are gifts of God in them. Under His hidden judgment, which is not unjust, some men are born feeble-minded; some, slow-witted and dull in understanding. Some have both gifts, being keen-witted and able to store up what they learn in the treasury of a very tenacious memory. Some are gentle by nature; others are easily aroused to anger for slight causes; while others are in between in respect to seeking revenge. Some are eunuchs; some are so cold they can scarcely be quickened; some are so lustful they can scarcely be restrained; and some are in between, both easily moved and languid. Some are very timid; others, very daring; others, neither. Some are joyful; others, melancholy; others are inclined to neither. None of the things I have mentioned arises from institution or design, but from nature, so that medical writers dare attribute them to bodily constitution. Whatever the solution after thorough investigation, even if all possible questions had been solved, we could still ask whether every man made his body for himself, and whether these natural evils he endures in greater or lesser degree must be attributed to his will. No one, in any way or for any reason, can escape suffering them in this life. Let the suffering be the greatest or the least, no one has a right to say to Him who made him, though He is omnipotent, just, and good: 'Why hast thou made me thus?'[8] And no one but the second Adam delivers man from the heavy yoke which lies upon the children of the first Adam.[9] How much more tolerable, then, to attribute what you say are virtues in the ungodly to the divine gift rather than only to their will; although they are ignorant of this until, if they are of the number of the predestined,

---

8 Isa. 45.9; Rom. 9.20.
9 Cf. Eccli. 40.1.

they receive the spirit which is from God and thus come to know the things given them by God.¹⁰

(17) But God forbid there be true virtues in anyone unless he is just,¹¹ and God forbid he be truly just unless he lives by faith, for 'He who is just lives by faith.'¹² Who of those wishing to be considered Christians, except the Pelagians alone, or, perhaps, you alone among the Pelagians, will call an unbeliever just, and an ungodly man just, and say a just man is in bondage to the Devil?—whether he be Fabricius, whether he be Scipio, whether he be Regulus, whose names you thought would frighten me, as though we were speaking before the ancient court of Rome. You may also appeal to the school of Pythagoras, or that of Plato, where the most erudite and learned in a philosophy far excelling the others in nobility said there are not true virtues except those in some way impressed on the mind by the form of the eternal and unchangeable substance which is God. In spite of this, I proclaim against you with all my divinely given liberty of godliness: 'True justice is not in those men' and 'He who is just lives by faith, faith comes from hearing, and hearing is by the word of Christ. For Christ is the consummation of the Law unto justice for everyone who believes.'¹³ How are those men just to whom the humility of the truly just is common? Pride kept them from following their understanding, 'Seeing that, although they knew God, they did not glorify him as God or give thanks, but became vain in their reasonings, and their senseless

---
10 Cf. 1 Cor. 2.12
11 Augustine's doctrine that virtue is not true virtue unless it is informed by faith is stated more rigidly here than elsewhere; it is a simple logical deduction from the truths that none is saved without baptism, and that God does not condemn what is good. Cf. St. Thomas' explanation of Augustine's meaning, especially in *Summa theologica*, 2-2, q. 23, a. 7.
12 Rom. 1.17
13 Rom. 10.4,17.

minds have been darkened. For while professing to be wise, they became fools.'[14] How can true justice be in those in whom there is not true wisdom? If you attribute true wisdom to them, there will be no reason for not saying they arrive at the kingdom of which it is written: 'The desire of wisdom bringeth to the kingdom.'[15] Therefore, Christ died in vain if men without the faith of Christ through other means or power of reasoning may arrive at true faith, at true virtue, at true justice, at true wisdom. As the Apostle most truly says about the Law: 'If justice is by the law, then Christ died in vain;'[16] it is also most true to say that, if justice is by nature and the will, then Christ died in vain. If any justice whatsoever is given through the teaching of men, then Christ died in vain, for what gives true justice also gives the kingdom of God. God Himself would be unjust if the truly just were not admitted to His kingdom, since the kingdom itself is justice, as it is written: 'The kingdom of God does not consist in food and drink, but in justice and peace and joy;'[17] and if the justice of the ungodly is not true justice, then whichever they have of the virtues allied with it are not true virtues (because failure to refer the gifts of God to their Author makes the evil men using them unjust); thus, neither the continence of the ungodly nor their modesty is true virtue.

(18) But you misinterpret the Apostle's words that 'Everyone in a contest abstains from all things,'[18] when you assert that flute-players and other common and infamous persons have continence, which Scripture says is so great a virtue that none can have continence except God give it.[19] When

---
14 Rom. 1.21,22.
15 Wisd. 6.21.
16 Gal. 2.21.
17 Rom. 14.17.
18 1 Cor. 9.25.
19 Cf. Wisd. 8.21.

those persons are entered in a contest they exercise restraint because of vain coveting of the crown. This vain, depraved, coveting prevails in them, and restrains other depraved covetings; for which reason they were said to be continent. But you, to the grave injury of the Scipios, have also given to stage-players the continence you praised so eloquently in them, forgetting that, when the Apostle exhorted men to virtue, he used a faulty human affection as an illustration; further, another passage of Scripture exhorting us to love of wisdom says it should be sought after like money.[20] Must we therefore think holy Scripture praises avarice? It is well known to what great efforts and pains lovers of money will patiently subject themselves, from what great pleasures they abstain, in their desire to increase their wealth or in their fear of diminishing it; with what great shrewdness they pursue gain, and how prudently they avoid losses; how they are usually afraid to take the property of others, and sometimes despise loss to themselves lest they lose more in its quest and litigation. Because these traits are well known, it is right for us to be exhorted so to love wisdom that we most eagerly seek it as our treasure, acquire more and more of it, suffer many trials, restrain desires, ponder the future, so that we may preserve innocence and beneficence. Whenever we act in this way we are in possession of true virtues, because our objective is true, that is, is in harmony with our nature in reference to salvation and true happiness.

(19) Virtue is not absurdly defined by those who say: 'Virtue is a habit of the soul, in harmony with reason and with the mean of nature.'[21] That is true, but they did not know what is in harmony with the nature of mortals as

---
20 Cf. Prov. 2.4.
21 Cicero, *De inventione* 2

that nature is to be freed and made happy. Not all men, by a mere natural instinct, would wish to be immortal and happy unless they could attain it. This highest good can come to men only through Christ, and Him crucified; by whose death death itself is conquered, and by whose wounds our nature is healed. Therefore, the just man lives by the faith of Christ. For by this faith he lives prudently, courageously, temperately, justly, and, thereby, correctly and wisely in all these virtues because he lives according to faith. If virtues do not help man to achieve that true happiness which true faith in Christ promises us as immortal, they can by no means be true virtues. Would it please you if we said the virtues of misers are true virtues, when they prudently ponder the ways of profit, courageously bear cruel and bitter experiences for the acquisition of money, temperately and soberly chastise the various desires in which a man revels; when they do not take the property of others and often scorn what they have lost of their own—something which seems to pertain to justice—and this they do lest they lose more of their own property in drawn out law suits? When something is done prudently, courageously, temperately, and justly, we have all four of the virtues which on your argument are true virtues, that is, they are true if we regard only what is done and not why is is done. Lest I slander you, I shall quote your own words. You say: 'The origin of all virtue is located in the rational soul, and all the affections through which we are good effectively or ineffectively are in our mind as in their subject; they are prudence, justice, temperance, and fortitude. Although the power for these affections is in all men by nature, they do not conspire to one end in all men, but, in accordance with the judgment of the will, to which they are subject, they are directed to either eternal or temporal things. When this happens they do not vary in what they are, nor in what they do, but only in what they deserve. Neither their name nor their kind can be dispensed with; they vary only between enrichment, when they seek a great reward, and frustration, if their quest is slight.' I do not know where you learned these things, but I believe you see even now that as a consequence we would have to regard as true virtue the prudence by which misers ponder the various kinds of profit; and the justice by which they sometimes, in fear of more serious loss of their own property, despise it; and the temperance by which they restrain their appetite for luxury, because it is costly, and are content with only the necessary food and clothing; and the fortitude by which, as Horace says: 'Through oceans they go fleeing poverty; through rocks and through fire';[22] and by which, as we know, some of them in the barbarian invasion could not be forced by any of the enemy's tortures to betray what they possessed. Therefore, these virtues which are so debased and deformed for such an end, and hence in no way genuine and true virtues, seem to you to be so true and beautiful 'that neither their name nor their kind can be dispensed with, but only the frustration resulting from the meagerness of their quest,' that is, judged by the fruit of earthly advantages, not of heavenly rewards. And the justice of Catiline will be none other than true justice: to hold many in friendship; to protect them by service; to share possessions with all; his fortitude will be true fortitude, which was able to endure cold hunger, and thirst; his patience will be true patience, which was incredibly enduring in fasting, in cold, and in vigil.[23] Who but the foolish could be wise in this fashion?

(20) But we see that you, a scholarly man, are deceived by the resemblance of these vices to the true; they seem near to virtues, neighboring on them, although they are

---
22 Horace, *Epistolae* 1.1.46.
23 Sallust, *De Catilinae conjuratione* 15.

as far from them as vices are from virtues. Constancy is a virtue whose contrary is inconstancy; there is, however, a vice bordering on it, so to speak—stubbornness, which seems to imitate constancy. May you be wanting in this vice when you recognize that what I say is true; lest, as though loving constancy, you might think you must persist stubbornly in error. Thus, not only are there vices contrary to the virtues, and plainly distinct from them—as rashness is contrary to prudence—but there are also vices which somehow border on the virtues, being similar, not in truth, but by a deceptive appearance. As a kind of neighbor to prudence we find, not rashness or imprudence, but cleverness, which is nevertheless a vice—although the words of Scripture: 'Wise as serpents,'[24] should be taken in good sense, while the words that in paradise 'The serpent was more cunning than any of the beasts,'[25] are taken in a bad sense. It is not easy to find names for all these vices which border on virtues, but, even if we cannot call them by name, we must beware of them.

(21) You know that virtues must be distinguished from vices, not by their functions, but by their ends. The function is that which is to be done; the end is that for which it is to be done. When a man does something in which he does not seem to sin, yet does not do it because of that for which he ought to do it, he is guilty of sinning. Not heeding this fact, you separated the ends from the functions and said that the functions, apart from the ends, should be called true virtues, and in consequence you involved yourself in such absurdities that you were obliged to call even that whose mistress is avarice true justice. If you think only of the function, then refusing to take another's property can look like justice. But, when someone asks why it is done,

---
24 Matt. 10.16.
25 Gen. 3.1.

and the answer is: 'In order not to lose more money in contention,' how could this work, serving avarice, belong to true justice? The virtues Epicurus introduced as handmaids of pleasure are such that they do whatever they do for the sake of obtaining or possessing pleasure. God forbid that true virtues serve anyone but Him to whom we say: 'Lord of virtues, convert us.'[26] Therefore, virtues which serve carnal pleasure or any temporal advantages or emoluments cannot be true. But virtues that render no service to anything are not true virtues. True virtues in men serve God, by whom they are given to men; true virtues in angels serve God, by whom they are also given to angels. Whatever good is done by man, yet is not done for the purpose for which true wisdom commands it be done, may seem good from its function, but, because the end is not right, it is sin.

(22) Therefore, certain good acts can be done when those who do them are not doing well. It is good to help a man in danger, especially an innocent man. But, if a man acts loving the glory of men more than the glory of God, he does a good thing not in good way, because he is not good when his act is not done in a good way. God forbid that a will be or be said to be good when it glories in others, or in itself, and not in the Lord. Neither may its fruit be said to be good, since a bad tree does not produce good fruit; rather, the good work belongs to Him who acts well even through evil men. Thus, it is impossible to say how mistaken is your opinion that 'All virtues are affections through which we are good either effectively or ineffectively.' It cannot be that we are ineffectively good, but, whatever we are ineffectively, we are not good from that aspect, since a good tree bears good fruit. Never be it said that the good God, by whom the axe is prepared for trees not bringing

---
26 Ps. 79.8.

forth good fruit, to be cut down and thrown into the fire, prepares the axe for good trees.[27] By no means, then, are men good ineffectively; but, of those who are not good, some are less evil and some are more evil.

(23) I do not see how it helps you to recall the people described in the Apostle's words: 'The Gentiles who have not the Law are a law to themselves, who show the work of the Law written in their hearts.' By means of these Gentiles you tried to prove that even those who are strangers to the faith of Christ can have true justice, for the Apostle says they 'do by nature what the Law prescribes.' In this passage you have clearly expressed the teaching by which you are enemies to the grace of God which is given through Jesus Christ our Lord, who takes away the sin of the world.[28] You introduce a race of men who can please God by the law of nature without the faith of Christ. This is the chief reason why the Christian Church detests you. But what do you want them to be? Are they to have true virtues and to be only ineffectively good because it is not for the sake of God? Or are some of them to please God and be rewarded by Him with eternal life? If you say they are ineffective, then of what use is it to them that, according to the Apostle, their own thoughts will defend them 'on the day when God will judge the hidden secrets of men'?[29] But if those whose own thoughts defend them are not ineffectively good, since they naturally do the work of the Law, and for this reason receive eternal recompense from God, then undeniably the reason they are just is that they live by faith.

(24) The testimony I cited from the Apostle—'All that is not from faith is sin'—you received as you pleased, and you did not expound it as it savors, but as you savor it. The

---

27 Cf. Matt. 7.17,18; 3.10.
28 John 17.29.
29 Rom. 2.14-16.

Apostle was talking first about food, but when he said: 'He who hesitates, if he eats, is condemned, because it is not from faith,' he wished to make a general statement about the kind of sin in question, concluding immediately, 'For all that is not from faith is sin.'[30] But I shall grant you that it should be understood only of food. What about the other testimony I cited in the same passage, which you did not challenge because you found no way to distort it to your point of view? I cited from the Hebrews: 'For without faith it is impossible to please God.'[31] In arriving at this statement, Paul discussed the entire life of man, in which the just man lives by faith; and, though it is impossible to please God without faith, virtues without faith please you, so that you say they are true virtues, and that they make men good.[32] Then, again, as though you regret praising them, you do not hesitate to call them ineffective.

(25) Thus, those who are just by the natural law please God and please by faith, because without faith it is impossible to please God—and by what faith do they please except by the faith of Christ? As we read in the Acts of the Apostles: 'In him God has defined the faith for all, by raising him from the dead.'[33] The reason they are said to do by nature the works of the Law without the Law is that they came to the Gospel from the Gentiles, not from the circumcision, to which the Law was given; they came by nature, because, that they might believe, their very nature was corrected through the grace of God. You cannot prove through them what you wish to prove—that even unbelievers can have true virtues—for those men are believers. If they have not

---
30 Rom. 14.23.
31 Heb. 11.6.
32 Cf. above, note 11. Augustine corrects the harsh impression produced by the first statement of this proposition, especially when he explains the good works of unbelievers, and asserts there are various degrees of eternal punishments.
33 Acts 17.31

the faith of Christ, then they are neither just nor pleasing to God, since without faith it is impossible to please God. Their thoughts will defend them on the day of judgment thus: that they may receive a more tolerable punishment, because in some way they did naturally the works of the Law, having the work of the Law written in the hearts to the extent that they did not do to others what they did not want done to themselves. But those men without faith sinned in that they did not refer their works to the end to which they should be referred. Fabricius will be punished less than Catiline, not because Fabricius was good, but because Catiline was more evil. Fabricius was less wicked than Catiline, not because he had true virtues, but because he did not deviate so much from the true virtues.

(26) Perhaps you will provide a place between damnation and the kingdom of heaven where even those who did not please God, whom it is impossible to please without faith, a faith they had neither in their works nor in their hearts, will exist, not in misery, but in everlasting beatitude? Do you envisage such a place for men who have shown a Babylonian love for their earthly fatherland, serving demons or human glory by civic virtue, which is not true virtue but resembles true virtue—for the Fabricii, the Reguli, the Fabii, the Scipios, the Camilii, and others like them[34]—as you do for infants who die without baptism? I do not believe your own state of destruction can flaunt this imprudence. You ask: 'Will those, then, in whom there was true justice be in everlasting damnation?' Words beyond impudence! There was not true justice in them, as I declared, because functions should not be weighed by the mere acts, but by their ends.

(27) With grace and wit, you, a very elegant and urbane gentleman, assert: 'If it be maintained that the chastity of

---

34 These men were Roman patriots, beloved by their countrymen, and distinguished by their lives and accomplishments.

unbelievers is not chastity, then for the same reason it must be said that the body of pagans is not a true body, and the eyes of pagans have not the sense of sight, and the crops growing in pagans' fields are not true crops, and many other consequences so absurd they could move an intelligent man to laughter.' Your laughter will move intelligent men, not to laughter, but to tears, as the laughter of the insane moves their sane friends to weeping. Do you deny, contrary to holy Scripture, that the soul of an unbeliever commits fornication; and do you laugh, and are you sane? Whence, how, and by what reason could this take place? This is neither true chastity nor true sanity. Indeed, I say, the chastity of the soul committing fornication is not true chastity, and the insanity of a man who in laughter says this shameful thing is true insanity. Far be it from us to say the body of pagans is not a true body, and all the rest. It does not follow that if the virtue in which an ungodly man glories is not true virtue, the body God makes is not a true body. We can clearly state that the brow of heretics is no brow, if we mean, not the member God made, but shame. What if I did not anticipate in my book your interpreting the words, 'All that is not from faith is sin,' to include even those things of unbelievers which are gifts of God, whether they are goods of the soul or of the body? It is there we find the things about which you vainly babble: body, eyes, and the other members. The crops growing in pagan's fields are also of this kind. Their creator is God, not the pagans. Did you not quote with the rest of my words the statement: 'For the soul and body, and whatever good of soul and body are natural to man, are gifts of God, even in sinners, because God, not they, made them'? The words, 'All that is not from faith is sin,' concern what sinners themselves do.'[35] If you had remembered this short but clear statement of mine, I do not

---
35 *De nuptiis* 1.4.

think you would have been so dishonest as to assert we could say: 'The body of pagans is not a body, and the eyes of pagans do not have the sense of sight, and the crops growing in pagans' fields are not crops.' Let me repeat these words of mine to you as though you had just awakened from sleep, since they may have slipped your mind. I said: 'These are gifts of God, even in sinners, because God, not they, made them. The words, "All that is not from faith is sin," concern what sinners themselves do.' When you make insane remarks and laugh, you behave like a lunatic, but, when you pay no attention and forget truths which, as I say, I stated just a short time before, and placed in the very work in which you seem to be answering me, then you resemble a sluggard more than a lunatic.

(28) You say you marvel 'that one so outstanding'—meaning me, and by way of ridicule—'does not see how much he helps me by asserting that some sins are conquered by other sins.' You go on to say: 'By all means, then, a man can be without sins, by his effort for holiness with God's help. For,' you say, 'if sins may be overcome by sins, how much more easily can sins be overcome by virtues?' This you say as though we would deny that the help of God is so great that, if He willed it, we could this day be without the evil concupiscences against which we must invincibly fight. Not even you will admit that this comes to pass, but, as to why it does not come to pass: 'Who knows the mind of the Lord?'[36] But it is not a little I know when I do know that, no matter what the cause, there is something in the hidden and lofty plan of God to explain why, as long as we live in this mortal flesh, there is in us something against which our mind must fight. This is why we say: 'Forgive us our trespasses.'[37] Speaking to you as man to man, and as a man

---

36 Rom. 11.34.
37 Matt. 6.12.

'whose earthy habitation presseth down the mind that museth upon many things,'[38] I say that, so far as the merits of the divinely instituted natures are concerned, there is nothing in creatures more excellent than the rational mind. It follows that a good mind has more delight and satisfaction in itself than it has in any other creature. How dangerous, yes, how pernicious, is this self-delight, since in its exultation it may give rise to the fever and disease of delusion, and this danger exists as long as it does not see, as it will indeed see in the end, the supreme and unchangeable Good, in comparison with which it will despise itself and will become vile to itself through love of Him, and it will be so filled by His great spirit that it will prefer the supreme Good to itself, not only with its reason, but also in eternal love. We should need a long time to demonstrate this; he realizes it who returns to himself when worn out with hunger, and says: 'I will get up and go to my father.'[39] We know, then, that we must live under daily remission of sins, in this place of infirmity, so that we shall not live in pride. And when the evil of pride will no longer be able to tempt the soul and there be nothing against which we must fight, then the soul will be so filled with the vision of the higher Good and so inflamed with love of it that it could not fail in its love of that supreme Good and come to rest again in self-delight. On account of this evil of pride not even the Apostle Paul was entrusted to his own free will, because he had not yet arrived at such perfect participation of that higher Good; and, lest he exalt himself, there was given him an angel of Satan to buffet him.[40]

(29) Whether the reason be this or something else much further beyond my grasp, I cannot doubt that, no matter how great our progress under this burden of a corruptible

---
38 Wisd. 9.15.
39 Luke 15.18.
40 Cf. 2 Cor. 12.7.

body, 'If we say that we have no sin, we deceive ourselves, and the truth is not in us.'[41] Hence, holy Church, even for those of her members in whom there is neither blemish of crime nor wrinkle of error,[42] despite your haughty opposition, never stops pleading with God to 'Forgive us our trespasses.' He who does not know your teachings is not aware of your immense arrogance and presumption of personal virtue when you say: 'By all means, then, a man can be without sins by his effort for sanctity, with God's help.' You wish to say that the effort for sanctity comes first, in man's will, without the help of God, and that God's aid is not gratuitous but justly due. Thus, you think a man can be without sins in this miserable life, so that he has no personal reason for saying: 'Forgive us our trespasses.'[43] You seem to have put it a little more reticently, since you did not say he can be without all sins, yet neither did you say you meant only some sins, not all. You measured your statement in such a way that it could be defended verbally both by us and by you, as though you blushed for your presumption. If you are among Pelagians, you can say the reason you did not say only some sins is that a man can be without all sins. If this is discussed among us, you can say the reason you did not say all sins is that you wished us to understand that every man needs to ask pardon for some sins. But we who know what you mean are not unaware of how you mean it.

(30) You say: 'If a Gentile clothes a naked man, is it a sin because it is not by faith?' In so far as it is not from faith it is truly sin—not that the thing done, clothing the naked, is a sin in itself; but only an ungodly man denies that it is sin not to give glory to the Lord in such a work, though enough has already been said for you to understand. Yet,

---

41 1 John 1.8.
42 Cf. Eph. 5.27.
43 Cf. above, pp. 83-84.

since the matter is important, attend a little longer. Yea, I shall quote your very words: 'If a Gentile,' who does not live by faith, 'clothes a naked man, delivers someone from danger, binds up an injured man's wounds, gives money in honest friendship, or cannot be compelled to bear false witness even when tortured,' I ask you whether he does these good works well or evilly. If he does them in an evil way, though they are good, you cannot deny that he who does anything in an evil way sins, regardless of what he does. But, since you do not wish him to sin when he does these things, you will surely say that he does good and he does it well. Therefore, a bad tree brings forth good fruit, and, according to the Truth, this cannot happen. Be in no hurry to express an opinion, but consider your answer carefully. Would you call an unbeliever a good tree? Therefore, he must be pleasing to God, since the good must be pleasing to the Good. What, then, of Scripture: 'Without faith it is impossible to please God'?[44] Will you answer that he is a good tree, not in so far as he is unbelieving, but in so far as he is a man? Then, of whom did our Lord say: 'A bad tree cannot bear good fruit'?[45]—for, whoever it be, it is either man or angel. But, if man, in so far as he is man, is a good tree, then surely an angel, in so far as he is an angel, is a good tree, for angels are the work of God who is the Creator of good natures. Therefore, there would be no bad tree of which it is said that it cannot bear good fruits. What unbeliever thinks so unbelievingly? Hence, it is not as man, which is the work of God, but as man of bad will, that someone is a bad tree and cannot bring forth good fruit. Would you still say an unbelieving will is a good will?

(31) Perhaps you will say a merciful will is good. This would be correct if mercy were always good, in the way in

---
44 Heb. 11.6.
45 Matt. 7.18.

which the faith of Christ, which works through love, is always good.⁴⁶ But there is a mercy that is evil, which respects the person of the poor in judgment,⁴⁷ for which King Saul finally deserved to be condemned by God, yet in mercy; when, through human affection, but contrary to the commandment of God, he spared the captive king.⁴⁸ Watch carefully; it may well be that the only good mercy is the mercy of this good faith. That you may understand without reservation, answer whether you think unbelieving mercy is good mercy. If it is a fault to have mercy in an evil way, it is undeniably a fault to have mercy unbelievingly. In itself, mercy out of natural compassion is a good work, but he who uses this good work unbelievingly uses it in an evil way, and he who does this good thing unbelievingly does it in an evil way; but whoever does something in an evil way sins.

(32) We gather from all this that even the good works of unbelievers are not good works of theirs, but are the works of Him who makes good use of evil men. But their sins are sins of theirs, by which they do good things in an evil way, because they do them, not with a believing but with an unbelieving will, that is, with a foolish and harmful will. No Christian doubts that a tree that can bring forth only bad fruit, that is, only sins, is a bad tree. For, whether you will or not, 'All that is not from faith is sin.'⁴⁹ Therefore, God cannot love those trees, and, if they remain such as they are, He plans to cut them down, because 'Without faith it is impossible to please God.' But I tarry here as though you yourself had not already called those trees barren. I ask you whether you are joking or raving when you praise the fruit of barren trees? Either there are no fruits, or they are evil

---
46 Cf. Gal. 5.6.
47 Cf. Exod. 23.3.
48 1 Kings 15.
49 Rom. 14.23.

and must not be praised; or they are good fruits and the trees are not barren, but those trees are good whose fruits are good, and they ought to please God, who cannot fail to be pleased with good trees. Then the Scripture, 'Without faith it is impossible to please God,' will be false. How does the last sentence cohere with the rest?

(33) Will your answer be anything but vain words? You say I asserted that 'men are sometimes ineffectively good, if by failing to do good acts for the sake of God, they do not obtain eternal life from Him.' Will the just and good God then send good men to eternal death? I regret to note how many unsound consequences follow when you think such things, and say such things, and write them down, and then find fault with me because I am not guilty of the same foolishness. Briefly, though you truly err in the matters themselves as much as a man can err, lest I may seem to fight against you over mere words: Understand what our Lord says: 'If thy eye be evil, thy whole body will be full of darkness. If thy eye be sound, thy whole body will be full of light,'[50] and from this learn that he who does not perform his good works with the intention of the good faith, the faith that works through love, his whole body, which is as it were composed of the works as members, will be darkened, that is, full of the blackness of sin. You will at least concede that the works of unbelievers which seem to you to be their own good works do not lead them to everlasting salvation and the kingdom. Realize we say that this good of men, this good will, this good work can be conferred on no one without the grace of God which is given through the one Mediator of God and men, and only through this good can man be brought to the eternal gift and kingdom of God. All other works which seem praiseworthy among men may seem to

---

50 Matt. 6.25,22.

you to be true virtues and they may seem to be good works and to be carried out without any sin, but as for me, I know this: They were not perfomed by a good will, for an unbelieving and ungodly will is not a good will. You call these wills good trees; it suffices for me that they are barren with God and therefore not good. They may be fruitful with those for whom they are also good, relying on your word, your praise, and, if you like, you as planter; yet, whether you will or no, I shall win my point that the love of the world by which a man is a friend of this world is not from God, and that the love of enjoying any creature whatsoever without love of the Creator is not from God; but the love of God which leads one to God is only from God the Father through Jesus Christ with the Holy Spirit. Through this love of the Creator everyone uses even creatures well. Without this love of the Creator no one uses any creature well. This love is needed so that conjugal modesty may also be a beatific good; and that the intention in carnal union is not the pleasure of lust but the desire for offspring. If, however, pleasure prevails and extorts an act for its own sake and not for the sake of propagating children, this sin will be pardonable, because of Christian marriage.

Chapter 4

(34) I did not write the words you quote from me, saying: 'The reason children are under the power of the Devil is that they are born of the union of bodies.' To say 'who are born of the union of the bodies' is not the same as to say 'because they are born of the union of the bodies.' The cause of the evil here is not their being born of the union of bodies, since, even if human nature had not been vitiated by the sin of the first man, children could not have been

generated except from the union of bodies. The reason those born of the union of bodies are under the power of the Devil before they are reborn through the Spirit is that they are born through that concupiscence by which the flesh lusts against the spirit and forces the spirit to lust against the flesh.[1] There would be no such combat between good and evil if no one had sinned. Just as there was no combat before man's iniquity, so there will be no combat after man's infirmity.

Chapter 5

(35) You argue against my words at length: 'Because we are made up of elements of unequal goodness, the soul ought to rule over the body. The one we have in common with the gods; the other, with the beasts. Therefore, that which is better, the soul endowed with virtue, should rule both the members of the body and its desires.' You fail to observe that desires are not ruled as members are. Desires are evils which we restrain by reason and fight against with our mind; members are goods which we move by the decision of the will, with the exception of the reproductive members, although they also are the work of God and are good. They are called *pudenda* because lust has greater power to move them than reason, although we do not permit them to commit the acts to which they urge us, since we can easily control the other members. But, when does a man use his good members badly except when he consents to the evil desires within him? Of these desires, lust is baser than others, and if not resisted it commits horrible impurities. Conjugal modesty alone uses this evil well. This lust is not an evil in beasts, because in them it does not

---

1 Gal. 5.17.

war against reason, which they lack. Why do you not believe that it could have been divinely granted to those in Paradise before there was sin that they might without any lust procreate children by tranquil action and the union or intercourse of the members of the body; or, at least, that lust in them was such that its action neither preceded nor exceeded the will? Or do you count it nothing to approve of lust unless it be approved as that which solicits the unwilling and even those who fight against it? This is the kind of lust over which the Pelagians glory, even in its strife, as though over a good. But the saints confess it with groaning, that they may be delivered from evil.

Chapter 6

(36) You slander me by saying that I said: 'in ridiculous contradiction, that some men derive guilt from a good deed, while others are holy through an evil deed,' because I said: 'By using the good of marriage without faith unbelievers turn it to evil and to sin; likewise, the marriage of believers turns the evil of concupiscence to the use of justice.'[1] I did not say that some men derive guilt from a good deed, but from an evil deed in which they use goods in an evil way; not that some are made holy through an evil deed, but from a good deed in which they use evils well. If you are unwilling to understand or are pretending not to understand, do not make it difficult for others who are both willing and able to understand.

---

1 *De nuptiis* 1.5.

Chapter 7

(37 You say: 'If anyone could be born with the evil, he could never pass to good by washing.' By the same reasoning, you could say that the body which is born mortal can never become immortal; if the second inference is false, so is the first. God did not create evil when He created man; rather, the good He created derives evil from the sin God did not create. He heals this evil, which He did not create, in the good which He did create.

(38) We do not say: 'The demons instituted the marriage union and the seminal union of the two sexes,' or that 'The union of the married for the purpose of generating is a diabolic act,' because all these were instituted by God and they all could have existed without the evil of concupiscence if the wound of the prevarication, from which arose the discord between flesh and spirit, had not been inflicted by the Devil. Why not consider your position, and blush for the garrulous loquacity from which came such wonders as: 'Demons seize the married in their union and prevent them from generating children to be freed by regeneration'? —as though the demon, could he do what he wished, would not constantly suffocate ungodly adults still under the power of the same demon, when he sees that they have decided to become Christians. It does not follow, as you imagine, that demons with threat and terror oppose parents as they generate those to be reborn, when the parents have come together for this very purpose, since by the creative power of God something is brought into being through the wound inflicted by the Devil, the wound in which the human race limps, and this offspring is to be transferred from Adam to Christ; but the legion of demons could not have had power even over the swine if Christ had not granted their request.[1]

---

1 Cf. Matt. 8.31,32.

Thus, He who knew how to make a crown for martyrs from the very persecutions He permitted the Devil to arouse makes good use of every kind of evil for the advantage of the good. But, even in those spouses who either do not think about the regeneration of their children, or even detest it, the legitimate union of the sexes for the purpose of generating is a good act of marriage, for the fruit of this act is the orderly begetting of children, even though some parents use this good in an evil and sinful way, glorying over propagating ungodly offspring, or over ungodly offspring already propagated. Whatever be the contagion or commission of sin by which men are stained, in so far as they are men, they are good; and, because they are good, it is good that they are born.

(39) It is not true that 'Adultery and all manner of perverse carnal commerce should be committed that there may be offspring.' You think you can force this absurd conclusion on us because we say that out of the evil of lust marriage produces the good of offspring. This perverse and false conclusion can by no means be deduced from our true and correct judgment. Our Lord's words, 'Make friends for yourselves with the mammon of wickedness,'[2] do not imply that we ought to add to our wickedness, to commit theft and rapine, so that we may enlarge our mercy and thus care for a greater number of saintly paupers. With the mammon of wickedness we should make friends who may receive us into everlasting dwellings; and from the wound of sin parents should beget children to be regenerated into eternal life. Just as we should not enlarge our wealth by wickedness, adding theft, fraud, pillaging, to provide for a greater number of needy just friends, so we should not add adultery, rape, fornication to the evil with which we are born, so that a more numerous progeny may be born

---
2 Luke 16.9.

from this source. It is one thing to make good use of an evil already in existence; quite another, to give rise to a new evil. The one is to produce a voluntary good out of an evil derived from the parents; the other is to add personal and voluntary evils to the evil derived from the parents. But there is certainly a difference. Using the mammon of wickedness for the needy is a laudable act, but restraint of carnal concupiscence by the virtue of continence is more laudable than its use for the fruits of marriage. The evil of carnal concupiscence is so great that it is better to refrain from using it than to use it well.

Chapter 8

(40) Next you introduce some other words of mine, and say a great deal of nothing against me, repeating what I have already answered in earlier arguments. If I indulged in the same sort of repetition, where would it all end? You make the futile allegation often used by your adherents against the grace of Christ: you say that in the name of grace we are saying that men are made good by fatal necessity, although those who are not yet able to talk oppose you strongly in voice and tongue. In your lengthy efforts to convince men of what Pelagius condemned in his audience by the Palestinian bishops, namely, that 'The grace of God is given according to our merits,' you do not mention any merits of infants through which those adopted as sons of God may be distinguished from those who die without receiving that grace.

(41) You calumniously assert that I say we should not expect any effort from the human will, since that would be contradictory to the passage of the Gospel where our Lord says: Ask and you shall receive; seek and you shall

find; knock and it shall be opened to you. For everyone who asks, receives; and he who seeks, finds; and to him who knocks, it shall be opened.'[1] Here it seems you already regard as merits preceding grace this asking, seeking, knocking, so that a due reward be given to such merits, and thus we speak in vain of grace, as though no grace had preceded and touched the heart that this blessed good might be asked of God, and sought of God, and that we might knock and, knocking, attain. In vain would it be written: 'His mercy shall prevent me';[2] in vain would be bidden to pray for our enemies,[3] if the conversion of averse and adverse hearts were not the work of grace.

(42) You cite an apostolic testimony, saying that God, who wishes all men to be saved and come to the knowledge of the truth,[4] opens to those who knock. You intend us to understand, by your teaching, that the reason all men are not saved and do not come to the knowledge of the truth is that they do not wish to ask, although God wishes to give; that they do not wish to seek, although God wishes to offer; that they do not wish to knock, although God wishes to open. By their very silence infants answer this notion of yours, for they neither ask, nor seek, nor knock—actually even while they are being baptized they sometimes scream, spit, and struggle against it—yet they receive and find it is opened to them, and they enter into the kingdom of God where they have eternal salvation and the knowledge of the truth. A far greater number of infants is not adopted for that grace by Him 'who wishes all men to be saved and come to the knowledge of the truth.' You cannot say to them: 'I would but thou wouldst not';[5] for, if He had willed,

---

1 Matt. 7.7,8.
2 Ps. 58.11.
3 Matt. 5.41.
4 Cf. 1 Tim. 2.4.
5 Matt. 23.37.

which of them who do not yet have the power to decide by their own will would have resisted His supremely almighty will? Then, why do we not accept the statement: 'Who wishes all men to be saved and come to the knowledge of the truth,' as we accept what the same Apostle says: 'From the justice of the one, the result is unto justification of life to all men'?[6] For God wishes that all those to whom grace comes through the justice of the One unto justification of life be saved and come to the knowledge of the truth. Else we may be asked: If God wishes all men to be saved and come to the knowledge of the truth, but they do not come because they do not wish to come, then why do so many infants dying without baptism not come to the kingdom of God where the knowledge of the truth is certain? Is it that they are not human beings, men, so that the words 'all men' do not apply to them? Could anyone say that God wishes indeed, but they do not wish, they who do not yet know how to wish or not to wish in such matters; when not even the infants who die after being baptized and, through that grace, come to the knowledge of the truth which is fully certain in the kingdom of God, when not even these come to the kingdom because of their own wish to be renewed by the baptism of Christ? If the reason the former are not baptized is not that they do not wish, and the reason the latter are baptized is not that they wish, then why does God, who wishes all men to be saved and come to the knowledge of the truth, not permit so many, who do not resist Him by any decision of their will, to come into His kingdom where there is certain knowledge of the truth?

(43) Perhaps you will say the reason that infants should not be counted in the number of all those whom God wishes to be saved is that infants are saved according to

---
6 Rom. 5.18.

the kind of salvation you understand herein: because, you say, they do not contract any sin. And, thus, a still geater absurdity follows. You make the benevolence of God greater for the most ungodly and most criminal than for the most innocent and the most free from every stain of sin. Because He wishes all the former to be saved, He must also wish that they enter into His kingdom, since this would follow if they are saved; but those who are not willing among them block up their own way. On the other hand, God does not wish to admit to His kingdom that immense number of infants who die without baptism, who, as you hold, are not impeded by any sin, and who, as no one doubts, cannot resist His will by a contrary will. It follows, then, that he wills all these to be Christians, but many of them are not willing; and He does not will all those to be Christians, yet none of them is unwilling. This is abhorrent to the truth. The Lord knows who are His,[7] and His will is certain about their salvation and entrance into His kingdom. Therefore, the statement, 'Who wishes all men to be saved and come to the knowledge of the truth,' should be interpreted as we interpret: 'From the justice of the one, the result is unto justification of life to all men.'

(44) If you think the apostolic testimony should be explained by saying that the word 'all' means the many who are justified in Christ (indeed, many others are not brought to life in Christ), you are answered that in the words, 'Who wishes all to be saved and come to the knowledge of the truth'—the 'all' means the many whom He wishes to come to the grace. It is much more fitting to say this, because no one comes but him whom He wishes to come. 'No one can come to me,' the Son says, 'unless the Father who sent me draw him' and 'No one can come to me unless it be given

---

7 Cf. 2 Tim. 2.19.

by him by my Father.'⁸ Therefore, all are saved and come to the knowledge of the truth at His willing it, and all come at His willing it. For those such as infants who do not as yet have the use of free will are regenerated by the will of Him through whose creative power they are generated; and those who have the actual use of free will cannot exercise it except through the will and assistance of Him by whom the will is prepared.

(45) If you ask me why He does not change the wills of all who are unwilling, I shall answer: Why does He not adopt through the laver of regeneration all infants who will die, whose wills are quiescent and, therefore, not contrary? If you found this too profound for you to investigate, it is profound for both of us, in both aspects: namely, why, both in adults and in infants, God wishes to help one and does not wish to help another. Nevertheless, we hold it to be certain and everlastingly firm that there is no injustice with God,¹⁰ so that He should condemn anyone who had done no wrong, and that there is goodness with God by which He delivers many without personal merit. In those He condemns we see what is due all, so that those He delivers may thence learn what due penalty was relaxed in their regard and what undue grace was given.

(46) You do not know how to consider these matters as becomes Christian hearts, and it is you who say they happen by fate. That is your statement, not ours: 'What is not the result of merit is the result of fate;' and, lest, according to your definition, whatever happens to men must happen by fate if it does not happen by merit, you do your best to assert both good and evil merit, lest denying merit you

---

8 John 6.44,66.
9 Cf. Prov. 8 (Septuagint).
10 Cf. Rom. 9.14.

have only fate. Thus, someone can make the following argument against you. First, you say that, if men are given things without personal merit, then there must be fate. Thus, we must admit merit, you say, for, if there is no merit, there must be fate. Therefore, infants, with no personal merit, are baptized by fate, and enter into the kingdom by fate; again, infants, with no demerit, are by fate not baptized, and by fate do not enter into the kingdom of God. Behold, sucklings unable to talk convict you of asserting fate. By our doctrine of the demerit or desert due to vitiated origin, however, we say one infant enters into the kingdom of God by grace,. because God is good; another infant deservedly does not enter, because God is just; there is no question of fate in either case, because God does what He wishes. But, although we know that one is condemned according to the judgment, and another is delivered according to the mercy, of Him whose mercy and judgment we praise with confidence,[11] who are we to ask God why He condemns the one instead of the other? Shall the object moulded say to him who moulded it: 'Why hast thou made me thus?' Is not the potter master of his clay, to make from the same mass of vitiated and condemned origin one vessel for honorable use according to mercy, and another for dishonorable use according to judgment?[12] He does not make both for honorable use, lest the nature think itself to have merited honor, as if guiltless; He does not make both for dishonorable use, that mercy may triumph over judgment.[13] Therefore, the condemned has no right to complain about his punishment, nor can the one gratuitously delivered glory proudly over his merit. Instead, he humbly gives thanks when he recognizes in

---
11 Cf. Ps. 100.1.
12 Cf. Rom. 9.20,21.
13 Cf. James 2.13.

the one required to pay the debt what under the same circumstances was bestowed upon himself.

(47) You assert that in another book I said: 'Free choice is denied if grace is commended; and, again, grace is denied if free choice is commended.' You slander me; this is not what I said, although because of the difficulty of this question it can seem and be thought that it was said. I do not object to giving my exact words, so that readers may see how you misrepresent my writings and how you take advantage of the incompetent or the ignorant, who mistake your loquacity for argument. In the last part of my first book to St. Pinianus, entitled *De gratia contra Pelagium,* I said: 'The problem of free will involves distinctions so difficult to make that, when free choice is defended, the grace of God seems to be denied; and, when the grace of God is asserted, free choice seems to be denied.'[14] You, an honest and truthful man, left out some of my words and gave your own construction. I said it is difficult to understand that problem; I did not say it is impossible to understand it; much less did I say what you falsely record as my words, 'Free choice is denied if grace is commended, and grace is denied if free choice is commended.' Report me correctly, and your slander vanishes. Put my words in their setting where I said 'seems,' and where I said 'it is thought,' and your deception in this important matter is revealed. I did not say that grace is denied, but that it seems grace is denied. I did not say that free choice is denied or lost, but that it is thought to be lost. And you promise that when the books themselves are examined, the ungodliness of my statements will be laid bare and destroyed. Who will look for wisdom in the disputant when he has seen the reliability of the liar?

(48) When you say: 'One does not praise grace by saying it gives to its own that which sins give to the ungodly,' you

---
14 *De gratia Christi* 52.

refer to conjugal modesty, which you think the ungodly possess. Contentious man, true virtue, not something fictitious or non-existent, is given through grace. But how do you unite modesty and virginity as though they were of the same kind? Modesty belongs to the soul; virginity, to the body. The body can lose virginity by violence, while modesty remains unharmed in the soul; and virginity may be unharmed in the body while modesty is corrupted in the soul by a wanton will. For this reason, I said, not true marriage or widowhood or virginity, but true modesty: 'We cannot speak of true modesty, be it conjugal or widowly or virginal, unless it be united with the true faith.'[15] They can indeed be spouses, or widows, or virgins, and not be modest, when they commit fornication through a vitiated will or think impurely about lustful actions. You say they have true modesty even with fornication in soul, of which all the ungodly are guilty according to Scripture.

(49) Who says: 'Evil exists in the conjugal members,' when marriage uses well the evil of concupiscence for the purpose of propagating children? This concupiscence would not be an evil if it were moved only to lawful union for the sole purpose of generating; but, as it is, conjugal modesty, resisting it, becomes the limit of evil and is therefore a good. Your slander, that 'Its crime goes unpunished because of religion,' is false because no crime is committed when someone, through a good coming from faith, uses well the evil of lust. Nor can it be said here, as you think: 'Let us do evil that good may come from it;'[16] because there is no evil in marriage as marriage. In those who were begotten by parents, the evil which marriage did not produce in them, but only discovered there, does not belong to marriage itself. In the case of the first couple, who had no

---
15 *De nuptiis* 1.5.
16 Rom. 3.8.

parents, the discordant evil of carnal concupiscence which marriage uses well was the result of sin, and not of marriage, which does not deserve condemnation from that evil. Why do you ask whether I should call the pleasure of intercourse of Christian spouses modesty or immodesty? Hear my answer: Not the pleasure, but the good use of that evil, is called modesty, and, because of the good use, the evil itself cannot be called immodesty. Immodesty is the shameful use of that same evil, just as virginal modesty is the refraining from using it; therefore, without detriment to conjugal modesty, evil is contracted from evil in birth, and it is to be purged in rebirth.

(50) 'But if the offspring even of the Christian spouses is brought forth stained with fault because of the evil of lust, it follows that virginal modesty is the bearer of happiness, and, since it is found in the ungodly,' as you say, 'those unbelievers who rise to the heights in the virtue of modesty will surpass the Christians who are disfigured by the plague of lust.' It is not as you say; you are greatly mistaken. Those who use lust well are not disfigured by the plague of lust, although they indeed generate those who are disfigured by the plague of lust and must therefore be regenerated. Nor is virginal modesty found in the ungodly, although virginity of the flesh may be found in them. True modesty cannot exist in a soul committing fornication. Therefore, the virginal good of the ungodly is not to be preferred to the conjugal good of the faithful. Spouses using this evil well are preferred to virgins who use that good in an evil way; therefore, when married persons use well the evil of lust, it is not true, as your slander says, that 'They enjoy impunity because of the faith.' Because of their faith, their chastity is a true, not a false, virtue.

(51) How are we concerned with your charge that the Manichaeans assert: 'He who with his conscience threatening

him commits murder is guilty because of his apprehensiveness, but, if he commits a crime with braggadocio, convinced that what he does in an evil way he does out of faith, he escapes guilt'? I never heard the Manichaeans say this. But, what if they actually say it, or you also slander them?—the Catholic faith, which we hold, and whose power we are urging on you, does not say this. We say that works which seem to be good works are not truly good without faith, because truly good works must be pleasing to God, whom it is impossible to please without faith.[17] Therefore, a truly good work cannot exist without faith. But the faith that works through love does not do works that are obviously evil, because love of neighbor does no evil.[18]

(52) You say: 'Therefore, natural concupiscence is good' (you are ashamed to call it carnal concupiscence) which, when it is kept in its moderated way, cannot be degraded by any aspersion of evil.' I ask you how it is kept in its moderated way; how it is kept there, except by being resisted? Why it is resisted, except to keep it from carrying out evil desires? Then, how is it good?

Chapter 9

(53) You refer to those words of my first book: 'Were not the first spouses, whose marriage God blessed, saying, "Increase and multiply," naked, and they were not ashamed?'[1] Then, why did embarrassment arise from those members after sin, unless there was an unseemly movement there, such as undeniably would not have existed in marriage

---

17 Cf. Heb. 11.6.
18 Cf. Gal. 5.6; Rom. 13.10.

---

1 Cf. Gen. 1.28; 2.25.

if men had not sinned?[2] When you saw my words so written in accordance with the Scripture that whoever has read this part of the Book of Genesis cannot hesitate to agree with what I said, you expended much effort in your contradictory prolixity, but you lack sincerity. You remained in your own evil judgment, although experience has shown you that you cannot overcome my true judgment. I shall pass over the gesticulations and violent contortions in your contradiction, as those of a man panting, unable to reach his goal, and, in the dust in which he envelops himself, pretending to have reached it. With the help of the Lord I shall lay hold of and destroy the essential parts of your argument, so that whoever reads carefully your works and mine may see the whole body lying in defeat—especially since the things you repeat in so great variety of forms have so often been fully answered by us.

(54) Among other things, you say that I thought I could show that God instituted an etherial marriage, because the first men in their embarrassment covered the members where lust arises. If marriage without lust must be etherial, it follows, on your authority, that bodies will be etherial where there will be no lust. Or do you so love lust that you force it upon risen bodies, as you also place it in paradise before sin? I do not deny, as you would have me deny, that 'the natural is that without which the nature does not exist,' but I say that that fault without which human nature is not born at present is called natural, yet it was not so constituted at the beginning. Therefore, this evil derives its origin, not from the first institution of the nature, but from the evil will of the first man; and it will not remain, but will either be condemned or healed.

(55) You compare my opinion to one of those insects which 'gives a foul stench after it has been crushed, just

---

2 *De nuptiis* 1.6.

as it is a nuisance when alive,' as though you were ashamed, as you say, to try to conquer me by crushing me, or that you are 'loathe to follow and destroy the filth' in which I took refuge. The reason you give is that your modesty, 'like the keeper of a temple, prohibits freedom of speech' in parts of the argument in which you might wear me down and destroy me, because you would be obliged to talk about shameful things. Why do you not prefer to talk about the good things you praise? Why do you not speak freely about the work of God, if its dignity remains inviolate and there is no sin from which it might rather produce modesty and repress freedom of speech?

Chapter 10

(56) You say: 'If there is no marriage without lust, then whoever condemns lust in general must also condemn marriage.' You could likewise say that all mortals must be condemned because death will be condemned. But, if lust belonged to marriage itself, there would be no lust before or outside marriage. You say: 'That without which there is no marriage cannot be called a disease, because there can be marriage without sin, while the Apostle says disease is sin.' We answer that not every disease is called sin. This disease is that punishment for sin without which human nature not yet healed in every part cannot exist. If lust were rightly said not to be evil simply because there can be no good of marriage without it, then, contrariwise, the body would not be good because without it there cannot be the evil of adultery. This is false; hence, the other is also false. Everyone knows that the Apostle was speaking to the married, commanding each to know how to possess his own vessel, that is, his wife, not in the disease of desire

like the Gentiles who do not know God.[1] Whoever reads what the Apostle says about this matter will pass you by. Do you not blush to introduce into Paradise and to attribute to the spouses before sin that disease, that lust, which you also shamefacedly admit to exist? Are you not covered with filth, crowning yourself, as it were, with the lust of flesh and blood as in a rose-colored flower of Paradise? And, as though gladly flushed with that color, you both blush and praise.

Chapter 11

(57) Does talking give you so much pleasure that you must try by a superfluous abundance of words to prove something we confess and teach, as though we denied it? Who denies that marriage would have existed even if sin had not preceded it? But it was to have existed so that the reproductive members would be moved by the will, like the other members, not aroused by lust; or (not to burden you with sorrow about lust) they would not have been aroused by lust such as now exists, but by lust obedient to the will. You labor so faithfully for your protege that you will endure force rather than not give lust, as it now is, a place in Paradise; not holding that it came from sin there, but that it would have existed if none had sinned. Thus, lust would have had to be opposed in that peace, or, if not opposed, would have had to be satisfied upon its demand. Alas for the holy delights of Paradise! Alas for the crowns of all bishops! Alas for the faith of all chaste men!

---
1 Cf. 1 Thess. 4.4-5.

Chapter 12

(58) In trying to show that not all things that are covered should be thought shameful because of sin, you make a multitude of vain observations about many parts which are covered by nature in our body, as though they, too, had been covered only after sin, when, you say, the first men made coverings after sin for parts neither shameful nor covered before sin. 'In Tully's book,' you say, 'Balbus and Cotta discuss the matter truly and carefully.'[1] You say you wrote down a few remarks to make me feel ashamed that I did not understand, under the guidance of sacred Law, concepts the Gentiles were able to attain by reason alone. You quote from Cicero the words of Balbus, to teach us what the Stoics held about the differentiation of male and female in dumb animals, and about the reproductive parts of the body and the astonishing lusts involved in carnal commerce. Nevertheless, before you quoted the words, whether they are Tully's or someone else's, you prefaced very carefully: 'He touches upon the difference of the sexes when he discusses beasts, for the sake of seemliness; he omits it in his description of man.' What do you mean by saying it is for the sake of seemliness? Is seemliness confounded in the sex of man, where God makes it more worthy as being in a more excellent nature? The Stoics have taught you to dispute about what is hidden; they did not teach you to blush about the shameful. You say: 'He gives a verbal description of man himself, showing the subjection of the stomach to the esophagus, being the receptacle of food and drink, while the lungs and heart draw the air from the outside. He names many wonderful effects in the multiple and tortuous stomach, which consists of sinews, and contains and protects what it receives, be it dry or moist'; and other observations of the

---
1 *De natura deorum* 2.

same kind, until you come to the part about how 'waste food is expelled by the alternating contraction and relaxation of the intestines.' Since he could also have described these processes in beasts, why did he choose man there, unless it be such things are not shameful, just as the facts about the reproductive members are not shameful in beasts, although they are shameful in man—the very reason, indeed, they were covered by fig leaves after sin. For, when his description of the human body approaches the extremity where the waste food is expelled, he says: 'It is not difficult to say how this takes place, but we shall omit it lest the discussion become somewhat unpleasant.' He does not say, lest it be embarrassing, or become somewhat shameful, but 'lest it become somewhat unpleasant.' Some things offend the senses because they are deformed; some make the mind ashamed, even though beautiful. The former detract from pleasure, the latter arouse lust, or are aroused by lust.

(59) How do these observations help you? You say: 'Because our Creator did not recognize any fault in His art obliging Him to hide so carefully our vital members.' God forbid that so great a craftsman recognize any fault in His art. But you yourself told us a while back why He covered them: 'Lest these members perish or offend.' But the members which the first couple covered were not in danger of perishing, nor did they offend when they were naked and were not ashamed.[2] The caution of modesty now keeps us from viewing those members, lest the seeing be not offensive, but pleasing. It is futile to hope the testimony of the Stoics could help your protege, no friend of theirs, for they find no particle of human good in the pleasure of the body. Moreover, they, as you, chose to praise lust in beasts rather than in man. Tully is quite in accord with their opinion when he says somewhere that he does not believe the good of a ram is the same as that of

---

2 Cf. Gen. 3.7; 2.25.

Publius Africanus. You had better follow his judgment in what you ought to hold about human lust.

(60) It gives us pleasure to discuss such writings, because some vestiges of truth are found in them. Meanwhile, I think you now admit that the words you quoted are of no avail against us. Note how my next answer will destroy your argument. In Book 3 of the *Republic,* the same Tully says that man 'was brought into life by nature, not as a mother, but as by a stepmother; naked, fragile, and weak in body, his soul much troubled, humbled by fears, soft in labors, prone to lust. In him, however, as though buried within, there is a divine spark of character and intellect.' What do you say to this? Tully did not say that this effect came from their evil conduct; rather, he blamed nature. He saw the reality, but did not know the cause. The reason there is a heavy yoke upon the children of Adam from the day of their coming out of their mother's womb until the day of their burial into the mother of all[3] was unknown to him, for he was not taught by sacred Scripture; he did not know original sin. If, however, he had sensed goodness about the lust you defend, the soul's proneness to lusts would not have displeased him.

(61) If you defend these things as a lesser good to which the soul, turning from the higher, ought not to incline—not because lust is a fault, but because it is only a slight good—then hear what Tully says more clearly, in the same Book 3, when he speaks of the science of ruling. 'Do we not see,' he says, 'that, to each thing which is best, dominion is given by nature herself, to the greatest advantage of the least things? Why does God command man; the soul, the body; reason, lust, anger, and the other vicious forces in the soul?' Do you see from his teaching how he must confess that the things you defend as good are vicious forces in the soul? Hear more. He says a little later: 'We should recognize different kinds

---

3 Cf. Eccli. 40.1.

of commanding and serving. The soul is said to command the body; it is also said to command lust. It commands the body as a king commands his subjects or a parent his children. It commands lust as a master commands a slave, since it coerces and breaks it. Kings, emperors, magistrates, fathers, peoples rule their subjects and associates as the soul rules the body. Masters harass their slaves as the best part of the soul, which is wisdom, harasses the vicious and weak parts of the same soul, such as lusts, anger, and the other disturbing forces.' Have you even more to say against us from authors of secular books? If you are looking for something to say in defense of your error (may God keep you from this) against the renowned bishops who treated of divine Scripture, if you seek to offer resistance to these holy men, will you not be bound to say Tully was foolish and as one demented? Hold your tongue about such books, and do not try insultingly to teach us anything from them; or testimonies you thought would sustain you will actually crush you.

Chapter 13

(62) Why did you foolishly think you could make an argument about the movement in the woman, of which she was also ashamed? It was not a visible movement the woman covered, when, in the same members, she sensed something hidden but comparable to what the man sensed, and they blushed at the mutual attraction, either each for each, or the one for the other. Your idle talk 'begs that modest hearers forgive and groan rather than take offense at this necessity.' Why does it embarrass you to discuss the works of God? Why do you ask to be forgiven for it? Does not your plea for pardon itself accuse lust? You say: 'If the male member had also been active before sin, then the offense introduced

nothing new.' It could certainly have been active earlier, but it was not then unbecoming so as to cause shame, because it was moved only by the command of the will, not by the flesh lusting against the spirit. Here we find the shameful newness which your innovation shamelessly defends. I have never, as you say, 'devotedly' found fault with the movement of the reproductive members in general, but I find fault with the movement produced by the concupiscence by which the flesh lusts against the spirit. When your error defends lust as a good, I do not know how your spirit lusts against it as an evil.

(63) You say: 'If this lust was in the fruit of that tree, it must come from God and must be defended as good.' We answer you that lust was not in the fruit of the tree; hence, the tree was good. But the disobedience of lust is evil and it arose against the disobedience that man committed in reference to the tree, God leaving him to himself. Never be it said that God might confer such a benefit from the good tree on any age of human life at any time that they would have an adversary in their members against which modesty would have to struggle.

(64) We know that 'The Apostle John did not find fault with the world, that is, the heavens and the earth and all the things that are in it as substances; it was made by the Father through the Son; for he said: "Because all that is in the world is the concupiscence of the flesh, and the concupiscence of the eyes, and the pride of life, which is not from the Father but is from the world".'[1] We know this, and I do not want you to teach it to us. But when you, wishing to explain the concupiscence of the flesh which he says is not from the Father, say that it should be explained as meaning licentiousness, I ask you what a man consents to if there is licentiousness, or what he fights against lest it exist; and then

---
1 1 John 2.16.

we are confronted with your protege. Will you continue to praise a thing such that there is licentiousness when you consent to it, and continence when you oppose it? I marvel that you must deliberate whether to revile it together with the licentiousness brought into being through assent to it, or to praise it along with the continence which wages against it the war in which modesty is the victory of continence, and licentiousness the victory of concupiscence. You would be an uncorrupted and honest judge if you praised continence and reviled concupiscence, but, as it is, you show partiality to the person of concupiscence (you should ask yourself why you fear to offend it), so that you do not blush to praise it together with its adversary, and you do not dare to revile it in its victory. God forbid that any man of God heed your vilification of licentiousness to approve your praises of concupiscence and believe from your words that that which he knows by personal experience to be evil is good. He who fights and conquers the concupiscence you basely praise will not possess the licentiousness you correctly revile. How shall we obey the Apostle John if we love the concupiscence of the flesh? You will answer: 'I do not praise that kind of concupiscence.' And what is the concupiscence John says is not from the Father? 'Licentiousness,' you say. But we are not licentious unless we love the concupiscence you praise; thus, when he says: 'Do not love the concupiscence of the flesh,' he does not wish us to be licentious. Thus, we are forbidden to love the concupiscence of the flesh you praise when we are forbidden licentiousness. But, what we are forbidden to love is not from the Father; hence, the concupiscence you praise is not from the Father. Two good things from the Father cannot be at odds with each other, and continence and concupiscence are at odds with each other. Answer which you want to say is from the Father. I see you are distressed, since you favor concupiscence but blush for continence. Let your modesty conquer and let your error be conquered by it. Since continence, which opposes the concupiscence of the flesh, is from the Father, receive from the Father the continence at whose exclusion you would rightly blush and overcome the concupiscence your perversity praised.

Chapter 14

(65) You saw fit to call the pleasures of all the senses to your assistance, as though the pleasure of the reproductive members would not be a sufficient advocate for itself without this auxiliary force. You say: 'We would have to admit that the senses of sight, hearing, taste, smell, and touch were conferred on us, not by God, but by the Devil, if we conceded that that concupiscence of the flesh we fight against through continence did not exist in Paradise before sin, and that it came from the sin which the Devil first persuaded man to commit.' You do not know, or pretend not to know that the quality, the usefulness, and the necessity of sensation through a sense of the body are not the same as lust for this sensation. The quality of sensation enables one according to his capacity to perceive the truth in corporeal things corresponding to their mode and nature, and to distinguish more or less accurately the true from the false. The usefulness of sensation enables us to judge things by way of approval or disapproval, acceptance or rejection, seeking or avoidance, in reference to our body and our way of life. Necessity for sensation arises when things we do not desire are borne in upon our senses. The lust for sensation with which we are here concerned impels us by the appetite of carnal concupiscence to sense something, whether we mentally consent to or resist it. This is contrary to love of wisdom and inimical

to the virtues; and, in regard to that part of it involved in the union of the sexes, it is the evil well used by marriage when the spouses procreate children through it and do nothing for its sake only. If you had wished or had been able to distinguish it from the quality, the usefulness, and the necessity of sensation, you would see how many useless things you said. Our Lord did not say: 'Whoever shall look on a woman,' but: 'Whoever shall look on a woman to lust after her has already committed adultery with her in his heart.'[1] Consider: He has briefly and clearly distinguished the sense of sight from the lust for sensation, as you would see if you were not obstinate. God made the one when He equipped the human body; the Devil sowed the seed for the other when he persuaded man to sin.

(66) Let godly men praise the heavens and earth and all they contain; but let it be in consideration of their beauty, not through ardent lust. A religious man and a miser praise the glory of gold in different ways; the one, piously to venerate the Creator; the other, in lust to possess the creature. The soul may indeed be moved to sentiments of piety upon hearing a divine hymn, yet even in this, if it is lust for the sound and not for the meaning, it cannot be approved; how much less, if delight is found in empty or even objectionable ditties? The other three senses are more like the body, and quite coarse, in a way, and their action is accomplished within the body, not projecting themselves outward. Odor is distinct from that which smells it; savor, from that which tastes; touch, for the most part, is distinct from that which touches, for smooth and rough are not the same as hot and cold; nor are these the same as the soft and hard, and heavy and light are different from all of them. When we act to avoid nuisances in all these sensible things, we are looking to our convenience, not lusting for pleasure. We may appropriately

---

1 Matt. 5.28.

receive the contraries of such nuisances provided none of them interferes with our health or our avoidance of pain or effort, yet those things should not be desired with lust when they are absent, though we receive them with a certain delight when present. It is not good to desire them, for such appetite must be brought under control and healed, no matter what its objects. What man, however carefully he disciplines carnal concupiscence, can, upon entering a room filled with the odor of incense, prevent it from smelling sweetly to him, unless he holds his nose or, by a very powerful act of the will, nullifies the senses of his body? But when he has left that room, will he desire it at his home, or wherever he has gone? And if he desires it, should he satisfy the desire, not restrain it, and thus not lust in spirit against the lusting flesh until he returns it to that health in which he will desire nothing of this sort? This is indeed the minimum, for 'He that contemneth small things shall fall by little and little.'[2]

(67) We need food for sustenance, but, when what is taken by mouth is not sweet, it cannot be retained and may often be spit out because of nausea; and we must also guard against harmful squeamishness. Therefore, the weak body needs not only food, but also the taste of food, not to satisfy lust, but to protect health. When nature in its way demands supplements which are absent, we do not say this is lust, but hunger or thirst. When the need has been satisfied, yet the love of eating tempts the soul, then we have lust, then we have the evil to which a man must not yield, but must resist. The poet described the two, hunger and the love of eating, when, judging that the companions of shipwrecked and wandering Aeneas had taken as much food as the need for refreshment requires, after the buffeting by the sea, he said: 'When hunger had been satisfied and the tables were

---

2 Eccli. 19.1.

removed.'³ But when Aeneas himself was a guest of King Evander, the poet thought it more seemly to show that royal banquets were more ample than necessity required. He was not content to say: 'When hunger had been satisfied'; he added, 'and the love of eating suppressed.'⁴ Much more, then, ought we to recognize the need for nourishment and distinguish it from the demands of lust for eating, since we are to lust in spirit against the lusting flesh, and to be delighted with the law of God according to the inner man, and not by lustful pleasures to cloud the serenity of our delight with the law. For that love of eating is to be controlled, not by eating, but by restraint.

(68) What sober-minded man would not prefer to take food, dry or moist, without any stinging carnal pleasure, if he could, as the air he draws in and lets out into the surrounding air by inhaling and exhaling? This food, consumed continually through mouth and nose, neither tastes nor smells, yet we cannot live without it even the shortest time, whereas we can live a very long time without meat and drink. We do not sense our need for air except when an obstruction closes our mouth and nose or, as much as the interference itself permits, we voluntarily inhibit the function of the lungs in which, as though by a bellows, we draw in and breathe out the vital draughts by alternating movement. How much more happy it would be if for long intervals we could, as we do even now, or for longer ones, take meat and drink without any of the enticing sweetness of taste, and thus get rid of a very great nuisance and danger? Those who in this life take food temperately are said to be continent and sober, and they deserve praise for it; there are some who take only as much as nature demands, or even less, preferring, if mistaken about the amount needed, to take less rather than

---
3 Virgil, *Aeneas* 1.216.
4 *Ibid.* 8.184.

more. Much more, then, should we believe that the honest way of taking food, in which the needs were taken care of and the natural measure never exceeded, existed in that dignity in which we believe the first men lived in Paradise.

(69) Although some writers on holy Scripture, by no means the least, are of the opinion that the first men did not need such food at all, so that only the pleasure and nourishment which delights and sustains the hearts of the wise could have existed in Paradise, I myself hold with those who, considering the words, 'Male and female he created them, saying, Increase and multiply and fill the earth,' interpret them as referring to visible and bodily sex. Hence, in view of what follows, 'And God said: Behold, I have given you every herb bearing seed upon the earth and all trees that have seed of their own kind to be your meat, and to all the beasts and to every fowl of the air and to all that move upon the earth and wherein there is life, that they may have to feed upon,'[5] they accept it in the sense that both sexes used the food for the body which the other animals used, and received fitting sustenance from it; that this was necessary for the animal body lest it suffer by want; but it was received in a certain immortal way, and from the tree of life, lest they die of old age. I would never believe that, in a place of such great happiness, either the flesh lusted against the spirit and the spirit against the flesh, and there was no internal peace; or that the spirit did not war against carnal desires, but carried out in the base service of lust everything lust suggested. We conclude, therefore, either that there was no carnal concupiscence in that place, but such was the manner of life that all necessities were taken care of by the proper functions of the members, without arousing lust (for the fact that the earth is not sowed by lust but by the voluntary actions of the farmers' hands does not make it true that

---

5 Gen. 1.27-30.

the earth does not itself conceive the fruits it bears); or, lest we seem too offensive to those who defend howsoever the body's pleasure, we may believe that in that place there was lusting of the carnal senses, but that, subject in every way to the rational will, it existed only when men needed to take cognizance of it for the health of the body or the progeny of the race; and then it in no way kept the mind from delight in lofty thoughts, and there was no meaningless or importune disturbance from it, and it contributed only to their advantage, and nothing whatever was done for its sake only.

(70) Those especially who war against lust know what a change has taken place. Whoever sees or hears anything, though seeing or hearing for some other purpose, is forced to recognize, even when not aware of any pleasure of touch, that a voluptuous thought may suddenly appear in matters not essentially allied with pleasure. Even when there is no attraction before the eyes, no sound in the ears, will not this thought, be it never so dormant or trite, seek to arouse disquieting memories associated with base pleasures and crowd in upon chaste and holy intentions with a certain uproar of sordid interruptions? When we come to the use of the pleasure needed to refresh our body, who can put in words how it will not permit us to find the measure of necessity and the limit for procuring health, but conceals them and passes them by, drawing us to whatever delectable things may be present; so that we think what is enough is not enough and freely follow its provocation, serving gluttony under the illusion of health? This evil we do is attested in drunkenness; heavy drinkers often eat less than enough to take away hunger. Thus, coveting knows not where necessity ends.

(71) The pleasure in eating and drinking may be tolerated when, with the strongest effort of will we can muster, we are

satisfied with less, rather than go to excess in food. We oppose this concupiscence by fasting and taking food sparingly; we use well this evil when we use it for nought but what is conducive to health. I say such pleasure may be tolerated, because its power is not so great that it interrupts and turns us away from thoughts of wisdom, if we should be engaged in such mental delight. We often not only think, but even dispute, about important matters at feasts, even between morsels of food and sips of drink; we pay close attention when listening and speaking; we learn what we wish to know, or recall if it is read to us. But that pleasure about which you argue with me so contentiously, does it not engage the whole soul and body, and does not this extremity of pleasure result in a kind of submersion of the mind itself, even if it is approached with a good intention, that is, for the purpose of procreating children, since in its very operation it allows no one to think, I do not say of wisdom, but of anything at all? But, when it overcomes even the married, so that they come together, not for propagation, but for carnal delight, which the Apostle says is concession not command,[6] and after that whirlpool the mind emerges and inhales, as it were, the air of thought, it may follow, as someone has truly said, that it regrets that close association with pleasure. What lover of the spiritual good, who has married only for the sake of offspring, would not prefer if he could to propagate children without it or without its very great impulsion? I think, then, we ought to attribute to that life in Paradise, which was a far better life than this, whatever saintly spouses would prefer in this life, unless we can think of something better.

(72) I beg you, do not let the philosophy of Gentiles be more honest than our Christian philosophy, which is the one true philosophy, for its name means the quest or love

---

6 Cf. 1 Cor. 7.6.

of wisdom. Consider Tully's words in the dialogue *Hortensius*,[7] which should delight you more than those of Balbus, who takes the part of the Stoics. What he says is true, but it concerns the inferior part of man, that is, his body, and it could not help you. See what he says about the quality of the mind over against the pleasure of the body. He says: 'Should one seek the pleasures of the body, which, as Plato said truly and earnestly, are the enticements and baits of evil? What injury to health, what deformity of character and body, what wretched loss, what dishonor is not evoked and elicited by pleasure? Where its action is the most intense, it is the most inimical to philosophy. The pleasure of the body is not in accord with great thought. Who can pay attention or follow a reasoning or think anything at all when under the influence of intense pleasure? The whirlpool of this pleasure is so great that it strives day and night, without the slightest intermission, so to arouse our senses that they be drawn into the depths. What fine mind would not prefer that nature had given us no pleasures at all?' These are words of one who had no belief concerning the life of the first man, the happiness of paradise, or the resurrection of bodies. Let us, then, who have learned in the true and holy philosophy of true godliness that the flesh lusts against the spirit and the spirit against the flesh,[8] blush as we hear the true judgments of the ungodly. Cicero did not understand this, yet he did not favor the concupiscence of the flesh as you do. Indeed, he vigorously condemned it; you not only do not do so, but you even become violently angry with those who do so. It is you who, like a cowardly soldier, thus praise the concupiscence both of the spirit and of the flesh, which oppose each other within you, as though you were afraid to have for an enemy the lust which would conquer the lust

---

7 This work is not extant.
8 Cf. Gal. 5.17.

of the spirit. Do not fear; act instead, and praise the concupiscence of the spirit, fighting the more keenly, the more chastely. You must fearlessly condemn the law warring against the law of your mind, by means of that same law of the mind against which it wars.

(73) Consideration of beauty, even corporeal beauty, whether visible as in colors and shapes, or audible as in songs and melodies, a consideration proper only to a rational mind, is not the same as the stirring of lust, which must be restrained by reason. The Apostle John says the concupiscence which lusts against the spirit is not from the Father.[9] None says it is good except he whose spirit does not love to lust against it. If the concupiscence in the action and heat of the reproductive members is not such as this, the spirit must not lust against it, lest, lusting against the gift of God, it be found ungrateful. Instead, let whatever it desires be given to it, since it is from the Father. If we are unable to give it its desire, let us ask the Father, not to remove or suppress it, but to satisfy the concupiscence He gave. If this wisdom is folly, then how can we liken concupiscence to food and wine and think we say something sensible when we say: 'Drunkenness does not condemn wine, nor does gluttony condemn food; and obscenity does not defame concupiscence,' when there is no drunkenness or gluttony or obscenity if the concupiscence of the flesh is conquered by the spirit which lusts against it? You say: 'Its excess is culpable.' You do not see, as you could very easily see if you were more eager to conquer it than me, that to avoid the evil of excess you must resist the evil of concupiscence itself. There are, then, two evils here. One of them is with us; the other we bring about if we do not resist the one with us.

(74) I stated above[10] that this is not an evil in beasts,

---

9 Cf. 1 John 2.16.
10 Above, pp. 199-200.

because in them it does not lust against the spirit. They lack the power of reason with which to subject lusts by overcoming them or to weary them by warfare. Who tells you that 'Sinning comes always from imitating beasts'? You strove at great length to refute this proposition which no one stated as an objection to you, and you idly assembled many of the observations about brutes which are used in the science of medicine. Although concupiscence is a good in a brute, to delight a nature unable to desire wisdom, let no one on that score think that the concupiscence of the flesh is not an evil. It is said to be a good for the brute, whose spirit it delights without opposition, but an evil for man, in whom it lusts against the spirit.

Chapter 15

(75) You have also invoked a great number of philosophers, so that, if the natural adroitness of brutes cannot help your protege, at least the errors of learned men may do so. But who does not see that you were seeking vainglory when you listed the names and different schools of learned men, since, on careful reading of your words, we see this has no bearing on our question? Let us read the list you have compiled: 'Thales of Miletus, one of the seven wise men; then Anaximander, Anaximenes, Anaxagoras, Xenophanes, Parmenides, Leucippus, Democritus, Empedocles, Heraclitus, Melissus, Plato, and the Pythagoreans'—each with his own dogma about natural phenomena. Who can hear this list and not be frightened by the clamor of names and the banding of schools, if he, as the majority of men, is not a scholar and think that you, who know such things, must be really important? That is the praise you sought, yet with all these names you have said nothing relevant to the matter

we are considering. You prefaced them with the statement: 'All the philosophers, when engaged in other matters, indeed worshiped idols with the people, yet when they tried to understand physical causes, with their many false opinions, they also grasped some truth which we may justly prefer to the vain obscurity of this dogma we are opposing.' To prove this you list the names of the natural philosophers I have just mentioned, together with their opinions about physical causes; either you would not or could not list them all. Here you deceived not the learned, but the inexperienced. You proposed to demonstrate that 'All the philosophers who have tried to understand physical causes can justly be preferred to this dogma we are opposing.' When you mentioned Anaximenes and his disciple Anaxagoras, not to mention the many other names, you were silent about another of his disciples, Diogenes, who, disagreeing with his teacher and with his fellow disciple, proposed his own dogma about the nature of things. If his theory disqualifies him from being preferred to us, what about all those who have philosophized about the nature of things, all of whom, according to you, should be preferred to us? That you might show this, have you not foolishly displayed your vanity in this useless enumeration of names and dogmas of philosophers? But you omitted one you should have noted, either in connection with his teacher or with his fellow disciple. Perhaps you feared your readers might think this was Diogenes the Cynic, and, thinking of the one of the same name, they might recall that the latter was a better patron of lust than you, since he was not ashamed to exercise it in public; whence that sect is known as Cynics, or Dogs. You, however, profess to be a champion of lust, but you blush for your protege; this ill becomes the fidelity and freedom of a patron.

(76) I ask you, if you prefer the philosophers to us, why did you not mention, instead, those expressly treating of

morals, that part of philosophy they call ethics and we call moral philosophy? This would have been most fitting for you who think the pleasure of the body is one of man's goods, although you admit it is a good inferior to the solid goodness of the mind. But who does not see the prospect confronting you? You feared lest you be thwarted in our discussion about pleasure by those more sound philosophers whom Cicero called a kind of consular philosophers because of their soundness, as well as by the Stoics themselves, most inimical to pleasure, whose testimony you thought should be quoted from Cicero's book, in the person of Balbus, but which was in no way helpful to you.[1] However, wishing to conceal their opinion that the pleasure of the body is not a good for man, you did not wish to mention the names and dogmas of philosophers concerned with moral questions, although this must be of prime importance if anything is to be proved from the philosophers. I shall not cite Epicurus, who put the whole good of man in the pleasure of the body, because you do not agree with him; let us take Dinomachus, whose dogma pleased you.[2] He taught that pleasure should be joined with moral soundness, so that pleasure, like moral soundness, might seem justly desirable in itself, just as moral soundness is desirable in itself;[3] but, when you observed that his discussion of morals is hostile to you, you feared to touch it. You see the number and character of the philosophers of great renown among the Gentiles, who must be preferred to you; especially so in our controversy. Before all is Plato himself, whom Cicero did not hesitate to call almost the god of philosophers.[4] Not even you could pass his name by when you were hurling against or preferring to our teaching the

---

[1] Above, p. 216.
[2] This philosopher and his teaching are discussed by Cicero (*De finibus* 5.8) and by Clement of Alexandria (*Strom.* 2.31).
[3] Cf. Cicero, *De finibus* 5; *Tuscul. qu.* 5.
[4] *De natura deorum* 2; *Ad Atticum*, Ep. 16.

physical, not the moral, dogmas of the philosophers. Plato said truly and earnestly that the pleasures of the body are the enticements and baits of evil.[5]

(77) Did you not think your cause somehow required you to tell what the philosophers you named thought about the production of man, since this is also included in the investigation of nature? You did not say anything, and rightly. What could they have learned or said about Adam, the first man, and his wife; about their first prevarication; about the cunning of the Serpent; about their nakedness without embarrassment before sin, always with embarrassment after sin? Could they have heard anything like the Apostle's words: 'Through one man sin entered into the world and through sin death, and thus death has passed unto all men; in whom all have sinned'?[6] What could men without knowledge of those writings and of this truth know about the matter? But you decided, and rightly, not to quote anything about the origin of man from the dogmas of those who abhorred our holy Scripture; much less can their statements about the beginnings of this sensible world help you—something we are not discussing. Truly, your mind has been subverted by the vanity of your boasting, as though you had learned something important from the works of the philosophers.

(78) It seems significant that some of them approximated the Christian faith when they perceived that this life, which is replete with deception and misery, came into existence only by divine judgment, and they attributed justice to the Creator by whom the world was made and is administered. How much better than you and nearer the truth in their opinions about the generation of man are those whom Cicero names in the last part of his dialogue *Hortensius,* who seemed

---

5 Above, p. 229.
6 Rom. 5.12.

to be drawn and compelled by the very evidence of things. After he had mentioned the many things we see and grieve over in human vanity and unhappiness, he said: 'From those errors and hardships of human life it happened that at times there was vision by the ancients, whether they were seers or interpreters of the divine mind, as found in sacred things and origins; who said we are born to atone by punishment for crimes committed in a higher life. We find in Aristotle a statement to the effect that we have been afflicted by punishment similar to one once given a group of men who, fallen into the hands of Etruscan pirates, were slaughtered with deliberate cruelty, and their bodies, part corresponding to part, were very neatly piled up, the living with the dead; thus it seems our souls are united with our bodies as the living were joined with the dead.' Did not the philosophers who thought these things perceive much more clearly than you the heavy yoke upon the children of Adam, and the power and justice of God, though not aware of the grace given through the Mediator for the purpose of delivering men? Following your suggestion, then, I have found in the writings of the Gentile philosophers a teaching that can justly be preferred to you, although you, who could find no such thing in them and were not willing to hold your peace, were the occasion of my discovering matter to be used against you.

Chapter 16

Do you realize that the Apostle's testimony you think is in your favor is against you; that when you say the members that were naked before sin and caused no embarrassment were shameful, you do not know what you are saying? I, not you, ought to have used this testimony of the Apostle:

'Much more those that seem to be the more feeble members of the body are the more necessary,' and so forth. But it is worth while considering how you happened to say these things. You say: 'It is time for us to use the authority of the Law in addition to the evidences of nature, to show that our members were so formed that some of them call for modesty while others enjoy freedom.' You continue: 'In confirmation, let us cite the teacher of the Gentiles, who writes to the Corinthians: "But as it is, there are indeed many members, yet only one body." ' Then you subjoin the Apostle's wonderful explanation of the unity and harmony of the members of the body, and you say: 'Because of seemliness, and because he mentioned only a few members of the whole body, he did not wish to refer directly to the reproductive members.' Do not your own words refute you? It follows that it was not possible to mention directly what God saw fit to make correctly, and the herald was ashamed to proclaim what the judge was not ashamed to make. How could this be true, unless by sinning we made unseemly what God by creation made seemly?

(80) You add the following apostolic testimony which you give as written: 'Much more, then, those that seem the more feeble members of the body are more necessary; and those that we think the less honorable members of the body we surround with more abundant honor, and our modest parts we surround with more abundant seemliness, whereas our seemly parts have no need of it. But God has so tempered the human body together in due portion as to give more abundant honor where it was lacking, that there may be no disunion in the body, but that the members may have care one for another.'[1] At these words you exclaim like a con-

---

1 Augustine's Scriptural quotation here agrees with certain modern translations, although it differs somewhat from that of the Confraternity Version. Cf. 1 Cor. 12.12,22,25.

queror: 'Behold one who truly understands the work of God; behold a faithful preacher of His wisdom.' You continue: 'The modest parts, he says, receive a covering of more abundant seemliness.' You thought, certainly, that your whole case should be bound to the words you read as 'the modest parts.' But, if you had read: 'our unseemly parts,' you would not have dared cite this testimony. For God in no way and certainly not before sin made anything unseemly in the members of the human body. Learn, then, what you do not know, since you were not willing to inquire earnestly. The Apostle said 'unseemly,' but some translators, among whom, I think, is the one you read, being a bit embarrassed, wrote 'modest' where he said 'unseemly.' This is proved by the codex itself from which you translated the Apostle's words. What you read as 'modest' is *aschêmona* in the Greek. But what follows, 'have more abundant seemliness,' is *euschêmosynên* in the Greek, which, fully translated, is 'seemliness.' It appears, then, that the members said to be *aschêmona* are said to be unseemly, or *inhonesta*, in Latin. Finally, the words 'our seemly parts,' correspond to the Greek *euschêmona*. But, even without considering the Greek, you should have been aware that parts receiving more abundant seemliness when veiled are unseemly, while those parts that do not need this are said to be seemly. For, what does 'our seemly parts have no need' mean, except that the parts needing it are unseemly? Therefore, when parts are veiled by the sense of decency of human nature, seemliness is applied to the unseemly. Their seemliness and honor consist in their covering: the more abundant the more unseemly they are. The Apostle surely would not have said this if he had been describing the body men had when they were naked and not ashamed.

(81) See how shamelessly you declare: 'Men were naked in the beginning because the art of covering themselves was

the result of human inventiveness, an art then unknown to them.' This means we must believe they were slothful before sin, and sin made them inventive and industrious. You conclude a multitude of vain arguments with eloquence and cunning by saying: 'The first men did not regard the reproductive members as diabolical or unseemly because they had sinned; rather, because they were afraid, they covered the members which retained the seemliness which was theirs at the beginning.' I answer that the members were not diabolical as to their substance, figure, and quality, which God made; but, if those same members remained in their former seemliness, why did the Apostle call them unseemly? It is well you admitted the former seemliness of the members; you could not have held anything else without blasphemy. Therefore, the Apostle has called unseemly things God made seemly. I ask the reason; if it was not from sin, whence is it? What removed seemliness from the seemly works of God, so that the Apostle might call them unseemly? Was it their position, in which we find the power of the Creator; or lust, in which we have the punishment of the sinner? Even now, what God produces there is seemly; what origin contracts, unseemly; yet, that there may be no disunion in the body, the instinct of the nature was divinely gifted so that the members may have care for one another and modest shame may cover what concupiscence deprived of seemliness.

(82) You ask: 'Why did Adam and his wife hide when they heard the voice of God walking in Paradise, when their girdles would have sufficed if they were ashamed of the nakedness of their reproductive members?'[2] Why do you say this when there is nothing for you to say? You do not see that, fearful in soul before the face of the Lord, they looked for even more hidden hiding places; the coverings about their

---
2 Gen. 3.8,7.

loins veiled the stirring they blushed to sense there. If they were not ashamed when naked, then they covered themselves because of shame. Unquestionably, the unseemly gives rise to shame. The reason it is said: 'They were naked and were not ashamed,'[3] is to show that, when later they covered the shameful parts, this was due to shame. Hence, when they hid amid the trees of Paradise, Adam answered: 'I heard your voice in Paradise and I was afraid, because I was naked.' The one is manifest shame; the other, depth of conscience, whose inner failure produced this manifest shame. Modesty produced the one; fear, the other; shameful concupiscence produced the one; conscience about to be punished, the other—somewhat like a madman who thinks by hiding his body he can escape what is only in his mind. What does it mean when the Lord says: 'Who has told thee that thou wast naked, but that thou hast eaten of the tree whereof I commanded thee not to eat?'[4] Why was their nakedness signified by the tasting of the forbidden fruit except to indicate that sin laid bare what grace had covered? The grace of God was indeed powerful when there was no lust in the earthy and animal body. Therefore, he who had nothing to be ashamed of in his naked body when clad in grace sensed what should be covered when he had lost grace.

(83) You say: 'We must not think the Devil had anything to do with producing the members of a man or with the activities of the members.' Why do you raise such vainly extravagant objections? Man's nature owes nothing to the Devil. But, by persuading man to sin, the Devil violated what God made well, so that the whole human race limps because of the wound made through the free choice of two human beings. Consider the wretchedness of the human race

3 Gen. 2.25.
4 Gen. 3.10,11.

which permeates your theories. You are a man; consider nothing human foreign to you.⁵ Be compassionate with those who must endure what you have escaped; yet, no matter how great the earthly happiness you may enjoy, you must daily cope with internal strife, if you truly practice what you profess. If this is not clear from what has been recalled, look at infants: see how many and how great are the evils they endure; in what vanities, torments, errors, and terrors they grow up. Error tempts adults, even those who serve God, to deceive them; labor and pain tempt them, to crush them; lust tempts them, to inflame them; grief tempts them, to prostrate them; pride tempts them, to make them vain. Who can easily explain all the ways in which the heavy yoke presses down upon the children of Adam? The evidences of our misery compelled pagan philosophers, having neither knowledge nor faith about the sin of the first man, to declare that we were born to atone by punishments for crimes committed in a higher life, and that our souls are united with our corruptible bodies in that same kind of torment with which some Etruscan pirates afflicted their captives, as though the living were joined with the dead. But the Apostle has voided the opinion that individual souls are united with different bodies in correspondence to the merits of a previous life. We must, then, hold that the reason for these evils must be either the injustice or impotence of God, or the punishment for the first and ancient sin. Since God is neither unjust nor impotent, there is only what you are forced unwillingly to confess: that the heavy yoke upon the children of Adam from the day of their coming out of their mother's womb until the day of their burial within the mother of all would not have existed if the offense by way of origin had not come first to deserve it.

---

5 Terence, *Heaut.* 1.1.25.

BOOK FIVE

Chapter 1

NOW THAT WE HAVE ANSWERED your first and second books, order demands we look at the contents of the third, and, with the Lord's help, give your noxious efforts a wholesome answer. In accordance with our plan, we shall pass over irrelevant matters so that readers may learn our position with profit and without loss of time. Why need I say anything about the usual vain remarks at the beginning of your book, about how concerned you are in the cause of truth, and the lack of so-called prudent men whom you delight in pleasing? This is the cry of all heretics ancient and recent, and it is a bit shabby and worn with use. Your intense pride forces you into a role and attitude that will be your undoing. It is not necessary again to refute your insulting slanders, seemingly aimed at one man, myself, while without mentioning their names you vent your spleen or blindness upon a multitude of Catholic teachers. I think I have answered your first two books to the satisfaction of all.

(2) You exaggerate the difficulty of knowledge of holy Scripture and say it is fitting for only the learned few:

namely, that God is the Creator of men and the universe; that He is just, truthful, and good; the generous bestower of His gifts on men. As you say, 'The one and the best reason for all striving for good is that God be honored.' And your honor of Him is such that you deny He is the deliverer of infants through Christ Jesus, which means Saviour, for you say they are washed by His baptism, yet not so as to obtain salvation from this, as though they do not need Christ the Physician. Julian shrewdly inspects the vein of human origin and actually pronounces them sound. How much better to have learned nothing at all than through supposed knowledge of the Law with your unseemly boasting—surely not under the guidance of God's Law, but rather by your own vanity—to have come to this ungodly presumption, inimical both to the Christian faith and to your own soul.

(3) You say my teaching is so deformed and groundless that it tries to ascribe injustice to God, the creation of man to the Devil, a substance to sin, and conscience without knowledge to infants. I reply briefly that our teaching is not deformed, because it proclaims One fair above the sons of men to be the Saviour of all men,[1] and, therefore, also of infants. It is not groundless, because it says man is like to vanity and his days pass away like a shadow,[2] not without reason, but through previous sin. It does not ascribe injustice to God, but justice, because it is not unjust that even infants suffer the many and great evils we constantly observe. It does not ascribe the creation of man, but the corruption of human origin, to the Devil; it ascribes to sin, not a substance, but the action, in the first men, and the contagion, in their posterity. It does not ascribe conscience

---

1 Cf. Ps. 44.3.
2 Cf. Ps. 143.4.

without knowledge to infants, in whom there is neither knowledge nor conscience; he in whom all have sinned knew what he was doing, and every man contracts evil from that source.

(4) But you, indeed, bar the way for the multitude of the ignorant, whom you say are simple men, busy with other affairs, without instruction, who by faith alone should enter the Church of Christ, lest they be easily frightened by obscure questions. Let them believe God is the true Creator of men, and, holding firmly that He is good, truthful, and just, let them preserve this judgment about the Trinity and embrace and praise whatever they hear that is in harmony with it; let no force of argumentation pluck it from them; rather, let them detest every authority and society which tries to convince them of the contrary. If you consider these words of yours, you will find them most telling against you, and that the one reason the Christian multitude, from whose inexperienced judgment you refer us to the few you regard as most prudent and learned, detests your innovation is that they believe that God, supremely just, is the Creator of men. And, because they see the sufferings of their own infants, they know that God, supremely just and supremely good, would not permit His image in infants to endure these evils if there were no original sin. If one of them, carrying his infant son, should come to you where none could hear, far from your malicious clamor, and rebuke you, saying: 'By the mind, intelligence, and reason in which I was made after the image of God, I do so love the kingdom of God that I should think it a great punishment for someone if he could never enter that kingdom,' are you, who do not belong to the ignorant mob, but are among the few very prudent men and are a lover of that kingdom, your love influenced by the ardor of the few and not cooled

by the tepid multitude, are you going to answer this man by saying that never to be able to enter the kingdom of God is no punishment at all? I do not believe you will dare say this even to one man whose power and testimony you do not fear. Therefore, when you give some sort of answer or remain silent (a demand of even human, let alone Christian, modesty), will he not force you to look at his infant son, and say to you: 'God is just. What evil forbids His innocent image from entering His kingdom, if it be not the sin which entered into the world through one man'?[3] I do not think you will find greater wisdom than this even among the very learned. But, if you put aside your impudence, you will find yourself more speechless than the infant.[4]

Chapter 2

(5) Let us consider the turn your argument takes after this prologue, where you brushed aside the ignorant and addressed yourself to the very learned few. I do not know what keen thought came to you about something you forgot in your second book, where you argued at such length about the shameful members which, after sin, shamefaced rational nature covered with fig leaves, and where you tried in vain to refute my conclusion that 'Embarrassment could have arisen from these members after sin only because in them there was an unbecoming activity.'[1] What so pleased you that you could not pass it by, even after ending the volume in which you considered the matter which such unending

---
3 Cf. Rom. 5.12.
4 'Speechless' is a play on the Latin *infans*, which means both 'infant' and 'speechless,' so that there is probably an allusion to a text of Scripture such as Wisd. 10.21.

---
1 *De nuptiis et concupiscentia* 1.5.

prolixity? You say it is written: 'And they made themselves coverings.'² This, you say, is another translation of the word we translate as girdles; that coverings can be understood as clothing for the whole body, which, you add, is the function of modesty. I marvel that the translator you read, if not a Pelagian, chose to translate the Greek *perizomata* as 'coverings.' If modesty, which you say is concerned with garments, is also found here, you will never try to tell us the first men learned the functions of modesty from sin as the teacher, so that before sin innocence and shamelessness dwelt together in them in harmony. By your argument, when they were naked and not ashamed, they were immodest, and their deep embarrassment come from the natural sense of shame; they were corrected from this depravity by sinning, and when the reprobate sense of prevarication became the teacher of modesty, wickedness made shamefaced those whom justice made shameless. But your words are so wretchedly shameless and indecently naked you cannot cover them, no matter how many leaves of words you sew together.

(6) You think to ridicule me, saying painters have taught me Adam and his wife covered the shameful members, and you bid me listen to the oft-quoted words of Horace: 'Power to try all figments alike has always belonged to poets and painters.'³ Not from a painter of insubstantial figures, but from the author of the holy Scripture, I learned that the first men were naked before they sinned, and they were not ashamed. God forbid so great innocence in them to make them ashamed. They sinned; they noticed; they blushed; they covered themselves.⁴ And yet you say: 'They sensed nothing unbecoming and new.' God forbid I say any Apostle or Prophet, or even any poet or painter, taught you

---
2 Gen. 3.7.
3 Horace, *De arte poetica* 9-10.
4 Cf. Gen. 2.25; 3.11.

this incredible shamelessness. The very men who, as it is elegantly said, have always had the power to try all figments alike would be ashamed to invent as a pleasantry what you are not ashamed to present for belief. That these two, innocence and shamelessness, the one the very best, the other the very worst, dwell together in agreement and concord is something no painter would dare picture, no poet would write; nor would any of them so despair of human judgment as to believe he had a similar power and not, rather, a senseless vanity to try even this figment.

(7) You say that, if the translation reading *perizomata*, that is, *praecinctoria*, be preferred, the sides were covered, not the thighs. First of all, I am sorry to see you so abuse the ignorance of those who do not know Greek that you do not give the opinion of those who know it. But, as a matter of fact, the Latin custom has adopted as its own the word *perizoma* we find in the Greek codices. When you say not the thighs but the sides were covered by a *perizoma*, I think you ridicule yourself. Does anyone, informed or uninformed, not know which parts of the body *perizomata* cover? This is a conventional name for certain garments listed in women's dowries: the girdles which bind the loins. Ask, then, and learn what I think you already know; but, even if you do not know, I wish you would avoid perverting, not human speech, but human clothing, by raising the *perizoma* up over the shoulders or saying the sides of those men were so covered by the *perizomata* that the genitals and the entire region of the loins, together with the thighs, were left naked. How can it help you and not me instead, when, no matter from what part of the upper body the veiling of the lower parts was suspended, both of them sensed the law in the members warring against the law of the mind,[5] aroused in each by the sight of the other, confounding

---

5 Cf. Rom. 7.25.

the wickedness of the disobedient by the novelty of its own disobedience? The more turbulent its activity, the more shameful must it have been, if the flesh whose sight titillated it need a more ample veil. Therefore, whether the coverings hung from the loins or from the sides, the shameful members were covered. These would not have been shameful if the law of sin had not warred viciously against the law of the mind. Where the reality itself is evident, we ought not add our own notions to the sense of divine Scripture, since this would not be merely human ignorance, but perverse presumption. The word *perizomata* indicates satisfactorily the parts of the body that were covered immediately after sin by Adam and his wife, who before sin were naked and were not ashamed. We see what they covered; to investigate further is extreme folly; still to deny what they sensed is extravagant shamelessness. Despite your stubborn opposition, you also know there is but one answer: Those men blushed at the activity of concupiscence in the reproductive members and wished to cover it. When you seek to raise the *perizoma* to the sides you either cover a part where you say the sinners experienced no evil, or basely expose what you admit had much greater need of covering.

Chapter 3

(8) You quote a passage from my book: 'Disobedient man was most deservedly repaid by the disobedience of his flesh, for it would be unjust if he who did not obey his master were obeyed by his own slave, which is to say by his own body.'[1] You try to show, in consequence, that the disobedience of the flesh must be praiseworthy if it is punishment for sin, and, as though this disobedience were a person, who

---
1 *De nuptiis* 1.7.

knowingly afflicted the sinner, you adorn it with lofty speech as 'an avenger of wrongs and therein a minister of God,' and consider it a great good. You do not see that by your reasoning you could praise the evil angels, who are, in fact, nothing but ungodly prevaricators, yet God inflicts punishment on sinners through them, as holy Scripture testifies: 'He sent upon them the wrath of his indignation; indignation and wrath through evil angels.'[2] Praise them, then; praise Satan their prince, because he also was an avenger of sin when the Apostle gave him one man for the destruction of the flesh.[3] You have spoken very openly against the grace of Christ, and are the proper choice to deliver a panegyric on Satan and his angels, through whom God executes judgment and exacts punishment of sinners, rewarding them according to their works, making the very worst and most damnable spirits the torment of those who are to be punished, using well both the evil and the good. Proclaim those very wicked powers, because through them evils are requited evil men, since you proclaim the concupiscence of the flesh because this disobedience has been given in retribution for the disobedience of the sinner. Praise wicked king Saul, because he also was a punishment for sinners, as the Lord says: 'I gave you a king in my wrath.'[4] Praise the demon that king suffered, because it also was punishment for a sinner.[5] Praise the blindness of heart that has befallen Israel, and do not be silent about why it is said: 'Until the full number of the Gentiles should enter,'[6] although you will perhaps deny this is a punishment. If you were a lover of the inner light, you would cry out that it is not merely

---

2 Ps. 77.49.
3 Cf. 2 Cor. 5.5.
4 Osee 13.11.
5 Cf. 1 Kings 16.14.
6 Rom. 11.25.

a punishment, but a very great punishment. This blindness in the Jews was the immense evil of their unbelief, and a great cause of the sin that they put Christ to death. If you deny that blindness was a punishment, you are suffering a like punishment. If you say it is a punishment, but not for sin, you admit that one and the same thing can be both sin and punishment; but, if not for sin, it must be an unjust punishment, and you make God either unjust, commanding or permitting it, or impotent, if it is inflicted and He does not avert it. If you admit it is also for sin, lest by not admitting this you show yourself blind in heart, then see what you do not wish to see, for the question you asked is now answered. The Devil and his angels and the evil kings were not only sinners themselves, but also torments of sinners, through the justice of God; nor are they made praiseworthy when through them just punishment is inflicted on those deserving it. Thus, we cannot conclude that because the law in the members warring against the law of the mind is just punishment for him who has acted unjustly, this law itself acts justly; and the blindness of heart which only God's illumination removes is not only sin, in which a man does not believe in God; as well as punishment for sin, in which a proud heart is punished by deserved censure; but also a cause of sin, when evil is committed in the error of that blind heart. In like manner, the concupiscence of the flesh against which a good spirit lusts is not only a sin, because it is disobedience against the dominion of the mind—as well as punishment for sin, because it has been reckoned as the wages of disobedience—but also a cause of sin, in the failure of him who consents to it or in the contagion of birth.

(9) Despite your prolix discussion of your blind and inconsiderate opinion, it is most certain that your contention has no foundation when you say this concupiscence of the flesh,

which we say is punishment for sin, is not only not reprehensible, but even praiseworthy. When you say: 'If lust is punishment for sin, then modesty must be abandoned, lest chastity, rebelling against God, be said to weaken the judgment He has passed,' and the other consequences of this vanity, the same could be said about blindness of heart, and in the same number of words—as though, if blindness of heart is punishment for sin, instruction must be abandoned, lest mental enlightenment, rebelling against God, be said to weaken the judgment He has passed. If this conclusion is absurd, your argument is likewise absurd; yet lust, which is the disobedience of the flesh, is punishment for sin. For knowledge should strive against blindness of heart, and continence should strive against lust, while patience should endure punishments which are neither error nor lust. Therefore, when with the gift of God a man lives by faith, God Himself is present to enlighten the mind and to overcome concupiscence, and also to endure trials to the end. The whole work is done rightly when God Himself is loved gratuitously; which is to say, when He is loved with the love that can come only from Him. If, however, one well pleased with himself and relying on his own strength is given up to his own proud desires, the evil grows as the other desires cease and, like one praiseworthy, he restrains them, but for the sake of this one proud desire.

(10) If you will forget your eagerness to be triumphant, and pay close attention to what you say you have read in other opuscula of mine, and have tried in vain to refute: 'There are not a few sins which are also punishment for sin,'[7] you will find this entirely true, as we have seen about blindness of heart. I ask, then, what you accomplished, what was the effect of your citing the apostolic testimony by which I proved this, as you read in another discussion of mine

---

7 *De natura et gratia* 25.

that he said of certain men: 'God has given them up to
a reprobate sense, so that they do what is not fitting'? You
try to say this is a use of hyperbole, the exaggeration of the
truth of things for the purpose of moving men's minds. You
do not hesitate to point out that this is what the Apostle
must have done. You assert that, inveighing against the
crimes of the ungodly, he exaggerates them by calling them
punishments, when he declares they are to him more like
men already condemned than merely guilty. By his own
words, however, not by what you would have him say, he
shows they are not only condemned, but also guilty; and
this not merely guilt from the past deeds because of which
they have been condemned, but they are also guilty in their
condemnation. For he shows they were guilty when he says:
'And they worshiped and served the creature rather than
the Creator, who is blessed forever. Amen.' He next shows
they were condemned because of this guilt when he says:
'For this cause God has given them up to shameful lusts.'
You hear him say it was for this cause, yet you foolishly ask
how we are to understand that God has given them up,
and are at great pains to show He gave them up by deserting
them, as you hold. But, no matter how He gave them up,
He gave them up for this cause, and He deserted them for
this cause. You also see the consequence of His giving them
up, no matter what the kind or manner of giving up. The
Apostle wishes to show the magnitude of the punishment
of being given up to shameful lusts, whether this be done
by desertion or by another way, explicable or inexplicable,
in which the supreme Good and ineffable Justice brings it
to pass. He says: 'For their women have changed the natural
use for that which is against nature, and in like manner
the men also, having abandoned the natural use of the
woman, have burned in their lusts for one another, men
with men doing shameful things and receiving in themselves

the fitting recompense of their perversity.' What could be plainer? What more direct? What more express? He says they received in themselves the fitting recompense; surely this was their being condemned to commit such great evils. Yet this condemnation is also guilt, by which they are more deeply involved; thus, those acts were both sins and punishments for preceding sins. Even more remarkably, he asserts that it was fitting they receive in themselves this recompense. The words immediately preceding these have the same general purport: 'They have changed the glory of the incorruptible God for an image made like to corruptible man and to birds and four-footed beasts and creeping things. Therefore, God has given them up in the lustful desires of their hearts to uncleanness,'[8] and the rest. Again you see the undeniable cause for which they were given up. He names the evil they had done previously, and adds: 'Therefore God has given them up in the lustful desires of their hearts.' Therefore, it is indeed a punishment for preceding sin; yet, it is also sin, as he next explains.

(11) In your argument to the contrary conclusion, you think you have the answer to your question in the Apostle's words that God gave them up to their own desires. You say they were already seething with desires for the foul deeds, and add: 'How can we think they fell into such deeds through the power of God, who gave them up?' I ask you then, what was the effect of His giving them up, and why does the Apostle say: 'God has given them up in the evil desires of their hearts,' if they were already somehow possessed by the evil desires of their heart? Does it follow that because someone has evil desires in his heart he consents to them to commit those evils? We see, then, that to have evil desires of heart is not the same as to be given up to them. Possession comes from the consent to them, and this takes

---
8 Rom. 7.23,28.

place when one is given up to them by divine judgment. For, if man is guilty from the mere sense of their seething and trying to draw him to evil deeds, though he does not go after them, though he is not given up to them, and he engages in glorious combats against them, if he is living in grace, if he is nonetheless guilty, we would read to no purpose: 'Thou shalt not go after thy lusts.' What do you say about him who observes what is written: 'If thou give thy soul her desires' (and this means her evil desires) 'she will make thee a joy to thy enemies and those who envy thee.'[9] Is a man guilty merely having in his soul those lusts to which he ought not to give his soul, lest she become a joy to the Devil and his angels, our enemies who envy us?

(12) When a man is said to be given up to his desires, then, he derives guilt from them because, deserted by God, he yields and consents to them, is conquered, seized, drawn, and possessed by them. 'For by whatever a man is overcome, of this also he is the slave;'[10] and the ensuing sin is his punishment for the preceding sin. Is sin not also punishment for sin where we read: 'For the Lord hath mixed for them a spirit of error, and he hath caused Egypt to err in all his works as a drunken man is seduced'?[11] Is not sin also punishment for sin where the Prophet says to God: 'Why hast thou made us to err, O Lord, from thy ways? Why hast thou hardened our heart, that we should not fear thee?' Is not sin also punishment for sin where he says to God: 'Behold, thou art angry, and we have sinned; therefore we have erred, and all of us have become as unclean'?[12] Is not sin also punishment for sin where we read about the Gentiles that Jesus Nave fought against because

---

9 Eccli. 8.30,31.
10 2 Peter 2.19.
11 Isa. 19.14.
12 Isa. 63.17; 64.5,6.

their heart was strengthened by the Lord and they warred against Israel to exterminate them?[13] Is not sin also punishment for sin where King Roboam did not listen to the good advice of the people, because, as Scripture says: 'The Lord was turned away from him, to make good his word which he had spoken in the hand of the prophet'?[14] Is not sin also punishment for sin where Amasias, king of Juda, did not wish to hear the good advice of Joas, king of Israel, not to go to war? We read: 'Amasias would not listen to him because it was the Lord's will that he should be delivered into their hands, because they sought the god of Edom.'[15] We can recount many other events clearly showing that from a hidden judgment of God comes perversity of heart, with the result that refusal to hear the truth leads to commission of sin, and this sin is also punishment for preceding sin. For to believe a lie and not believe the truth is indeed sin, but it comes from the blindness of heart which by a hidden but just judgment of God is also punishment for sin. We see this also in what the Apostle says to the Thessalonians: 'For they have not received the love of truth, that they might be saved. Therefore God sends them a misleading influence that they may believe falsehood.'[16] See, the punishment for sin is sin. Each part is clear, brief, spoken by him whose words you have tried in vain to distort to your own meaning.

(13) What do you mean by saying: 'Even when they are said to be given up to their lusts, we should understand they are forsaken by divine patience, not compelled to sin by divine power,' as though this same Apostle did not mention both of them, patience and power together, when he says: 'What if God, wishing to show his wrath and to make known

---

13 Cf. Josue 11.20.
14 3 Kings 12.15.
15 2 Par. 25.20.
16 2 Thess. 2.10.

his power, endured with much patience vessels of wrath ready for destruction'?[17] Which of the two, patience or power, do you find in the words of Scripture: 'And when the prophet shall err and speak a word, I, the Lord, have deceived that prophet, and I shall stretch forth my hand upon him and will cut him off from the midst of my people Israel'?[18] Whichever you choose, even if you admit both, you must surely see that the false speech of this prophet is both sin and punishment for sin. Will you also say that the words, 'I, the Lord, have deceived that prophet,' should be interpreted as though God deserted him that he might be deceived in return for past misdeeds and thus err? Say what you will, he was punished for sin in such a way that he sinned prophesying something false. Hear Micheas the Prophet: 'I saw the Lord sitting on his throne, and all the army of heaven standing by him, on his right hand and on his left. And the Lord said: Who will deceive Achab the king of Israel, that he may go up and fall in Ramoth Galaad? And one spoke words of this manner and another otherwise and there came forth a spirit before the Lord and said: I will deceive him. And the Lord said: By what means? And he said: I will go forth and be a lying spirit in the mouth of all his prophets. And the Lord said: Thou shalt deceive him and shalt prevail. Go forth and do so.'[19] How will you answer these words? The king himself sinned by believing the false prophet, but this itself was also punishment for sin, by the judgment of God sending the evil angel, that we may understand more clearly how the psalm says He has sent the wrath of His indignation by evil angels.[20] Did He err or act unjustly or rashly when He sent the wrath? God forbid; the words, 'Thy judgments are as the

---

17 Rom. 9.22.
18 Ezech. 14.9.
19 3 Kings 22.19-22.
20 Cf. Ps. 77.49.

deep sea,'²¹ were not spoken in vain. It is not in vain that
the Apostle exclaims: 'O the depth of the riches of the
wisdom and of the knowledge of God! How inscrutable are
his judgments, and how unsearchable his ways! For who
has known the mind of the Lord; or who has been his
counsellor? or who has first given to him that recompense
should be made him?'²² None He chooses is worthy; but,
choosing, He makes them worthy. Yet He punishes none
who does not deserve it.

Chapter 4

(14) You tell us the Apostle says: 'The goodness of God
is meant to lead thee to repentance.' This is very true; but
He leads him whom He has predestined, even though that
man himself be unrepentant, in hardness of heart treasuring
up wrath to himself on the day of wrath and of the revelation
of the just judgment of God, who will render to every man
according to his works.¹ No matter how great the patience
He reveals, who will repent unless God Himself grants it?
Have you forgotten that the same teacher says: 'In case
God should give them repentance to know the truth, and
they recover themselves from the snare of the devil'?² But
His judgments are as the deep sea. We know that, if we
permit those we govern to commit crimes before our eyes,
we shall stand guilty with them; yet how innumerable are
the crimes God permits men to commit before His eyes,
which He would by no means permit if He willed not to
do so; yet God is just and good. Showing patience, He

---
21 Cf. Ps. 35.7.
22 Rom. 11.33-35.

1 Rom. 2.4-6.
2 2 Tim. 2.25,26.

makes room for repentance, not wishing that any should perish,³ for 'The Lord knows who are his,'⁴ and 'All things work together unto good,' but 'for those who have been called according to his purpose'; for not all who have been called have been called according to His purpose. 'Many are called, but few are chosen.'⁵ Those elected, then, are those called according to His purpose. Thus, he says elsewhere: 'Through the power of God, who has saved us and called us with a holy calling; not according to our works, but according to his purpose and the grace which was granted us in Christ Jesus before this world existed.'⁶ Again, after saying: 'All things work together for good, for those who have been called according to his purpose,' he adds: 'for those whom he has foreknown he has also predestined to become conformed to the image of his Son, that he should be the firstborn among many brethren. And those whom he has predestined, them he has also called; and those whom he has called, them he has also justified; and those whom he has justified, them he has also glorified.'⁷ These have been called according to His purpose; therefore, they have been chosen, and that before the foundation of the world,⁸ by Him who calls things that are not, as though they were;⁹ but they have been chosen through the election of grace. Thus the same teacher says about Israel: 'There is a remnant left, selected out of grace.' And, lest it be thought they were chosen before the foundation of the world, from works that were foreknown, he adds: 'And if out of grace, then not in virtue of works; otherwise grace is no longer grace.'¹⁰

---
3 Cf. 2 Peter 3.9.
4 2 Tim. 2.19.
5 Matt. 22.14.
6 2 Tim. 1.8 9.
7 Rom. 8.28-30.
8 Cf. Eph. 1.4.
9 Cf. Rom. 4.17.
10 Rom. 11.5,6.

Of the number of the elect and predestined, even those who have led the very worst kind of life are led to repentance through the goodness of God, through whose patience they were not taken from this life in the commission of crimes; in order to show them and their co-heirs the depth of evil from which the grace of God delivers man. Not one of them perishes, regardless of his age at death; never be it said that a man predestined to life would be permitted to end his life without the sacrament of the Mediator. Because of these men, our Lord says: 'This is the will of him who sent me, the Father, that I should lose nothing of what he has given me.'[11] The other mortals, not of this number, who are of the same mass as these, but have been made vessels of wrath, are born for their advantage. God creates none of them rashly or fortuitously, and He also knows what good may be made from them, since He works good in the very gift of human nature in them, and through them He adorns the order of the present world. He leads none of them to the wholesome and spiritual repentance by which a man in Christ is reconciled to God, whether His patience in their regard be more generous or not unequal. Therefore, though all men, of the same mass of perdition and condemnation, unrepentant according to the hardness of their heart, treasure up wrath to themselves on the day of wrath when each will be repaid according to his works, God through His merciful goodness leads some of them to repentance, and according to his judgment does not lead others. Our Lord says He has the power to lead and draw men: 'No men can come to me unless the Father who sent me draw him.'[12] Did He not lead the sacrilegious and ungodly King Achab to repentance, or, at least, show patience and magnanimity and long-suffering to that king, who had already been led astray

---
11 John 6.39.
12 John 6.44.

and deceived by the lying spirit? Was not the result of his being deceived accomplished in him immediately after his death?[13] Who can say he did not sin by believing a lying spirit? Who can say the sin was not punishment for sin and the judgment of God, to execute which He chose the lying spirit, whether that spirit was sent or only permitted to go? Who but a man saying what he wishes and not wishing to hear the truth says this?

(15) Who is so foolish that, when he hears what is sung in the psalm: 'Do not give me up, O Lord, from my desire to the wicked,'[14] he says this man was praying that God should not be patient with him, as though, as you say, 'God does not give a man up so that evils are done except to show His patient goodness'? Do we not ask daily: 'Lead us not into temptation,'[15] lest we be given up to our lusts? For everyone is tempted by being drawn away and enticed by his own concupiscence.[16] Do we, therefore, ask God not to show His patient goodness, and not, rather, invoke His mercy? What sane man understands this; indeed, what maniac says this? Therefore, God gives men up to shameful lusts that they may do what is not fitting; but He gives them up fittingly, and these acts not only are sins, as well as punishments for past sins, but also they demand future punishments, just as He gave Achab up to the lie of the false prophets, and gave Roboam up to false advice.[17] God, knowing how to work his just judgments not only in the bodies of men, but also in their very hearts, acts in marvellous and ineffable ways; not causing evil volitions, but using them as He wishes, since He cannot will anything unjustly. Being gracious, He hears; angry, He does not hear; and

---

13 Cf. 3 Kings 22.
14 Ps. 139.9.
15 Matt. 6.13.
16 Cf. James 1.14.
17 Cf. 3 Kings 12.

again, gracious, He does not hear; angry, He hears. Being gracious, He spares; angry, He does not spare; and again, being gracious, He does not spare; angry, he spares; and in all things He remains good and just. Who is able to comprehend these things? Indeed, what man under pressure of the corruptible body, even though he already have the pledge of the Holy Spirit, is able to comprehend and search out His judgments?

(16) But you, a very subtle and intelligent man, say: 'One must proclaim the justice and praiseworthiness of lust if by disobeying it punishes him who has not obeyed God.' If you were wise, you would see it must be by wickedness that the lower part of man wars against the higher and better part; yet it is just for a wicked man to be punished by the wickedness of his own flesh, as the wicked king was punished by the wickedness of the malignant spirit. Will you praise the malignant spirit? Speak out, why do you hesitate? It becomes you, an enemy of the gratuitous goodness of God, to be the encomiast of a lying spirit. You will easily find something to say. You have its praises at hand, if you apply to that spirit the praise of lust you thought to deduce from my statement that 'It would be unjust if he who did not obey his Lord were obeyed by his own slave; that is to say, by his own body.'[18] This you deny, and deride as false, and, wanting to show the absurdity you think follows if my words are true, praise lust as 'the avenger of sin.' You will certainly not deny that the lying spirit was an avenger of wickedness, since by deceiving him it drew the ungodly king to the death he deserved. Consider: I say here, too: 'It would be unjust if he who did not believe the true God were deceived by the false.' Praise the justice of falsehood; say what you said in praising lust: 'Nothing can be more praiseworthy than lust, if the repayment of wickedness is

---
18 *De nuptiis* 1.7.

committed to it; if it avenges injury to God; if it can have no association with sin, in order to qualify for the office of avenger.' By this very subtle interpretation, all your words rightly serve to praise the unclean spirit. Be consistent, then, and either be the herald in this case for the lying spirit, or refuse to speak for rebellious lust.

(17) Why do you take refuge in a most obscure question about the soul?[19] In Paradise, rebellion certainly began in the soul, whence began consent to breaking the commandment; this is why the Serpent said: 'You shall be as gods.'[20] But the whole man committed the sin, and it was then that the flesh was made sinful flesh, whose faults can be healed only by the likeness of sinful flesh. In order, then, that, unless what is born be cleansed by rebirth, soul and body shall be equally punished, both are faulty when derived from man, or the one is corrupted in the other as in a faulty vessel, and this contains the hidden justice of the divine law. I should be more pleased to learn which of the two is true than to give my own opinion, lest I dare say what I do not know. But this I know: that one of them is true which the true, ancient, and Catholic faith, which believes and asserts original sin, shall hold is not false. This faith must not be denied. Latent facts about the soul may either be discussed in leisure time or, like many other things in this life, may remain

---

19 This obscure question about the soul concerns the production of man by carnal generation. Pelagians seems to have denied the possibility that the soul itself is transmitted through human seed by propagation, and to have made this an important part of their argument against the Catholic doctrine about original sin, because they thought they could deny that the soul, created immediately by God, could be born under sin. Augustine leaves the question about the nature of the production of the human soul unsolved, although he takes pains to show that, whatever be the answer, it cannot affect the doctrine about original sin. Cf. *De peccatorum meritis et remissione* 3.10.18; *De anima et ejus origine;* and the answer given by St. Thomas in *Summa theologica* I, q. 118.
20 Gen. 3.5.

unknown without injury to our salvation. Whether it be in infants or in adults, we must be more concerned with the aid by which the soul is healed than with the fault by which it has been vitiated; but, if we deny it has been vitiated, then neither will it be healed.

(18) I cannot account for the remark you make after you cite the Apostle's words: 'And their foolish heart was darkened.'[21] You say: 'We should note he says foolishness is the cause of all evils.' It is not fully established that the Apostle said this, but I shall not argue the point; rather, I ask why you said it. Was it because infants cannot properly be called foolish, since they are not as yet able to partake of wisdom, and you, wishing men to believe there can be no evil in infants, think this conclusion follows if foolishness is the cause of all evils? We should need a very subtle and elaborate investigation to learn whether the first men became proud in virtue of foolishness or whether pride made them foolish, but, for the present, I merely ask if anyone does not know that all men, whosoever come to be wise, come to it out of foolishness. Unless, perhaps, by a very great and extraordinary grace of the Mediator, some of his messengers could have passed to wisdom, not out of foolishness, but directly out of infancy. If you say this can happen by nature without the faith of the Mediator, you expose the secret poison of your heresy, for we see clearly that the sole result of your defense and praise of the nature is that Christ died in vain, whose faith, which works through love,[22] we say is lavishly bestowed even on those congenitally feeble-minded. For there are men born with such sluggish wits that they seem more like cattle than men. The feeble-mindedness which is obviously natural in them is so extreme that you, who say there is no original sin, could find nothing in them to deserve

---

21 Rom. 1.21.
22 cf. Gal. 2.21; 5.6.

it. Do we not know from daily experience in human activities that at first an infant is wise about nothing; he grows, and is wise about vain things; and then, if he belongs in the portion of wisdom, he is wise about the right, and therefore passes from infancy to wisdom through an intermediate foolishness. You see, then, how human nature which in infants you by your praises would refuse a savior, as though it were sound, brings forth fruit of foolishness sooner than wisdom; and you do not wish to see the fault in its root—or, worse still, you see it and deny it.

Chapter 5

(19) You quote some other words of mine, slanderously asserting I contradict myself when, after saying the disobedience of the body was given to disobedient men as punishment, I immediately named the parts of the body, and said they obey the command of the will.[1] When I stated the second proposition, I excluded the reproductive members from what I meant by the 'body'; hence, it is true that the body serves the will in the activities of the other members, and the body does not serve the will in the activity of the reproductive members. My words do not contradict each other, although they permit you to contradict me by not understanding them or keeping others from understanding them. If a part of the body could not be called 'the body,' the Apostle would not have said: 'The wife has not authority over her body, but the husband; the husband likewise has not authority over his body, but the wife.'[2] By the body he means the members of the body through which sex is distinguished and the act of union is performed. Could you say

---
1 *De nuptiis* 1.7.
2 1 Cor. 7.4.

a man has not authority over his body if in the Apostle's words you understand the whole body consisting of all the members? In accordance with the Apostle's use, then, I also used the word 'body' to mean the reproductive members; and those members are not moved by the will, like the hand and the foot, but by lust, as is acknowledged by common sense, which derides your confounding the self-evident, and forcing us to speak at length about the shameful, where decency calls for indirectness. It is quite enough for me that he who reads my words which you think to refute, and sees how you would distort them, understands what I meant by 'body.'

(20) Anyone who hears you accuse me of contradicting myself, and reads what I wrote, and recalls that the Apostle also called the reproductive members 'the body' will see your accusation is false. You, who find contradictions in my arguments, and pounce upon them, must defend the consistency of your own, where you begin by saying: 'When it comes to semination of offspring, the members created for this purpose co-operate with one another upon mere command by the will, and they obey the mind unless impeded, either by infirmity or by excess,' but later you hold that 'This activity of the body must be included among the many whose order and disposition are hidden, requiring not the command, but the consent of the will.' Here you give partial acceptance to the evident truth, but you should have retracted what you said earlier. How do those members, by your first statement, 'co-operate with one another upon mere command of the will, and obey the mind,' if, by your second statement, they require, 'not the command, but the consent of the will, as do hunger, thirst, and digestion'? You are at great pains to find something to say, but it is against you rather than against me. In this matter, however, no pains would be necessary if modesty were present. What good does it do you to feel shame, as you say, and be shocked beyond words when forced by necessity

to speak about such things; when you do not blush to give a written judgment against which you yourself, when disturbed by self-evident truth, immediately give another judgment? Even your mentioning shamefacedness is shameless. It is enough for me, however, because it exposes you, who are not ashamed to praise lust, yet say you are ashamed to discuss the works of lust.

(21) Was it an important discovery that after I said: 'It was given power that it might move the other members,' I added: 'when the body is free from impediments and in good health'? Sleep and drowsiness, when they overcome men against their will, are impediments by which the agility of the members is hindered. When you say: 'Nor do the members follow our will if we wish what their special powers will not bear,' you do not note that for this very reason I said at the beginning: 'That they may be moved to suitable works.' If we wish them to do what their nature will not permit, they do not follow our will to acts not suited to them; nevertheless, when we move them by will and they obey, we do not need the help of lust. When we wish to stop moving them, we stop immediately, and the stimulations of lust do not rouse them in opposition to the will.

(22) When you say: 'The reproductive members also obey the command of the soul,' you speak of a new kind of lust, or, perhaps, of a very ancient lust such as could have existed even in Paradise if no one had sinned. But why should I discuss this here, when your next words eliminate it from consideration? You say: 'Such lust is not moved by command of the soul, but awaits its consent.' This is not, however, a reason for comparing lust with hunger and other vexations. It is true no one suffers hunger, feels thirst, or digests his food at will, since these are needs to refresh or relieve the body, and we must help it in these needs lest it be injured or kill. But does the body kill or suffer injury if assent is not

given to lust? Distinguish, then, the evils we endure through patience from the evils we restrain through continence, for the former also are evils we can experience in the body of this death. Who can know with certainty or explain fitly the magnitude and tranquillity of our power in the happiness of Paradise, even over the actions by which food is eaten and digested? God forbid we think any sensation could have caused us internal or external pain, or any feeling of effort wearied our senses, or shame embarrassed us, or sensation of heat burned us, or cold injured us, or horror offended us.

(23) Thus, you are not ashamed to proclaim your very beautiful handmaid, whose exact name I am ashamed to say even in reproach; and you do not blush to say you think: 'It is the more to be commended because the other parts of the body serve it, that it may be more ardently aroused; be it the eyes for lusting, or the other members, in kisses and embraces.' You have found a way to subject men's ears to its reign, resurrecting an ancient and very glorious title, when you repeat the story Cicero tells in his *Counsels*: 'When, as sometimes happens, the intoxicated youths had been aroused by the sound of the flutes and had begun to break down the door of the house of a chaste woman, Pythagoras is said to have asked the flute-player to sing a spondee. As she did so, their wild licentiousness was stilled in the slowness of the measures and the gravity of the song.' You see how fittingly I said lust has, in a way, a personal right by which the other senses serve it in advancing to its work or resting from its commotion as it sees fit. The reason I said this is, as you admit, 'A man consents to it instead of commanding it.' For, even the fact that 'It may be aroused by other stimuli than its own, or weakened or quieted by moderation,' as you say later, would certainly not be true if it were servant to man's will. I grant that women, whom you would make immune to this activity, can be subjected to the concupiscence

of men, even when they experience none of their own; yet, we may ask Joseph how intensely women can be affected by its onslaught.³ You, a man of the Church, ought to be better instructed by the music of the Church than by Pythagoras. Think what David's lyre did for Saul, who was harassed by an evil spirit, but recovered from this disturbance when the holy man played his lyre;⁴ beware of thinking the concupiscence of the flesh is a good, merely because it is sometimes checked by musical sounds.

Chapter 6

(24) You exclaim: 'How fitting it was for Jeremias, with the chorus of the Prophets and all the saints, to cry out: 'Who will give water to my head, and a fountain of tears to my eyes,'¹ that he might bewail the sins of the foolish people; and this, because the Church of Christ expelled the teachers of the Pelagian error. If you wish to weep wholesomely, weep for this, that you are involved in that error, and let your tears wash you clean of the new plague. Are you ignorant, or have you forgotten, or do you wish not to know that the holy, the one, the Catholic Church was also signified by the word 'Paradise'?² What wonder you are expelled from this Paradise, when you want to introduce the law in the members warring against the law of the mind into the Paradise from which we were expelled by the Lord and to which we cannot return

---
3 Gen. 39.
4 1 Kings 16.

---
1 Jer. 9.1.
2 An obscure reference to a figurative sense of Scripture, probably based on an allegorical interpretation of the word 'Paradise.' This particular exegesis, beloved of Ambrose and often used by Augustine, is insisted on by neither, and seems never advanced as more than an accomodation of the literal sense.

unless in this Paradise we conquer this law? For, if the concupiscence you defend does not truly war against the law of the mind, no saint engages in any combat against it. But you have admitted that the saints 'engage in glorious combats' against that concupiscence you defend. Therefore, this concupiscence is what wars against the law of the mind in the body of this death, and from which the Apostle says the grace of God through Jesus Christ our Lord delivers him.[3] Do you begin to see the fountain of tears with which the enemies of this grace should be lamented, and the great pastoral care with which they must be avoided, lest they draw others with them to destruction? For by your innovation you 'increase the depravity of the latter times' which is in all heretics. It is you who are the 'ruin of morals' when you try to subvert the foundations of the very faith upon which morals must be built. It is you who are 'the destruction of modesty' when you are not ashamed to praise what modesty itself combats. The Church, which is called a virgin, ought certainly to hear this, so that she may be on guard against you. Matrons, holy virgins, all Christian modesty ought to hear this. They do not, as you charge they do, 'assert with the Manichaeans that a compulsion to evil exists in their own flesh.' The Manichaeans falsely assert an evil in the flesh, co-eternal with God, having the nature of substance. Christians declare with the Apostle: 'I see another law in my members, warring against the law of my mind,'[4] but this other law, by the grace of God through Jesus Christ our Lord, is under the power of the mind, to be chastised in the body of this death; to be dissolved in the death of the body; to be healed in the resurrection of the body and the death of death. They hold this holy profession, not in mere habit of dress, but in habit

---

3 Rom. 7.23-25.
4 *Non usque adeo putandum est perisse frontem de rebus;* an allusion to Persius, *Sat.* 5.103,101.

of both mind and body, by resisting the concupiscence of the flesh—a work which can be done here; not by being entirely without concupiscence of the flesh—an effect which cannot be achieved here. Let them hear us, then, so that until they are entirely without concupiscence they may be on guard against you. Suppose two men were asked to speak in a holy auditorium—one censuring lust, the other praising it—and all the saints were asked to choose which they preferred to hear. What do you think the combats of celibates, the modesty of the married, the chastity of all would say? Would they close their ears to the censure of lust and joyfully listen to its praises? We cannot believe propriety has so disappeared[5] that this evil could come to pass, except, perhaps, in an auditorium where Celestius or Pelagius presides over the assembled disciples while you perform.

Chapter 7

(25) You quote my words: 'When the first men sensed this activity in their flesh, unseemly because disobedient, they blushed at it and covered those members with fig leaves, so that this activity they could not control at will they might at least cover at will when ashamed; and thus by covering, because it shamed, the thing that gave unseemly pleasure they might achieve what seemliness required.'[1] You boast vainly of having already destroyed the force of my statement in the arguments of your second book and the first part of the third, which I am now answering but now, because I said: 'The activity which was unseemly because disobedient,' you want it thought I said it is subject neither to the body nor to the soul, 'but always with the indomitable power of a wild beast.' I never said it is a power; it is a fault. If it

---

1 *De nuptiis* 1.7.

does not act by lusting, what is meant by saying chastity opposes it by exercising continence? And where are those glorious combats of the saints you say they wage against it? About modesty, you say what I say; we serve it when we attack lust, when we repress and restrain it and permit it nothing unlawful. You, not I, however, call good the need to assault, to repress, to restrain lust lest it draw us to the unlawful acts it always desires. Let the chaste decide which of us speaks the truth; and let them not attend your words, but their own experience. Let the Apostle decide, who says: 'I see another law in my members, warring against the law of my mind.'

(26) You say: 'The Paternians and the Venustian heretics, who resemble the Manichaeans, hold that the Devil made man's body from the loins to the feet, but God placed the upper parts upon this as on a kind of pedestal.[2] No effort is required of man except that he preserve the purity of the soul, which they say dwells in the stomach and the head. It is no concern of his, they say, if the pubic region is covered with filth and all kinds of impurity.' 'That they may render base service to lust,' you conclude, 'they invariably give it a title to a realm of its own'; and this you find akin to my statement that 'What the first men could not move at will they veiled at will when ashamed; lust, not obeying the will, inflamed the body in its own right.' Can you escape the force of truth by invoking falsehood and slandering us? What I wrote in my book—would you had yielded to it, rather than offer resistance—is far from the Paternians and Venustians. In accordance with the Catholic faith, I attribute the whole man—that is to say, the whole soul and the whole body—to God the Creator, supreme and true; the Devil vitiated, but did not create, human nature or any part of it. We must fight against the Devil's wound, which, with

---

2 Augustine describes this obscure sect in *De haeresibus* 85.

God's help, is to be tended and healed until we shall be entirely freed from it; nor can man, with what purity he has in his life, keep the soul by which his body lives all pure if he consents to concupiscence of the flesh to commit crime and uncleanness. As to your slander, what have you to object to my words? If this means nothing to you, behold, I condemn and anathematize what you say the Paternians and Venustians hold; I add the Manichaeans; I execrate, I condemn, I anathematize, I detest them together with all the other heretics. What more can you ask? Get rid of the slander; fight with your own strength, not with fraud. Answer: Where does that come from, which, unless resisted, will not permit man to be chaste? It cannot be a nature and substance, as the Venustians and Manichaeans believe; if not a fault of a nature, what is it? It rises up, I repress it; it resists, I restrain it; it fights, I oppose it. In my whole soul and my whole body I have as my Creator the God of peace. Who has sowed this war in me? Apostle, answer our question: 'Through one man sin entered into the world and through sin death, and thus death has passed unto all men in whom all have sinned.'[3] But Julian would not have it so. Blessed Apostle, say to us: 'If anyone should preach a gospel to you other than that which we have preached to you, let him be anathema.'[4]

(27) You say that, if I hope to establish that the evil of lust is invincible, I make myself the advocate of depravity; but, if I say I regard it as a natural evil, yet conquerable, that is, one that can be guarded against, you immediately present your theory from another approach and say: 'Then men are able to avoid all sins, since they are able to overcome the evil of concupiscence. For, if lust is a natural evil and it can be overcome by love of virtue, much more will this love overcome all vices coming from the will alone.' We have

---
3 Rom. 5.12.
4. Gal. 1.9.

answered these arguments in many ways. As long as we live here, where the flesh lusts against the spirit and the spirit against the flesh,[5] no matter how mightily we prevail in combat and do not yield our members to sin as weapons of iniquity, obeying its lusts,[6] nevertheless—not to mention the sensations of the body and the excesses of sudden pleasure in things it is lawful to use—certainly in our affections and thoughts, 'If we say that we have no sin, we deceive ourselves and the truth is not in us.'[7] It is vain for you to rush to another side of your theory, unless you wish in sacrilegious presumption to reject the words of the Apostle John. To return to the present question, then, I say lust is natural, since every man is born with it; you, indeed, state this more fully, since you say the first man was created with it. I say lust must be overcome, and, to be overcome, must be opposed. You also say this, lest you hear in return what you say to me: 'You profess yourself an advocate of depravity when you deny lust must be overcome'; it certainly cannot be overcome unless there is combat against it. Since we both say lust is natural and conquerable, our dispute concerns whether we must overcome good or evil. Do you not see how absurdly you wish to expel this enemy, lust, yet do not wish to complete the discussion of its evil? Thus, if the Devil does not overcome you in the adversity of concupiscence, he will overcome you in the perversity of your opinion.

(28) Are you not as yet able to understand that we by virtue do not war against our nature, but our fault? For we do not overcome good with good, but evil with good. In whose company is lust overcome? In whose company does it overcome? When lust conquers, the Devil also conquers; when lust is conquered, the Devil is also conquered. Whom

---

5 Cf. Gal. 5.17.
6 Cf. Rom. 6.13,12.
7 1 John 1.8.

lust overcomes and by whom it is overcome is its enemy; in whose company it conquers and is conquered is its author. Open your eyes, I ask you, and see what is in plain sight. There is no fighting without evil, for, when there is fighting, it is either good against evil, or evil against evil; or, if two goods oppose each other, their opposition itself is a great evil. When the elements composing the body, although they are contraries, fail to keep peace and harmony among themselves, disease and sickness arise. Who will dare say any one of these elements is not good, since every creature of God is good, and cold and heat bless the Lord in the canticle of the three children?[8] They are contraries, yet in harmony for the preservation of things; but, when they disagree and oppose one another in the body, our health is disturbed. All this, as death itself, comes to us from the propagation of that sin, for no one will assert we should have had to suffer in the blessedness of Paradise if no one has sinned. The qualities of corporeal things, tempered by contrary qualities accompanying them in the body that we may be in good health, are good in their respective kinds, yet their disagreement produces bad health. But besides these are also those covetings of the soul which are said to be 'of the flesh,' because it is according to the flesh that the soul lusts when it so lusts that the spirit, that is to say, the higher and better part, must oppose it. These faults do not require physicians of bodies; they are cared for by the medicinal grace of Christ: first, so that they do not hold man guilty; next, so that they do not overcome him in combat; and finally, that they may be completely healed, leaving no trace. Since to love evils is evil, and to desire goods is good, and since this combat will not cease as long as we live here where the flesh lusts against the spirit and the spirit lusts against the flesh, who will deliver me from the body of this death, unless it be the grace

---

8 Cf. Dan. 3.67.

of God through Jesus Christ our Lord? Your detestable doctrine is inimical to this grace.

(29) You, a very courageous man, if not a supervisor of nocturnals, at least a preacher and herald of wars, say: 'The opinion holding that in Paradise the reproductive members could have obeyed the command of the will is soft and effeminate.' The more power the soul has over lust the more effeminate it seems to you, a chaste man! We shall not contend with you about the absence or presence of lust in Paradise, nor offend the love we see you owe it, but at least put it under the command of the will in that place of happiness. Remove from there that most evident combat which arises when the mind resists its activity, remove the very wicked peace arising when the mind is servant in its dominion, and certainly, because you do not now see such lust as could have existed there, you will confess, compelled by shame if not recalled by reason, the original fault in lust as it now exists, serving which we perish, and which we must combat lest we serve. Consider what you praise, not fearing you yourself may be told you incite men to commit crimes lest they oppose concupiscence, which you commend as a natural good. How can it help you if you seem to censure its excesses when you approve its activity? It exceeds the lawful limit whenever we yield to its movements. But it is an evil even when we do not yield, because evil is resisted lest the goodness of chastity be destroyed if this evil is not resisted. Since you say it is naturally good, you shrewdly decree man must always consent to it, in order not to oppose a natural good by unjustified resistance. Indeed, in this way your opinion that man can be without sin if he wishes can very easily be proved, for there is no way to do the unlawful when whatever pleases is lawful, since, you say, what naturally pleases is good. Let us enjoy present pleasures to the full, let us amuse ourselves in their absence

with thoughts of them, as Epicurus advocated, and we shall be without sin and not deprive ourselves of any good. Let us not resist natural movements because of any doctrinal opinion, but, as Hortensius says: 'Man would be obedient to nature, sensing without a teacher whatever nature desires.'[9] A nature which is good cannot desire what is evil, or we must deny good to the good; therefore, let whatever this good lust desires be done, lest he who resists the good himself be evil.

(30 You will deny you hold this, and say it is unjust to suspect you of thinking something you do not say. Then do not do what you would not have done to you, by asserting that we 'invite men to knavish pleasures when we repeat to them the Apostle's words: "I know that in me, that is, in my flesh, no good dwells." '[10] Although they do not fulfill the good they wish, so that they no longer lust, nevertheless they do good, so that they no longer go after their own lusts.[11] If you think you are teaching chastity when you say: 'Do not be overcome by good, but overcome good with good,' how much more do we teach chastity when we say: 'Be not overcome by evil, but overcome evil with good.'[12] See how unjustly you refuse to believe that we oppose what we censure, but you will not have it thought you wish to enjoy what you praise. How can enemies of lust not be chaste, if its friends can be chaste? In this work, then, we refute in you only this: denying original sin and refusing to infants the Savior Jesus, you wish to introduce into Paradise before sin the law of sin warring against the law of the mind. We do not wish to judge what we do not see or hear. What a professed encomiast of lust may do in secret is not our concern.

---
9 Cicero, *Hortensius*.
10 Rom. 7.18.
11 Cf. Eccli. 18.30.
12 Rom. 12.21.

Chapter 8

(31) You quote the distinction I made between marriage and concupiscence in the first men: 'What they afterwards accomplished in propagation is the good of marriage; what they earlier covered in confusion is the evil of concupiscence.'[1] You think this distinction erroneous, because, as you say: 'Whatever is good must share its commendation with that without which it cannot exist.' By this reasoning, you would have one and the same commendation of marriage and lust. Hear briefly how your supposedly definitive judgment is answered. In the first place, the universe of things God created cannot exist without evils, but it does not follow that evils must share the praises of the goods. Secondly, if 'Whatever is good must share its commendation with that without which it cannot exist,' then it must by all means be true that evil must share its reproach with that without which it cannot exist. Therefore, we must revile the works of God, just as we revile the evils incapable of existence without them. There can be no evil except in the work of God, and no evil anywhere if there were no work of God. You have something near at hand: revile the members of the human body as you revile adultery, which cannot exist without those members. If do not wish to do so, lest you seem plainly insane, then it is possible that the good of marriage need not share its commendation with the lust without which it cannot now exist, just as no evil must share its reproach with the work of God, without which it can never exist. Just as your definition is false and vain, so also are the consequences you draw from it.

(32) I never said: 'The pleasure of the flesh is invincible,' although you say this is my usual wording. Both you and I say it can and should be overcome; but you say as a good to

---

[1] *De nuptiis* 1.8.

be overcome by another good warring against it, while I say as an evil by a good warring against it. You say it can and should be overcome by man's own powers, while I say it is to be overcome by the grace of the Saviour, so that it may be overcome, not by another kind of coveting, but by the charity of God, which is poured forth in our hearts, not by our own powers, but by the Holy Spirit who has been given to us.[2]

(33) You repeat that you used, vainly, the testimony of the Apostle to demonstrate something about the embarrassment of these men and the covering of the members you called 'modest,' but he called unseemly. We have investigated this matter quite thoroughly. You vainly take refuge in Balbus and the writings of the philosophers, as though Balbus might make you speak when you can find nothing to say about the embarrassment of the first men. But if you would yield to true judgments, found in at least some of the philosophers' writings, you would not fail to hear them say pleasures are the enticements and baits of evils, and that lust is a faulty part of the soul. Balbus' observation that the digestive parts of our body are removed from the power of our senses is true, because the things we digest offend our senses; they do not entice us; thus, the parts by which waste is voided are naturally hidden by more prominent parts around them, just as they were concealed when those men were naked and were not ashamed, but directly after sin they concealed, not hidden parts, but members in plain sight. The more their vision was drawn by delight and not offended in revulsion, the more those members aroused your protege and the greater the concern of modesty to cover them.

(34) If you are not trying to deceive, you have failed to understand what I meant by limping and arrival.[3] By

---
2 Rom. 5.5.
3 *De nuptiis* 1.8.

'arrival' I did not mean the man born of marriage, as you think or pretend to think; I meant the good which marriage possesses in the end to which its office tends, even if none be actually born. The man sows the seed; the woman receives it; and precisely this much the married are able to accomplish by their own activity. I said they could not arrive at this end without 'limping,' that is to say, without lust. That offspring be conceived and born is the divine work, not the human, yet it is with this intention and wish that marriage achieves even that good which belongs to its own work. But because the offspring itself is born to condemnation unless reborn, Christian marriage, inasmuch as the goal of its journey is not merely the end to which its own work tends, but the purpose of the will, presses onward even to this: that it may generate men to be regenerated, and this is why modesty in it is true modesty, that is, modesty pleasing to God. For without faith it is impossible to please God.[4]

Chapter 9

(35) You turn next to the passage where we discussed the Apostle's testimony: 'That everyone of you learn how to possess his vessel,' that is to say, his spouse, 'not in the disease of lust, like the Gentiles who do not know God.'[1] Commenting on these words, I said: 'Conjugal, that is to say, lawful and honest, intercourse is not forbidden. He says the reason for this act must be desire for offspring, not pleasure of the flesh, so that what cannot be done without lust must be done in such a way that it is not done for the

---
4 Cf. Heb. 11.6.

---
1 1 Thess. 4.4,5.

sake of lust.'² You exclaim: ' "O the depth of the riches of the wisdom and knowledge of God!" '³ who decreed that, besides the future retribution for our works, a large part of the judgment shall consist in the actions of free will. It is most just that the good and the evil each be left to himself, so that the good may rejoice in himself, while the evil endures himself.' Your exclamation has nothing to do with the matter in which you find it forceful. Your outcries do not remove the weight upon you when you maintain the ungodly dogma in which you say the good is also left to himself by divine judgment, so that the grace of God is not necessary for one able to guide himself. God forbid this be so; indeed, those who are left to themselves are not good, because they are not sons of God. 'Whoever are led by the Spirit of God, they are sons of God.'⁴ I think that in this judgment you will recognize the apostolic teaching by which your teaching is overcome.

(36) One of your contradictions I ought not to pass by in silence. Do you remember your lengthy argument against the very evident truth stated by the Apostle, when you said: 'By no means can anything be both sin and punishment for sin'? How can you have forgotten your prolixity so that you now praise the depth of the riches of the wisdom and the knowledge of God because He decreed that, besides the future retribution for our works, a large part of the judgment shall consist in the action of free will? You declare: 'It is most just that the good and the evil each be left to himself that the good may rejoice in himself,' surely in a good work, 'while the evil endures himself,' surely in an evil work. This evil work is indeed his sin, because he does

---
2 *De nuptiis* 1.9.16.
3 Rom. 11.13.
4 Rom. 8.14; Wisd. 1.13.

something evil, and also punishment for sin, because he endures his evil self, so that a large part of the judgment by which goods are rendered the good, evils the evil, shall consist in the action of free will; that is, a good man rejoices in himself acting rightly, while an evil man endures himself sinning. You see how boastfully you are brandishing your futile and blunted weapons while you are exposed where you are vulnerable; indeed, you wound yourself. You slanderously boast that my words contradict one another, although I did not say: 'The union of bodies was instituted by the Devil,' for, even if no one had sinned, children would not have been born except by the union of the two sexes. I said: 'The disobedience of the flesh which appears when the flesh lusts against the spirit is a result of the diabolic wound.' You boast because I said: 'The law of sin warring against the law of the mind was inflicted in vindication by God, and is therefore punishment for sin,' and you find these two statements contradictory, as though it could not be true that one and the same evil is inflicted on sinners both by the Devil's iniquity and God's justice. Yet, the Devil himself both besets men by his own malevolence and by God's judgment is permitted to harm sinners. Holy Scripture itself cannot be said to contradict itself when it says: 'God made not death,' and also says: 'Life and death are from the Lord God.'[5] For the cause of death is he who deceived man, the Devil; God inflicted death, not as its first author, but as the avenger of sin. You yourself answered the question fully when you said that man has been left to himself, so that his being a torment to himself comes from the divine judgment and also from his own free will. It is not contradictory that in his punishment he himself is the author, God the avenger.

(37) You take advantage of the less gifted. I do not wish

---

5 Eccli. 11.14.

to say you also do not understand, cannot distinguish these two, and, in malevolent calculation or deep blindness confuse the voluntary and the voluptuous, so that, just as the words sound the same to dull ears, you hope to convince the dull of heart that the things themselves are the same. This is the source of your thinking, or wishing others to think, my statements are contradictory, as though I disapproved what I had earlier approved or accepted what I earlier rejected. Hear my open declaration, and understand it, or permit others to understand, raising no more mists of obscurity about the serenity of the most sincere truth. Just as it is good to use evils well, so it is honest to use the unseemly well. Not because of the beauty of the divine work, but because of the ugliness of lust, the Apostle calls these members of the body unseemly.[6] The chaste are not bound by a necessity to depravity, for they resist lust lest it compel them to commit unseemly acts; yet not even honorable procreation can exist without lust. In this way in chaste spouses there is both the voluntary, in the procreation of offspring; and the necessary, in lust. But honesty arises from unseemliness when chaste union accepts, but does not love, lust.

(38) Since it is your custom joyfully to report any conclusions of secular authors which you think will help you, examine honestly, if you can, what the poet says about Cato: 'He is a father to the city, a husband to the state; devoted to justice; servant of strict honesty; good in all things. No sudden pleasure rises to take him unawares.'[7] That is the sort of man Cato was. Whether it was true virtue and honesty which was praised in him is another question. But, regardless of the end to which he referred his acts, he certainly did not procreate children without pleasure. Yet, sudden pleasure did not take Cato unawares and take a

---
6 Cf. 1 Cor. 12.23.
7 Lucan, *Pharsal.*

part for itself, because he did not do for the sake of pleasure what he could not do without pleasure. He did not possess his vessel in the disease of lust—although he did not know God—if he was such a man as he is said to have been. Yet you do not wish to understand the Apostle's words: 'That every one of you learn how to possess his vessel, not in the disease of lust like the Gentiles who do not know God.'

(39) You do well to distinguish between the lesser good of marriage and the greater good of celibacy, but you are unwilling to put aside this dogma wholly inimical to grace. You say: 'Our Lord honored the glory of celibacy with free choice, saying: "Let him accept it who can" '—as though it were accepted, not by the gift of God, but by freedom of choice. You are silent about what He said earlier: 'Not all accept this teaching, but those to whom it has been given.'[8] Note what you say and what you leave unsaid. I think your conscience must disturb you, but, if this gives rise to perverted shame, the need to defend a hasty judgment overcomes wholesome fear. You censure only excess and never cease to praise lust itself; nor do you heed or sense or understand that what temperance must oppose, lest it exceed the limits of necessity, is evil.

(40) You think the Apostle's warning against possessing one's vessel in the disease of lust refers only to fornication, not to marriage, and thus you remove from the union of the married all the honesty of temperance, so that none could possess his vessel in the disease of lust, no matter what the passion drawing him to this in his wife. For, if you thought there should be moderation there, you could also have censured the excess of concupiscence in marriage itself, and seen that the Apostle's 'disease of lust' signifies this excess, instead of your groundless denial that 'his vessel'

---

[8] Matt. 19.12,11.

means a man's wife. The Apostle Peter in this matter also uses the word when he tells husbands to honor their wives as weaker vessels and as co-heirs of grace, and adds: 'See to it your prayers be not hindered.'[9] He speaks as his fellow Apostle, who prescribed conjugal temperance for times of prayers, and by concession permitted union with the spouse for pleasure, not for offspring.[10] Let Christian marriage hear this, let it not listen to you, who would have it not restrain concupiscence, but satisfy it whenever aroused, and thus secure its dominion. Let the faithful of Christ who are bound in marriage hear this, I say, that they may by consent establish times of temperance for prayer; and when, because of their intemperance, they return from prayer to the same habit, they may also know how to say to God: 'Forgive us our trespasses.'[11] For, what so great a teacher says by concession is surely a matter of indulgence, not command.

Chapter 10

(41) You quote my words commending the intention of truly godly, because Christian, spouses who generate children in this world that the children may be regenerated in Christ, for the sake of the other world.[1] You remark you have already destroyed the force of my argument in your second book, where anyone wanting to know what I answered you may read it. No one should commit adultery even if he intends to generate men to be regenerated, just as no one should steal even intending to provide for needy paupers;

---
9 Cf. 1 Peter 3.7.
10 1 Cor. 7.5-6.
11 Matt. 6.12.

---
1 *De nuptiis* 1.9.

although this may be accomplished, not by theft, but by good use of the mammon of wickedness, so that they may receive you into the everlasting dwellings.[2] Thus, children should be generated, not by adultery, but by good use of the evil of lust, with the intention of reigning with them in eternity.

(42) You give elegant praise to your protege when you truly say that one cannot think about anything else during intercourse. This is entirely true. What can one think about when the very mind with which he thinks is so absorbed in this carnal pleasure? He whose words I quoted in the foregoing book spoke well when he said: 'When its activity is most intense, it is most hostile to philosophy. Intense pleasure of the body is incompatible with great thought. What man, under the power of this the most intense of pleasures, can use his mind or carry on a process of reasoning, or think about anything at all?'[3] Not even you could have made a more serious charge against the lust you praise except by admitting that in its onslaught no one can think about what is holy. But, when a religious man uses this evil well, he first thinks about its good use and thus thinks to experience lust in intercourse, although he cannot think about this when experiencing it. In like manner, one thinking about his health can decide to go to sleep, although he cannot think about this when sleeping. But, when sleep fills the members, it is not in opposition to the will, because it takes from the will the power of command, turning the soul to visions in dreams, wherein future events are often revealed. If, then, there was this alternation between wakefulness and sleep in Paradise, where there was no evil of concupiscence, the dreams of that sleep were as happy as the life of the wakeful.

---

2 Cf. Luke 16.9.
3 Cicero, *Hortensius*.

(43) You boastfully and vainly say I put parents on a par with those who murder their own children, declaring that they cause their offspring to be born under condemnation. While you are elevating yourself on the exultation of your own eloquence, in the furor you create for yourself, you forget God. Why not make these complaints to the very Creator of men, instead of those who beget them, since He is certainly the Author and Creator of all goods; yet He does not cease to create those He has foreknown will burn in eternal fires, nor is aught but goodness imputed to Him because He creates them. Certain infants, even those baptized, He does not take from this life as adopted into the eternal kingdom, and does not confer on them the great benefit given him of whom we read: 'He was taken away lest wickedness alter his understanding.'[4] Yet, nothing is attributed to God except justice and goodness, by which from goods and evils He makes all things well and rightly. You see how much more understandable it is that nothing be imputed to parents, undeniably ignorant of their children's future, except that they choose to have children.

Chapter 11

(44) You quote from the Gospel: 'It were better for that man if he had not been born.'[1] But was his birth not due more to the work of God than his parents? Why did not God, foreknowing the evil that lay before him and which parents cannot know, give the better portion to His own image? Those who understand rightly know that nothing is attributed to God except what is proper to the goodness

---

4 Wisd. 4.11.

1 Matt. 26.24.

of the Creator. In like manner, without any difficult investigation, we must attribute to parents their wish to have children, although they know nothing of their future. But I do not say that children who die without the baptism of Christ will undergo such grievous punishment that it were better for them never to have been born, since our Lord did not say these words of any sinner you please, but only of the most base and ungodly. If we consider what He said about the Sodomites, which certainly He did not mean of them only—that it will be more tolerable for one than for another in the day of judgment,[2] who can doubt that non-baptized infants, having only original sin and no burden of personal sins, will suffer the lightest condemnation of all? I cannot define the amount and kind of their punishment, but I dare not say it were better for them never to have existed than to exist there. But you, also, who contend they are, as it were, free of any condemnation, do not wish to think about the condemnation by which you punish them by estranging from the life of God and from the kingdom of God so many images of God, and by separating them from the pious parents you so eloquently urge to procreate them. They suffer these separations unjustly, if they have no sin at all; or if justly, then they have original sin.

(45) You next quote the words in which I related how honorably the ancient fathers used their wives, and you say: 'They did not seek offspring with the intention of generating those to be washed as culprits by baptism, since the baptism by which we are now adopted had not yet been instituted.'[3] What you say about baptism is true, yet it is not a reason for thinking that, even before circumcision had been given, the servants of God did not help their children by any sacra-

---

2 Cf. Matt. 10.15; 11.24.
3 Cf. *De nuptiis* 1.9.

ment of the Mediator, since, indeed, faith in the Mediator who was to come in the flesh existed among them; although for some necessary reason Scripture did not reveal the nature of their sacrament. For we read of their sacrifices,[4] by which was figured the blood which alone takes away the sin of the world;[5] and, more openly, we read that, during the Law, sacrifices for sins were offered at the birth of infants. Can you answer what sins they were offered for? Think, also, that the soul of the infant of one of those fathers would perish from his people unless he were circumcised on the eighth day,[6] and answer what there could be in him whom you deny is subject to original sin to deserve that he must perish?

Chapter 12

(46) You have many objections to make about my declaration about 'Joseph, whose wife was Mary,' as I stated according to the Gospel.[1] You try to show that 'because there was no intercourse, there was no marriage.' By your reasoning, then, when the married cease to have intercourse, they are no longer spouses and the cessation will be divorce. Lest this come to pass, the decrepit must according to their power behave as the young, not sparing bodies worn with age from the act in which you, who profess celibacy, take such great joy. In order to remain spouses, let them not think of age, where the incentives of lust are concerned. If this pleases you, look to it. Nevertheless, because human soundness agrees that the motive in taking a wife is the procreation of offspring, regardless of how weakness yields

---
4 Cf. Lev. 12.
5 Cf. John 1.29.
6 Cf. Gen. 17.14.

---
1 *De nuptiis* 1.10.

to lust, I note, in addition to the faithfulness which the married owe to each other so that there be no adultery, and the offspring, for whose generation the two sexes are to be united, that a third good, which seems to me to be a sacrament, should exist in the married, above all in those who belong to the people of God, so that there be no divorce from a wife who cannot bear, and that a man not wishing to beget more children give not his wife to another for begetting, as Cato is said to have done.[2] This is why I said the full number of the three goods of marriage is found in what I declared by the Gospel was a marriage: 'Faithfulness, because no adultery; offspring, our Lord Christ; and sacrament, because no divorce.' And thus my statement that the full number of the goods of marriage, that is, this threefold good, was fulfilled in the parents of Christ does not, as you think, imply I meant to say that whatever is otherwise is evil. I say that there is another way in which marriage is good when offspring can be procreated only through intercourse. If there were another way to procreate, yet the spouses had intercourse, then they evidently must have yielded to lust, and made evil use of evil. But, since the two sexes were purposely instituted, man can be born only from their union, and thus spouses by their union for this purpose make good use of that evil; if, however, they seek pleasure from lust, this use is excusably evil.

(47) You say: 'It was only the common opinion that Joseph was her husband.' You would have us think Scripture was merely giving an opinion, not a fact, when it said that the Virgin Mary was his wife. Now, we hold that one of the Evangelists could have written in this way when relating either his own words or those of another man, and thus speaking according to men's opinions; but was the angel, speaking as one person to one person, merely giving an

---

2 Plutarch, *In vita Catonis;* Lucan 2.

opinion instead of a fact, contrary to his own knowledge and that of his hearer, when he said to Joseph: 'Do not be afraid to take to thee Mary thy wife'? And what was the purpose of listing the generations up to Joseph,[3] if not because the male sex has the place of honor in marriage? You were afraid to meet this argument in the book you are answering.[4] The Evangelist Luke says of our Lord: 'Being, as was supposed, the son of Joseph'[5]; because it was so supposed in order that it might be thought He was really begotten through the marriage union of Joseph. Luke wished to remove this false opinion, not to deny, contrary to the angel's testimony, that Mary was Joseph's wife.

(48) You yourself admit that 'He received the name husband from the faith of the betrothal.' This faith certainly remained inviolate. When he saw the holy Virgin already fruitful with the divine gift, he did not seek another wife, although he would never have sought the Virgin herself if she had not needed a husband. He did not think the bond of conjugal faith should be dissolved because the hope of carnal intercourse had been taken away. But think what you will about that marriage; we do not say, as you calumniate us: 'The first spouses were so instituted that they would have been spouses without the carnal union of the two sexes.' The point at issue between us is this: whether before sin the flesh lusted against the spirit in Paradise; or whether this does not now take place in spouses, when conjugal modesty itself must restrain the excess of this same concupiscence; whether this opposing force to which man may not consent, lest it proceed to its excesses, is not an evil; whether he in whom you deny any evil exists is not born of and with this concupiscence; and whether any man can be delivered

---

3 Cf. Matt. 1.20,16.
4 *De nuptiis* 1.12.
5 Luke 3.23.

from this inborn evil except by regeneration. In these matters your ungodly innovation is silenced by the ancient tradition of the Catholic truth.

Chapter 13

(49) You thought is is necessary to assemble testimonies from holy Scripture to prove something about which there was no question between us, namely, that man was created by God—which we may not deny about the least of worms. Do you not in all this seem to be unusually prolix, for purposes of your own? When you were making extended use of the testimony of holy Job, why did it not occur to you that that man of God, when talking about human sins, said no one on earth, not even a day-old infant, is free from sin?[1] Who but a man refusing to believe God exists, or cares for the things of the earth, will deny that mercy is bestowed on the great and the small by Him from whom the salvation of men and beasts comes, and who makes His sun rise on the good and the evil?[2] As though we had somehow disagreed about this matter, you try to teach it through the testimony of holy Job, because he said: 'Thou hast put me together with bones and sinews; thou hast granted me life and mercy.'[3] It is possible he did not refer to all men, but was only giving thanks for himself, that God had not deserted him who had been born carnally, and that He who created him had shown him mercy so that he might live truly, that is, live justly; or, perhaps, because the life he had been allotted at birth was a paltry thing, he added 'and mercy,' lest he remain by nature a son of wrath even

---
1 Cf. Job 14.5 (Septuagint).
2 Cf. Matt. 5.45.
3 Job 10.11,12.

as all the rest, to remain among the vessels of wrath and not be made one of the vessels of mercy.

(50) I no longer know how many times we have answered why a believer is not guilty of the evil always near him and existing in his members, while the newly born contracts guilt from this evil; for rebirth, not birth, conferred this benefit on the believer. Therefore, the offspring can be delivered from guilt only as his parent was delivered.

Chapter 14

(51) Dialectics has taught you an impressive truth: 'That which inheres in a subject cannot exist without the thing which is the subject of its inherence.' You conclude: 'Therefore, the evil which inheres in the parents as its subject cannot transmit its guilt to something else to which it does not extend, that is to say, to the offspring.' What you say would be correct if the evil of concupiscence did not extend to the offspring from the parents; but, because no one is seminated without it, no one is born without it. How can you say it does not extend to that to which it passes? Not Aristotle, about whose Categories you are foolishly wise, but the Apostle, says: 'Through one man sin entered into the world, and it has passed unto all men.'[1] Dialectics is not false, but you do not understand its teaching. What you have taken from dialectics is true; things which inhere in a subject, such as qualities, cannot exist without the subject in which they inhere, as color or form inheres in a subject body. But they pass to other things by affecting them, not by emigrating, as Ethiopians beget black men because they themselves are black, although the parents do not transfer like a coat the color of their bodies to their offspring. By means

---
1 Rom. 5.12.

of the quality of their own bodies, they affect the body which is propagated of them. It is even more wonderful when the qualities of corporeal things pass to incorporeal beings, yet this happens when we somehow derive the corporeal forms we see and store them up in memory, and carry them with us wherever we go. These forms are not separated from the bodies whose forms they are, yet they pass to us in a marvellous way when our senses are affected by them. Now, they pass from the spirit to the body in the same way in which they pass from the body to the spirit. The various colors of Jacob's rods affected the mothers of lambs, and this passed to their souls; then, passing from the souls of the ewes by the same kind of influence, those colors appeared in the bodies of the lambs.[2] The well-known medical authority, Soranus, writes and confirms by an historical example that such can also take place in human offspring. He narrates that the tyrant Dionysius, because he was deformed and did not wish his son to be like himself, used at time of intercourse to place before his wife a portrait of an extremely handsome man, so that she, desiring its beauty, might absorb it, and this effect might be transmitted to the offspring she conceived.[3] For, when God creates something having a nature, He does not remove the laws He has given to the movements of that nature. In like manner, then, although these faults are in a subject, they may pass from parents to

---

[2] Cf Gen. 30.37-42.
[3] When he considered this book in his *Retractationes* (2.62), Augustine said: 'In the fifth volume of this long and elaborate work, I mentioned a deformed husband who at the time of intercourse used to place before his wife a beautiful portrait, lest she bear deformed children. I gave the man a name as though this were certain knowledge, although it was not certain, for my memory deceived me. Soranus, the medical authority, wrote that a Cyprian king actually used to do this, but Soranus did not give the name of that king.' Soranus was a physician of Ephesus, who practiced his profession first at Alexandria and later at Rome, A.D. 98-138.

children, not by wandering from their own subject to another, as those Categories you have read most truly show is impossible, but, as you do not understand, by affecting the offspring and by contagion.

Chapter 15

(52) Why did you strive by elaborate arguments to arrive at the sea of ungodliness revealed in your words: 'The flesh of Christ, because He was born of Mary, whose flesh like that of all the rest came from propagation from Adam, will not differ from sinful flesh, and we should not find any distinction expressed in the Apostle's words[1] that He was sent in the likeness of sinful flesh'? You dare insist: 'There is no sinful flesh, lest the flesh of Christ also be this.' Then what is the likeness of sinful flesh, if there is no sinful flesh? You say I have not understood the Apostle's meaning; but neither have I explained his words in such a way that we might believe, as you teach, that a thing resembles something non-existent. If these are the words of one demented, and it cannot be doubted that the flesh of Christ is not sinful flesh but like to sinful flesh, what remains but to hold that, excepting His flesh, all other human flesh is sinful flesh? We see, moreover, that the concupiscence through which Christ willed not to be conceived produced the propagation of evil in the the human race, for though the body of Mary was thence derived, it did not transmit concupiscence to the body it did not thence conceive. Moreover, whoever denies that the reason the body of Christ is said to be the likeness of sinful flesh is that all other flesh of men is sinful flesh, and so compares the flesh of Christ with the flesh of

---
1 Cf. Rom. 8.3.

other men as to assert they are of equal purity, is a detestable heretic.

(53) You think you have found something important and argue at length that, 'Even if the born contract evil from their parents, it would be cleansed by the power of God, because He Himself forms them in their mother's womb. As though we denied this last, you give many testimonies from Scripture to prove we are formed by Him, and you quote from the Book of Ecclesiasticus, which says the works of God are hidden works.[2] You immediately add your own voice: 'This judgment refutes the vanity of those who believe the depths of nature can be comprehended by investigation.' Apply this to yourself, and do not try rashly to define the origin of the soul, which cannot be comprehended by any absolutely certain reasoning or any unambiguous passage of Scripture. Speak rather like that very wise woman, the mother of the Machabees, whose words to her sons you quote: 'I know not how you were formed in my womb.'[3] We surely cannot think she meant their bodies, which she had no doubt she conceived from male seed. She truly did not know whether the souls of her children were derived from the father's seed, or began to exist in her womb from somewhere else; nor was she ashamed to confess her ignorance, that she might avoid temerity. What do you mean, then, when you ask: 'Why would not the children be cleansed in the work itself, so that the hands of the Creator would purify them of the defilements attributed to the parents?' You do not see this could also be said about the manifest bodily faults with which not a few infants are born; yet, let none ever doubt that the true and good God forms all bodies. Nevertheless, from the hands of so great a Creator proceeds a multitude not only of faulty things, but even such monsters that they

---

2 Cf. Eccli. 3.22 23.
3 2 Mach. 7.22.

are called 'errors of nature' by some who, unable to search out the divine power, what God does and why, are ashamed to confess they do not know what they do not know.

(54) When we consider the passing of original sin to all men, we see that because it passes by means of the concupiscence of the flesh, it could not have passed to flesh that a virgin conceived, not through concupiscence. You quote from another book I wrote to Marcellinus, of holy memory, and you attribute to me the statement: 'All who were to come from this stock Adam infected in himself.' Christ did not come into His mother's womb thence, whence Adam infected all. I shall repeat the most important parts of my argument, since you did not wish to quote them, for reasons that will soon become clear. I said: 'By this hidden corruption, that is, his carnal concupiscence, he infected in himself all who were to come from his stock.'[4] Thus, he did not infect flesh in whose conception this corruption was not present. The flesh of Christ received mortality from the mortality of His mother's body, because it found her body mortal; it did not contract the taint of original sin, because it did not find the concupiscence of one carnally seminating. But, if He had received only the substance of the flesh from His mother, and not mortality, His flesh not only could not have been sinful flesh; it could not have been the likeness of sinful flesh.

(55) You equate me and my teaching with the error of Apollinaris, who, you say, 'denied that bodily senses existed in Christ'; so that you may create confusion everywhere for the uninformed, lest they see the light of truth.[5] The bodily

---

4 *De peccatorum meritis et remissione* 1.10.
5 In the *Opus imperfectum contra Julianum,* Augustine denies that the doctrine here stated by Julian is genuinely Apollinarian. Apollinaris did not deny that Christ had the sense faculties of the body: he denied that the Word of God assumed a human soul when He assumed human nature.

senses, without which no man living in the body ever has been or is or will be, are not the same as the concupiscence by which the flesh lusts against the spirit. Before sin, the first man existed without this concupiscence, and he had a human nature such as we have been shown in Christ, for Christ was created from a woman, without the activity of concupiscence, as the first man was created from earth. But Christ also assumed from the woman the infirmity of mortality, and before sin this infirmity did not exist in the flesh of the first man. Christ assumed it that His flesh might be what the flesh of the first man at the first had not been: the likeness of sinful flesh. That He might give us an example of suffering, He who had no iniquity of His own bore the iniquities of others; He bore us, not in covetings, but in sorrows.

(56) Therefore, those born of Adam must be transferred, reborn, to Christ, lest the image of God perish from the kingdom of God. Man generated from the condemned origin must be generated with this evil. God forbid, however, that as you calumniate us, we 'place the regenerated under necessity to commit evil, God giving the gifts of virtues.' Although we see another law in our members, warring against the law of our mind, we are not thereby forced to commit crimes; he whose spirit lusts by the spiritual gift against the concupiscence of the flesh is worthy of praise. No matter where you turn, how you boast, what you accumulate, how you expand and sputter—what the good spirit combats is not good.

(57) You say: 'An unlike nature could not have given us an example.' It could, indeed; what else is meant when He exhorts us to imitate the Father, who makes His sun rise upon the good and the bad, so that by His example we may love our enemies?[6] But the nature of the man Christ

---

6 Cf. Matt. 5.44,45.

was not unlike our nature; it was unlike our fault. He alone of all men born was born without fault. As to our life imitating Christ: that He is also God while we are only men makes a great difference, for no man can be as just as the man who is also God. You say something important and true when you cite the testimony of the Apostle Peter: 'He did no sin';[7] and note the Apostle holds this statement that Christ did no sin sufficient to prove there was no sin in Him. 'Thus he teaches,' you conclude, 'that He who did not sin could not have had sin.' Entirely true; for certainly the adult would have committed sin if there was sin in the infant. The reason that, except for Him, there is no man who has not committed sin after reaching majority is that, except for Him, no man is without sin at the beginning of infancy.

(58) You say: 'Remove the cause of the example, and you take away its value for us.' No wonder you find nothing but an example in Christ, since you attack the help of grace, of which He was the fullness. You say: 'In the hope of being without evil, we seek the supports of the faith; yet we are not without power, since manliness itself remains after baptism.' By manliness you mean the concupiscence of the flesh; the thing indeed remains against which the spirit must lust, lest man already reborn be enticed and drawn away by his own concupiscence. But, surely, the concupiscence which wars in order to draw man away, even if it does not do so when the spirit lusts against it and resists—and therefore it does not conceive and bring forth sin,[8] is not a good. About this concupiscence the Apostle says: 'For I know that in me, that is in my flesh, no good dwells.'[9] If Christ had had in His nature this thing which is not good, He would not have healed it in ours.

---

7 1 Peter 2.22.
8 Cf. James 1.14,15.
9 Rom. 7.18.

Chapter 16

(59) You quote again from my book, where I said: 'Conjugal intercourse performed with the intention of generating children is not itself sin, because the good will of the soul directs and does not follow the consequent pleasure of the body.'[1] You argue against this that 'Sins do not arise from a thing which is free from the sin.' You think thus to destroy the original sin which none destroys except the Saviour you deny to infants; but He destroys it by freeing them from it, not by denying its existence. Conjugal intercourse with the intention of generating children is not sin, because it uses well the law of sin, that is to say, the concupiscence existing in the members of the body and warring against the law of the mind. If this concupiscence does not bind the parent by guilt, but only because he was regenerated, no wonder it binds the one born, because he was generated from it; therefore, in order that he do not remain guilty, he also must be regenerated. If you could understand how your statement that 'Sins do not arise from a thing which is free from sin' helps the Manichaeans, you would wish to delete it from your book and from the hearts of all who have read it. If sins do not arise from a thing which is free from sin, then, as the Manichaeans say, sins have a nature of their own from which they arise. In Book I of this work I showed how you aid the Manichaeans by other declarations of the same kind.[2] What you say here has the same effect. Do you not see that if we are to overcome the Manichaeans, in addition to our concern with the special error by which you are Pelagians, we must also overcome statements of yours like this? You say: 'Sins do not arise from a thing which is free from sin,' but this is contradicted by the truth, which answers

---
1 *De nuptiis* 1.13.
2 Cf. above, pp. 46-53.

you and the Manichaeans, in this opinion you share with them. The angel God created was free from sin; the man God first created was free from sin. Thus, whoever denies sins arise from things free from sin either is himself a Manichaean or inadvertently bears witness for the Manichaeans.

(60) You quote other words of mine and argue as though I had said that, when lust serves the married in propagating offspring, it is then honorable. You may think what pleases you, but I never said this, and never held it. How is lust honorable as a servant when its master, the soul, must suppress it lest it rush to the excess in which its freedom consists? Thus, we do not say what you attribute to us: The use of lust always means guilt. As though we said it, you conclude we say: Adulterers sin less than husbands, because lust serves the married in sinning, but it commands adulterers. Since I do not make the first assumption, I do not care what conclusion you draw from it. I say to use lust is not always sin, because to use well an evil is not sin, nor does good use by a good man mean the thing itself must be good. Of two men it is written: A learned son will be wise, but he may use an imprudent minister';[3] is it then good to be imprudent, since the wise use the imprudent well? Thus, the Apostle John does not tell us not to use the world, but says: 'Do not love the world,' in which he also puts the concupiscence of the flesh.[4] Whoever uses something and does not love it is as though using and not using, because he does not use it for its own sake, but for something else he so beholds and so loves that he uses the other even though he does not love it. This is why John's fellow Apostle says: 'Who use this world as though not using it.'[5] What is it to use as though not using, except that

---
3 Prov. 10 (Septuagint).
4. 1 John 2.15,16.
5 1 Cor. 7.31.

they do not love what they are using, it being something they would otherwise do well not to use? This may also be seen in those things in the world which are good, but in such a way that they should not be loved. Who can justly say money itself is evil? Yet, none who loves it uses it well. How much more is this true of lust? For an evil spirit lusts after money, but money, unlike lust, does not lust against the good spirit; thus, both he who denies it is evil sins, and he who uses this evil does not sin. You argue: 'If lust is evil, it binds the married, whom it obeys, in greater guilt than the adulterers it dominates.' Your argument would be correct if we actually said that the married who use the evil of concupiscence only for their office of generating children use it for evil purposes, as a murderer uses a servant to commit his crime. But we say the office of procreation is good in the married, even though the one born contracts from the contagion of the first sin the wound which can be healed in him when he is reborn. It follows that good spouses should use the evil of concupiscence just as the wise use an imprudent minister for good works.

(61) But you, with your sharp sight, censure and think execrable not the mode, not the genus, but only the excess of this pleasure, because, as you say: 'It can be kept within the limits granted by the sovereign power of the mind.' Let the sovereign power of the mind bring it about, if it can, that lust does not arouse itself to go beyond the limits set by the mind. If the mind cannot do this, then it must resist and keep in check the faithless enemy constantly trying to transgress these limits. You protest we bear witness that there is total contempt for it in virgins and celibates. Do virgins and celibates, then, not war against the concupiscence of the flesh? What do they oppose in those glorious combats you proclaim, so that they may preserve virginity and celibacy? If they fight, they try to ex-

pel evil, and where but in themselves? Therefore, they also truly say: 'In me, that is, in my flesh, no good dwells.'

(62) You say: 'Marriage is nothing else but the union of bodies.' Next you say something true, that 'Propagation cannot take place without mutual desire and the union of bodies and the natural act.' But, do you deny that adulterers come together with mutual desire in the natural act and the union of bodies? Therefore, you have not given the definition of marriage. Marriage itself is not the same as that without which not even marriage can propagate offspring. Men can be born without marriage, and there can be spouses without the union of bodies; otherwise, to say no more, they will not be spouses when old, and either unable to have intercourse or since they have no hope of offspring, blush and do not wish to perform that act. You see, then, how ill considered is your definition that marriage is nothing else but the union of bodies. It would be more tolerable if you said marriage is not begun except through the union of bodies, because men take wives for the purpose of procreating children, and this cannot be done in any other way. But the union of bodies for the purpose of procreation would have taken place differently if there had been no sin; God forbid we think that that most honest happiness in Paradise always obeyed an aroused lust, and that that peace of soul and body held a cause of internal warfare in the first nature of man. If there was no need either to serve lust or to war against it, then either lust did not exist there or was not such as it is now, for at the present time whoever does not wish to serve lust must war against it; whoever neglects the fight must serve it. Of the two, the one, though praiseworthy, is an affliction; the other is base and wretched. In this world, then, one of these is necessary for the chaste, but in Paradise both were unknown to the blessed.

(63) You think to find another contradiction in my book,

and quote the passage where I distinguished the office of propagation from the desire for carnal pleasure, saying I assert that to have intercourse only when intending to generate offspring, wherein there is no guilt, is not the same thing as to desire carnal pleasure in union, although, provided this is with the spouse, the guilt in it is venial.[6] In so far as all who see the truth agree with me about this, you can find no evidence here of contradiction. Listen once more to the same words, for this should be brought home to the minds of those you want to deceive. You slander us, saying we 'permit base and criminal men to excuse themselves when they commit unspeakable impurities, by saying they did so against their will, therefore have not sinned,' as though we did not much more vigorously exhort them to fight against lust. If you, however, despite your saying lust is good, do not wish us to think your war against that good is growing cold or at least lukewarm, must we not just so much more wakefully and ardently fight against evil? We say it is against our will that our flesh lusts against our spirit, but not that our spirit lusts against our flesh; and through this good concupiscence the married refrain from using the lust of the flesh except for the purpose of generating offspring, and thus they make good use of evil, which good use makes for honest and truly nuptial union. Use for the sake of pleasure, not for offspring, makes this union culpable, yet it may be venial when it is with the spouse. But the reason everyone born, even of honest union, contracts that which is washed away at rebirth is that the evil used well by the goodness of marriage exists even in honorable union. But what is against them at birth is not against them after rebirth; whence it follows that is is also against him who is born of them if he be not reborn.

---

6 *De nuptiis* 1.7.

(64) In the midst of your twisted arguments against my words you do not see you are once more helping the Manichaeans. You think a man born of conjugal union does not contract original sin, because, you say, 'Guilt cannot be brought forth from a work which has no guilt.' Why were the guilt of angel and the guilt of man brought forth from the work of God where there was not guilt? See how well you testify for those you so detest you try to conceal what you hold against the absolutely firm Catholic faith. If, by your definition, 'Guilt cannot be brought forth from a work which has no guilt,' then consider, since none of God's works has guilt: Whence was guilt brought forth? This Manichaeus, with your help, wishes to introduce another nature which by his foolish wisdom is an evil nature, to be regarded as that whence guilt arises, for, by your words, 'Guilt cannot be brought forth from a work of God.' Can this Manichaeus be overcome unless you are also overcome with him? Both angel and man are works of God, without guilt; yet guilt was brought forth from them when through the free will given them without guilt they withdrew from Him who is without guilt, and they were made evil, not through admixture of evil, but through failure from good.

(65) You say I praise the celibacy of the Christian era, not to inspire men to virginity, but to condemn the goodness of marriage, although this good was instituted by God. Not to be unduly disturbed by malicious suspicions about my soul, you say as though to test me: 'If you are really inviting men to strive for continence, you will admit that the virtue of chastity can be possessed by those who wish, in such a way that whoever wishes may be holy in body and soul.' I answer that I admit it, but not in your sense. You attribute this to the powers of the soul itself; I attribute it to the will helped by the grace of God. But what must be suppressed by the command of the soul, lest we sin? In

order not to say with the Manichaeans, then, that this evil is mixed with us from an alien, evil nature, we must confess that in our nature there is something like a wound which must be healed; that the guilt for it has now been healed by regeneration.

(66) It was in vain you listed the many wiles of the heretics with whom you compare me, and whose number I pray you may not increase. You say I must feel the weight of the Apostle's words naming the heretics who forbid marriage,[7] as though I said: 'After the coming of Christ, marriage is filthy.' Listen to what we actually say, and, when you have heard it often and in many ways, you may perhaps no longer dissimulate the truth by simulating deafness. We do not say marriage is filthy, since incontinence must be stayed by the soundness of marriage, lest it fall into damnable baseness. But the Christian teaching does not say what you say, in your own words: 'Man is fully capable of regulating the activities he possesses by birth.' We do not say this; we say what the Apostle says: 'Each one has his own gift from God.'[8] We say what our Lord says: 'Without me, you can do nothing' and 'Not all can accept this teaching, but those to whom it has been given';[9] although He could have said, if your opinion were true, that not all accept this teaching, but only those who wish. I ask you: What sort of activities had by birth do you say a man is able to regulate—good or evil? If good, the spirit lusts against good, and two goods are hostilely opposed in man, and this opposition of two goods could not be good. But if these are evil activities, you admit that in man there are evil activities he possesses by birth, against which chastity fights. Not to be obliged to agree with the Manichaeans that there

---

7 Cf. 1 Tim. 4.3.
8 1 Cor. 7.7.
9 John 15.5; Matt. 19.11.

is a mixture of an alien nature of evil in us, you had better admit our original sickness. This sickness is the evil which conjugal modesty uses well; it is the evil to which the incontinent apply the remedies of marriage, and against which celibates fight in glorious combats. I think, however, the promise I made when I began my answer to your arguments involving real difficulties will be more suitably fulfilled if I do not exceed the number of your books. This, then, shall end my fifth book, so that your last may be refuted from another standpoint.

BOOK SIX

Chapter 1

WE HAVE ANSWERED your third volume and now answer the fourth; with God's help we shall give you charity as well as truth. Whoever has these two will never be guilty of folly or envy,[1] two vices discussed at length at the beginning of your volume. Error must yield to truth, envy to charity. When you speak of folly, saying: 'It is the mother of all vices,' you quote Scripture: 'God loveth none but him that dwelleth with wisdom.'[2] Ask yourself seriously whether the childish vanity which man must necessarily pass through on his way from infancy can dwell with wisdom. Consider the first-fruit born of the root you praise and think of the change required that he may be loved by God, who loves none but him who dwells with wisdom. God removes what He hates from predestined infants

---
[1] The English words, 'foolishness,' 'folly,' 'wisdom,' and 'vanity,' which, as they occur in Scripture, often have a less common if not archaic sense, have been kept in this translation in order to preserve the Scriptural allusions given by them.
[2] Wisd. 7.28.

that His love may be for those who, delivered from vanity, may dwell with wisdom. If the last day takes them from the breast, will you dare say they dwell with wisdom outside the kingdom of God, which, according to you, 'the good of inviolate and guiltless nature' does not permit them to enter unless the grace of the true Saviour shall redeem and deliver them from the folly of deceitful speech? I shall say nothing of those who are feeble-minded by nature, who in the words of Scripture are more to be mourned than the dead.[3] The grace of God is indeed able to deliver them from so great an evil through the blood of the Mediator; but how could they have fallen into so great an evil unless by divine decree there was a punishment due a vitiated origin?

(2) Truly there is reason for censuring, and grievously censuring, 'those who fail to learn the known and do not hesitate to disapprove the unknown.' Could you not say this of those born feeble-minded? You can find no way in which the evil could have befallen them under a just God, if children do not contract from their parents something deserving punishment. You say we are senselessly envious of you, in a sort of 'midday of known truth, where there is no shadow of the unknown.' But you who are without envy, why do you not see great evils in infants? God is good, God is just; there is no such thing as a nature of evil mixed with our own, as the Manichaeans hold. Whence come the great evils of men— I do not mean moral evils, but evils in the very wits with which they are born—if human origin is not vitiated and there is no condemned mass? Do not you, who are free of feeble-mindedness and envy, make envy appear both sin and punishment for sin? Is not envy the sin of the Devil? Is not that which 'immediately harasses the one in whom it arises' a punishment for sin? These are your own words, yet you thought by constant repetition to argue acutely, saying: 'One

---

[3] Cf. Eccli. 22.13.

and the same fault cannot be both sin and punishment for sin.' But, since you are without envy, you could scarcely see in your other book the envy about which you speak here, and thus because you do not envy me, you contradict yourself.

Chapter 2

(3) After your prologue, where, as usual, you seek to prove what I already hold, that 'God is the Creator of men,' you introduce my words: 'A man born of the concupiscence of the flesh is born to the world and not to God. He is born to God when he is reborn of water and Spirit.'[1] Mistakenly, you took these words to mean that whatever pertains to the world pertains to the Devil, because I said somewhere else that 'Those who are born of the union of bodies belong by right to the Devil' and also 'they are rescued from the domain of darkness when they are regenerated in Christ.' I shall answer your false accusation. You would like to have men think I said the world belongs to the domain of the Devil in such a way that the Devil either made the heavens and the earth and all things in them or that he controls them. I never said this; on the contrary, I detest, I refute, I condemn anyone who says it. I speak of the world as our Lord did when He said: 'The prince of this world is coming.'[2] He did not mean the Devil is the prince of the heavens and the earth and all things that were made through the Word, through the same Christ Himself, whence it is said: 'The world was made through him.'[3] He meant: 'The whole world is in the power of the evil one'; and again: "All that is in the world is the concupiscence of the flesh and the concupiscence of the

---
[1] *De nuptiis et concupiscentia* 1.21.
[2] John 14.30.
[3] John 1.10.

eyes, and the pride of life, which is not from the Father, but from the world.'⁴ The heavens and the earth are from the Father through the Son; also, the angels, the constellations, the trees, the animals, and men in their very substance as men are from the Father through the Son. The prince of the world is the Devil, and the world which is in the power of the wicked one means all men subject to eternal condemnation unless delivered therefrom and redeemed by the Blood which was shed for the remission of sins, and thus no longer under the prince of sinners. To this world, whose prince is the one about whom He who overcame the world says: 'Behold, the prince of the world is coming, and in me he has nothing,'⁵ I say man is born to this world until he is reborn in Him who overcame the world and in whom the Prince of this world has nothing.

(4) What is this world of which the Saviour of the world and the conquerer of the world says: 'The world cannot hate you, but it hates me, because I bear witness concerning it that its works are evil?'⁶ Are the works of the earth and the sea, of the heavens and the constellations, evil works? Surely, this world is man. And no one is chosen for deliverance out of this world except by the grace of God through Jesus Christ the Lord, who gave His own flesh for the life of the world; and this He would not have done if the world had not been in death. Which world is this about which He said to the Jews: 'You are of this world and I am not of this world'?⁷ Which is this world from which Jesus chose His disciples so that they were no longer of the world, and thus the world would hate them who were no longer of it? The Saviour of the world, the Light of the world, says: 'These things I command you, that you love one another. If the world hates you, know

---
4 1 John 5.19; 2.16.
5 John 16.33; 14.30.
6 John 7.7.
7 John 8.23.

that it has hated me before you. If you were of the world, the world would love what is its own. But because you are not of the world, but I have chosen you out of the world, therefore the world hates you.'⁸ If He had not added: 'I have chosen you out of the world,' we could think He said: 'You are not of the world,' in the way in which He said of Himself: 'I am not of the world.' But He was not likewise first of the world and then chosen out of it so as not to be of the world. What Christian would say this? Nor is it true the Son of God was of the world inasmuch as He deigned to be man; how can this be so unless because in Him there was not sin, which is the reason every man is born first to the world, not to God; and, to be born to God, he who shall be reborn so as no longer to be of the world must be chosen out of the world? Therefore He casts out the prince of this world, and testifies: 'Now is the judgment of the world; now will the prince of the world be cast out.'⁹

(5) Unless, perhaps, your rashness causes you to say I hold that infants are not chosen out of the world when they are washed by the baptism of Him of whom it is said: 'God was truly in Christ, reconciling the world to himself.' If you, denying that infants are of the world, deny they belong to this reconciliation, I do not know by what effrontery you are in the world. If you admit they are chosen out of the world when they pass into the Body of Christ, then it is necessary they be born to the world out of which they are chosen for rebirth, for they are born through the concupiscence of the flesh; reborn through the grace of the Spirit. The concupiscence of the flesh is of the world; grace came into the world that those who were predestined before the world may be chosen out of the world. When the Apostle says: 'God was truly in Christ, reconciling the world to himself,' he adds

---

8 John 15.18,19.
9 John 12.31.

immediately how He did this: 'not reckoning against men their sins.'[10] Therefore, the whole world was guilty from Adam, God not withholding His creative power from His own work, although the seeds already instituted had been vitiated by the paternal prevarication. When the world is reconciled through Christ, it is delivered from the world, when it is delivered by Him who came into the world, not to be chosen, but Himself to choose, not by election of merits, but by election of grace, because a remnant is saved according to the election of grace.[11]

Chapter 3

(6) You next quote my words: 'Regeneration alone remits the guilt of concupiscence, and thus generation continues to contract it.' I added immediately: 'Therefore, what is generated must be regenerated, so that what has been contracted may be remitted in that same way, for it cannot be remitted otherwise.'[1] In another futile attempt to conceal your suspicion that baptism is superfluous in infants, you say: 'The grace of the mysteries of Christ is rich in many gifts.' Whether you will or not, we hold that infants believe in Christ through the hearts and voices of those who carry them. Hence, the sentence of our Lord, 'He who does not believe shall be condemned,'[2] also pertains to them. For what reason, and in what justice, if they contract no sin by way of origin? You say: 'Here, rather, He approves them as His own, because, even before they could use their will, He exalts what He has done in them.' If He approves these as His own, then He does not

---

10 2 Cor. 5.19.
11 Cf. Rom. 11.5.

1 *De nuptiis* 1.21.
2 Mark 16.1.

approve as His own those to whom He does not give added favors. But, since the others are also His, and for the same reason, that He created them, why does He not also approve of them as His own? Here you say nothing to exclude fate or respect for persons. Then, admit grace with us. What else is there, if none of these? In one and the same situation, one is left, by an act of justice, not by fate; another is taken, by the gift of grace, not by merit.

(7) Your contention that infants are not cleansed even of original sin by regeneration is without foundation. He who said: 'All we who have been baptized into Christ Jesus have been baptized into his death,' surely did not except infants when he said 'all who.' What is it to be baptized into the death of Christ but to die to sin? He also says of Him in another passage: 'The death that he died he died to sin once for all.' This was said because of the likeness of sinful flesh, because of which there is also the great mystery of His cross, where 'our old man is crucified with him that the body of sin may be destroyed.' If infants, then, are baptized into Christ, they are baptized into His death; but if they are baptized into His death, they who have been united with Him in the likeness of His death die to sin. 'For the death that he died, he died to sin once for all, but the life that he lives, he lives unto God.' And what does it mean to be united with Him in the likeness of His death except what follows: 'Thus do you consider yourselves also as dead to sin but alive to God in Christ Jesus.'[3] Are we to say that Jesus died to sin which He never had? God forbid. Yet, that He died to sin, He died once for all; His death signified our sin through which death itself came. When He died to death—that is, so that He would no more be mortal—He is said to have died to sin. Through His grace we in the sinful flesh carry out what He signified in the likeness of sinful flesh, so that as He by dying to the

---
3 Rom. 6.3.11.

likeness of sin is said to be dead to sin; so, whoever is baptized into Him dies to that same reality of which His flesh was a likeness. And as there was true death in His true flesh, so there is true remission in true sins.

Chapter 4

(8) If that whole passage of the Apostle's letter fails to overcame your perversity, you are obdurate indeed. Though everything he says when he writes to the Romans to commend the grace of God through Jesus Christ is connected with it, we cannot quote and discuss the entire Epistle now, for it is very long. Let us, then, consider the chapter we have been dealing with, where he says: 'God commends his charity towards us because when as yet we were sinners Christ died for us.'[1] You would have infants excluded from this statement. May I ask you: If they are not among sinners, how did He who died for sinners die for them? You will answer He did not die for sinners only, although He died also for sinners. Nowhere will you find in the sacred authors that Christ died also for those who had no sin at all. But see how hard pressed you are by valid testimonies. You say He died also for sinners; I say He died for none but sinners. Thus, if I am right, you must answer that if infants are bound by no sin, He did not die for infants. The Apostle says to the Corinthians: 'Since one died for all, therefore all died, and Christ died for all.'[2] You must admit, then, that Jesus died for none but the dead. Then, who are the dead in this passage? Those who have departed from the body? Who is so foolish as to think this is wise? The dead, then, for all of whom Christ died, should be understood in the way in which he says elsewhere: 'And

---

1 Rom. 15.8,9.
2 Cor. 5.14,15.

you, when you were dead by reason of your sins and the uncircumcision of your flesh, he brought to life along with him.'³ Again, he says: 'One died for all, therefore all died,' showing it cannot be so that He died for any but the dead, for from the fact that one died for all he proved that all died. I repeat, I re-enforce, I hold this openly. Accept it, for it brings health, and I do not want you to die. 'One died for all, therefore all died.' See how he insists it follows that all died if He died for all. Since this death is not in the body, it follows that all for whom Christ died died in sin. No one who is a Christian will deny or doubt it. Hence, if infants contract no sin, they are not dead. If they are not dead, He who died for none but the dead did not die for them. If you will heed your first volume, where you said: 'Christ died also for infants,' you cannot deny that they contract original sin. Whence did they die, if not for this reason? Because of what death of infants did He die who died for none but the dead? You admit He died for infants. Then return with me to the discussion of the Epistle to the Romans.

(9) The Apostle says: 'God commends his charity towards us, because when as yet we were sinners, Christ died for us.' 'When we were yet sinners,' he says, that is, when we were dead, 'Christ died for us. Much more, now that we are justified by his blood, shall we be saved through him from the wrath. For if when we were enemies we were reconciled to God by the death of his Son, much more, having been reconciled, shall we be saved by his life.' This is what he says elsewhere: 'God was truly in Christ, reconciling the world to himself.'⁴ He continues: 'Not this only, but we exult also in God through our Lord Jesus Christ.' He says: 'Not only saved, but also exulting, through whom we have now received reconciliation.' Then, as though someone asked why the

---
3 Col. 2.13.
4 2 Cor. 5.19.

reconciliation was made through one man, the Mediator, he says: 'Therefore as through one man sin entered into the world and through sin death, and thus death has passed unto all men; in whom all have sinned.' Then, what of the Law? Was it able to reconcile? No, he says: 'For until the Law sin was in the world,' that is, not even the Law could take away sin. 'But sin is not imputed when there is no law.' There was sin, to be sure, but sin was not imputed because it was not recognized. We read in another passage: 'For through law comes recognition of sin.'[5] 'And yet death reigned from Adam until Moses,' because its kingdom was not taken away even through Moses, that is, not through the Law.' But it reigned even over those who did not sin.' Why did it ruie them if they did not sin? This is why: 'in the likeness of the transgression of Adam, who is the form of the one to come.'[6] Adam gave to his posterity, even though not having sins of its own, the form that those begotten through his carnal concupiscence should die from the contagion of the paternal sin.[7] The Apostle says: 'But not like the offense is the gift. For if by the offense of the one many died, much more the grace of God and the gift in the grace of the one man Jesus Christ abounded unto the many.' It has surely abounded much more, because those in whom it abounds die in time, but will live eternally. 'Nor is the gift as it was in the case of one man's sin, for the judgment was from one man unto condemnation, but grace is from many offenses unto justification.' Truly, that one sin was able to draw to condemnation; yet grace

---

5 Rom. 3.20.
6 'In similitudine,' inquit, 'praevaricationis Adae, qui est forma futuri.' Dedit enim ex se formam posteris suis, quamvis peccata propria non habentibus, ut peccati paterni contagione morerentur, qui per ejus carnalem concupiscentiam gignerentur.
7 Augustine was also familiar with the more common interpretation of this passage of Scripture, and he accepted it without question, as is shown by his remarks on Chrysostom's statement about it, in Book 1; cf, above, pp. 32-33.

has taken away not only the one sin, but also the many that have been added to it. 'For if by reason of the one man's offense death reigned through the one man; much more will they who receive the abundance of the grace and of the gift of justice reign in life through the one Jesus Christ.' He repeats the earlier sense because those who reign eternally will have much greater power in life than death with its temporary sway: 'Therefore as from the offense of the one man the result was unto condemnation to all men; so from the justice of the one the result is unto justification of life.' He says it is all, in both instances, because none is unto death except through the former, and none is unto life except through the latter. 'For as by the disobedience of one man many were constituted sinners, so also by the obedience of the one the many will be constituted just. Now the law intervened that the offense might abound. But where the offense has abounded, grace has abounded yet more; so that as sin has reigned unto death, so also grace may reign by justice unto life everlasting through Jesus Christ our Lord.'

(10) 'What then shall we say? Shall we continue to sin that grace may abound? By no means!' If we continue in sin, of what benefit is grace? He continues: 'For how shall we who are dead to sin still live in it?' Mark what follows: 'Do you not know that all we who have been baptized into Christ Jesus have been baptized into his death?' Are baptized infants included or not? If not, then these words are false: 'All we who have been baptized into Christ Jesus have been baptized into his death,' because infants, you say, have been baptized, but not into His death. Since what the Apostle says is true, there can be no exception. If you think he means only adults with the use of free will when he says all, our fear is idle when we hear the words of our Lord: 'Unless a man be born again of water and the Spirit.' Here you have an important summation: Say Christ also was speaking only of adults, and

infants were not included in the universality of His words. What use is it for you to investigate the matter of baptism, asking whether there is eternal life outside the kingdom of God, or whether so many innocent images of God are deprived of eternal life and thus committed to eternal death? If you dare not say this because of the universality of His words: 'Unless a man be born again of water and the Spirit, he cannot enter into the kingdom of God,'[8] you are confronted with the same universality in the words of the Apostle: 'All we who have been baptized into Christ Jesus have been baptized into his death.' Therefore, infants also who have been baptized into Christ have died to sin because they have been baptized into His death. We reach the same conclusion from previous statements: 'How shall we who are dead to sin still live in it? As though we asked what it is to die to sin, he answers: 'Do you not know that all we who have been baptized into Christ Jesus have been baptized into his death?' This he proves by what he said before: 'How shall we who are dead to sin still live in it?' Thus, those who know they were baptized into the death of Christ when they were baptized into Christ may also know that they have died to sin, because to be baptized into the death of Christ is nothing else but to die to sin. To explain the matter even more clearly: 'For we were buried with him by means of baptism into death, in order that just as Christ has arisen from the dead through the glory of the Father, so we also may walk in newness of life. For if we have been united with him in the likeness of his death, we shall also be so in the likeness of his resurrection. For we know that our old man has been crucified with him in order that the body of sin may be destroyed, that we may no longer be slaves to sin; for he who is dead is acquitted of sin. But if we have died with Christ, we believe we shall also live together with Christ; for we know that

---

8 John 3.5.

Christ, having risen from the dead, dies now no more, death shall no longer have dominion over him. For the death that he died he died to sin once for all; but the life that he lives, he lives unto God.'[9] If, therefore, infants do not die to sin, they are not baptized into the death of Christ. If they are not baptized into the death of Christ, they are not baptized into Christ, for 'All we who have been baptized into Christ Jesus have been baptized into his death.' But they are indeed baptized into Christ; therefore they die to sin. To what sin but original sin, which they have contracted? Let men's arguments cease: 'The Lord knows the thoughts of men, that they are vain.'[10] He has hidden these things from the wise and prudent, and revealed them to little ones.[11] If you do not like the Christian faith, say so; you will not find another Christian faith. There is one man unto life; there is one unto death. The one is only man; the other is God and man. Through the one the world was made the enemy of God; through the other the world chosen from the world is reconciled to God. For, 'As in Adam all die, so in Christ all will be made to live. Therefore even as we have borne the image of the earthy, let us also bear the image of the heavenly.'[12] Whoever tries to undermine these foundations of the Christian faith will himself be destroyed, but they will remain firm.

Chapter 5

(11) In my book there is a true statement which you do not accept: 'That what has been remitted in the parent is contracted in the offspring happens in wondrous manner;

---
9 Rom. 5.8,6,11.
10 Ps. 93.11.
11 Cf. Matt. 11.25.
12 1 Cor. 15.22,48.

yet it does happen, and, because the manner is not easily understood nor easily expressed, it is not admitted by unbelievers.'[1] Why do you give my words dishonestly as though I had said: 'Reason cannot understand it, nor words express it?' You leave out what I really said: that it is not easily understood or expressed. It is not the same to say a thing cannot be done at all and to say it cannot be done easily; your statement is more than calumny. No matter what difficulty there may be in the thought and word, this has been proclaimed throughout the whole Church and believed from ancient times as the true Catholic faith. The Church would not exorcise and exsufflate the infants of the faithful if she were not rescuing them from the power of darkness and from the prince of death. I wrote this in my book which you are supposedly refuting, but you were afraid to mention it, as though you yourself would be exsufflated by the whole world, if you were to contradict this exsufflation by which even from infants the prince of this world is cast out.[2] Your meaningless arguments are not against me, but against our common spiritual mother; you would not have her bring forth children now in the way she brought you forth. You strike her very heart by what you regard as adequately sharp weapons, summoning arguments from the justice of God against the justice of God, from the grace of God against the grace of God. This, then, is the true justice of God: if the heavy yoke upon the children of Adam from the day of their coming out of their mother's womb[3] is not unjust. How is that heavy yoke not unjust if there is no evil in infants which makes it just that a heavy yoke oppress them? This is the true grace of God: when thing and word are in agreement. How could this be if grace exsufflates him in whom it knows there is nothing

1. *De nuptiis* 1.21.
2 *Ibid.* 1.22.
3 Cf. Eccli. 40.1.

to expel, if it washes him in whom it knows there is nothing to wash away?

(12) Would you or your associates believe you are saying anything, if with a pure mind you could realize how great is the evil of concupiscence of the flesh (when what is born of it must needs be reborn, and what is not reborn must be condemned); if you could realize what grace confers when, making full remission of sins in him, it absolves man of the guilt of this evil, by which concupiscence made him guilty by way of origin; even though it itself remains and the spirit of the one regenerated wars against it, either using it well in the lesser contest, or refraining entirely from its use, in the greater contest? For we are aware of this evil in its opposition or our restraint of it. Just as the guilt which was remitted only by regeneration was not sensed when it inhered, so its removal is accepted by faith, but not sensed by the flesh or the mind. Thus you throw yourself into the obscurity of this matter, and against a truth which cannot be demonstrated for the perception of extremely carnal men. But your keenness for battle is in proportion to your unbelief.

(13) But, 'Transform thyself as thou wilt, and collect what strength of courage or skill is thine,'[4] 'All we who have been baptized into Christ Jesus have been baptized into his death.' Hence, it is true we died to sin in the death of Christ, a death without sin. As a result, both adults and infants have died. It is not true that the former and not the latter, or the latter and not the former, but 'All we who have been baptized into Christ Jesus have been baptized into his death.' 'Therefore, we were buried with him by means of baptism into death.' This includes infants, because 'All we who have been baptized into Christ Jesus have been baptized into his death.' And as Christ has risen from the dead through the glory of the Father, so we also may walk in newness of life. For if we have

---

4 Virgil, *Aeneas* 12.889-890.

been united with him in the likeness of his death, we shall be so in the likeness of his resurrection also.' Infants have also been united in the likeness of His death, for this applies to all who have been baptized into Christ Jesus. 'For we know that our old man has been crucified with him.' What old man, unless it be 'All we who have been baptized into Christ'? Infants must be included, because they have been baptized into Christ. And what is the meaning of 'our old man has been crucified with him'? He says: 'In order that the body of sin may be destroyed, that we may no longer be slaves to sin.' Because of this body of sin, 'God sent his Son in the likeness of sinful flesh.'[5] By what impudence do you deny that infants also have the body of sin, when his words refer to all who have been baptized into Christ? 'For he who is dead is acquitted of sin. But if we have died with Christ, we believe that we shall also live together with Christ; for we know that Christ, having risen from the dead, dies now no more, death shall no longer have dominion over him. For the death that he died, he died to sin once for all, but the life that he lives, he lives unto God.' He says: 'Thus do you consider yourselves also dead to sin but alive to God in Christ Jesus.' To whom is he speaking? Are you fully attentive? Surely he is speaking to those to whom he said: 'If we have died with Christ.' And who are they except those to whom he said: 'Our old man has been crucified with him in order that the body of sin may be destroyed'? Who are they but those to whom he said: 'We have been united with him in the likeness of his death'? Who are they except those to whom he said: 'We were buried with him by means of baptism into death'? You will discover to whom he spoke if you will read the earlier words with which these are connected: 'Do you not know that all we who have been baptized into Christ Jesus have been baptized into his death?' What did he mean when he said this? Read back

---

5 Rom. 8.3.

a bit and you will find: 'How shall we who are dead to sin still live in it?' Then, either acknowledge that infants died to sin in baptism and confess that they had original sin to which to die, or admit frankly that they were not baptized into the death of Christ when they were baptized into Christ, and then accuse the Apostle of lying when he said: 'All we who have been baptized into Christ Jesus have been baptized into his death.'

(14) I hold on to the celestial weapons that conquer Celestius; to them I commit my faith and my speech. Your arguments are human; these weapons are divine. 'Who can understand sins?'[6] Are they, then, not sins? Who understands the original sin which is remitted in a regenerated parent yet passes to the offspring and remains there unless the offspring also is regenerated? Is it, then, not sin? 'One died for all, therefore all died.' With what heart, what speech, what countenance do you deny that infants have also died, when you do not deny Christ died for them? What is the meaning of their baptism if Christ did not die for them? 'For all we who have been baptized into Christ Jesus have been baptized into his death.' But, if the one who died for all died also for infants, then infants also have died together with all. And because they have died in sin they also die to sin to live to God when they are reborn through God's grace. What if I cannot explain how the living generates the dead (a parent dead to sin and living to God generates one dead in sin so that by regeneration he may die to sin and live to God); is it false because this cannot be explained in words or only with the greatest difficulty? Deny, if you dare, that he is born dead for whom you do not deny that Christ died. 'One died for all, therefore all died.'[7] These are the words of the Apostle but they are our weapons. If you are not prepared to oppose

---
6 Ps. 18.13.
7 2 Cor. 5.14.

them, then remember you must believe without doubting, even if you do not understand. A man born spiritually who begets carnally has both seeds: the immortal seed whence he has life and the mortal seed whence he generates the dead. The death of Christ would not have been necessary to give life to the offspring if the offspring were not born dead. 'One died for all, therefore all died.' You will not raise them from that death by exclaiming they are not dead. Rather, you will keep them from life if through the devices of ungodly arguments you attack the faith of their parents through which alone they can be restored to life.

Chapter 6

(15) We have now reached your wordy and pretentious discussion in which you try to refute an illustration I thought might throw a little light on a matter very difficult to understand; namely 'that the seed of an olive tree may degenerate into a wild olive.' You sought to brush it aside in the statement: 'Illustrations are of no value when used in reference to something that of its very nature cannot be defended.' Why, then, does the Apostle, immediately after raising the question of how the dead rise again, and with what body, undertake to show by an example a thing unknown and of which we have no experience? He says: 'Senseless man, what thou thyself sowest is not brought to life unless it dies.'[2] His example is not altogether inappropriate for the matter in hand. Wheat is cleansed of chaff as man is cleansed of sin, yet other wheat sprouts from it with chaff.

---

1 The wild olive, or oleaster, is used in Africa even today in propagation of the olive by grafting. Augustine develops this illustration in detail and uses it more than once in *De nuptiis et concupiscentia;* cf. 1.21,37,38.
2 1 Cor. 15.36.

(16) What did you have in mind about the crocodile when you said: 'Albinus affirms that it is the only animal whose upper jaw moves. The fire which means destruction to most things is sport for the salamander.' Are not these examples rather against you than for you, since you have found something which shows the possibility of what is generally denied? Hence, when you categorically deny that those who beget can transmit to their offspring something which they themselves do not have, then if something is found which can do this, you are refuted; just as the crocodile refutes him who says that animals can move only their lower jaw, and he who says no animal can live in fire is unanswerably silenced when given the facts about the salamander. When you declare that 'Natural things cannot be transformed by an accident,' it follows that if only a single person be found who, maimed by chance, generates offspring with the same faults, so that the accident in the parent becomes natural in the offspring, your statement is nullified. Again you say: 'A parent cannot transmit to his offspring that which he himself does not have.' Will not your statement be invalidated if it is shown that offspring with all their members intact may be born of parents who have lost some of their members? Our elders report they both knew and saw Fundanius, a Carthaginian orator, who accidentally lost the sight of one eye and generated a son with only one eye. This example answers your proposition that 'Natural things cannot be transformed by an accident.' That which was an accident in the father was natural for the son. Your other proposition, 'Parents cannot transmit to their offspring what they themselves do not have,' is answered in the case of another son of Fundanius, who, as is usual, was born with two eyes, from a parent who had but one eye. There are numberless children born with sight from blind parents, who transmit to their offspring what they themselves

do not have. In your blind observations you resemble these parents more than do their own offspring.

Chapter 7

(17) Although many of your words are irrelevant, you urge me to keep to the point, saying: 'We marvel less at things we can fully grasp. Against this fault in human curiosity the divine plan has provided that the earth produce very many things distinguished by very many properties.' This is indeed the usefulness of the hidden works of God, lest they be despised because common and cease to be wonderful because comprehended. We read in Scripture: 'Just as thou knowest not how the bones are joined together in the womb of her who is with child, so thou knowest not the works of God who is the maker of all.'[1] You have said truly that because we marvel less at things we can fully grasp, the works of God are incomprehensible, in order to oppose such curiosity. Why, then, do you try by human conjecture to destroy what you are much less able to comprehend in the divine reason? I did not say (as you falsely accuse me): 'It can be understood by no reasoning,' but: 'It cannot be understood by an easy reasoning.' What if God has also willed to conceal this matter in the way He conceals many things, so that it is beyond investigation and comprehension by human conjecture? If this were also done to keep human curiosity from holding as common what it fully grasps, are you then bound to array yourself against your mother the Church with your puny reasons that are like little parricidal daggers, and thus look for the hidden force of her sacrament by which she conceives those infants who, though born of parents already cleansed, have also to be cleansed? Thus you seek, not gently, but laceratingly, the

---
1 Eccli. 11.5.

bones in the womb of her who is with child. If I did not hesitate to tire the reader, I could overwhelm you with a thousand things that creep incomprehensibly as though through deserted wildernesses, acting contrary to the usual way of nature; such as seeds degenerating, not to a different genus (not even the wild olive differs from the cultivated olive as does the vine), but to what might be called a like unlikeness. Thus, the wild vine is unlike the cultivated vine, yet the wild vine may be produced from the seed of the vine. Why may we not hold that this was the will of the Creator: so that we might believe that the seed of man can contract a fault which is not in those by whom it is begotten; so that the baptized also would hasten with their infants to His grace, which rescues men from the power of darkness and transfers them to His kingdom—as no doubt your father hastened with you, not knowing how ungrateful you were going to be for that grace.

(18) As a very keen observer of nature you have discovered its limits and its laws, saying: 'By the very nature of things it cannot be proved that parents transmit what it is believed they do not possess. If they transmit it, they have not lost it.' These are Pelagian doctrines you ought now to reject, since you have read and quoted from our work to worthy Marcellinus.[2] Pelagius, in his first period, said of believing parents: 'They could not have transmitted to their posterity what they themselves in no way possessed.' The falsity of this proposition is clearly shown by examples: some already given, some I shall mention briefly now. Is there any part of the foreskin retained by a circumcized man, whence a man may yet be born with a foreskin? Therefore, what is no longer in man is derived from the seed of man. We believe the commandment to circumcize infants on the eighth day was divinely given to the ancient fathers to signify the regenera-

---

2 *De peccatorum meritis et remissione* 3.3,8,9.

tion which is made in Christ, who after the seventh day, the Sabbath, on which He lay in the tomb delivered up for our sins, rose again on the following day, that is, on the eighth day in the sequence of the weeks, rose again for our justification.³ Anyone with even the slightest knowledge of sacred Scripture knows that the sacrament of circumcision was a figure of baptism, for the Apostle says in the clearest terms of Christ: 'Who is the head of every Principality and Power, in whom too you have been circumcised with a circumcision not wrought by hand, but through putting off the body of the flesh, a circumcision which is of Christ. For you were buried together with him in baptism, and in him also rose again through faith in the working of God who raised him from the dead. And you, when you were dead by reason of your sins and the uncircumcision of your flesh, he brought to life along with him, forgiving you all your sins.'⁴ The circumcision wrought by hand, given to Abraham, is a likeness of the circumcision not wrought by hand, which is now made in Christ.

(19)⁵ It cannot be said that this foreskin is the body, while that which is contracted by way of origin is a fault; and that, although the foreskin has been cut off, its force cannot have been removed from the seed, while the fault which is not the body but is an accident cannot reside in the seed after it has been removed by pardon. No cunning can support this, since it is refuted by the divine authority commanding that that special part of the body be cut off for the purging of this fault. This fault would never have come to the infants from whom it had to be removed by circumcision, unless it had been in the seed. If it had never come

---
3 Cf. Rom. 4.25.
4 Col. 2.10.13.
5 Paragraph 19 is omitted in the three Vatican and the two Gallican manuscripts.

to them, then it would never have had to be removed through that circumcision of the body. Since an infant has no personal sin, then it must be original sin that was taken from them by that remedy without which their soul would perish from their people. Such a thing would not happen under the just God unless there were guilt by which it might happen. Since this is not personal guilt, it can only be the guilt of vitiated origin.

(20) The circumcized transmits to the man born of him something he himself does not possess. What, then, about your proposition: 'From the very nature of things, it cannot be proved that men transmit what it is believed they do not possess'? The foreskin is good, not evil, because God made it—as you have argued at length in regard to the wild olive. We answer this objection of yours: The wild olive is naturally good, but in the language of mysteries it signifies evil, as do wolves, foxes, swine wallowing in the slough of filth, the dog returning to its own vomit. They are all good in nature, just as sheep are good. God made all things very good.[6] But in sacred Scripture wolves signify wicked men; sheep signify the good. When we discuss the difference between good men and bad, we use these likeness, not as they are in themselves in nature, but according to their signification in literature. Thus, the foreskin is a part of the human body, the whole of which is a good substance, a natural good; but by figure it signifies an evil, when an infant is commanded to be circumcized on the eighth day because of Christ, in whom the Apostle says we have been circumcized by circumcision not wrought by hand, the circumcision wrought by hand undeniably prefiguring it. Thus, the foreskin is not sin, but it signifies sin, and, above all, original sin, for the origin of those who are born is through that member, and through that sin we are said to be by nature children of wrath, for

---
6 Gen. 1.31.

that member also properly called nature. The circumcision of the flesh, then, more than refutes with certainty your supposedly general proposition that 'From the very nature of things, a parent cannot transmit to his offspring what he himself does not possess.' Since the foreskin signifies sin, and since something no longer in the parent is found in the offspring, it follows that the original sin which has already been remitted in rebaptized parents remains in the infants, unless they also are baptized, that is, cleansed by spiritual circumcision. Thus, what you deny is most true; for those who deny original sin can find no reason why the infant of whom it is said: 'That soul shall be destroyed out of his people unless he is circumcised on the eight day,'[7] should perish under the just judge.

(21) Let us leave the forests of wild olives and the mountains of olives of Africa and Italy. Let us not ask the husbandmen, who would probably give you one answer and me another, with no easy solution for either of us, whether a tree planted by way of experiment will yield shade to our children's children on a later day.[8] We have an olive tree, not African, not Italian, but Hebrew, in which we, being a wild olive, rejoice to be grafted.[9] To that olive tree was given the circumcision which solves the question for us without argument. The offspring contracts the foreskin which the parent no longer possesses; the parent did not have it, yet handed it down; lost it, yet transmitted it; and this foreskin signifies sin. Thus, the sin also can cease to be in the parents, yet pass to the children. Even the infant bears mute witness: My soul shall be destroyed out of my people if I am not circumcized on the eighth day; you who deny original sin and confess a just God, tell me how I have sinned. Since your loquac-

---

7 Gen. 17.14,12.
8 Cf. Virgil, *Georgics* 2.58.
9 Cf. Rom. 11.16-24.

ity cannot give a reasonable answer to the mutely pleading infant, it would be better for you to join your voice to ours, which is in union with the voice of the Apostles. We are free to inquire about the kinds and the existence of other contagions of sins from parents—whether the quest be easy, difficult, or even impossible. But the words 'Through one man sin entered into the world and through sin death, and thus death has passed unto all men; in whom all have sinned.'[10] must be believed in the sense that all men, for all of whom Christ died, died in the sin of the first man; and that all whosoever are baptized into Christ die to sin.

Chapter 8

(22) You claim that in some of my statements which you seek to refute I tried to arouse the people against you. I said: 'The Christian faith which recent heretics have begun to attack never doubts that those who are washed in the laver of regeneration are redeemed from the power of the Devil; and those who have not yet been redeemed by this regeneration, even infant children of redeemed men, are captive under the power of that same Devil, unless they also are redeemed by the same grace.'[1] In proof, I said: 'The goodness of God, of which the Apostle says: "Who hath rescued us from the power of darkness and transferred us into the kingdom of his beloved Son,"[2] applies to all ages of men.' If this statement has aroused the people against you, should you not, rather, be impressed by the fact that Catholic belief is so widespread and deeply rooted in all, even in popular

---

10 Rom. 5.12.

1 *De nuptiis* 1.22.
2 Col. 1.13.

knowledge? Indeed, it was necessary that all Christians know everything that has to be done for their infants in reference to the Christian mysteries. But why do you say that I have 'forgotten about the single combat and have taken refuge in the people'? Who promised you a single combat with me? Where? When? With what witnesses? With what rules? You say: 'Rejoicing that offer of treaty stays the war.'[3] Thus, the strife of all is to cease when ours ceases. God forbid that I among Catholics should arrogate to myself the role you are not ashamed to assume among Pelagians. I am but one of many who refute your profane innovations, each according to his ability, as God has apportioned to each of us the measure of faith.[4] Before I was born to this world and before I was reborn to God, many Catholic teachers had already refuted your future errors. In two of the foregoing books I spoke of them as clearly as I knew how. You have a court of appeal, if it is still your pleasure to rave against the Catholic faith.

(23) You are not ridiculing the members of Christ when you call them 'workmen of the stalls.' Remember, God chose the weak things of the world to put to shame the strong.[5] What do you mean by saying that when you begin to give them evidence they will become even more aroused against me? Do not lie to them, and this will not happen. Despite your slander, I do not assert that those I know have been redeemed by the blood of Christ are 'the property of the Devil.' I do not 'ascribe marriage to the Devil,' in so far as it is marriage. I do not regard him as 'the author of the reproductive members of the body.' I do not assert that the Devil 'arouse men to none but unlawful acts,' or that 'he impregnates women,' or that 'he is the creator of infants.'

---
3 Virgil, *Aeneas* 12.109
4 Cf. Rom. 12.3.
5 Cf. 1 Cor. 1.27.

If you accuse me of such things to the people, you are lying. And if any of them should believe you and become angry at me, he would be deceived but not enlightened. Those who know both of us and also know the Catholic faith do not wish to be enlightened by you; rather, they avoid you lest you take from them what they already know. Many among them learned, even before my time, these things which your new error attacks. Since I only discovered, did not cause, their association with the truth you deny, how could I be the author of this which you think their error?

Chapter 9

(24) You ask: 'Explain how sin can justly be ascribed to that person who did not will to sin and was not able to sin.' The commission of personal sins is not the same as the contagion of another's sin, considering a man actually living his own life. If you were not intent on distorting the correct meaning to your perverted notion you would understand how the Apostle explains this briefly when he says there was one man in whom all sinned. In that one all died, so that another one man might die for all. 'Since one died for all, therefore all died'[1] for whom Christ died. Deny, then, that Christ also died for infants, so that you may exclude them from the number of the dead, that is, from the contagion of sins. You ask: 'How could a matter of will be mixed with the creation of the seeds?' If this could not happen, we could have no reason to say that infants not yet departed from the body are dead. If Christ also died for them, they also died; 'Since one died for all, therefore all died.' Do you not realize, Julian, these are not my words, but the words of the Apostle? Why do you ask me how this took place, when you

---

1 2 Cor. 5.15.

see it did take place, in some way or other, if you believe the Apostle, who could by no means have spoken falsely about Christ and about those for whom Christ died?

(25) One minded as you could speak as perversely and erroneously about God as you do about infants; saying that God is ever more active for the gain of His own enemy, because He does not cease to create, nourish, and clothe those He knows will not only be under the power of the Devil for a time, but will burn forever with him, and He also sustains them in life and health as they continue to sin wickedly. God acts in this way because He knows how to use well both the good and the evil; and the Devil cannot by any device of wickedness withdraw even himself, let alone those whom he oppresses and deceives, from the power of God. Thus, those who are rescued from the power of the Devil do not belong to the Devil; while those who really belong to him are, as he himself, in the power of God.

(26) How vain, then, is your self-styled acumen when you assert: 'The Devil and God entered into a covenant with each other, to the effect that whatever is laved belongs to God; whatever is born belongs to the Devil, in accordance with the law,' as you say, 'that God through payment of the power He has pledged shall make fertile the union of the sexes which the Devil instituted.' The Devil did not institute the union of the sexes, because this would have existed if no one had sinned; but in such a way that your protege either would not have existed or would not have been restless. Moreover, the power of God by which He makes fruitful the wombs of women is not a power payable on demand, but free and all-powerful, even when the womb bears diabolical vessels. Just as God gives to evil men, so, too, free from all necessity, through His invincible power and faultless truth, He gives with gratuitous goodness growth, form, life, health, and welfare to seeds vitiated from their origin,

yet in which the substance God created is good. Because what is laved and what is born are equally in the power of God, as also the Devil himself, for what purpose did you distinguish the two? Did you wish to say it is better to be born than to be laved; or that it is better to be laved because this also involves being born? For one who has not been born cannot be laved. Did you consider them of equal value? If you think it is better to be born, you do injury to spiritual regeneration, for then by a sacrilegious error you put carnal generation above it. It would seem you do not wish to say 'what is reborn,' but prefer 'laved,' seeking to dishonor God by the use of an ignoble word, and thus to make it appear we hold that the Devil and God divided shares between them. You could have said 'what is reborn' or 'what is regenerated' or, finally, you could have said 'what is baptized,' since Latin usage understands this Greek derivative to apply only in the sacrament of regeneration. You did not choose to say any of these, but chose the word that would make what you were saying contemptible. No one could prefer born to reborn, or to regenerated, or to baptized, but you thought that born might easily be preferred to laved. But, if to be laved and thus bear the image of the heavenly man is better than to be born and thus bear the image of the earthy,[2] the two as far apart as heaven and earth, then your invidious division vanishes. Nor should we be surprised that God would claim for Himself the image of the heavenly man received in His sacred laving, while He permitted the image of the earthy man, soiled with earthy impurity, to be under the power of the Devil until he be reborn in Christ to receive the image of the heavenly man.

(27) Perhaps you regard being laved and being born as of equal value, so that infants not yet reborn may be

---
2 Cf. 1 Cor. 15.49.

thought not to be under the Devil, for then God and the Devil seemingly would have equal shares, God claiming the laved for Himself; the Devil, the born. But, if to be laved had the same value as to be born, you would persuade men it is needless to be laved, because to be born, having the same value, is sufficient. We are thankful that you do not believe this. You do not permit the born to enter the kingdom of heaven unless they are laved; thus, you judge it much better to be laved than to be born. Take thought, then, and see to it you do not think it unworthy that those who are not admitted to the kingdom of God must be under the power of him who fell from the kingdom of God, and that those who do not have life must be under him who lost life. Infants do not have life unless they have Christ, and they unquestionably cannot have Christ unless they put Him on, as it is written: 'All you who have been baptized into Christ have put on Christ.'[3] The Evangelist John testifies that they do not have life unless they have Christ, when he says: 'He who has the Son has life; he who has not the Son has not life.'[4] They, then, who do not have life, for whom Christ died that they might have it, are rightly regarded as dead: 'One died for all, therefore all died.' He died, as we read in the Epistle to the Hebrews: 'That through death he might destroy him who had the empire of death, that is, the devil.'[5] It is any wonder, then, that infants, as long as they are dead and before they begin to have Him who died for the dead, are under him who has the empire of death?

---

3 Gal. 3.27.
4 1 John 5.12.
5 Heb. 2.14.

Chapter 10

(28) You list propositions the Christian faith truly cannot doubt, including statements we also taught in this form, even to our admitting the truth of the words that 'There can be no sin of man without the act of free will.' For not even this original sin which is contracted would have existed without the act of free will by which the first man sinned, through whom sin entered into the world and passed to all men.[1] But there are distinctions governing correct understanding of your statement: 'A man is not held liable for another's sins.' I shall not now note that David sinned and for his sin one thousand men fell in battle;[2] that one sinned against the interdict and the anathema of avenging justice fell upon those who had not sinned and had not known of the commission of the crime.[3] The nature of such sins or punishments is another question which ought not to detain us here. In a way, the sins of our parents are said to be another's sins, and, in a way, they are also our own. They are another's by right of ownership of the action; they are ours by means of contagion of offspring. If this were false, the heavy yoke upon children of Adam from the day of their coming out of their mother's womb would in no way be just.[4]

(29) You quote the Apostle's words: 'All of us must be made manifest before the tribunal of Christ, so that each one may receive what he has won through the body, according to his works, whether good or evil.'[5] How do you understand these words in reference to infants? Will they also appear before the tribunal of Christ or not? If they will not, how

---

1 Cf. Rom. 5.12.
2 Cf. 2 Kings 24.
3 Cf. Josue 7.
4 Cf. Eccli. 40.1.
5 2 Cor. 5.10.

does this passage help you when it does not apply to those whose case we are now considering? If they will appear, how will they who have done nothing receive what they have done, unless we must ascribe to them their believing or not believing through the hearts and mouths of those bearing them? He says: 'What he has won through the body,' which refers to one now living his own life. How can an infant receive good that he may enter into the kingdom of God, if each one receives for what he has done, unless what an infant has done, that is, believed through another, belongs to him? If, then, that he has believed, this is his, that he may receive the kingdom of God; so, too, if he has not believed, this is his, that he may receive the judgment of condemnation. For the Gospel also says: 'He who does not believe shall be condemned.'[6] The words of the Apostle, 'All of us must be made manifest, so that each one may receive according to his works, whether good or evil,' leave no middle course. You see, then, how inadequate is your position. You would not have an infant receive evil from another's sin, yet you would have him receive from another's good work, not just any good, but the kingdom of God. It is another's work when he believes through another, just as it was another's work when he sinned in another. Moreover, we do not doubt that every sin is cleansed by baptism; but man is cleansed by rebirth, and, therefore, what regeneration alone can destroy, generation does not cease to contract.

(30) When you say: 'Concupiscence is not in constant rebellion against the soul,' you at least admit that it does indeed rebel; you do not admit it is a penalty that you wage this internal warfare? You say: 'God should be the Creator of only such infants as are worthy of His hands,' and you add: 'that is, of innocents.' Does not he who says that only works beautiful and sound are befitting the hands of God

---

6 Mark 16.16.

seem to surpass you in piety and praise of God? But many are born deformed, many diseased, many horrible and monstrous, yet we hold that none but the good and true God could have created the whole substance, together with all its parts and whatever exists and lives by way of substance.

(31) You demand I explain 'how the Devil dares to claim for himself infants created in Christ, that is, in His power.' You must answer, if you can, how the Devil openly, not obscurely, claims infants harassed by unclean spirits. If you say they have been delivered up to him, we both see the torment; you must say what deserves it. We both perceive the punishment; but you who say that nothing deserving of punishment is contracted from parents, while we both confess God is just, must prove, if you can, that there is in infants guilt deserving such punishment. Do you not realize this is part of the heavy yoke upon the children of Adam from the day of their coming out of their mother's womb until the day of their burial in the mother of all? The human race is so consumed by various afflictions under this yoke that it would seem men's being made children of mercy from children of wrath as promised is preparation for the future world, but in this world even the children of mercy are harried from birth to death under this same yoke. Yes, even baptized infants are at times subjected to attacks by demons, in addition to other evils of this life, although they have been rescued from the power of darkness lest it draw them to everlasting punishment.

(32) You repeat some statements I have already answered,[7] yet I ought not to disregard them even now. 'When God gives the glory of regeneration to infants who have nothing of their own to deserve either good or evil,' you say, 'He teaches us they are under His providence, His justice, His dominion, and in the lavishness of His inestimable bounty He anticipates their will.' How have they offended God,

---

7 Cf. above, pp. 112-114.

those innumerable infants, equally innocent and pure, created by God Himself after His own image, from whom He withholds this gift and does not anticipate their will by the lavishness of His inestimable bounty, segregating that multitude of His own images from His own kingdom? If it will not be an evil for them, it follows that this multitude of innocent images of God will not love the kingdom of God. But, if they will love it, and love it as much as innocents ought to love the kingdom of Him by whom they are created after His own image, will they suffer no evil from the very separation? Finally, no matter where they may be and no matter how subject to God, a judge not compelled by an immovable fate, no respecter of persons, they will not be in the happiness of that kingdom with those who are likewise without anythink of their own to deserve either good or evil. But, if they had deserved nothing evil, they would never be deprived of the enjoyment of so great a good, in the same situation. As we have often said, in the words of the Apostle, in the vessels of wrath God makes known the riches of His glory towards the vessels of mercy, in order that the latter may not glory in the merits of their life when they realize that He could most justly have rendered to them what they see has been rendered to those who were perfect peers in their death.

(33) If you would be wise, apply also to infants what the Apostle tells us God the Father has done: 'Who has rescued us from the power of darkness and transferred us to the kingdom of his beloved Son'; and again: 'We were by nature children of wrath, even as the rest.'[8] For all are rescued from the power of darkness and were children of wrath when they die to sin. But they die to sin in order to live to God when they are baptized into the death of Christ. Indeed, all are baptized into His death when they are baptized into Christ.

---
8 Col. 1.13; Eph. 2.3.

Since infants are also baptized into Christ, they die to sin and are rescued from the power of darkness where they were by nature children of wrath. You say that the Apostle's words, 'by nature children of wrath,' can be interpreted as 'entirely children of wrath.' Here note that the ancient Catholic faith is opposed to you, for there is scarcely a Latin codex—if you have not tampered with them—in which the words 'by nature' are not found. The ancient translators should surely have avoided it, unless this was the ancient faith which your innovation has just now begun to oppose.

Chapter 11

(34) Remarkable man that you are, you do not care to be numbered among the common people. You once more reject the judgment of the people, after so many arguments with which you were trying to arouse them more seriously against me than they had been aroused against you. You have seen, however, that your arguments had no effect on people rooted in the truth and antiquity of the Catholic faith; so you turned to rail against the people by describing and deriding special groups of that multitude of Christians deservedly hostile to you. Then, referring to scholastic *auditoriales*, you say they will cry out against me: '*O tempora, O mores.*'[1] But you must be in awe of the judgment of the people, since you were able to find among them a witness so clamorous you thought it could frighten me with the words of Tully, stirring them up by saying I hold that the reproductive members of the body come from a source other than that of the whole body. Suppose I answer and say: This is a lie, for it is not what I think. I blame lust, not the members; I am concerned with a fault, not a nature. The man who

---

1 Cicero, *Orat. 1 in Catil.* and *act 6 in Verrem.*

slanders me to you dares to sing the praise of lust in the Church of Christ, before the Master who is in heaven. If you were fellow students, no master would assign him such matter to declaim, lest he offend everyone's modesty. Would they not rather use against you those other, really appropriate words of Cicero: 'Modesty fights on this side; impudence comes from you. Here is continence; there, lust.'[2]

(35) Those men you say have deserted your teaching, converted or returned to the Catholic faith, and whom you say you can expose as guilty of misconduct are not known to me. You seem to be in such dread of them that you dare not give their names, lest, perhaps, when they hear your false charges against them they may accuse you of more credible, if not truer, offenses. Whoever they may be, if they are truly wise they will do nothing against you, but spare you, instead, in accordance with the words of the Apostle, 'Not rendering abuse for abuse.'[3] At least you will not refuse to listen to the admonition of him in whose words you were pleased to exclaim: '*O tempora, O mores!*' Hear him, at least, 'So that you may put yourself as far from licence with words as you are remote from depravity'—if, indeed, you are remote from it—and not say of others what you blush to hear said falsely of yourself. I must inform the readers that in persons I know who with the vow of celibacy have renounced the Pelagian heresy, I know no such things as you have charged against I know not whom. But I am not concerned with the kind of men and women you so deceive as to say that I hold: 'Lust cannot be restrained even in a body decrepit with age.' Because I know it can be restrained and must be restrained I know it is evil. Let him who denies it is evil look to how he may possess that good which is attacked by the lust that he admits, whether he will or not, must be restrained.

---

2 Cicero, *Orat.* 2 *in Catil.*
3 1 Peter 3.9.

I declare that lust can be restrained, not only by the senile, but also by the young; but I marvel much that lust can be praised by celibates.

(36) Who of us has ever said: 'The evil which infants contract can exist, or at some time has existed without the substance in which it inheres'? As though we held this, you appeal to dialecticians as judges, and you scoff at the people as though I were citing you before them to judge about matters in which they have no competence. Truly, if you had not learned these things the Pelagian system would have lacked the architect it needed. If you would live, do not love the wisdom of words by which the cross of Christ is made void.[4] We have already discussed[5] how good and evil qualities may pass from one substance to another, not by migrating, but by affecting the substance. If you scorn the judgment of the people, then consider the judges I mentioned in the first two books, judges of outstanding authority in the Church of Christ.

Chapter 12

(37) Why do you accuse Zosimus, of blessed memory, bishop of the Apostolic See, of prevarication, to protect your own baseness?[1] He was in accord with his predecessor, Innocent, whom you feared to mention. You preferred Zosimus because he dealt more leniently with Celestius at first, when Celestius promised to correct any of his statements that were unacceptable, and agreed to abide by the judgment of Innocent's letters.

(38) Recall how insolently you sought to damage us in

---

4 Cf. 1 Cor. 1.17.
5 Cf. above, pp. 291-293.

1 Cf. Introduction, pp. xi-xii.

regard to the dissent of the Roman people in the election of the Pope.² Would you say men act this way by their own will? If you deny they do, how will you defend free choice? But if you admit they do, how can you call it 'the vengeance of God,' and abandon your own teaching while pretending you have been divinely vindicated? Or will you sometime concede what you have been stubbornly and contentiously denying: that by a hidden judgment of God there may be something in the very volitions of men which is both sin and punishment for sin? If you had not been thinking this, you would never have said an act of men may be the vengeance of God. But when something similar happened in the case of blessed Damasus and Ursicinus, the Roman Church had not yet condemned the Pelagians.

(39) You say that I also have changed my opinions, and that at the beginning of my conversion I agreed with you. You deceive or are deceived in misrepresenting what I say now, or in not understanding, or, worse, not reading what I said then. I have always held from the beginning of my conversion, and I now hold, that through one man sin entered into the world and through sin death, and thus death has passed to all men; in whom all have sinned.³ There are books extant which I wrote as a layman at the very beginning of my conversion. I was not then as learned in sacred Scripture as later on, yet I held and also said, when there was need to speak, nothing on this matter except what the whole Church has from the earliest times learned and taught; namely, that the human race, as a consequence of original sin, has deservedly fallen into these great and manifest miseries in which man is like to vanity: his days pass away like a shadow; all things are vanity and every man living.⁴

---

2 A schism arose at the death of Zosimus (418), when certain men contended for Eulalius against the legitimately elected Boniface.
3 Cf. Rom. 5.12.
4 Cf. Ps. 143.4; 38.6.

He alone can give deliverance who said: 'The truth shall make you free' and 'I am the truth' and 'If the Son makes you free you will be free indeed.'[5] Truth alone frees from vanity, but this is according to grace, not according to debt; through mercy, not merit. As we were made subject to vanity through judgment, so it is through mercy that we are made free by truth, and we confess that our good merits themselves are but the gifts of God.

Chapter 13

(40) Let us now discuss your slanderous accusation against me: 'The baptized are cleansed only in part.' You say this appears much more clearly in my sermons. You then proceed to quote from some of the sermons in which you say this appears. I thank you; my words are:[1] 'The concupiscence of the flesh should not be imputed to marriage, but tolerated. It is not a good coming from the natural marriage union, but an evil added accidentally from the ancient sin. For this reason, even of just and legitimate marriage between children of God, not children of God, but children of this world are generated. Although those who generate have been regenerated, they do not generate from that by which they are children of God, but from that by which they are children of this world. Our Lord's words are: "The children of this world generate and are generated."[2] From that by which we are still children of this world our outer man is being cor-

---

5 John 8.32; 14.6; 8.36.

1 *De nuptiis* 1.19,20.
2 Luke 20.34. The text quoted by Augustine reads: '*Filii hujus saeculi generant et generantur.*' He uses this text and this form of it as the minor premiss of a similar argument in *De peccatorum meritis et remissione* 1.20.27.

rupted; and from this same thing children of this world are generated. From that by which we are children of God our inner man is being renewed day by day.³ Although the outer man also is sanctified through the laver and receives the hope of future incorruption, and is therefore rightly said to be the temple of God⁴—this is said, not only because of our present sanctification, but also because of that hope of which we read: "But we ourselves also who have the first-fruits of the Spirit —we ourselves groan within ourselves, waiting for the adoption as sons, the redemption of our body." If the redemption of our body is awaited, as the Apostle says, surely that which is awaited is still hoped for and is not yet possessed.' My words contain nothing a baptized person does not find in himself, when he says with the Apostle: 'We ourselves groan within ourselves.' And elsewhere: 'For we who are in this tent sigh under our burden.'⁶ The relevant words in the Book of Wisdom are: "The corruptible body is a load upon the soul and the earthly habitation presseth down the mind that museth upon many things."⁷ You, as though already dwelling among the angels in heaven, ridicule the words of weakness and mortality. You explain them, not according to my sense, but according to your deceit, and state untruly that I said: 'Grace does not perfectly renew man.' Note what I actually said: 'Grace perfectly renews man, since it brings him even to immortality of body and full happiness.' It perfectly renews man now, also, as regards deliverance from all sins, but not as regards deliverance from all evils, nor from every ill of mortality by which the body is now a load upon the soul.

---

3 Cf. 2 Cor. 4.16.
4 Cf. 1 Cor. 3.16.
5 Rom. 8.23.
6 2 Cor. 5.4.
7 Wisd. 9.15.

This is the groaning which the Apostle acknowledges also as his own when he says: 'We ourselves groan within ourselves.' But it is by the same baptism here received that a man reaches the perfection hoped for. Not all the children of this world are children of the Devil, although all children of the Devil are children of this world. For there are children of God who are still children of this world, for which reason they also join in marriage. But by the flesh they do not beget children of God, for, in order that they themselves might be children of God, they were born not of blood, not of the will of man, and not of the will of the flesh, but of God.[8] Even now through baptism sanctification is conferred on the body also, yet the corruption of the body, which also is a load upon the soul, is not now taken away. Though the bodies are chaste when the members do not serve the desires of sin and have therefore begun to belong to the temple of God, there is something in this whole structure that grace may make perfect as long as the flesh lusts against the spirit to stir up evil movements that must be restrained, and the spirit lusts against the flesh, that holiness may abide.[9]

Chapter 14

(41) Who does not know what you, an outstanding teacher, affirm: 'The flesh is said to lust because the soul lusts carnally.' There can be no concupiscence of the flesh apart from the soul. Concupiscence is so proper to a living and sentient nature that it does not cease even when restrained by the chastity of a eunuch; less troublesome for him, for where

---
8 Cf. John 1.13.
9 Cf. Gal. 5.17.

there is less fuel there is less desire. It exists, nonetheless, and must be curbed by modesty, lest the eunuch, though incapable of intercourse, attempt that wickedness for which we are told Calligonus, the eunuch of the younger Valentinian, convicted on the charge of a harlot, was put to death. The words of Ecclesiasticus, 'He seeth with his eyes and groaneth, as an eunuch embracing a virgin, and sighing,'[1] would not apply unless eunuchs were also moved by the affections of carnal concupiscence, although without the carnal effects. Thus, in movements according to the spirit the soul sometimes opposes other movements of itself according to the flesh. Conversely, in movements according to the flesh, it opposes others which it has according to the spirit, and this is why we say the flesh lusts against the spirit and the spirit lusts against the flesh. But this is also why 'it is being renewed day by day,'[2] for the soul does not fail to make progress in virtue as it gradually diminishes the carnal desires to which it does not consent. It is to those already baptized that the Apostle says: 'Mortify your members, which are on the earth.' In this same passage he also mentions fornication, evil concupiscence, and covetousness.[3] Then, how does a man already baptized mortify the fornication which he no longer commits, and, according to you, has nothing to mortify? How, I ask, can he obey the Apostle's words and 'mortify fornication,' unless he wars to expel the desires to which he does not consent; for, even though these desires do not cease to exist, the desire diminishes daily in those making progress and not committing fornication in consent or in deed? This is realized in the temple of God when, with God's help, we carry out God's commands. The

---
1 Eccli, 30.21.
2 2 Cor. 4.16.
3 Cf. Col. 3.5.

works of the spirit are built up; the works of the flesh are mortified: 'For if you live according to the flesh you will die, but if by the spirit you put to death the deeds of the flesh you will live.' That they may know they can do this only through the grace of God, he says: 'For whoever are led by the Spirit of God, they are the sons of God.'[4] Therefore, whoever are led by the Spirit of God mortify by the spirit the deeds of the flesh.

(42) The baptized have, then, something to do in themselves, that is, in the temple of God which is first being built, and then will be dedicated at the end. It is built after the captivity, as the title of the psalm indicates: when the enemy who had taken them captive has been expelled. There is something noteworthy in the order of the psalms. The psalm of the dedication of the house precedes in order of numbering the psalm of the building of the house. The psalm of the dedication comes first, because he is singing of the house of which its Architect says: 'Destroy this temple and in three days I will raise it up.'[5] The later psalm, when the house was being built after the captivity, foretold the Church. Moreover, its opening words are: 'Sing to the Lord a new song, sing to the Lord all the earth.'[6] Let no one foolishly think that a baptized man is already perfect, therefore, merely because it has been said: 'For holy is the temple of God, and this temple you are,' and: 'Do you not know that your members are the temple of the Holy Spirit, who is in you, whom you have from God?'[7] In another passage he says: 'For you are the temple of the living God,'[8] and similar expressions. It is even now called a temple, and

---
4 Rom. 8.13,14.
5 John 2.19.
6 Ps. 95.1,2.
7 1 Cor. 3.17,16.
8 2 Cor. 6.16.

while is is being built our members here on earth are mortified. Though we, even now dead to sin, live to God, there is still something in us to mortify in order that sin reign not in our mortal body so that we obey its lusts.[9] The full and perfect remission of sins has freed us from subjection to them, yet they must be combated even by the chaste. One of these is also the concupiscence which is used well by modest spouses, but when it is used well, good is born of evil not without evil, and thus must be reborn to be delivered from evil. What God creates and man generates is indeed good, as far as it is man. But it is not without evil, for regeneration alone delivers a man from the evil which generation contracts from the first and great sin.

(43) You would have it seem incredible that 'In the womb of a baptized woman, whose body is the temple of God, there be formed a man who must be under the power of the Devil unless he be reborn from God to God,' as though it were not more remarkable that God should operate even where He does not dwell. He does not dwell in a body subject to sins, yet He forms a man in the womb of a harlot. He reaches everywhere because of His purity and nothing defiled comes into Him.[10] It is much more remarkable that He sometimes adopts for a son one whom He forms in the womb of an impure woman; and sometimes does not accept for a son him whom He forms in the womb of his own daughter. The one is baptized, by what providence I know not; the other dies suddenly and is not baptized. God, in whose power are all things, receives one whom He has formed in the dwelling of the Devil into fellowship with Christ, and He does not wish that one He formed in His own temple should be in His kingdom. Or, if He wishes it,

---

9 Cf. Rom. 6.11,12.
10 Cf. Wisd. 1.4; 7.24,25.

why does He not do what He wishes? What you are accustomed to say about adults does not apply here, that is, that God wishes and the infant does not wish. Here, where there is no immovable fate, no careless chance, no personal dignity, what remains except the depths of mercy and of truth? From consideration of these two men, the one through whom sin entered into the world, and the other who takes away the sin of the world, let us try, in an incomprehensible matter, to comprehend that all children of this concupiscence of the flesh, no matter whence they are born, deservedly come under the heavy yoke of the children of Adam, and all the children of spiritual grace, no matter whence they are born, without their own merit arrive at the sweet yoke of the children of God. Hence, he has his own condition, whoever is so formed in the body of another, which is the temple of God, that he himself is not the temple of God simply because formed in the temple of God. That the body of his mother is the temple of God is the gift of grace, not of nature, and this grace is not conferred by conception but by regeneration. For, if what is conceived in the mother belonged to her body in such a way as to be regarded part of it, an infant still in the womb would not again be baptized after birth if the mother had been baptized in urgent danger of death. But, as it is, when the infant also is baptized, he is not held to have been baptized twice. He did not belong to his mother's body when he was in her womb; one not the temple of God was created in the temple of God. Thus, an unbeliver is created in a believing woman, and the parents transmitted to him the unbelief which they did not have when he was born from them, but which they themselves had when they were likewise born. They transmitted something no longer in them because of the spiritual seed by which they were regenerated, but it was in the carnal seed by which they generated him.

(44) Although man's body is also sanctified in sacred baptism, it is sanctified so that through the remission of sins he is not bound by any guilt for past sins, nor for the concupiscence of the flesh which exists in him. Every man at birth is necessarily answerable by the guilt of this concupiscence, and will be until death, if he is not reborn. Where have you heard or read that I say: 'Men are not renewed through baptism, but only as though renewed; not freed, but as though freed; not saved, but as though saved'? God forbid I call vain the grace of that laver in which I was reborn of water and the Spirit; the grace through which I was delivered from the guilt of all sins, whether derived at birth or contracted by wicked living; the grace through which I know how to avoid temptation when drawn away and enticed by my own concupiscence, and I am heard when I say with the faithful: 'Forgive us our trespasses';[11] the grace I hope will make me free in eternity where there will be no law in my members warring against the law of my mind.[12] I do not make void the grace of God. You, its enemy, seem to be seeking an empty boast by introducing Epicurus, 'who said that the body and blood of the gods was not body and blood, but only as though body and blood.'[13] In this instance you are as inept as you seem erudite, for this matter from the writings of the philosophers is irrelevant to our question. Who has said: 'Everything that happens in the present age is culpable'—when Christ Himself did so many good things on earth—but in order to deliver us from this present evil age?

---

11 Matt. 6.12.
12 Cf. Rom. 7.23.
13 Cicero, *De natura deorum* 3.

Chapter 15

(45) I observe how carefully and fittingly you quote the testimony of the Apostle: 'We are saved by hope,' and the rest, to 'the redemption of our body.'[1] You say: 'The resurrection will not take away any sins, but will only make return for the deserts of individuals.' You continue: 'God will reward each one according to his own works,' yet you do not say for what works of their own He will give His kingdom to infants. Indeed, no sins are remitted in the kingdom, but, if none were remitted in that last judgment, I think our Lord would not have said about a certain sin: 'It will not be forgiven him, either in this world or in the world to come';[2] and the thief who said: 'Remember me when thou comest into kingdom,'[3] surely hoped his sins would be forgiven. We shall not now give a hasty judgment on this question, since it is very profound. But we may ask why God forgives no sins for His children in the kingdom—unless it be because He finds nothing to forgive? There could not be sins where the spirit, let alone not consenting with the concupiscence of the flesh, does not even lust against the flesh, because the flesh also does not lust against the spirit. The flesh will be perfect in that ineffable health which even baptism, remitting all sins as it does, does not effect at the present time; for the evils of carnal lusts remain after baptism, when there is progress in glorious combats with these evils by the married, and in still more glorious combats by the continent, as you yourself admit.[4] I do not know what misfortune keeps you from hearing yourself when you speak for the truth.

---
1 Rom. 8.24,23.
2 Matt. 12.32.
3 Luke 23.42.
4 Cf. above, pp. 143-144.

(46) In describing the supreme happiness of the resurrection, you say: 'None of the just will longer bruise his body and subject it to servitude; none will longer humble his soul on hard pallets in the squalor of his members.' Why, then, does he who in baptism lost every evil do such things? Why does he dare bruise the temple of God? Then why does he invite God's presence, or beg His mercy, or placate His wrath, not by a sweet odor, but by the squalor of His temple? Does he chastise, tame, conquer, suppress no evil in the temple of God, not even in the bruising and squalor of the temple of God? Do you not understand, do you not perceive that when he is so vehemently persecuting his own body, if he is not persecuting something displeasing to God, he is to no purpose doing grave injury to God by persecuting God's temple? Why do you vacillate, why do you hesitate to admit this openly? That which the man whose bruises and squalor you mention persecutes in his flesh is that of which the Apostle says: 'I know that in me, that is, in my flesh, no good dwells.'[5] Why do you deny that this is the voice of a baptized man, when you recognize in the bruises of the body and the squalor of the members the deeds of this voice? These are not things the saints bear in patience under scourges from God or from enemies; they in their continence inflict these things on themselves. Does this not come from the spirit lusting against the concupiscence of the flesh, something of which you are aware? When you were discussing the happiness of the future life, you said: 'No one will face reproaches undismayed, no one will offer his cheek to blows, nor his back to lashes. None will strive to make strength from weakness, or to unite frugality with poverty, or magnanimity with mourning.' Why were you unwilling to say: 'or chastity with concupiscence of the flesh,' but

---

5 Rom. 7.18.

hastened to conclude with: 'nor will patience mourn with grief'? You mention only what comes from outside and must be borne with courage, not that which disturbs us from within and must be overcome with chastity. Do you perhaps regard us as sluggish because we do not understand something you already mentioned when you spoke of the bruises of the body and the effort and squalor of the members? When this affliction comes not from an enemy, but the courageous afflicts himself, then there is within him an enemy that must be overcome.

(47) You must recall that you did not explain why the Apostle, already adopted in the laver of regeneration, was 'waiting for the adoption'?[6] You say again: 'No one hates his own flesh.' Who denies this? Yet you assert the flesh must be brought to subjection by rigorous discipline. Again you speak the truth, but are deaf to your own teaching. Why do the faithful mortify the flesh, if in baptism nothing remains to lust against the spirit? Why, I ask, does the temple of God mortify itself, if there is nothing in it to resist the Spirit of God? On the other hand, such a thing would not only exist there, but would inhere in a seriously harmful way, if the guilt by which it bound him had not been dissolved through the remission of sins. It is dissolved through indulgence, then, because it bound harmfully. It is mortified through continence lest it conquer in the conflict. It must be kept from doing harm until it has been so healed that it does not exist at all. For this reason, all sins, both those contracted by the way of origin and those added later, in ignorance or knowingly, are remitted in baptism. The Apostle James says: 'Everyone is tempted by his being drawn away and enticed by his own concupiscence. Then when concupiscence has conceived, it

---

6 Rom. 8.23.
7 James 1.14.

brings forth sin.'⁷ These words distinguish the thing brought forth from the one giving birth. The one giving birth is concupiscence; the thing brought forth is sin. But concupiscence does not give birth unless it conceives; it does not conceive unless it entices, that is, unless it obtains willing consent to commit evil. Therefore, man's battle against concupiscence consists in keeping it from conceiving and giving birth to sin. If concupiscence also is consumed when all sins, that is, all the brood of concupiscence, have been remitted in baptism, how, in your words, will the saints fight to keep it from conceiving, 'in bruises of the body and the squalor of the members, the mortification of the flesh'? How, I say, will the saints wage war against concupiscence with bruises, squalor, and mortification of the temple of God, if concupiscence itself is taken away by baptism? Concupiscence, then, remains; nor do we lose it in the laver of regeneration, if we did not lose there the sense by which we perceive that it remains.

(48) How can any man be so impudent and imprudent, so obstinate, obdurate, and obstructive, finally so foolish and beside himself as to confess that sins are evil and yet deny that the lust for sins is evil, even when the spirit lusting against it does not permit it to conceive and give birth to sins? Must not an evil of this kind and so great bind man in death and carry him to final death merely because it is in him, unless its bond be loosed in that remission of all sins which is accomplished in baptism? Hence, the chains stretching from the first Adam can only be broken in the second Adam. By these chains of death, I say, infants are dead, not in the familiar death which separates the soul from the body, but in the death binding all for whom Christ died. As the Apostle says, and as we have often repeated: 'Since one died for all, therefore all died, and he died for all in order that they who are alive may live no longer for themselves, but for him who died for

them and rose again.'⁸ The living are those for whom He who was living died in order that they might live; more plainly, they are freed from the chains of death, they for whom the one free among the dead died.⁹ Or, still more plainly: they have been freed from sin, for whom He who was never in sin died. Although He died once, He dies for each at that time when each, whatever his age, is baptized in His death; that is, the death of Him who was without sin benefits each man at the time when, having been baptized in His death, he who was dead in sin shall also die to sin.

Chapter 16

(49) You insist on the testimony of the Apostle from 'Do not err, neither fornicators nor idolators,' and the rest, to the conclusion, 'they will not possess the kingdom of God.' But the doers of these deeds are those who consent with the actions of that concupiscence you praise, to commit all manner of evil and depravity. When he says: 'And such were some of you, but you have been washed, but you have been sanctified,'¹ he also says they have been changed for the better; not so as to lose concupiscence, a condition never realized in this life, but so that they do not obey it, a condition that can be found in a good life. Thus they may know they have been delivered from its bondage, and this can only be effected through regeneration. You are much mistaken in thinking: 'If concupiscence were an evil, he who is baptized would lose it.' Such a man loses every sin, but not every evil. More plainly, he loses all guilt for all evils, but not all evils. Does he lose bodily cor-

---

8 2 Cor. 5.14,15.
9 Cf. Ps. 87.6.

---

1 1 Cor. 6.9,10.

ruption? Is this not an evil weighing down the soul, so that he erred who said: 'The corruptible body is a load upon the soul'?[2] Does he lose the evil of ignorance through which men unwittingly commit innumerable evil deeds? Is it a slight evil not to perceive the things that are of the Spirit of God? The Apostle says about baptized persons:[3] 'The sensual man does not perceive the things that are of the Spirit of God, for it is foolishness to him and he cannot understand, because it is examined spiritually.' Later on, he says: 'And I, brethren, could not speak to you as to spiritual men but only as carnal, as to little ones in Christ. I fed you with milk, not with solid food, for you were not yet ready for it. Nor are you now ready for it, for you are still carnal. For since there are jealousy and strife among you, are you not carnal, and walking as mere men?' See what evils he names as coming from the evil of ignorance; and I think he is not talking to catechumens. How would his hearers be infants in Christ unless they had already been reborn? If you still do not believe, note what he says to them a little later: 'Do you not know that you are the temple of God, and that the Spirit of God dwells in you?' Do you still doubt or deny that none but the baptized in whom the Spirit of God dwelt could have been the temple of God? At least consider what he said to them: 'Were you baptized in the name of Paul?' Therefore, they did not lose this great evil of ignorance in the laver of regeneration, where they unquestionably lost all sins. And through this evil of ignorance the things of the Spirit of God were foolishness to the temple of God, in which dwelt the Spirit of God. If they made progress from day to day, however, and continued to walk in the way at which they had arrived, then with the aid of sound doctrine the evil would be diminished. Are we, then, to believe that in this life it can be not merely diminished, but even

---

2 Wisd. 9.15.
3 1 Cor. 2.14,15; 3.1,2,16; 1.13.

eliminated; yet after baptism—or should we say in baptism—Does anyone doubt that concupiscence can be diminished in this life, but not entirely eliminated?

(50) All past guilt of these evils, then, is washed away in the sacred font. They are remitted in the reborn; diminished in those making progress. Ignorance is diminished in ever-increasing brilliance of truth. Concupiscence is diminished in ever-increasing ardor of charity. None of the goodness of these two comes from us, for 'We have received not the spirit of the world, but the spirit that is from God, that we may know the things that have been given us by God.'[4] Concupiscence is worse than ignorance, because to sin in ignorance without concupiscence is lesser sin; but concupiscence without ignorance makes sin more serious. Moreover, ignorance of evil is not always evil, but lust after evil is always evil. It is sometimes useful to be ignorant of a good, in order to learn of it at an opportune time; it is never possible that man's good be lusted after by carnal concupiscence, since not even offspring itself is desired by the lust of the body, but by the intention of the soul, even though offspring is not sowed without the lust of the body. For, indeed, we are concerned with that concupiscence by which the flesh lusts against the spirit; not with the good concupiscence by which the spirit lusts against the flesh,[5] and by which is desired the continence through which concupiscence is overcome. By this concupiscence of the flesh no one ever desires any good of man, unless the pleasure of the flesh is the good of man. If the sect of Dinomachus,[6] which joins moral soundness with sensual pleasure, pleases you, as you indicate somewhere, that good which the admittedly sounder philosophers of this world also called 'Scylla-like,' that is, a compound of human and animal

---
4 1 Cor. 2.12.
5 Cf. Gal. 5.17.
6 Cf. above, p. 233.

nature; if your opinion favors this monster, we shall be satisfied with your admission that one pleasure is lawful, another unlawful. The concupiscence which seeks both of them indiscriminately is evil, unless it be restrained from unlawful pleasure by lawful pleasure. This evil is not laid aside in baptism, but the baptized, already freed from its obligation, through the grace of regeneration, overcome it wholesomely to keep it from drawing them to the unlawful. That it exist not at all at the time of the resurrection in a body which lives and does not sorrow is the reward of those who have fought against it faithfully, and, the sickness healed, are to be clothed in blessed immortality. It will not exist in those who do not rise to life; not for their happiness, but penally non-existent, and this not because each will be cleansed of it, but because at that time its activity, being turned about, no longer moving towards pleasures, will only face torments.

Chapter 17

(51) Let us examine your very excellent acumen in refutation of my statement: 'The concupiscence of the flesh is put away in baptism, not so as not to exist, but so as not to be imputed for sin. But even though its guilt has been removed, concupiscence remains.'[1] Most astute of men, you argue against my words as though I said baptism delivers concupiscence itself from guilt, because I said: 'When its guilt has been removed,' as though 'its' meant a guilt by which concupiscence is guilty, and I said when such guilt has been removed, concupiscence would be absolved.[2] If that had been

---
1 *De nuptiis* 1.28.
2 This chapter shows more clearly the nature of the genuine difficulty stated by Julian, to which Augustine refers in passing in Book 2; cf. p. 66.

my thought, I surely would not have said it is evil, but that it had been evil. Thus, according to your remarkable intelligence, when you hear that the guilt of murder in someone has been removed, you must hold that not the man but murder itself has been absolved of guilt. Who can understand it in this way except one who does not blush to praise what he is forced to combat? Moreover, how can you boast and exult in refuting a statement which is plainly yours, not mine? You point out what should be affirmed against those who say that through baptism concupiscence of the flesh is sanctified and made believing in those in whom it nevertheless remains after their regeneration. It is more appropriate, however, for you who proclaim that concupiscence is good to say of it what you say of infants: 'The good of sanctification is added to its natural goodness, and the concupiscence of the flesh is a holy daughter of God.' But we declare it is evil; nonetheless, it remains in the baptized, even though its guilt—not a guilt by which it itself is guilty, since it is not a person, but the guilt by which it made man guilty by way of origin—has been remitted and made void. God forbid we assert the sanctification of that with which those who have been regenerated and have not received the grace of God in vain must battle as with an enemy in civil war and from which plague they must desire and hope to be healed.

(52) If your reason for saying that no evils remain in those who have been baptized is to avoid the conclusion you draw—that evils are baptized and sanctified—consider the absurd consequences. If we must hold that whatever is in a man when he is baptized is also baptized and sanctified, then you must say that the waste which is being evacuated through digestion in the intestines and bladder is baptized and sanctified. You must say that a man is baptized and

sanctified when in his mother's womb, if necessity compels that a pregnant woman receive this sacrament; and thus the one born would no longer need to be baptized. Finally, you must say that even fevers are baptized and sanctified when the sick are baptized, so that works of the Devil are also baptized and sanctified; as, for instance, if the woman whom Satan had bound in sickness for eighteen years[3] had been baptized before she was cured. What shall I say about the evils of the soul itself? Consider how great an evil it is to regard the things of the Spirit of God as foolishness; yet, such were the men the Apostle fed with milk, not with solid food. Are you going to say the great evil in that foolishness was baptized and sanctified because it was not taken away by baptism? So also, then, concupiscence which remains as something to be combated and healed, even though absolutely all sins are remitted in baptism, is not only not sanctified, but must rather be made void lest it hold the sanctified liable to eternal death. If those men who were fed with milk and not with solid food, being as yet sensual, not perceiving the things of the Spirit of God because they persisted in their foolishness, had died at that age of the mind, not of the flesh, when as new men they were called little ones in Christ, they would not have been bound by any guilt for this foolishness. For, of all the evils which they had to put off, after regeneration, by death or spiritual progress, as well as before, the gift conferred by regeneration removed forthwith the guilt of these evils by the remission of sins, but not as yet the cure of all diseases. But this guilt must bind those generated according to the flesh, for it is remitted only for him who is regenerated according to the spirit. Through the one Mediator of God and men the human race is delivered from the death to which it was most justly condemned; not

---

[3] Cf. Luke 13.11.

only the death of the body, but also the death by which those were dead for whom One died. And because He died for all, therefore all died.

Chapter 18

(53) Do you not see the irrelevance of your joyful account of the differentia of qualities because I mentioned quality when I said: 'Concupiscence does not remain in the manner of a substance, a kind of body or spirit; it is an affection, an evil quality, like sickness.'[1] First you say I have changed my mind and forgotten the whole book in which I asserted that lust is a substance. If you will honestly and carefully analyze my book, you will find that I do not even once say lust is a substance. Some philosophers have, indeed, asserted it is a faulty part of the soul—and, surely, a part of the soul is a substance since the soul itself is a substance—but I say lust is the fault itself by which the soul or any part of the soul is faulty in this special way, and, consequently, when every fault is cured, the entire substance is sound. I think those philosophers themselves were using a figure of speech when they gave the name lust to a faulty part of the soul in which the fault called lust exists, just as the word house is used for a household.

(54) By incautious use of your oversharp dialectical weapons and your boastfully trying to frighten us you have dealt your own group a mortal blow. In dividing and defining and also describing the differentia of qualities you say, among other things: 'The third kind of quality includes affection and affectional quality.' You continue: 'Affection is put in the category of quality because it is a principle

---

1 *De nuptiis* 1.28.

of qualities. The momentary and transient passions and reactions of soul or body are also placed here. On the other hand,' you say, 'affectional quality, arising from more powerful causes, so inheres in the things in which it is found that it can be separated only by powerful counterforces or not at all.' Your explanation is adequate for those who are competent, but, since those of our readers who are not familiar with this matter should not be neglected, I shall by illustration supply what I think is missing. As to the soul, then, a fright is an affection; timidity is an affectional quality. A fit of anger is not the same as surliness; intoxication is not the same as chronic alcoholism. The latter are affectional qualities; the former are affections. As for the body, we have pale and pallid, blushing and ruddy, and others for which we have no familiar names. Since you say: 'Affectional quality, arising from more powerful causes, so inheres that it can be separated from things only by powerful counterforces or not at all,' then, when a man is said to be evil according to affectional quality, are you not afraid a good will can never exist there, or cannot have any effect? Do you not admit that that unfortunate man, whoever he is, or was, or will be, was certainly crying out against such a quality in the words: 'To wish is present with me, but I do not find the strength to accomplish what is good'? Here, at least, you will confess the necessity of the groaning in the words: 'Who will deliver me from the body of this death? The grace of God through Jesus Christ our Lord.'[2]

(55) No matter how great your dialectical manipulation in dealing with the inexperienced, you will be fully exposed by the manifest truth. I say that the fault by which the flesh lusts against the spirit is inborn in man, from his vitiated origin, as a kind of bad health. I say that conjugal modesty

---
2 Rom. 7.18,24,25.

uses this evil well when it uses it for the purpose of generation; however, in this good use of evil we do not praise the evil itself, but him who uses it. The evil is not innocent, but the user: when he brings it about that his own evil which he uses well does not harm him, just as death is the sinner's torment, but by good use of evil may become the martyr's merit. Thus, Christian baptism gives us perfect newness and perfect health from those evils by which we were guilty, not from the evils we must still combat lest we become guilty. These, too, are in us and they are not another's, but our own. After baptism we see men resist the habit of drunkenness, surely a bad habit which they brought upon themselves and did not contract in birth. They resist it lest it draw them to their ways of evil habit, yet they resist evil when through continence they deny to concupiscence what is desired through habit. In like manner, against the concupiscence of the reproductive members which is born in us through original sin, a widow combats more vigorously than a virgin, and a harlot who wants to be chaste combats more vigorously than a woman always chaste. The greater the power given concupiscence by habit, the greater the effort of the will striving to overcome it. From and with this evil of man, man is born; and this evil is of its own self so great and has so powerful an obligation to the condemnation of man and his separation from the kingdom of God that, even though it is contracted from regenerated parents, it can be dissolved only as it was dissolved in them, by regeneration, and the prince of death can be cast out of the offspring only by that one remedy by which he was cast out of the parents. The quality of evil does not wander from substance to substance as from place to place, leaving the place where it was, so that the same quality which formerly was here would now be there; rather, by a kind of contagion, another quality of the same kind is produced, as often happens when the diseased bodies of parents affect the body of their offspring.

(56) What did you mean when you said: 'Closing the gymnasium of Aristotle and returning to sacred Scripture,' and added: 'Concupiscence is a sensation; it is not an evil quality. Therefore, when concupiscence is diminished, sense-perception is diminished." Is not the concupiscence of the flesh daily diminished through concupiscence for chastity and continence? Would you not agree that he who finds fornication less and less inviting is being healed of the disease of fornication, even though he broke with its works in a single resolve and never commits them again from the day he received the laver of regeneration? Again, would you not agree that a man baptized after a habit of drunkenness, who never drinks to excess after that time, is daily being healed of that disease as he has less and less desire to drink than formerly? The sensation is not concupiscence, the sensation is that by which we perceive we have greater or lesser concupiscence. It is like the passions of the body, where pain is not a sensation; the sensation is that by which pain is perceived. Nor is the sensation disease, but that by which we perceive we have disease. If he who renounces fornication and drunkenness and refrains from such acts becomes good forthwith, and that by a good quality, should he not hear: 'Behold thou art cured. Sin no more,'[3] and deservedly be called chaste and sober? If, subsequently, by the impetus of the good concupiscence by which he battles the evil concupiscence for fornication and drinking, he becomes such as he was not as yet at the time of his conversion, that is, experiencing fewer desires for sins, so that he no longer wages such combats against those evils as formerly—not because virtues are diminished but because enemies are fewer; not in absence of battle but in increasing victory—will you hesitate to pronounce him better? And

---
3 John 5.14.

whence, I ask you, except that the good quality has increased and the evil quality diminished? This he did after baptism; he did not fully accomplish it in baptism. Full remission of sins is completely accomplished in baptism, yet there remains an ever-watchful and ever-ready warfare for improvement against the many turbulent desires within ourselves. For this reason, even the baptized are told: 'Mortify your members which are on earth,' and: 'If by the spirit you put to death the deeds of the flesh, you will live,' and 'Strip off the old man.'[4] These things, then, are said in great accord with truth, with no reproach to baptism.

(57) · If you did not wish to be contentious, I think you would now see how correctly we understand what you are trying to explain differently. When the Prophet said: 'Who forgives all thy faults'—something which is done by the remission of all sins—he immediately added: 'Who heals all thy diseases,'[5] he means us to understand the evils with which the saints will never finish their internal warfare until those evils are healed or, as far as possible in this life, progressively diminished. Not even when the virtue of chastity stands unshaken is there no sickness by which the flesh lusts against the spirit. When there is no sickness, the spirit does not lust against it, because it lusts in order at least by not consenting to obtain health, since it is unable to do so by not fighting. We are speaking of that whose resistance to us we perceive within us; if an alien nature, we must get rid of it; if our own, it must be healed. If we say it is an alien nature and must be got rid of, we agree with the Manichaeans. Let us, then, confess it is our own nature which must be healed, and thus we shall at the same time be clear of Manichaeans and Pelagians.

---

4 Col. 3.5; Rom. 8.13; Col. 3.9.
5 Ps. 102.3.

Chapter 19

(58) 'The wound inflicted on the human race by the Devil compels whatever is born through it to be under the Devil's power as though by right he plucked the fruit from his own branch.'[1] You quote these words from my book to refute them; you captiously suggest I say: 'The Devil is the author of human nature and the maker of the very substance in which man consists,' as though you could call a wound in the body a substance. Perhaps the reason you think I said the Devil is the creator of the substance is that in the simile I used the word 'branch,' and a branch is undoubtedly a substance. Why did you pretend to be so uninformed as not to know that things which are substances may be used as similes of things not substances? Perhaps by your dialectics you wanted to calumniate the words of our Lord: 'Every good tree bears good fruit, but the bad tree bears bad fruit.'[2] Who but one not knowing what he says would assert that badness is goodness, or good or evil works, which our Lord wants us to understand by the fruits of those trees, are substances? Who, if he knows what he is saying, will deny that trees and their fruits are substances? Thus we see that things which are substances have been used as similes of things not substances. If we regard the good and bad trees, not as the goodness and badness of man, but as the men themselves who are the subjects of these qualities, that is, goodness in the good, badness in the bad, so that the substances themselves, the men themselves, are to be the trees, it surely follows that only the inexperienced would say that their fruits (which are nothing other than their works) are substances, although none but the inexperienced would deny that fruits of all trees, from which the simile is taken, are

---

1 *De nuptiis* 1.26.
2 Matt. 7.17.

substances. Thus, it is proper to use a substance as a simile of something not a substance. In this way I used correctly the simile of a substance for the fault which the Devil inflicted like a wound on the human race, although the fault is by no means a substance, in order that I might call it a branch and also speak of its fruits, meaning those faults with which, you denying but the truth proving, men are born—and from which they will eternally perish from the kingdom of God unless they are reborn by the liberating truth.

(59) I said the Devil is the corrupter, not the creator, of the substance. Through what he inflicted he subjected to himself what he did not create, the just God bestowing this power on him. He cannot withdraw from God's might either himself or what is subject to him, since the reason a second birth was instituted is that the first was condemned. Yet the goodness of God is shown even in this condemned birth, so that from the accursed seed a rational nature is formed, and by this most bounteous goodness the very great multitude of wicked men is most evidently nourished and is also given growth by a hidden work of God. If this goodness of God's action were withdrawn from the formation and care of the seeds and from the quickening of living beings, not only would begetting not come to pass, but things already begotten would be reduced entirely to nothing. Since only foolish ungodliness would reproach God with the fact that men damnable because of their corrupted will are alive because He who quickens all things gives them life, why should we think it abhorrent to the works of Him who is the Creator of all things that men damnable in virtue of their corrupted origin are born by His creative power, and are elevated from this due condemnation when regenerated through the Mediator, and that, by mercy not due them but gratuitously bestowed on those whom He chose before the foundation of this world through election of grace, and

not in view of works past, present, or future? Otherwise, grace is no longer grace.³ This is most obvious in the case of infants, where we cannot speak of past works, since they did not exist; nor present, because infants do nothing; nor future, when they die in infancy.

(60) I surely said: 'Just as sins that have passed in their action remain in their guilt; conversely, concupiscence can remain in its action and pass in its guilt.'⁴ You say this is false; truth proves it true. Since you cannot refute it, you try to create confusion for the inexperienced by dialectics, saying you do not know in what system of logic I could have found the convertibility of all contraries. If I sought to explain your statement, especially for those who know nothing of dialectics, I would probably need a whole volume. But your words, 'The convertibility of all contraries cannot be found in any system of logic,' will suffice for the present, for here you show there can be conversion of some, not all; therefore, among the some, I find these. If you had said there can be no conversion of contraries, and thus shown the contraries I gave cannot be converted because none is convertible, I would have had to show that some can be converted and that those I named are among the some; that is, whether just as it is true that sins remain in their guilt, although they are past in their action, so it is true that concupiscence may remain in its action and pass in its guilt. In your desire to disprove this, you say something I did not say. I spoke of the concupiscence which exists in the members and wars against the law of the mind,⁵ even though its guilt has passed in the remission of all sins; just as sacrifice offered to idols and thereafter not repeated is past in the action but remains present in its guilt unless remitted through pardon.

---
3 Cf. Rom. 11.6.
4 *De nuptiis* 1.28,30.
5 Cf. Rom. 7.23.

To sacrifice to idols is of such nature that, after the deed has been done, it itself passes, and when that same deed is past, its guilt remains present and must be remitted by pardon. The concupiscence of the flesh, however, is such that it remains in man warring against it through continence, even though its guilt, which was contracted by generation, has already been completely ended by regeneration. It remains in its action, not by drawing away and enticing the mind and with the mind's consent conceiving and bringing forth sins, but by arousing evil desires the mind must resist. For this excitement of desires is itself the action of concupiscence, even when, in the absence of the mind's consent, the effect does not follow. In addition to this action, that is, besides this stimulation, there is in man another evil, whence arises this stimulation which we call desire. There is not always a desire present for us to fight. There is no desire when there is nothing to be lusted after by the musing mind or by the senses of the body; but an evil quality, although not aroused by any temptation, may still exist in us, as timidity exists in a timid man when he is not frightened. When occasion for lusting arises, yet no evil desire is excited, not even against our will, we have full health. This fault, then, could not but hold man in guilt, even if he is born of chaste spouses by good use of the evil of concupiscence, and, although this evil remains, that guilt is removed through the grace of God by which we are delivered from all evil. For the Lord not only forgives all our iniquities, but also heals all our diseases. Recall what our Deliverer and Saviour Himself replied to those who told Him to leave Jerusalem: 'Behold, I cast out devils and bring perfect health today and tomorrow, and the third day I am to end my course.'[6] Read the Gospel and see how much later He suffered and rose again. Did

---

6 Cf. Luke 13.32.

He, then, lie? God forbid. He signified something relevant to our question. The expulsion of devils signified the remission of sins; the production of perfect health is that made in progress after baptism; on the third day is the consumation He also showed us in the immortality of His own flesh, that is, the beatitude of incorruptible joy.

(61) You mention sacrilegious sacrifice as an instance of what you mean, saying: 'Whatever comes under this head can be illustrated in a single case. If a man has once sacrificed to idols, he can be charged with the ungodliness of his deed until he obtains pardon, and the guilt remains after the action has ended. By no means,' you continue, 'can it happen that the action remains and the guilt departs, so that in consequence he continues to sacrifice, yet is free from impiety.' What you say about sacrifice to idols is most true. It is an action fully accomplished in the deed itself, and, if it occurs again, it is another deed. But the ungodliness by which these deeds are done remains present until he renounces idols and believes in God. Sacrifice to idols is a passing fact, not an enduring fault; but the ungodliness by which sacrifice was made resembles that concupiscence by which adultery is committed. Take away the error, however, which held ungodliness as godliness, and who will find pleasure in sacrificing to idols, or sense any desire to do so? Your instance is not really similar: passing sacrifice is in no way like that abiding concupiscence which, through constant stimulation to the unlawful desires chastity resists, still seeks to disturb one who no longer commits what he once by consenting habitually committed; but now no more, when he is firmly fixed in the belief and knowledge that these things are not to be done. Knowledge does not put an end to concupiscence, so that it does not exist; it must be restrained by continence and kept from reaching its goal. Sacrifice is no longer present in its action, since the action has passed;

it is not present in the will, for the error in which it was done has been removed; yet the guilt of it remains present until dissolved in the laver of regeneration by the remission of all sins. Conversely, though the guilt of evil concupiscence has been dissolved through that same baptism, concupiscence itself abides until healed with the medicine that brings perfection, by Him who after casting out devils brought perfect health.

(62) You yourself admit that guilt for past sin remains present unless washed away in the sacred font. What is this guilt and where does it remain in a man now reformed and living rightly, but not yet delivered by remission of sins? Is this guilt a subject, that is, a substance, like spirit and body, or is it in a subject, as fevers and wounds are in the body, and avarice and error in the soul? You will say it is in a subject, since you will not call guilt a substance. In what subject? Why not quote your own answer? You say: 'When its action is past, its guilt remains present in the conscience of the offender until it is remitted.' It is in a subject, then, in the soul of him who remembers his transgression and is troubled by a scruple of conscience until relieved by the remission of the offense. If he forgets his transgression and is not stung by his conscience, where will this guilt be, since you concede it remains present after the sin is past until it is remitted? It is not in the body, because it is not one of the accidents proper to bodies; it is not in the soul, because it has been forgotten. Yet it is present. Where, then? This man is now living well, committing no sin; you cannot hold the guilt of sins remembered remains present, but not the guilt of those forgotten; it by all means remains until it is remitted. Where, then, does it remain except in the hidden laws of God written somehow in the minds of the angels; in order that there be no wickedness unpunished except what the blood of the Mediator expiates. By the sign of His cross the waves of bap-

tism are consecrated so that they may wash away the guilt written as in a bond in the knowledge of the spiritual powers through which punishment for sins is required. All born carnally in the flesh of the flesh are born subject to this bond, to be freed from the debt of it by the blood of Him who was born in the flesh and of the flesh indeed—yet not carnally but spiritually, for He was born of the Holy Spirit and the Virgin Mary. Of the Holy Spirit, that in Him there be no sinful flesh; of the Virgin Mary, that the likeness of sinful flesh be in Him. For this reason He did not fall subject to that bond, and He freed its subjects from it. For iniquity is not absent when in one man his higher powers serve the lower, or his lower powers rebelliously resist the higher, even when not permitted to prevail. If man suffered this iniquity from an external enemy, another man, it would not exist in him, and it would be punished apart from him. Since it is in him, then either he will be punished with it, or, if he has been delivered from its guilt, it remains to fight against the spirit—not so that it will send him who is no longer guilty to any torments after death or estrange him from the kingdom of God or hold him under any condemnation; and again, not so that by separation as of an alien nature we lose it entirely; but, since it is a sickness of our nature, so that it may be healed in us.

Chapter 20

(63) Because of this fault, then, as I wrote in the book you are attacking, 'Human nature is condemned, and because of this which is the cause of the condemnation, it is also subject to the condemned Devil, for the Devil himself is also an unclean spirit: good, indeed, because spirit; evil, because unclean. He is a spirit by nature, unclean by fault; of these

two, the one is from God, the other from himself. Hence, men, adults as well as infants, are in bondage to him, not because they are men, but because they are unclean.'[1] You oppose these words from my book by saying: 'The formula found in the Devil should also apply to an evil man, so that none is condemned except from faults of his own will, and thus there can be no sin by way of origin. Otherwise,' you say, 'we cannot approve of the work of Him who made even the Devil good.' You fail to note that God did not create the Devil from another Devil, nor from another angel, who, though good, had that law in his members warring against the law of his mind, through which and with which every man is born of a man. This argument might help you if the Devil begat sons as man does, and we denied they were subject to the paternal sin. As it is, however, it is something different to talk about him who was a murderer from the beginning, because by misleading the woman he slew man at the beginning when man was made, and who through free choice did not stand in the truth,[2] and, falling, hurled man down with him; this, I say, is not the same as 'Through one man sin entered into the world and through sin death, and thus death has passed unto all men; in whom all have sinned.'[3] These words clearly teach original sin common to all men, apart from the personal sins of each one.

(64) 'Whoever marvels that a creature of God is subjected to the Devil, let him marvel no more, for a creature of God is subjected to a creature of God, the lesser to the greater.'[4] When you quoted this statement of mine why did you not add my next words, showing that by the lesser to the greater I meant the human to the angelic—unless in this mis-

---
1 *De nuptiis* 1.25,16.
2 John 18.44.
3 Rom. 5.12.
4 *De nuptiis* 1.26.

representation you saw an opportunity to introduce some Aristotelean Categories to the confusion of the inexperienced, who, in their ignorance, would mistake your obscurity for light. Your heresy has been reduced to the point where your followers sigh to find in the Church no dialectical judges of the Peripatetic and Stoic schools, who would acquit you, as you say. What point, what purpose, has your statement that 'greater and lesser belong in the class of finite quantity'? You say: 'Not only are contrary predicates incompatible in quantity—a property it shares with quality and the other predicaments; it also has no contrary—a property common by definition to quantity and substance. But good and evil are contraries.' You would never introduce this if you thought your readers or hearers would understand it. Does it follow that unclean man should not be subjected to unclean angel merely because the quantity by which an angel is greater than man is not only unable to have contrary predicates at the same time, but also has no contrary, as though man then should have been subjected to the Devil if he were found to be his contrary; and evils should not be subjected to evils merely because it seems only goods are contrary to evils, not evils to evils? How sterile the thought; how inept the conclusion. Is not a servant subject to his master; good servant to good master, and evil to evil, and evil to good, and good to evil? Is not a wife subject to her husband; good wife to good husband, evil to evil, and evil to good, and good to evil? Then, what has the compatibility or incompatibility of contrary predicates in this thing or that to do with the power or reason by which the one is subjected to the other, whatever they may be? You would not utter these inconsiderate words if you cultivated the wisdom contrary to the folly that suggests them to you.

(65) How shall we characterize your statement: 'If what

is becomingly ordered is from God, and what is from God is good, then it is good to be subject to the Devil, for thus the order God instituted is observed'? You continue: 'It follows that is must be evil to rebel against the Devil, for this disturbs the order God instituted.' You could then say that farmers resist God and disturb His order by ridding the fields of the thorns and thistles God commanded them to bring forth to sinners.[5] If what is becomingly ordered is from God and is good, you could say by your reasoning that to be in Gehenna is a good for the evil, for thus the order instituted by God is observed. Why do you add: 'It follows that it must be evil to rebel against the Devil, for this disturbs the order God instituted'? Why do you say this? Who rebels against the Devil unless he has been delivered from the Devil's power through the blood of the Mediator? It would have been better, then, not to have an enemy than to overcome him; but, because human nature was subjected to an enemy as the just desert of sin, man must first be rescued from his power, that he may fight him; then, if his life in this flesh is prolonged, he is assisted in the conflict that he may overcome the enemy; and finally the victor will be beatified, that he may reign, and at the very end he will ask: 'Death, where is thy devouring?'[6] or, in the words of the Apostle: 'Death, where is thy victory? Death, where is thy sting?'[7]

Chapter 21

(66) You were at pains to quote some statements from

---
5 Cf. Gen. 3.14.
6 Osee 13.14.
7 1 Cor. 15.55.

the works of a Manichaean for comparison with my opinion,[1] although I not only detest and condemn in faith and word the mixture of two natures, one good, one evil, from which springs their whole imaginary raving, but I also oppose it by resisting and refuting you, their supporter. When truth cries out against them, that evils come only from goods, you cry back, for them and with them, against the truth: 'The work of the Devil is not permitted to pass through the work of God'; 'The root of evil cannot be located in the gift of God'; 'The reason in things will not permit evil to come from good or the unjust from the just'; 'Sins do not arise from a thing which is free from sin'; 'Guilt cannot be produced from a work which does not have guilt.'[2] From all these propositions we must conclude, as do the Manichaeans, that evils do not come from goods; hence, we must say evils come only from evils. How, then, can you accuse anyone of crime by calling him a Manichaean, and seem their adversary, when you are so dependent on them that you and they stand or fall together? We dealt with this matter somewhat more fully in Book 1 of this work, and more briefly in Book 5.[3] A few words more will suffice for the present.

(67) I have often pointed out how much your heresy in general helps the Manichaeans, and how again this should not be passed by. The Manichaeans call our attention to the number of evils in infants, which Cicero also mentions in what I quoted above from his *Republic*:[4] Listing some of those evils, he says: 'Man has been thrust into these miseries by nature, more a stepmother than a mother.' To

---
1 Long extracts from a letter by a Manichaean, quoted by Julian for the purpose named here, are reproduced by Augustine in *Opus imperfectum contra Julianum* 3.172-187.
2 Cf. above pp. 45-54.
3 Cf. above, pp. 298-299, 303-305.
4 Cf. above, p. 218.

this they add the many and various evils we see endured, not, indeed, by all infants, yet by a great many—even to possession by devils. The Manichaeans conclude by saying: 'Since God is just and omnipotent, whence does His image in infants suffer such evils unless there is really, as we hold, a mixture of two natures, good and evil?' Catholic truth refutes them by confessing original sin through which the human race was made the sport of demons and the progeny of mortals was destined to laborious misery. This would not be so if human nature through free choice had remained in the state in which it was first created. You who deny original sin must forthwith affirm God is either impotent or unjust, since under His power His image in infants, with no personal or original sin to deserve punishment, is afflicted with such evils; for they cannot cultivate virtue through them, as you correctly say about adults, who have the use of reason. Since you cannot say God is impotent or unjust, the Manichaeans will confirm against you their wicked error about a mixture of two substances mutually hostile to each other. Thus, it is not true that no fuller's herb can cleanse me of the Manichaean infection, as you say. By your petulant words you do injury to the laver of regeneration which I received in the bosom of my Catholic mother. The baneful poison of the ancient dragon has become so much a part of you that you not only label Catholics with the infamous name of Manichaeans, but by your perverse teaching you also help the Manichaeans themselves.

Chapter 22

(68) In another book addressed to Marcellinus, I said: 'The children of the woman who believed the Serpent and was corrupted by lust are not liberated except through the

Son of the Virgin who believed the angel and brought forth without lust.'[1] You quoted this as though I had said that the Serpent had intercourse with Eve, just as the Manichaeans in their madness say that their 'prince of darkness', who, they say, is the father of the woman herself, had lain with her. I made no such statement about the Serpent. Will you, contrary to the Apostle, deny that the mind of woman was corrupted by the Serpent? Are you not aware of the words of the Apostle: 'I fear lest, as the Serpent seduced Eve by his guile, so your minds may be corrupted and fall from a single devotion to Christ.'[2] From this kind of corruption by the Serpent, then, also found when evil companionships corrupt good morals, the lust for sin entered into the mind of the woman, so that, when the man had also been corrupted by prevarication, that for which they blushed and covered the shameful parts followed in the flesh; not at the approach of the Devil in bodily union, but upon the departure of the spiritual grace of God.

(69) Your whole argument has not, as you boast, rendered void my assertion of the evil of carnal concupiscence and the existence of the original sin; yet marriage remains praiseworthy, since it uses well an evil not made by it, but one it found already present. Indeed, you have not overcome even the Manichaeans, whom you help more than hinder; you first, and also all the followers of the common Pelagian innovation and error. In Book 1 of this work I gave an abundant and more certain answer from the testimonies of the Catholic treatises of St. Basil of Caesarea and St. John of Constantinople, although you say these are in accord with your opinion.[3] I showed how by failing to understand some of their words you, with remarkable blind-

---
1 *De peccatorum meritis et remissione* 1.28.
2 Cor. 11.3.
3 Cf. above, 1.5-6.

ness, attack their teaching, which is the Catholic teaching. And in Book 2 I said enough to show it is no 'conspiracy of lost men,'[4] but the pious and faithful consensus of the holy and learned fathers of the Catholic Church which resists your heretical novelties, for the ancient Catholic truth. You say we offer 'the people's muttering alone' against you; but it is not alone, since it rests on the authority of very great teachers, and it is also just, because it does not wish you, who also know this very well, to destroy the salvation of infants, which is in Christ.

Chapter 23

(70) You say I explain incorrectly the whole chapter of the Apostle where he says: 'I know that in me, that is, in my flesh, no good dwells,' and the rest up to: 'Unhappy man that I am, who will deliver me from the body of this death?' You exaggerate, since I am neither the first nor the only one to understand as it should be understood in truth this passage which destroys your heresy; indeed, at first I understood it in a different way, or, better, did not understand it, as some of my earlier writings will testify.[1] I did not see how the Apostle could say: 'But I am carnal,' since he was spiritual, and how he was held captive under the law of sin in his members.[2] I thought this could be affirmed only of those so completely under the power of concupiscence that they must always do its bidding. It would

---

4 Cf. above, pp. 35-37.

1 The unsound earlier opinion is expressed in *Ad Simplicianum* 1. q. 1; *Expositio epistolae ad Romanos,* prop. 41,42; *Expositio epistolae ad Galatas* 5. The better, later opinion is well expressed in *De gratia Christi* 45; *Contra duas epistolas Pelagianorum* 1.17-25; *Retractationes* 1.23.24; 2.1; *Contra Julianum* 2.3.
2 Cf. Rom. 7.14,18,24.

be unreasonable to think this of the Apostle, since an innumerable multitude of saints lust with the spirit against the flesh. Later on, I yielded to better and more enlightened minds, or, rather, to truth itself, and I heard in the words of the Apostle the groaning of the saints in their battle against carnal concupiscence. Although the saints are spiritually minded, they are still carnal in the corruptible body which is a load upon the soul.³ They will, however, be spiritual also in body when the body sown animal will rise spiritual.⁴ They are still prisoners under the law of sin, inasmuch as they are subject to stimulations by desires to which they do not consent. Thus I came to understand this matter as did Hilary, Gregory, Ambrose, and other holy and renowned teachers of the Church, who saw that the Apostle, by his own words, fought strenuously the same battle against carnal concupiscences he did not wish to have, yet in fact did have.⁵ You yourself have acknowledged that the saints engage in glorious combats against such stimulations, which must first be combated, lest they dominate; then, healed, that they may be entirely exterminated.⁶ When we fight, we at once recognize the words of the fighters. In this way it is not we who live, but Christ lives in us, if, for waging war against concupiscences and for complete victory over our enemies, we trust in Him and not in ourselves. For 'He has become for us God-given wisdom, and justice and sanctification, and redemption'; so that, as it is written: 'Let him who takes pride take pride in the Lord.'⁷

(71) It is not, as you think, contradictory that he who says: 'It is no longer I that live, but Christ lives in me,' should also say: 'I know that in me, that is, in my flesh, no

---
3 Cf. Wisd. 9.15.
4 Cf. 1 Cor. 15.44.
5 Cf. above, pp. 59-67.
6 Cf. above, pp. 147-148.
7 1 Cor. 1.30,31.

good dwells.'[8] As far as Christ lives in him, so far does he attack and conquer, not good, but the evil dwelling in his flesh. No man's spirit lusts rightly against his own flesh unless the spirit of Christ dwells in him. God forbid, then, that we say what you accuse us of saying: 'The Apostle spoke as though pretending to resist, but being led to a harlot by the hand of deadly pleasure,' when he actually said: 'It is no longer I who do it,'[9] to show that mere stimulation by lust, without consent to sin, really produces the concupiscences of the flesh.

(72) Why do you try in vain 'to transfer these words to the pride of the Jews, as though the Apostle were identifying himself with those who despised the gifts of Christ as not necessary for them'? You yourself suspect this is true; would that you so understood those gifts of Christ as to believe they are at least of some avail in overcoming concupiscence. You say the Jews despised them, 'Because He pardoned sins which the law warned them to avoid,' as though the effect of the remission of sins were that man's flesh lust not against his spirit.[10] We have the words, 'I know that in me, that is, in my flesh, no good dwells,' and similar statements. You are not departing from your teaching that the grace of God through Jesus Christ our Lord is concerned only with the remission of sins, and in such a way that it does not help us that we may avoid sins and overcome carnal desires, by pouring forth charity in our hearts through the Holy Spirit who has been given to us.[11] You forget that he who says: 'I see another law in my members, warring against the law of my mind,' and that he can be delivered from this evil only by the grace of God through Jesus Christ our Lord,

---
8 Gal. 2.20; Rom. 7.18.
9 Rom. 7.17.
10 Cf. Gal. 5.17.
11 Rom. 5.5.

is not a Jew, nor is he struggling because he has sinned, but lest he sin.

(73) You asserted that 'The Apostle purposely exaggerates the forces of habit.' Does not one baptized battle against that force? If you deny it, you contradict all Christian experience. But, if he battles, why not recognize the voice of the warrior in the words of the Apostle? You say: 'Through the good law and through the holy commandment wicked men acted savagely, because no amount of knowledge can inspire virtue if there is not the will.' Astute thinker! Outstanding interpreter of the divine words! What about the words of him who says: 'That which I will, I do not'; 'To wish is in my power'; 'I do that which I do not wish'; 'I am delighted with the law of God according to the inner man.' You hear this and say there is not virtue because there is not will. There was not only the will, but also virtue, lest he consent with the concupiscence of the flesh which in these evil proddings was serving the law of sin. He did not yield to the stimulations, nor offer his members as weapons of iniquity;[12] yet, sensing what he did not wish, in his flesh lusting against the spirit, he said in truest chastity: 'I myself with my mind serve the law of God, but with my flesh the law of sin.'[13] You quote the Apostle's words: 'The law indeed is holy, and the commandment holy and just and good. Did then that which is good become death to me? By no means! But sin, that it might be manifest as sin, worked death for me through that which is good, in order that sin, by reason of the commandment, might become immeasurably sinful.'[14] This can well be understood of his past life when he was under the law, not yet under grace. He uses the past tense when he says: 'For I had not known sin save

---

12 Rom. 6.13.
13 Rom. 7.25.
14 Rom. 7.12.17.

through the Law'; and 'I had not known concupiscence'; and 'Sin worked in me all manner of concupiscence'; and 'Once upon a time I was living without law'—this when he was not yet able to use reason. Again: 'When the commandment came, sin revived, and I died'; and 'Sin, having taken occasion from the commandment, deceived me, and through it killed me'; and 'That which is good became death to me.' In all these passages he refers to the time when he was living under the Law, and, not as yet helped by grace, was overcome by carnal concupiscence. When he says: 'The Law is spiritual, but I am carnal,' he shows what he suffers when now in the conflict. He does not say he had been carnal or he was carnal, but 'I am carnal.' He distinguishes the times more clearly when he says: 'It is no longer I who do it, but the sin that dwells in me.' It is no longer he who produces the evil desires with which he does not consent to commit sin. By the name of the sin that dwells in him he indicates concupiscence itself, because it was made by sin and, if it draws and entices one consenting, it conceives and brings forth sin. The next words of the Apostle, up to the words: 'Therefore I myself with my mind serve the law of God, but with my flesh the law of sin,'[15] are the words of one now under grace, but still battling against his own concupiscence, not so that he consents and sins, but so that he experiences desires which he resists.

(74) None of us accuses the substance of the body; none accuses the nature of the flesh. Vainly you show the innocence of what we do not say is evil. We do not deny that evil desires of concupiscence are in us; but, if we live rightly, we do not consent to them. They must be chastised; they must be restrained; they must be attacked; they must be overcome—nonetheless, they are with us, and they are not another's. Nor are they goods of ours, but evils. Mani-

---
15 Rom. 7.7-25.

chaean folly says they are distinct from us and outside us. Catholic truth says they have not been healed.

Chapter 24

(75) With remarkable abandon—madness, rather—you attack that most fundamental teaching of the Apostle: 'Through one man sin entered into the world and through sin death, and thus death has passed unto all men; in whom all have sinned.' In vain you offer a new interpretation, distorted and abhorrent, declaring that 'By these words he meant us to understand the one "in whom" (or "in which") all have sinned, as though he had said "because of which all have sinned, as it is said: "In what doth a young man correct his way?" '[3] By your reasoning, we must not hold that all men have sinned by way of origin in one man, as it were in common, in the oneness of the mass, but that all have committed their sins because of the sinful act of the first man, that is, when they imitate him, not when they are generated from him. 'In whom' (or 'in which') and 'because of which' do not always admit of the same interpretation. A man commits a sin because of something he proposes to himself, with the result that he commits a sin, or because of what is somehow the cause of his sinning. It is most unreasonable to say: That because of which this particular man committed a murder is Adam's eating fruit from the forbidden tree in Paradise—when as a matter of fact he killed someone in a robbery without any thought of

---

1 Cf. above, p. 9, note 8. This chapter merely shows the impossibility of the Pelagian reading of this text of Scripture; Augustine does not base his argument for the truth of his teaching on this text or on his special reading of it.
2 Rom. 5.12.
3 Ps. 118.9.

Adam, but because of the gold he hoped to take from his victim. Every personal sin has a cause because of which it is committed, even if no one should think about what the first man did, either in itself or as an example. That because of which Cain committed his sin was not Adam's sinful act, although Cain knew Adam, his father. That because of which Cain killed his brother is well known; it was not because of what Adam did, but because he envied his brother's good.

(76) The testimonies you cite do not support your theory. 'In what doth a young man correct his way' may well be read as 'Because of what' does he accomplish this correction —as is clear by the words that follow it: 'by observing thy words.' That because of which he corrects his way is his thinking about God's words as they should be thought about, and, in thinking about them, observing them, and, in observing them, living rightly. Thus, his observing God's words is precisely the cause of his correcting his way. The words of most blessed Stephen, 'Moses fled in this word,'[4] may be properly understood as 'because of this word.' He heard it, he feared it, he thought about it, so that he fled; it was the cause of his flight. None of these expressions refers in any way to a kind of imitation in which one man imitates another without thinking of him at all. Therefore, that because of which someone sinned cannot be said to be the sinful act of another, if the sinner neither existed in that other by way of origin nor gave him any thought in his own sin.

(77) You say: 'If Paul was talking about the transmission of sin,[5] it would have been more fitting to say that sin has passed to all men because all men have been generated of the pleasure of spouses; and he would have added that it passed to all men in that they have come from the corrupted

---

[4] Acts 7.24.
[5] *Tradux peccati.*

flesh of the first man.' One might answer you that, in the same way, if the Apostle had been talking about the imitation of sin, it would have been more fitting to say that sin passed to all men because there had first been Adam's example; and he would have added that it passed to all men in that all have sinned by imitation of that one man. Now, the Apostle, if he had been talking for your or my approval, would have spoken in one of these two ways. Since he did neither, would you have us believe his words state neither original sin as Catholics teach, nor sin by imitation, as the Pelagians teach? I think not. Take away what can be proposed with equal force from either side, and, without arguing, consider what the Apostle says and note what he had in mind when he said it, and you will find through one man the wrath of God upon the human race, and through one man reconciliation with God for those who are delivered gratuitously from the condemnation of the whole race. The former is the first Adam, made from earth; the latter is the second Adam, made from a woman. There, however, the flesh was made through the Word; here, the Word Himself was made flesh, so that we might live through His death; forsaking whom, we died. The Apostle says: 'God commends his charity towards us, because when as yet we were sinners, Christ died for us. Much more now that we are justified in his blood shall we be saved through him from the wrath.'[6]

(78) Of this wrath he says: 'We were by nature children of wrath even as the rest.'[7] Of this wrath Jeremias says: 'Cursed be the day wherein I was born.'[8] Of this wrath holy Job says: 'Let the day perish wherein I was born.'[9] Of this wrath the same Job says again: 'Man born of a woman, living for a short time, is filled with many miseries.

---
6 Rom. 5.8,9.
7 Eph. 2.3.
8 Jer. 20.14.
9 Job 3.3.

Who cometh forth like a flower and is destroyed, and never continueth in the same state. And dost thou think it meet to open thy eyes upon such a one and to bring him into judgment with thee? Who can make him clean that is conceived of an unclean seed? Not even one, although he lived but one day on the earth.'[10] Of this wrath the Book of Ecclesiasticus says: 'All flesh grows old like a garment; for the covenant of the world shall surely die'; and again: 'From the woman came the beginning of sin, and by her we all die'; and yet again: 'Great labor is created for all men, and a heavy yoke is upon the children of Adam from the day of their coming out of their mother's womb until the day of their burial into the mother of all.'[11] Of this wrath Ecclesiastes says: 'Vanity of vanities, and all is vanity. What hath a man more of all his labor that he taketh under the sun?'[12] Of this wrath the voice of the Apostle: 'Creation was made subject to vanity.'[13] Of this wrath the psalm laments: 'Behold thou hast made my day measurable, and my substance is nothing before thee. And indeed all things are vanity, every man living.'[14] Of this wrath another psalm also laments: 'Things that are counted nothing shall their years be. In the morning man shall flourish and pass away; in the evening he shall fall, grow dry, and wither. For in thy wrath we have fainted away and are troubled in thy indignation. Thou hast set our iniquities before the eyes, our life in the light of thy countenance. For all our days are spent; and in thy wrath we have fainted away. Our years shall be considered as a spider.'[15]

(79) No man is delivered from this wrath of God unless

---

10 Job 14.1-5 (Septuagint)
11 Eccli. 14.18,12; 25.33; 40.1.
12 Eccle. 1.2,3.
13 Rom. 8.20.
14 Ps. 38.6.
15 Ps. 89.5-9.

he is reconciled with God through the Mediator, wherefore the Mediator Himself says: 'He who is unbelieving towards the Son shall not see life, but the wrath of God rests upon him.'[16] He did not say it will come, but 'it rests upon him.' Therefore, both adults, through their own heart and voice, and infants, through that of another, believe and confess so they may be reconciled to God through the death of His Son, lest the wrath of God rest upon them whom their vitiated origin makes guilty. The Apostle says: 'When as yet we were sinners, Christ died for us. Much more now that we are justified by his blood shall we be saved through him from the wrath. For if when we were sinners we were reconciled to God by the death of His Son, much more, having been reconciled, shall we be saved by his life. And not this only, but we exult also in God, through our Lord Jesus Christ, through whom we have now received reconciliation. Therefore as through one man sin entered into the world and through sin death, and thus death passed unto all men; in whom all have sinned.' The Apostle's purpose is quite evident. By all means deprive infants of that reconciliation which is made through the death of the Son of God who Himself entered into the world without sin, and thus let the wrath of God rest upon them because of him through whom sin entered into the world. Where is your doctrine of imitation when you read: 'For the judgment was from one man unto condemnation, but grace is from many offenses unto justification'?[17] Why grace from many offenses unto justification, except because there were many other sins for grace to destroy all at once, besides that one sin of origin? Otherwise, there would be condemnation from many sins men committed by imitating the one, just as there is justification from many sins, after the remission of which they

---
16 John 4.36.
17 Rom. 5.8-12,16.

breathe again unto grace. But that one sin was enough, which, also, by itself sufficed for condemnation, while grace was not content to destroy only that one, but also all the additional sins, that justification might be made by the remission of all sins. Hence it is said: 'The judgment was from one man unto condemnation, but grace is from many offenses unto justification.' For, just as infants do not imitate Christ because they cannot do so, yet can receive His spiritual grace, so without imitating the first man, they are nonetheless bound by contagion from his carnal generation. If you hold they are strangers to the sin of the first man because they do not imitate him by their own will, by the same reasoning you estrange them from the justice of Christ because they do not imitate Christ by their own will.

(80) Since you do not wish to understand the 'many' he said later as meaning the 'all' he said first, you declare he said 'many' to keep us from thinking he meant 'all'. You could do likewise about the seed of Abraham to whom all nations were promised,[18] and say not all nations were promised him, because we read in another passage: 'I have made thee a father of many nations.'[19] Sound thinking shows that Scripture speaks in this way because there can be an 'all' which are not 'many,' as we speak of all the Gospels, yet they are only four in number. There can also be 'many' which are not 'all,' as we say many believe in Christ, yet not all believe; the Apostle says: 'All men have not faith.'[20] In the words, 'In your seed all nations will be blessed' and 'I have made thee a father of many nations,' it is clear that the same nations that are all are also many, and the same that are many are all. Similarly, when it is said that through one, sin passed unto all, and later, that through the dis-

---
18 Cf. Gen. 22.18.
19 Hen. 17.5.
20 2 Thess. 3.2.

obedience of one, many were constituted sinners, those who are many are also all. In like manner, when it is said: 'By the justice of the one the result is unto justification of life to all men,' and again: 'By the obedience of the one many will be constituted just,'[21] none is excepted; we must understand that those who are many are all—not because all men are justified in Christ, but because all who are justified can be justified in no other way than in Christ. We can also say that all enter a certain house through one door, not because all men enter that house, but because no one enters except through that door. All, then, are unto death through Adam; all unto life through Christ. 'As in Adam all die, so in Christ all will be made to live.'[22] That is to say, from the first origin of the human race, none is unto death except through Adam, and through Adam none is unto anything but death; and none is unto life except through Christ, and through Christ none is unto anything but life.

(81) In abominable perversity you attack the Christian religion when you would have us think not all, but many, have been condemned through Adam or delivered through Christ. If some are saved without Christ, then some are also justified without Christ; therefore, Christ died in vain. For there must have been another way, as you wish, in nature, in free choice, in the law, natural or written, by which they who so wished could be saved and be just. Who but the unjust would bar the just images of God from the kingdom of God? Perhaps you will say it is accomplished more easily through Christ. Could you not also say this of the Law—that there is justice through the Law, but more easily through Christ? Yet the Apostle says: 'If justice be by the Law, then Christ died in vain.'[23] Therefore, besides

---
21 Rom. 5.12,18,19.
22 1 Cor. 15.22.
23 Gal. 2.21.

the one Mediator of God and men, the man Christ Jesus,[24] there is no other name under heaven whereby we must be saved.[25] For this reason it is said: 'In Christ all shall be made alive,' because in Him God has defined the faith for all, raising Him from the death.[26] By proclaiming the nature as guiltless, and the power of free will and the law, whether the natural law or the law given through Moses, your dogma would persuade men that there is indeed some need for Christ, yet it is not necessary to pass into Christ for eternal salvation, because, it says, the way through the sacrament of His death and resurrection is more commodious (if you grant that much), not because there cannot be another way. Considering, therefore, how much Christians ought to detest you, renounce your opinion even in our silence.

Chapter 25

(82) For the last and supposedly strongest argument for your case, you refer to the prophetic testimony of Ezechiel, were we read that there will no longer be a proverb in which they say the fathers have eaten sour grapes and the teeth of the children are on edge; the son will not die in the sin of his father nor the father in the sin of his son, but the soul that sins, the same shall die.[1] You do not understand that this is the promise of the New Testament and of the other world. For the grace of the Redeemer brought it to pass that He cancelled the paternal decree,[2] and each man shall account for himself. On the other hand, can

---

24 Cf. 1 Tim. 2.5.
25 Cf. Acts 4.12.
26 Cf. Acts 17.31.

---

1 Cf. Ezech. 18.2-4.
2 Cf. Col.2.14.

any one count the many passages in Scripture where sons are bound by the sins of their parents? Why did Ham sin and vengeance was declared against his son Chanaan?[3] Why was the son of Solomon punished for the sin of Solomon by the breaking up of the kingdom?[4] Why was the sin of Achab, King of Israel, visited upon his posterity?[5] How do we read in the sacred books: 'Returning the iniquity of the fathers into the bosom of their children after them' and 'Visiting the iniquity of the fathers upon the children unto the third and fourth generation'?[6] The number here can be taken for all the descendants. Are these statements false? Who would say this but the most open enemy of the divine words? The carnal generation even of the people of God of the Old Testament, which generates into bondage,[7] binds children for the sins of their parents; but, just as spiritual generation has changed inheritances, so it has also changed the threats and promises of punishments and rewards. The Prophets spoke these things, foreseeing in spirit; Jeremias even more clearly, when he said: 'In those days they shall say no more the fathers have eaten sour grapes and the teeth of their children are set on edge; but every one shall die for his own iniquity; every man that shall eat the same grapes, his own teeth shall be set on edge.' It is manifest that this was said in prophecy, just as the New Testament itself, at first hidden, and afterwards revealed through Christ. Finally, that we may not be disturbed by the words I have quoted and many others of like importance, about returning the sins of the parents upon the children—words written truthfully, yet which might be thought contrary to this pro-

---

3 Cf. Gen. 9.22-25.
4 Cf. 3 Kings 12.
5 Cf. 3 Kings 21.
6 Jer. 32.18; Exod. 20.5.
7 Cf. Gal. 4.24.

phecy—he solves this very vexed question by adding: 'Behold the days shall come, saith the Lord, and I will make a new covenant with the house of Israel, and with the house of Juda, not according to the covenant which I made with their fathers.'[8] In this new covenant through the blood of the Mediator, the paternal decree having been cancelled, man by rebirth begins to be no longer subject to the paternal debts that bind him at birth, as the Mediator Himself says: 'And call no one on earth your father,'[9] inasmuch as we find another birth by which we shall not succeed our father, but shall live forever with the father.

Chapter 26

(83) If you are not too obstinate, Julian, I believe you will see I have answered and refuted all the arguments you have brought forth in your four volumes to show that we should not believe in original sin and that we cannot regard the concupiscence of the flesh as evil without also condemning marriage. It has been shown that he alone is not bound by the ancient paternal debt who has changed inheritance and father; where he who is himself adopted through grace discovers the sole co-heir who is heir through nature; that carnal concupiscence does not inflict death after death on him alone who in the death of Christ has found the death by which he dies to sin and escapes the death by which he had been born in sin. For, one died for all: therefore, all died;[1] and He died for all. Nor can there ever live any for whom He did not die, who, Himself alive, died for the

---

8 Jer. 21.24-32.
9 Matt. 23.9.

---

1 Cf. 2 Cor. 5.14.

dead. Denying these things, attacking them, trying to destroy these defenses of the Catholic faith and to rend the very sinews of the Christian religion and of true godliness, you dare assert you are waging war on the ungodly, when as a matter of fact you are using the weapons of ungodliness against the mother who gave birth to you spiritually. You dare join the line of the holy Patriarchs, Prophets, Apostles, martyrs, and priests, even when the Patriarchs say to you: Sacrifices for sins were offered even for new-born infants;[2] and: Not even an infant of one day upon the earth is clean of sin;[3] when the Prophets say to you: We are conceived in iniquities;[4] when the Apostles say to you: 'All we who have been baptized into Christ Jesus have been baptized into his death, so that we are dead to sin, but alive to God in Christ Jesus';[5] when the martyrs say to you: 'Those born carnally according to Adam contract the contagion of the ancient death in their first birth, so that not their own, but another's, sins are remitted for infants in baptism';[6] when the priests say to you: 'Those formed in carnal pleasure come under the contagion of sins even before they experience the gift of this life.'[7] You presume to associate yourself with these men whose faith you seek to destroy. You say that any association with Manichaeans would conquer you, yet you have so strengthened them that you and they stand or fall together. You are mistaken, my son, wretchedly mistaken, if not also detestably mistaken. When you overcome the animosity that possesses you, you will possess the truth that has overcome you.

---

2 Cf. Lev. 12.
3 Cf. Job 14.5 (Septuagint).
4 Cf. Ps. 50.7.
5 Rom. 6.3,11.
6 Cyprian, *Ep.* 64 *ad Fidum.*
7 Ambrose, *De sacramento regenerationis.*

INDEX

INDEX

Abimelech, 140, 141
Abraham, 124-126, 134, 135, 137, 141, 391
Achab, 255, 258, 259, 394
accident, 18
Adam, xiii, 5-44, 56-58, 76, 77, 95, 96, 118, 124, 139, 152, 158, 159, 201, 218, 234, 236, 240, 293, 295, 296, 312, 316, 319, 337, 386-388; as figure of Christ, 32, 40
adultery, 47, 48, 80, 81, 120, 121, 123, 132, 138, 141, 147-155, 202, 283, 284, 288, 299, 365
Albinus, 325
Amasius, 254
Ambrose, St., 10-13, 26, 36, 38, 43, 52-54, 58-60, 65, 67-86, 92, 94, 97, 99-101, 107, 132, 136, 149, 267 n., 382, 396 n.
Ammonianus, Bishop, 22, 39
Anaxagoras, 231, 232
Anaximander, 231
Anaximenes, 231, 232
angels, 45, 50, 52, 156, 187, 195, 248, 255, 310, 376

Apollinaris, 295, 296
Aristotle, 13, 98, 102, 111, 235, 291-293, 366
Augustine, St., works: *Contra duas epistolas Pelagianorum*, 105 n., 381 n.; *Contra Faustum*, 6 n.; *De anima*, 261 n.; *De bono conjugali*, 134 n.; *De gratia Christi*, 209 n., 381 n.; *De haeresibus*, 270 n.; *De natura et gratia*, 250 n.; *De nuptiis*, xii, 105 n., 147 n., 159 n., 163 n., 168 n., 169 n., 177 n., 191 n., 210 n., 213 n., 244 n., 247 n., 260 n., 263 n., 269 n., 276 n., 277 n., 279 n., 283 n., 286 n., 287 n., 289 n., 298 n., 302 n., 309 n., 312 n., 320 n., 324 n., 331 n., 345 n., 360 n., 363 n., 368 n., 370 n., 375 n.; *De peccatorum meritis et remissione*, 261 n., 295 n., 327 n., 345 n., 380 n.; *Opus imperfectum contra Julianum*, 137 n., 295 n., 378 n.; *Retractationes*, 292 n., 381 n.

Balbus, 277
baptism, 6, 8-10, 14-44, 71, 73, 75-78, 83, 88, 93-97, 108, 112-115; a cross, 32-34; efficacy of, 56-68; graces of, 204-206, 345-377; necessary, not superfluous, 312; none saved without, 17, 22, 28, 29, 39, 181; redeems from original sin, 286; remission of sins by, 312-374
Basil, St., 18-22, 26, 36, 39, 43, 97, 136, 380
Battifol, P., xii
body, 20, 85, 88, 114-116, 118, 120, 122, 123, 127, 201, 216-219, 236-240, 269-274, 280, 291, 301; afflictions in the, 114-118, 180, 234, 262, 273, 292, 294, 295, 308, 325; and generation, 263-266, 268, 292
Boniface, Pope, 344 n.

Caecilianus, Bishop, 8
Cain, 82, 387
Calligonus, 348
Camilius, 190
Carthage, Conference of, 108, 109, 114; Councils of, xi, xii, 14
Catiline, 185, 190
Cato, 281, 288
Cayré, F., xii
Celestius, xi, 24, 99-101, 107, 108, 114, 269, 323, 343, 344
celibacy, 131-133, 144, 158, 269, 270, 282, 300, 303; and concupiscence, 172-175; *see also* continence; virginity
Cetura, 126
Chanaan, 394
chastity, 20, 76, 80 n., 81, 87, 91, 102, 131-133, 136, 143-145, 158, 164, 168, 190, 191, 210-212, 250, 269-271, 274, 281, 303, 365
Christ, as God and man, 295; Incarnation of, 9, 10; as liberator of infants, 6, 25, 28, 107, 116, 159, 180, 313; as Mediator, 15, 16, 85 n., 177, 197, 235, 258, 262, 287, 308, 316, 362, 369, 373, 377, 390-393; name of, 37; not of this world, 310, 311; as Physician, 242, 273; as Samaritan, 10, 38; as Saviour, 16, 26, 37, 112, 114, 122, 135, 242, 275, 277, 308, 310, 371; Son of God, 7 n., 20
Chromatius, Bishop, 22, 39
Cicero, 101, 183 n., 216-219, 223 n., 229, 234, 235, 266, 275 n., 284 n., 341 n., 342 n., 352 n., 378
circumcision, and baptism, 77, 78, 138, 139, 287, 327-330
Clematius, Bishop, 22, 39
Clement of Alexandria, 223 n.
concupiscence, 61-65, 72-81, 85 n., 91, 94-96, 119, 130-134, 138, 161, 309, 311, 381; compared to idolatry, 371-373; and generation, 198; a good only in

beasts, 231; in infants, 312-374; invariably evil, 130-158, 169-176, 220-232; and marriage, 5, 6, 265-305; not in Christ or Mary, 293-296; overcome by grace, 162-166, 273, 274; *see also* grace; marriage; original sin

continence, 74, 75, 79, 150, 151, 161, 172, 203, 221, 222, 250, 270; *see also* celibacy; virginity

conscience, 242, 243, 282

Cynics, 232

Cyprian, St., 7, 8, 26, 28, 62, 65, 67, 77, 86, 87, 91, 97, 101, 103, 135, 136, 396 n.

Damasus, Pope, 344

David, 11, 60, 75, 79, 108, 267, 337

death, 29, 32-34, 40, 63-65, 67, 73, 129, 157, 163, 184, 214, 268, 273, 280

Democritus, 231

Devil, 7, 11, 16 n., 19, 28, 32, 38, 40, 49, 50, 56-60, 67, 69, 70, 72, 86, 97, 102, 114, 116, 117, 123, 124, 128, 138, 148, 168, 169, 181, 193, 198, 199, 202, 222, 223, 239, 248, 253, 256, 261, 272, 280, 308-311, 331-336, 339, 347, 368-380; not author of men and marriage, 111, 112, 121, 122, 137, 152, 156-159, 201, 242, 270, 271

Dinomachus, 233, 359

Diogenes, 232

Dionysius, 292

Diospolis, Council of, xi

Donatism, xi, 109, 110, 135

Donatus, 8

Eleutherius, Bishop, 22

Empedocles, 231

Epicureanism, 148, 149, 187, 233, 274, 352

Eulalius, 344 n.

Eulogius, Bishop, 22, 39

Eutonius, Bishop, 22, 39

Eve, 7, 11, 19, 21, 38, 39, 75, 76, 160, 236, 380

evil, 56, 60, 66-68, 92, 95, 96, 118, 145, 150, 154-156, 170, 174, 176, 202, 204, 250, 262, 263, 272, 273, 290, 293, 299, 300, 304, 307, 308, 340, 361, 365, 367; constraint of, 341, 342; and good, 44-54, 118-121, 137-140; nature and origin of, 16-24, 44-54; *see also* sin; vice

exsufflation, 16, 22, 116, 320

Fabius, 190

Fabricius, 181, 190

faith, 6, 250; and justice, 18-195; and true chastity, 210-212

Fidus, Bishop, 22, 39

first-born, 7, 257

first-formed, 7, 9

Fundanius, 325

generatio, 40 n.

generation, 12, 34-41, 58, 75, 77, 81, 94, 119-128, 133, 145, 147, 148, 154, 155, 159, 160, 166, 168, 198-203, 261 n., 263-266, 279, 280, 284, 286, 288, 290, 296, 298-304, 312, 324, 345, 346, 361, 362, 365-367

Good, Supreme, 44, 45, 51, 54, 59, 251

grace, 8, 17, 19, 32-34, 41, 56-67, 75, 78, 82-85, 87, 91, 95, 105 n., 107, 129, 137, 248, 257, 268, 279, 311-313, 345-377, 383, 390, 391; anticipates will, 204; and baptism, Pelagian view of, 112-114; fatalism and, 204-209; gratuitousness of, 150, 151, 178, 203; makes will efficacious, 178, 179; only man merits, 178, 207, 208; overcomes concupiscence, 162-166, 273, 274; and will, 178-188, 203-212

Gregory Nazianzen, St., 16-18, 22 n., 26, 39, 63-65, 67, 91, 97, 100, 101, 103, 136, 382

Ham, 394
happiness, natural desire for, 183, 184
Heraclitus, 231
Hilary, St., 9, 26, 38, 65, 87-91, 97, 100, 101, 103, 136, 382
Horace, 185 n., 245 n.

infants, 116, 117; baptism of, 112-115, 128, 129, 138; birth of, no evil, 147, 148; and original sin, 168, 314-341; and wisdom, 262, 263; *see also* baptism; concupiscence; generation; original sin

Innocent I, Pope, xi, 14, 15, 26, 39, 97, 101, 103, 136

Irenaeus, Bishop, 7, 37, 38, 101, 103, 136

Isaac, 127, 128, 138, 139
Ishmael, 126
Isidore, 127 n.

Jacob, 292
Jerome, St., 42, 97, 101, 103, 136
Joas, 254
John Chrysostom, St., xi, 25-31, 34-36, 39-43, 97, 101, 103, 136, 316 n., 380
Jonas, 42
Joseph, St., 287
Jovinian, 6
Jovinus, Bishop, 22, 39
judgment, divine, 247-256, 279, 280; mankind, 139, 308, 316, 337, 353-357
jus liberorum, 127
justice, 308, 313, 320, 335, 336; and faith, 180-195; and God, 180, 182, 207, 208, 242-244, 256, 257, 285; and ignorance, 140, 141; and mercy, 140; and providence, 117, 118

Lazarus, 28, 29, 40

Leucippus, 231
loin-cloths, 76, 77, 245-247
Lord's Prayer, 62, 63, 107, 170, 194, 259, 283
Lucan, 281 n., 288 n.

Manichaeism, xi, 4-6, 13-20, 24, 27, 28, 30, 36, 42-55, 62, 63, 71, 91, 108, 128, 135-137, 163, 212, 268, 270, 271, 298, 299, 303, 304, 308, 367, 378-380, 385, 396
Marcellinus, 295, 327, 379
marriage, 6, 47, 48, 56-60, 93, 94, 119-128, 134, 158; and concupiscence, 5, 198-203, 210-212, 223, 265-290, 298-305; and desire for children, 285, 286; does not require activity of concupiscence, 155-158, 161, 215, 216; goodness in, 117, 119-123, 133, 134, 148, 152-158, 165, 166, 176, 202, 278, 279, 298-305, 379-381; moderation in, 80, 81, 94, 96, 131, 132, 142, 150, 172, 203, 282, 283; purpose of, 298-304; remedial aspect of, 144, 170; *see also* concupiscence; generation
Mary, Virgin, 6, 7, 374, 380; did not transmit concupiscence, 293-295; marriage of, 287-289; *see also* virgin birth
Maximianists, 110
Melchiades, Bishop, 8
Melissus, 231

Memor, 13
mercy, 195, 196; of God, 69, 84, 90, 91, 129, 135, 204, 208, 258-260, 345, 369
Milevis, Council of, xi
modesty, 80 n., 270; conjugal, 169-177, 198, 199, 210-212, 214, 215, 217
Moses, 32, 316, 387

natura, 44 n.
naturale, 44 n.
nature, 44-54, 59, 63, 69, 70, 78, 93, 117, 119, 124, 128, 148, 153-157, 180, 184, 193, 218, 232-235, 258, 297, 303, 304; perfectibility of, by grace, 162, 166; vitiation of, by the first sin, 117, 118, 124, 128, 129
Novatians, 59
Nymphidius, Bishop, 22, 39

olive, wild, 324, 325, 327, 330
Olympia, 28
Olympius, Bishop, 8, 38, 97, 101, 103, 136
origin, 57 n.
originale, 57 n.

Parmenides, 231
Paternians, 270, 271
Pelagianism, xi-xviii, 5, 13, 28, 30 n., 36, 40, 41, 43, 64, 74, 91 n., 98-101, 107, 108, 112, 136, 149, 150, 173, 200, 203, 236, 245, 267, 298, 327, 344, 367, 380, 386 n., 388

403

Pelagius, 15, 22-24, 36, 39, 98-101, 107-109, 114, 129, 269, 327
Peripatetics, 376
Persius, 268 n.
Pius IX, Pope, 134 n.
Platonism, 13 n., 43, 79, 94, 98, 181, 229, 231, 233, 234
pleasure, 222-231, 365-367
Plutarch, 288 n.
Polemo, 13, 43
Porphyry, Bishop, 22, 39
Prat, F., 9 n.
prayer, 62, 84, 145; *see also* Lord's Prayer
predestined, 180, 256-258, 307
Primian, 110 n.
Providence, 81, 82, 85, 118, 124, 125, 138, 143, 147, 156-158, 166, 339, 350; *see also* Christ, as Mediator; as Saviour
pudicitia, 80 n.
punishment, deserved, 240; divinely inflicted, 247-256, 259, 280, 286; eternal, 189, 190; and pagan philosophers, 235, 240; *see also*, body, afflictions in
Pythagoras, 181, 231, 266, 267

reason, 66, 68, 98, 102, 199, 243
redemption, 6, 58, 78, 82-93, 112, 114, 116, 122, 128, 129, 139, 148, 290, 291, 298, 302, 312, 389-393; *see also* Christ

Regulus, 181, 190
repentance, 256-260
Reticius, Bishop, 8, 38, 97, 101, 103, 136
Roboam, 254, 259

Sallust, 107, 185 n.
Sara, 124-126, 134, 135, 137, 140, 141
Saul, King, 196, 248, 267
Scipio, 181, 183, 190
Scripture, Holy, citations from, or references to:
Acts, 157, 189, 387, 393
Colossians, 315, 328, 331, 340, 348, 367, 393
1 Corinthians, 10, 19, 26, 63, 79-81, 85, 121, 132-134, 145, 150, 168, 170, 181, 182, 228, 236, 263, 281, 283, 299, 304, 314, 319, 324, 332, 335, 343, 346, 349, 357-359, 377, 380, 382, 392
2 Corinthians, 3, 67, 71, 86, 102, 154, 175, 193, 248, 312, 315, 323, 333, 337, 346, 348, 349, 357, 395
Daniel, 273
Ecclesiastes, 389
Ecclesiasticus, 57, 113, 115, 118, 139, 162, 180, 218, 224, 253, 275, 280, 294, 308, 320, 326, 337, 348, 389
Ephesians, 68, 90, 129, 194, 257, 340, 388
Exodus, 196, 394

Ezechiel, 255, 393
Galatians, 20, 62, 97, 130, 151, 161, 168, 182, 196, 199, 212, 229, 262, 271, 272, 336, 347, 359, 383, 392, 394
Genesis, 21, 29, 50, 72, 76, 77, 82, 124, 138, 140-142, 160, 186, 212, 213, 217, 226, 238, 239, 245, 261, 267, 287, 292, 329, 330, 377, 391, 394
Hebrews, 189, 195, 212, 278, 336
Isaias, 57, 83, 121, 180, 253
James, 149, 170, 208, 259, 297, 355
Jeremias, 267, 388, 395, 396
Job, 58, 88, 89, 96, 149, 290, 388, 389, 396
John, 15, 17, 27, 77, 88, 109, 113, 118, 129, 188, 207, 258, 287, 304, 309-311, 318, 345, 347, 349, 366, 375, 390
1 John, 87, 146, 147, 149, 170, 194, 220, 221, 230, 272, 299, 310, 336
Josue, 254, 337
1 Kings, 196, 248, 267
2 Kings, 337
3 Kings, 254, 255, 259, 394
Leviticus, 287, 396
Luke, 10, 11, 68, 193, 202, 284, 289, 345, 353, 362, 371
2 Machabees, 294
Mark, 117, 312, 338
Matthew, 3, 16, 19, 21, 46, 47, 49, 56, 83, 88, 96, 107, 114, 131, 141, 149, 170, 186, 188, 192, 195, 197, 201, 204, 223, 257, 259, 282, 283, 285, 286, 289, 290, 296, 297, 304, 319, 352, 353, 368, 395
Micheas, 255
Osee, 248, 377
2 Paralipomenon, 254
1 Peter, 58, 114, 283, 297, 342
2 Peter, 253, 257
Philippians, 178, 179
Proverbs, 54, 87, 106, 179, 183, 207, 299
Psalms, 9-12, 37, 38, 57, 58, 60, 75, 84, 85, 89, 90, 106, 114, 129, 149, 150, 174, 177, 187, 204, 208, 242, 248, 255, 256, 259, 319, 323, 344, 349, 357, 367, 386, 389, 396
Romans, 9, 20, 26, 27, 32, 40, 41, 60, 72-74, 78, 92, 95, 107, 115, 124, 126, 131, 137, 139, 141, 142, 153, 160-164, 170, 174, 178, 180-182, 188, 189, 192, 196, 205, 207, 208, 210, 212, 234, 244, 246, 248, 252, 255-257, 262, 268, 271, 272, 275, 277, 279, 291, 293, 312-316, 319, 322, 328, 330-332, 337, 344, 346, 349, 350, 352-355, 364, 367, 370, 375, 381, 383-386, 388-390, 392, 396
1 Thessalonians, 80, 215, 278
2 Thessalonians, 254, 391
1 Timothy, 95, 204, 304, 393
2 Timothy, 206, 256, 257

Tobias, 11
Wisdom, 20, 138, 182, 193, 244, 279, 285, 307, 346, 350, 358, 382

---

sensation, 222-231, 347, 348, 366
Septuagint, 54, 57, 179, 207, 290, 299, 389, 396
shame, 76, 77, 124, 163, 212-222, 235-240, 244-247, 269, 270, 277
sin, 5, 8, 11, 12, 16, 17, 23-27, 30-32, 34, 39, 50, 58, 59, 64-67, 70-73, 79, 85 n., 90, 95, 96, 138, 149, 153, 173, 191, 192, 231, 242, 274, 333-336; and punishment, 243-256: remission of, by baptism, 312-362; visited on children, 393-395
sin, original, 5-44, 47, 50, 55-64, 69, 81, 82, 93, 97, 113, 116, 122, 141, 153, 198, 218, 253, 290, 312-396; and baptism, 159, 162; concerns moral philosophy, 232-235; distinct from personal sin, 25-35; a supernatural mystery, 140, 141; voluntary character of, 137-140; *see also* baptism; redemption
Sodom, 142, 143, 286
Solomon, 394
Soranus, 292
soul, 63, 69, 85, 114-116, 118, 177, 184, 193, 194, 199, 261 n.; origin of, 261, 262, 294; Plato on, 79

Spirit, Holy, 10, 12, 14, 25, 39, 57, 64, 86, 113, 129, 161, 198, 260, 279, 311, 317, 349, 374, 383
Stephen, St., 387
Stoics, 112, 216, 229, 233, 376
substance, 18, 19

Terence, 240 n.
Thales of Miletus, 231
Thomas Aquinas, St., 80 n., 85 n., 181 n., 261 n.
Trinity, 44, 243
Turbanus, 135

Ulpian, 127 n.
Ursicinus, 344

Valentinian, 348
Valerius, Count, xiii
Venustians, 270, 271
vice, 64, 69, 70, 80, 84, 86, 87, 179-188, 307; *see also* evil; sin
Virgil, 136 n., 224, 225, 321 n., 330 n.
Virgin birth, 6, 7, 10, 12, 58, 65, 66,·70, 94, 97, 293
virginity 144, 145, 172, 210, 268, 300, 303, 365; *see also* celibacy
virtue, 30, 32, 59, 63, 67, 91, 140, 141, 149, 150, 163-165, 177, 181, 199; and justice, 181; true and false, 179-197, 211
virtus, 32 n.
vitium, 44 n.

will, 18, 19, 30 n., 39, 41, 45, 56, 57, 62, 66, 69, 105 n., 107, 116, 140, 153, 162, 176, 193, 195, 278-282, 337; body subject to, 263, 274; and grace, 178-188, 203-212; and punishment, 344, 345

Xenocrates, 13, 43
Xenophanes, 231

Zoboennus, Bishop, 22, 39
Zoninus, Bishop, 22, 39
Zosimus, Pope, xii, 14, 15 n., 343, 344

www.ingramcontent.com/pod-product-compliance
Lightning Source LLC
Chambersburg PA
CBHW032023290426
44110CB00012B/642